OCR A LEVEL

PSYCHOLOGY

AS and YEAR 1

Second Edition

OCR
Oxford Cambridge and RSA
This is an OCR endorsed resource.

D0317332

Matt Jarvis • Julia Russell
Lizzie Gauntlett • Fiona Lintern

WORTHING
COLLEGE LIBRARY

WORTHING COLLEGE LIBRARY

45293

OXFORD

OXFORD
UNIVERSITY PRESS

Great Clarendon Street, Oxford OX2 6DP

Oxford University Press is a department of the University of Oxford.

It furthers the University's objective of excellence in research, scholarship, and education by publishing worldwide in Oxford New York Auckland Cape Town Dar es Salaam Hong Kong Karachi Kuala Lumpur Madrid Melbourne Mexico City Nairobi New Delhi Shanghai Taipei Toronto

With offices in

Argentina Austria Brazil Chile Czech Republic France Greece Guatemala Hungary Italy Japan South Korea Poland Portugal Singapore Switzerland Thailand Turkey Ukraine Vietnam

Oxford is a registered trade mark of Oxford University Press in the UK and in certain other countries

© Oxford University Press 2015

The moral rights of the authors have been asserted

Database right Oxford University Press (maker)

First published 2015

All rights reserved. No part of this publication may be reproduced, stored in a retrieval system, or transmitted, in any form or by any means, without the prior permission in writing of Oxford University Press, or as expressly permitted by law, or under terms agreed with the appropriate reprographics rights organization. Enquiries concerning reproduction outside the scope of the above should be sent to the Rights Department, Oxford University Press, at the address above

You must not circulate this book in any other binding or cover and you must impose this same condition on any acquirer

British Library Cataloguing in Publication Data
Data available

978 019 833275 6

10 9 8 7 6 5 4 3 2

MIX
Paper from responsible sources
FSC® C007785
www.fsc.org

Printed and bound by Bell & Bain Ltd, Glasgow

Paper used in the production of this book is a natural, recyclable product made from wood grown in sustainable forests. The manufacturing process conforms to the environmental regulations of the country of origin.

Acknowledgements

The authors would like to thank Minh Ha Duong, Commissioning Editor, and Patricia Briggs, Project Manager. Minh Ha is a very good organiser and has kept things moving with some very clever lateral thinking, and Patricia has been not only consistently helpful and efficient, but is always fun to work with, and her suggestions are unfailingly helpful.

The publishers would like to thank the following for permission to reproduce photographs: **p5**: sculpies/Shutterstock; **p7**: Sopotnicki/Shutterstock; **p8**: From the film Obedience (c) 1968 by Stanley Milgram; (c) renewed 1993 by Alexandra Milgram and distributed by Alexander Street Press; **p9**: From the film Obedience (c) 1968 by Stanley Milgram; (c) renewed 1993 by Alexandra Milgram and distributed by Alexander Street Press; **p13**: From the film Obedience (c) 1968 by Stanley Milgram; (c) renewed 1993 by Alexandra Milgram and distributed by Alexander Street Press; **p15**: markos86/Shutterstock; **p25**: NY Daily News Archive via Getty Images; **p30**: Janine Wiedel/REX; **p31**: blvdone/Shutterstock; **p33**: Lisa S./Shutterstock; **p44**: Sebastian Kaulitzki/Shutterstock; **p45**: With kind courtesy of Elizabeth Loftus Ph.D., University of California, Irvine; **p47**: Dmitry Kalinovsky/Shutterstock; **p50**: IS_ImageSource/iStockphoto; **p53**: StockLite/Shutterstock; **p56**: bibiphoto/Shutterstock; **p63**: (l) Anton Oparin/Shutterstock, (r) With kind permission from iDichotic; **p67**: Monkey Business Images/Shutterstock; **p69**: Suslik1983/Shutterstock; **p71**: Figures provided by Daniel Simon, www.dansimons.com www.theinvisiblegorilla.com; **p81**: Pressmaster/Shutterstock; **p83**: With kind permission from Albert Bandura; **p84**: With kind permission from Albert Bandura; **p89**: Sura Nualpradid/Shutterstock; **p91**: With kind permission from www.avitamedical.com; **p100**: Diego Cervo/Shutterstock; **p106**: Monkey Business Images/Shutterstock; **p115**: PATRICK LANDMANN/SCIENCE PHOTO LIBRARY; **p129**: Moving Moment/Shutterstock; **p131**: (t) ArtFamily/Shutterstock, (b) Luis Santos/Shutterstock; **p133**: PR MICHEL ZANCA/ISM/SCIENCE PHOTO LIBRARY; **p143**: Blakemore, C. & Cooper, G.F. (1970) Development of the brain depends on the visual environment. Nature 228: 477 478; **p145**: Alena Ozerova/Shutterstock; **p148**: StevenRussellSmithPhotos/Shutterstock; **p149**: Bikeworldtravel/Shutterstock; **p150**: GEOFF TOMPKINSON/SCIENCE PHOTO LIBRARY; **p151**: (t) ALFRED PASIEKA/SCIENCE PHOTO LIBRARY, (bl) ARTHUR GLAUBERMAN/SCIENCE PHOTO LIBRARY, (br) SCIENCE PICTURES LIMITED/SCIENCE PHOTO LIBRARY; **p163**: Caroline Purser/Getty Images; **p165**: Paul Banton/Shutterstock; **p166**: Franz Pfluegl/Shutterstock; **p168**: Brian Harris/REX; **p169**: With kind permission from Professor Simon Baron-Cohen; **p179**: Susan Law Cain/Shutterstock; **p184**: Zern Liew/Shutterstock; **p185**: © AF archive/Alamy; **p188**: sakhorn/Shutterstock; **p195**: inxti/Shutterstock; **p199**: T and Z/Shutterstock; **p219**: Lonely/Shutterstock; **p221**: © Janine Wiedel Photolibrary/Alamy; **p222**: Monkey Business Images/Shutterstock; **p225**: Fuse/Getty Images; **p229**: © Burntlight/Alamy; **p232**: © UpperCut Images/Alamy; **p235**: © dominic dibbs/Alamy; **p237**: (t) © Sally and Richard Greenhill/Alamy, (b) Roman Pyshchyk/Shutterstock; **p247**: Eric Isselee/Shutterstock; **p248**: (l) Figures provided by Daniel Simon, www.dansimons.com, (r) OHA 316: Steggerda Collection, Box 5, Folder 1 (Courtesy of the National Museum of Health and Medicine); **p249**: nspimages/iStockphoto; **p253**: Monika Wisniewska/Shutterstock; **p254**: Darren Green/Shutterstock; **p258**: Lonely/Shutterstock; **p262**: Reprinted with permission of the British Psychological Society; **p265**: Sebastian Kaulitzki/Shutterstock; **p268**: © Giovanni Gagliardi/Alamy; **p271**: © Newscast/Alamy; **p272**: PATRICE LATRON/LOOK AT SCIENCES/SCIENCE PHOTO LIBRARY; **p275**: author image; **p276**: Halina Yakushevich/Shutterstock; **p277**: Tomasz Trojanowski/Shutterstock; **p279**: Jacek Chabraszewski/Shutterstock; **p301**: © Russell Glenister/Corbis; **p304**: © Pawan Kumar/Reuters/Corbis; **p306**: Dan Piraro; **p307**: Jane September/Shutterstock; **p310**: Jorge Casais/Shutterstock; **p312**: JOHANNES EISELE/AFP/Getty Images

Artwork: Six Red Marbles; Patricia Briggs

Cover photo by Tischenko Irina/Shutterstock

Index by Indexing Specialists.

The authors and publishers are grateful to the following for permission to reprint copyright material:

BMJ Publishing Group for table from P.M. Watts, B. Clements, S.G. Devadason and G.M. Chaney: 'Funhaler spacer: improving adherence without compromising deliver', Archives of Diseases in Childhood, 88 (British Paediatric Association, 2003).

Guardian News & Media for extract from 'Do as you're told' by Nicci Gerrard, The Observer Review, 12 Oct 1997, copyright © Guardian News & Media 1997.

New York Times, via PARS International Corporation for extract from '37 who saw murder didn't call the police: Apathy at stabbing of Queen's woman shocks Inspector' by Martin Gansberg, New York Times, 27 March 1964, copyright © 1964 The New York Times. All rights reserved; protected by the Copyright Laws of the United States. The printing, copying, redistribution, or retransmission of this Content without express written permission is prohibited.

PNAS for figures from B.J. Casey et al: 'Behavioural and neural correlates of delay of gratification 20 years later', Proceedings of the National Academy of Sciences 108:36 (2011); and from E.A. Maguire et al.: 'Navigation-related structural changes in the hippocampi of taxi drivers', Proceedings of the National Academy of Sciences 97 (2000), copyright © 2000 by the National Academy of Sciences, USA.

Sage Publications, Inc. for table from R. Levine, A. Norenzayan and K. Philbrick: 'Cross-cultural differences in helping strangers', Journal of Cross-cultural Psychology 32:5 (Western Washington State College/ International Association for Cross-Cultural Psychology, 2001).

Solo Syndication for the Daily Mail for 'Is Peppa Pig making toddlers naughty?' by Katharine Faulkner, Daily Mail, 9 Jan 2012.

John Wiley and Sons for extracts from Kang Lee, Catherine Ann Cameron, Fen Xu, Genyao Fu & Julie Board: 'Chinese and Canadian children's evaluations of lying and truth-telling', Child Development 68:5 (1997), copyright © 1997 by The Society of Research in Child Development, Inc.

Every effort has been made to contact copyright holders of material reproduced in this book. If notified, the publishers will be pleased to rectify any errors or omissions at the earliest opportunity.

WORTHING COLLEGE

This resource is endorsed by OCR for use with specification AS Level GCE Psychology and H567 A Level GCE Psychology.

In order to gain OCR endorsement this resource has undergone an independent quality check. OCR has not paid for the production of this resource, nor does OCR receive any royalties from its sale. For more information about the endorsement process please visit the OCR website www.ocr.org.uk

45293

PICKABOOK   28/09/15

£24.99

CONTENTS

INTRODUCTION

Welcome to our book!

In this book we focus on core studies, and on the methods of psychology research. The studies are grouped according to the British Psychological Society's classification of the areas for studying psychology, and we devote a chapter to each of these, with pairs of studies — one classic and one more contemporary — sharing a theme, to help you learn about how psychology has changed over time.

Ten AS-level studies cover one theme from each of the five approaches, while twenty A-level studies represent two themes from each approach. The table below shows the core studies by approach. The first row in each approach represents the AS-level content. Throughout the book, A-level only content is indicated by a red corner flag or the use of red highlighting, as in the table below.

Key theme	Classic study	Contemporary study
Chapter 1: Social psychology		
Responses to people in authority	Milgram (1963) Obedience page 6	Bocchiaro *et al.* (2012) Disobedience and whistle-blowing page 14
Responses to people in need	Piliavin *et al.* (1969) Subway samaritan page 24	Levine *et al.* (2001) Cross-cultural altruism page 31
Chapter 2: Cognitive psychology		
Memory	Loftus and Palmer (1974) Eyewitness testimony page 45	Grant *et al.* (1998) Context-dependent memory page 51
Attention	Moray (1959) Auditory attention page 62	Simons and Chabris (1999) Visual inattention page 69
Chapter 3: Developmental psychology		
External influences on children's behaviour	Bandura *et al.* (1961) Transmission of aggression page 82	Chaney *et al.* (2004) Funhaler study page 88
Moral development	Kohlberg (1968) Stages of moral development page 98	Lee *et al.* (1997) Evaluations of lying and truth-telling page 103
Chapter 4: Biological psychology		
Regions of the brain	Sperry (1968) Split-brain study page 116	Casey *et al.* (2011) Neural correlates of delay and gratification page 129
Brain plasticity	Blakemore and Cooper (1970) Impact of early visual experience page 140	Maguire *et al.* (2000) Taxi drivers page 148
Chapter 5: The psychology of individual differences		
Understanding disorders	Freud (1909) Little Hans page 164	Baron-Cohen *et al.* (1997) Advanced theory of mind page 168
Measuring differences	Gould (1982) Bias in IQ testing page 178	Hancock *et al.* (2011) The language of psychopaths page 184

The book is designed to help you engage as deeply as possible with the subject matter of psychology, but also to be clear about the requirements for doing well in your exams. For every core study there are summaries, regular question spotlight features, and practice questions with sample answers and comments.

As well as the five approaches, you also need to know about two perspectives on psychology — behavioural and psychodynamic — which are considered in detail in Chapter 6. Chapter 7 then provides everything you will ever need to know at AS and first-year A-level about carrying out psychological research.

If you enjoy the subject and are thinking about continuing beyond AS/Year 1, turn to page 320, where we offer some advice about taking psychology further.

Good luck and enjoy!

C1 SOCIAL PSYCHOLOGY

Social psychology is concerned with how people interact with one another. In this chapter we will look at four studies.

For AS we consider two studies that highlight the theme of responses to people in authority:

1 Milgram's (1969) study of destructive obedience. This was a laboratory-based study of obedience in which participants who believed they were taking part in a learning experiment were ordered to give electric shocks to a person they believed to be another participant.

2 Bocchiaro et al.'s (2011) study of disobedience and whistle-blowing. This was a simulation in which participants were presented with an unethical request. A different group were asked what they would do if faced with that request.

For A level we additionally look at two studies paired around the theme of responses to people in need:

3 Piliavin et al.'s (1969) study of bystander behaviour. Unlike the first two studies, this was a field experiment carried out on underground trains. The aim was to see how people would respond to the collapse of a fellow passenger.

4 Levine et al.'s (2001) study of cross-cultural altruism. This was a field experiment carried out in 23 countries in which people were presented with non-emergency situations in which a stranger needed help.

We will look at these studies in detail, evaluating and exploring applications of each. We also consider them in their pairs, using them to think about the key themes. Finally we will use them to explore issues of social psychology, looking at the strengths and limitations of this area.

MILGRAM'S STUDY OF DESTRUCTIVE OBEDIENCE

Milgram, S. (1963) Behavioural study of obedience. *Journal of Abnormal & Social Psychology,* **67**: 371–378

IN BRIEF

Aim: To investigate the tendency for destructive obedience.

Method: 40 male volunteers were told they were taking part in a learning experiment. They took the role of teacher, giving what they thought were painful shocks to a confederate whom they believed to be a fellow participant taking the role of learner. Shocks increased by 15V for every wrong answer and went up to a maximum of 450V.

Results: 100% of participants gave at least 300V and 65% gave the full 450V. Most participants displayed signs of stress while giving the shocks.

Conclusion: People are surprisingly obedient to orders given by people in authority. However they become distressed when obeying orders to hurt another person.

KEY IDEAS

Obedience means following a direct order. This is different from compliance, which means going along with what someone wants you to do, or **conformity**, which means behaving in the same way as those around you. Remember that Milgram was studying **destructive obedience**, which means following an order to harm someone. Destructive obedience is generally necessary in order for genocide to take place. **Genocide** is the systematic attempt to wipe out an ethnic group.

CONTEXT

Most of the time we are told that **obedience** is a good thing. If your teacher tells you to get your book out or to answer a question, you might not want to do it but you probably accept that the most socially appropriate behaviour is to obey. You probably also accept that your teacher has the right to give you an instruction of this kind. But what if you were ordered to do something that caused harm or distress to another person? This type of obedience, in which people obey orders to cause harm, is called destructive obedience. Social psychologists such as Stanley Milgram have been particularly interested in **destructive obedience**. As the member of a European Jewish family that had left Europe for America, Milgram was profoundly affected by the atrocities committed by Nazi Germany against Jewish people and other minority groups. One of the key features of the Nazi atrocities was the extent to which people displayed destructive obedience. Many ordinary people obeyed destructive orders that led to the systematic mass murder of minority groups, including Jews, Romanies, Communists, Trade Unionists, and people with disabilities.

Early psychological research into the Holocaust focused on the idea that something distinctive about German culture or personality led to the high levels of **conformity** and obedience necessary for **genocide** to take place. This is known as the **dispositional hypothesis**. While Milgram was interested in this idea, he was also interested in the social processes that take place between individuals and within groups. The idea that we can explain events such as the Holocaust by reference to the social processes operating in the situation, rather than the characteristics of the individuals involved, is called the **situational**

hypothesis. In his early work Milgram worked with another famous social psychologist, Solomon Asch. Together they studied people's tendency to conform to group pressure. Milgram went on to investigate the tendency to obey destructive orders from individuals in positions of authority.

KEY IDEAS

There is a tension in social psychology between explanations that focus on the individuals involved in a social situation and those that focus on the situation itself. These explanations are known respectively as the **dispositional hypothesis** and the **situational hypothesis**.

ACTIVITY ✳

It can be hard to picture the sort of real-life situation in which destructive obedience occurs. Read the following account of a massacre that took place in Poland in 1942.

DO AS YOU'RE TOLD
by Nicci Gerrard

In the early hours of 13 July 1942, the 500 men of the German Reserve Police Force Battalion 101 – middle-aged family men, too old for the army, barely trained and stationed in Poland – were addressed by their leader, Commander Trapp. In a voice shaky with distress he told them of their next assignment: to seek out and kill the 1800 women and children in the nearby village of Jozefow. Then, astonishingly, Trapp told them he knew what a repugnant task some might find it, and that anyone could stand out with no punishment and no reprisals. Out of 500, only 12 men stood out.

During that terrible day, a further 10–20% managed to evade their duty; many more became distressed but continued to carry out the orders. Quite a few exhibited no signs of distress. A few seemed to enjoy themselves.

Source: **The Observer Review,** *12 October 1997*

Figure 1.1
Ordinary Germans obeyed orders that
led to millions being killed in extermination camps.

Q

1   How might the behaviour of Battalion 101 be explained using the dispositional hypothesis and the situational hypothesis?

2   What do you think you would have done if you were in Battalion 101?

DO IT YOURSELF

Design and carry out a study to test the percentage of people nowadays who believe they would give a helpless person potentially fatal shocks under orders. How do your results compare to Milgram's, and what might this tell us?

KEY IDEAS

Remember that the **sample** is the group of people who took part in the study. The **sampling method** is the way the people in the sample were selected.

Public Announcement

WE WILL PAY YOU $4.00 FOR ONE HOUR OF YOUR TIME

Persons Needed for a Study of Memory

*We will pay five hundred New Haven men to help us complete a scientific study of memory and learning. The study is being done at Yale University.

*Each person who participates will be paid $4.00 (plus 50c carfare) for approximately 1 hour's time. We need you for only one hour: there are no further obligations. You may choose the time you would like to come (evenings, weekdays, or weekends).

*No special training, education, or experience is needed. We want:

Factory workers	Businessmen	Construction workers
City employees	Clerks	Salespeople
Laborers	Professional people	White-collar workers
Barbers	Telephone workers	Others

All persons must be between the ages of 20 and 50. High school and college students cannot be used.

*If you meet these qualifications, fill out the coupon below and mail it now to Professor Stanley Milgram, Department of Psychology, Yale University, New Haven. You will be notified later of the specific time and place of the study. We reserve the right to decline any application.

*You will be paid $4.00 (plus 50c carfare) as soon as you arrive at the laboratory.

- -

TO:
PROF. STANLEY MILGRAM, DEPARTMENT OF PSYCHOLOGY, YALE UNIVERSITY, NEW HAVEN, CONN. I want to take part in this study of memory and learning. I am between the ages of 20 and 50. I will be paid $4.00 (plus 50c carfare) if I participate.

NAME: (Please Print). . . . .

ADDRESS . . . .

TELEPHONE NO. . . . . Best time to call you . . . .

AGE. . . . . . OCCUPATION. SEX . . . . . .
CAN YOU COME:

WEEKDAYS . . . . EVENINGS . . . . . .WEEKENDS. . . . .

Figure 1.2
Milgram's advertisement

BEFORE THE MAIN PROCEDURE

Before carrying out the main study, Milgram told psychology students about his procedure. This would involve ordering people to give electric shocks to a helpless man (actually an actor) whom they believed to be a fellow participant. The electric shocks would increase in intensity up to 450V. On average students estimated that only 1.2% of participants would obey the orders and give all the shocks.

AIM

The aim of the study was to investigate how obedient people would be to orders from a person in authority that would result in pain and harm to another person. More specifically, the aim was to see how large an electric shock participants would give to a helpless man when ordered to by a scientist in his own laboratory.

METHOD

Design

Milgram himself described his original study as a laboratory experiment. Technically it might more accurately be called a pre-experiment, because it had only one condition. The results from this condition then served as a baseline for a number of variations in follow-up studies. The dependent variable (DV) was the obedience. Obedience was operationalised as the maximum voltage given in response to the orders.

Participants

Forty men aged 20–50 were recruited by means of a newspaper advertisement. The **sample** was therefore mostly a volunteer or self-selecting sample. They were from a range of backgrounds and held a range of jobs: 37.5% were manual labourers, 40% were white-collar workers, and 22.5% were professionals. All were from the New Haven district of North America.

Procedure

Participants were recruited by means of a newspaper advertisement. They were promised $4.50 for their time, including 50 cents for travel It was made clear that payment was for turning up to the study, and was not conditional on completing the procedure. When each participant arrived at Yale University he was introduced to a man he believed to be another participant. The two men were then briefed on the supposed purpose of the experiment, which was described to them as to investigate the effect of punishment on learning.

In fact the other man was working for Milgram. He was a 47-year-old Irish-American accountant. He had been selected for the role because he was mild-mannered and likeable. People who help with experiments in this way are known as confederates or stooges.

The **naïve participant** and the confederate were told that one of them would play the role of teacher and the other the learner. They drew slips of paper from a hat to allocate the roles, but this was fiddled so that the naïve participant was always the teacher and the confederate was always the learner. They were then immediately taken to another room where the learner was strapped into a chair and electrodes were attached to him. They were shown the electric shock generator. This had a row of switches, each labelled with a voltage, rising in 15-volt intervals from 15V up to 450V. Participants were told that the shocks could be extremely painful but not dangerous; they were each given a 45V shock to demonstrate.

There was a wall between the teacher and learner, so that the teacher could hear but not see the learner. The procedure was administered by an experimenter, played by a 31-year-old male biology teacher. The participant (in the role of teacher) read out word pairs to test the confederate (in the role of learner). Each time the confederate-learner made a mistake, the experimenter ordered the teacher-participant to give a shock. The shock got larger by 15V for each mistake. The confederate-learner did not really receive shocks, but there was no way for the teacher-participant to know this.

Up to 300V the confederate-learner did not signal any response to the shocks. However, at 300V and 315V, he pounded on the wall. He was then silent and did not respond to further questions. This suggested that he was hurt, perhaps unconscious, or even dead. When participants turned to the experimenter for guidance, they were told to treat no response as incorrect and to continue to give the shocks. When they protested, they were given a series of verbal prods to encourage them to continue.

Each participant was considered to have completed the procedure either when they refused to give any more shocks, or when they reached the maximum voltage on the shock machine. They were then interviewed and de-hoaxed. During their interview they were asked to rate on a scale of 0–14 how

Figure 1.3
Milgram's electric shock machine

KEY IDEAS

A **naïve participant** is one who does not know the purpose of the procedure in which they are taking part. It is common practice not to explain the purpose of the study they are taking part in so as to reduce the likelihood that their behaviour is affected by their view of the study.

WEB WATCH @

You can see footage of Milgram's experiments and various replications online. Videos are sometimes available on YouTube, or try www.psychexchange. co.uk/videos/view/20257

Figure 1.4
In a particularly brutal variation on the basic procedure, participants were ordered to force the stooge's hand onto the electrode.

TABLE 1.1 DISTRIBUTION OF MAXIMUM VOLTAGES GIVEN

Voltage	Number of participants
0–285	0
300	5
315	4
330	2
345	1
360	1
375	1
390	0
405	0
420	0
435	0
450	26

painful the last few shocks they gave were. They were told that the shocks were not real, that the learner was unharmed, and that the real purpose of the study was to investigate obedience.

RESULTS

Quantitative and qualitative data was gathered. The 'headline figures' were quantitative, in the form of the average voltage that participants went up to, and the number of participants giving each voltage. The average voltage given by participants was 368V. 100% of participants gave 300V or more; 65% gave the full 450V. Remember that psychology students had on average estimated that only 1.2% of participants would do this! In their post-experiment interviews, their average rating of how painful the shocks were was 13.42 out of a maximum of 14.

Qualitative data was gathered in the form of the comments and protests participants made during the procedure, and in the form of observations of their body language. Most participants showed signs of tension during the procedure. Signs included groaning, sweating, biting lips, and stuttering. Fourteen giggled nervously. One had such a severe seizure that the procedure was stopped. One observer noted:

> 'I observed a mature and initially poised business man enter the laboratory smiling and confident. Within 20 minutes he was reduced to a twitching, stuttering wreck, who was rapidly approaching the point of nervous collapse.' *(p. 377)*

Most participants protested against the procedure, although the verbal prods were in most cases sufficient to get them to continue giving the shocks.

CONCLUSIONS

Milgram drew two main conclusions from this study:

1 People are much more obedient to destructive orders than we might expect, and considerably more than psychology students suggested in their estimates. In fact, the majority of people are quite willing to obey destructive orders.
2 People find the experience of receiving and obeying destructive orders highly stressful. They obey in spite of their emotional responses. The situation triggers a conflict between two deeply ingrained tendencies: to obey those in authority, and not to harm people.

Results supported the situational hypothesis rather than the dispositional hypothesis.

Explaining the high levels of obedience

Milgram identified nine possible factors in the situation that might have contributed to the high levels of obedience seen.

1 The study was carried out in a respectable environment of a top university.
2 The aim of the study appears to be a worthwhile one.

'I observed a mature and initially poised business man enter the laboratory smiling and confident. Within 20 minutes he was reduced to a twitching, stuttering wreck, who was rapidly approaching the point of nervous collapse.'

3 The learner appears to have volunteered and so has an obligation to the experimenter.

4 The teacher too has volunteered and so has an obligation to the experimenter.

5 Features of the design, for example payment, increase this sense of obligation.

6 From the perspective of the teacher, he might equally well have been unlucky enough to have been the learner and to have endured the shocks.

7 The rights of the participant to withdraw and the scientist to expect compliance are not obvious.

8 The participants were assured that the shocks were not dangerous.

9 The learner has appeared to be comfortable with the procedure for the first 300V.

Later variations on the procedure

What we have described here is Milgram's first published study, but over the following 10 years he refined his procedure. (This is why, if you watch footage of the procedure, some details might differ from the original procedure in the first published study.) As well as refining the basic condition, Milgram also tested the effect of a number of variations. Results are shown in the form of the percentage of participants who went to the maximum 450V in each condition. In general, giving the participant greater distance from the learner, or less personal responsibility for decision-making, increased obedience, while reducing the apparent power of the experimenter, or making the situation appear less respectable or scientific, reduced obedience.

TABLE 1.2 PERCENTAGE GIVING 450V IN VARIATIONS IN THE MILGRAM PROCEDURE	
Victim is silent throughout	100%
Standard procedure	65%
Location in seedy office	48%
Victim in same room	40%
Orders given by phone	20.5%
No lab coat	20%
Fellow participants disobey	10%
Participant chooses voltage	2.5%

These variations have been replicated many times by different researchers. Luttke (2004) reviewed these studies and concluded that Milgram was right about some but not all of his conclusions. In particular, the presence of disobedient participants and the physical closeness of the learner reliably reduces obedience. However, most studies have found that varying the location of the study makes little difference to obedience.

QUESTION SPOTLIGHT!

Milgram has been challenged on the ethical issues raised by his procedure. *How does his procedure stand up against the following ethical principles?*

1 Harm and distress
2 Right to withdraw
3 Real consent
4 Deception
5 Debriefing

See p.29 for an explanation of these principles.

QUESTION SPOTLIGHT!

Remember that **quantitative** data comes in the form of numbers, while **qualitative** data comes in the form of words, in this case what participants said and what observers said about their non-verbal communication. This study is a good example of the benefits of having both sorts of data. *If you had only quantitative data from this study – i.e. the figures for how obedient people were – what incorrect conclusions might you reach?*

EVALUATION

The research method

The study was a laboratory procedure. (It was called an experiment by Milgram, although technically we should now describe it as a pre-experiment.) Laboratory studies come with a set of strengths and limitations. Because the procedure takes place in a highly controlled environment it is possible to eliminate many extraneous variables and be reasonably confident that it is the independent variable we are interested in that is affecting the dependent variable. Laboratory procedures are straightforward to replicate, making them reliable. The potential weaknesses with laboratory studies lie in the realism of the environment and participants' tasks. It is hard to set up laboratory procedures in which people behave as they would in real life.

Quantitative and qualitative data

A strength of Milgram's study was the recording of both quantitative and qualitative data. It therefore has the strengths of both types of data (see p.282 for a discussion). In this case, having both types of data was important in drawing the correct conclusions. If we had only the figures for how many people went to what voltage we might conclude that people were uncaring and did not mind harming someone. However, when we add the qualitative data it becomes clear that, although people were highly obedient, they also found the experience highly stressful.

Ethical considerations

By modern standards, Milgram's procedure raises a number of ethical issues. First, he caused participants considerable distress, if only for a few minutes. He might even have put their health at risk – remember that one participant suffered such a severe seizure that the procedure had to be stopped. He did not obtain informed consent because participants agreed to take part in a learning experiment not a study of obedience. His payment of participants might also have compromised informed consent because they might have felt obliged to continue once they saw what the procedure involved. Participants were deceived about several things: the purpose of the study, the nature of the confederate, the reality of the 'shocks', and the apparent suffering of the learner. Perhaps most seriously, participants were effectively denied their right to withdraw by the use of the verbal prods. Although they could have withdrawn, they didn't feel that they could. Only 35% withdrew from giving all the shocks.

At the time of the study Milgram was in the process of applying for membership of the American Psychological Association. His application was suspended while he was investigated over these ethical issues, but he was able to justify his procedure and was found to have acted properly. The following arguments went in his favour:

- Although participants were deceived this is sometimes allowed within ethical codes provided it is essential for design, and provided participants are fully debriefed at the earliest opportunity. Milgram provided a thorough de-hoax and debrief, and participants generally left the study happy.
- Although participants were distressed for a short time, the vast majority said that they were glad they had taken part and that they had learned something useful.
- Most importantly, the study was an important one, especially given the historical period and the importance of gaining a better understanding of the Holocaust. It is not considered ethically acceptable to replicate the Milgram procedure now.

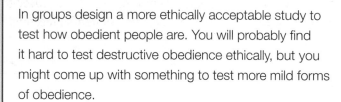

STRETCH & CHALLENGE

In groups design a more ethically acceptable study to test how obedient people are. You will probably find it hard to test destructive obedience ethically, but you might come up with something to test more mild forms of obedience.

Validity

We have said that a potential weakness in laboratory studies is their realism. There are two aspects to this realism: the environment and the task. Milgram's procedure took place in an artificial environment that was rather different to those in which most atrocities take place. On the surface, the task facing Milgram's participants is also artificial – we don't find ourselves operating electric-shock machines very often in real life. Therefore, it can be argued that Milgram's study is low in ecological validity. However, Milgram was clever in selecting both an environment and a task that represent quite well some of the features of the situation in which atrocities take place

- The situation was respectable and the experimenter was in a position of legitimate authority in that environment. People tend to obey orders to participate in atrocities only when those giving the orders have real status and authority. The experimenter wore the lab coat – the uniform of the scientist – in the same way as military leaders wear uniforms as a visible mark of their authority.

- Participants were told that the experiment was for the advancement of science – a noble aim. When leaders are ordering people to commit atrocities they generally claim that they are for the good of the country or the community. So participants were influenced in the same way as are those who commit atrocities.
- The electric shocks increased in small increments of 15V. In this way, each decision to obey was only a slight move from the one before. This is similar to the 'slippery slope' people find themselves on when receiving orders to act aggressively to their victims in real-life atrocities. For example, people might receive orders at first just to transport victims, then to mistreat them at their new location, then finally to kill them.

Reliability

Remember that reliability means consistency. A procedure is reliable if we can precisely replicate it, and when we consistently get the same results when we do replicate it. We have said that laboratory experiments are generally easy to replicate, and Milgram's procedure has been replicated many times. Although there is debate over the reliability of some of his variations, the results of the basic procedure have proved to be very consistent. Thus we can say that Milgram's procedure has good reliability.

Sampling bias

The sample was made up of 40 men from the same region in the USA. This is a fairly average sample for a laboratory study, neither particularly a strength nor a weakness. The fact that the sample was all male and all came from the same area makes it tricky to generalise from the results of the original study to the whole population. Remember, however, that the intention was always to replicate the study in different populations, so this is not a serious weakness.

The volunteer/snowball sampling method is a more serious problem. Self-selection and snowballing are the most unrepresentative of all the sampling methods. Most people do not volunteer for anything so, by definition, volunteers are not typical people! Allowing snowballing compounds this problem because participants tend to invite other people who are like themselves to take part.

Practical applications

This is an important strength of Milgram's research. Understanding the circumstances in which people will obey destructive orders has proved useful in understanding atrocities, even allowing the International Criminal Court in some cases to predict atrocities before they take place (Alexander, 2009). Understanding obedience has also had some more surprising benefits. Influenced by Milgram's research, Tarnow (2000) analysed records of 37 plane crashes, and suggested that in 25% of cases the crash was a direct result of the pilot's obeying orders from the ground. These results have clear implications for accident prevention.

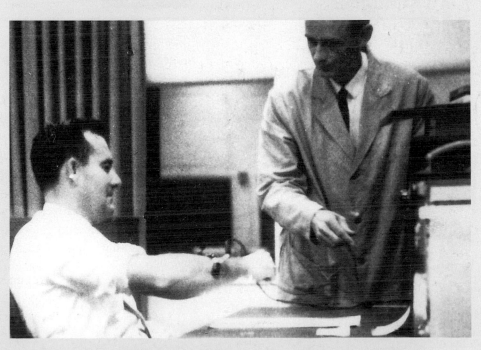

Figure 1.5
The experimenter wore a lab coat
as a visible mark of his authority.

BOCCHIARO *et al.*'s EXPERIMENT INTO DISOBEDIENCE TOWARDS UNJUST AUTHORITY

Bocchiaro, P., Zimbardo, P.G. and Van Lange, P.A.M. (2012) To defy or not to defy? An experimental study of the dynamics of disobedience and whistle-blowing. *Social Influence,* **7**: 35–50.

IN BRIEF

Aim: To see how many people will comply with an unethical request and how many will respond by 'whistle-blowing' to a higher authority. A secondary aim was to compare actual rates of disobedience and whistle-blowing to estimated rates.

Method: 149 students were given an unethical request, to write a statement designed to convince other students to participate in a traumatic sensory deprivation experiment. Participants were then left alone to see what they would do. In a separate procedure 138 students were told about the scenario and asked both what they would do, and what they thought the average student would do.

Results: When questioned, most participants said that they would report the unethical experiment and that the average student would disobey. However, 76.5% actually obeyed and only 9.4% 'blew the whistle.'

Conclusion: Although most people believe they will disobey unethical instructions and report unethical conduct, in practice the majority comply with unethical instructions.

 KEY IDEAS

Whistle-blowing involves informing the appropriate authorities about unethical practice, in particular unethical professional practice.

CONTEXT

The authors were inspired by Milgram's research into destructive obedience. However, they noted that Milgram's research focused on obedience and did not tell us much at all about disobedience. One of their aims therefore was to discover more about disobedience, specifically disobedience to unjust authority. Procedures such as Milgram's are generally discouraged now, on ethical grounds, so it was not possible to replicate or extend his research. Instead a new way was required of researching obedience in response to destructive instructions.

Aside from obeying or disobeying such instructions, there is a third option, known as whistle-blowing, which involves reporting an unethical incident to higher authorities. **Whistle-blowing** is a very challenging option because it involves 'taking on' your immediate superiors, those who have authority over you. The authors note that there is a lack of research into this option and point out that very little is known about what whistle-blowers think or feel when they make the decision to blow the whistle. Neither is much known about whether whistle-blowers have particular psychological characteristics in common, such as personality.

There are various ways in which whistle-blowing could be investigated. One way is to interview whistle-blowers after the fact. However, the authors rejected this approach because participants may have had considerable time since the event to draw their own conclusions about why they acted as they did. The authors also rejected a scenario-based method of investigation, in which people are asked how they would act in particular situations, on the basis that this has poor validity unless the situation is a very familiar one.

Milgram did not just investigate obedient behaviour, he also researched participants' beliefs about how obedient they thought people would be when given destructive orders. He found that people tended to wildly underestimate rates of obedience. Bocchiaro *et al.* picked up on this idea. As well as carrying out an experiment to see how many people obeyed, disobeyed and blew the whistle, they also surveyed people to gather information about estimated responses. It was predicted that participants would underestimate the tendency for compliance with unethical instructions.

Bocchiaro *et al.* also picked up on the distinction between dispositional and situational factors affecting obedience and compliance, and their participants were assessed for dispositional characteristics, including personality and social values.

Figure 1.6
The decision to blow the whistle on bad practice is a difficult one.

AIM

The main aim of the study was to investigate the rates of obedience, disobedience and whistle-blowing in a situation where no physical violence was involved but where it was quite clear that the instructions were ethically wrong. There were two additional aims:

1   To investigate the accuracy of people's estimates of obedience, disobedience and whistle-blowing in this situation.
2   To investigate the role of dispositional factors in obedience, disobedience and whistle-blowing.

METHOD

Pilot studies

Eight pilot studies, involving a total of 92 participants, were carried out in order to be sure that the procedure was both credible (i.e. they didn't realise that they were being deceived), and ethically acceptable to participants. It was found that from the participants' perspective the procedure was both believable and ethical.

Participants

All participants were undergraduate students from the VU University of Amsterdam. Ninety-two people took part in the pilot studies, and a further 149 in the main experimental procedure (96 women and 53 men, with a mean age of 20.8 years). The sample consisted of volunteers recruited by flyers posted in the university cafeteria. In addition, 138 different participants were surveyed about how they believed they would respond in the experimental situation.

MATHS MOMENT

In this study, 3.6% of participants in the comparison group said they would obey, 31.9% believed they would disobey, and 64.5% said they would blow the whistle. Express these figures as a ratio and as fractions.

QUESTION SPOTLIGHT!

Be aware that questions might focus on the headline figure of obedience and whistle-blowing rates, or they might look at the estimates or the dispositional factors. Make sure you can answer any of these.

Design and procedure

The main study was carried out in laboratory conditions. Each participant was paid seven euros or given course credits. They arrived alone and were met by a stern experimenter who informed them that they were carrying out research into sensory deprivation. They said that in their last study all participants had panicked, and some had asked for the procedure to be stopped – which it had not been. They aimed to carry out a similar study but were waiting for ethical approval from the university. Each participant was instructed to write a statement to convince other students to take part in the sensory deprivation procedure. They were told that they had to use at least two words from the choice of 'exciting', 'incredible', 'great' and 'superb', and not to mention the negative effects of sensory deprivation. They were also offered regular paid work in the future.

The participant was then left alone in a room with a computer on which to compose their statement, a mailbox, and some ethics committee forms. If a participant believed the study was unethical they had the option of completing a form and putting it in the mailbox. Obedience/disobedience was assessed by whether or not the participant composed the statement. Whistle-blowing was assessed by whether they completed an ethics form and mailed it.

After seven minutes the experimenter returned and led the participant back to the first room, where they were given a set of dispositional measures:

- The HEXACO-PI-R personality test, which measures six personality traits: honesty-humility, emotionality, extraversion, agreeableness (niceness), conscientiousness, and openness to experience.
- The Decomposed Games measure of social values, i.e. the extent to which personal values are oriented towards benefit for all or just for the self.
- Religiosity was assessed by asking participants about their religious affiliation (i.e. what their religion was), frequency of worship, and extent of faith.

Participants were then debriefed, with a particular emphasis on why they had been deceived in the course of the study. They gave written consent for their data to be used. The whole procedure took around 40 minutes.

Separately, 138 different participants were asked to estimate likely obedience levels in this situation. They were provided with a detailed description of the procedure and asked 'what would you do?' and 'what would the average student at your university do?'

RESULTS

There was a dramatic difference between the estimates of obedience gathered in the second procedure, and the actual rates seen in the first, experimental procedure. Only 3.6% of participants believed that they personally would obey, and 64.5% believed that they would blow the whistle. The remaining 31.9% believed that they would disobey. In relation to the average student estimates were somewhat more accurate but obedience was still underestimated; 18.8% were estimated to obey, 43.9% to disobey and 37.3% to blow the whistle. In fact 76.5% obeyed, 14.1% disobeyed and only 9.4% blew the whistle. Among the whistle-blowers, the majority (6%) had obeyed by writing a message.

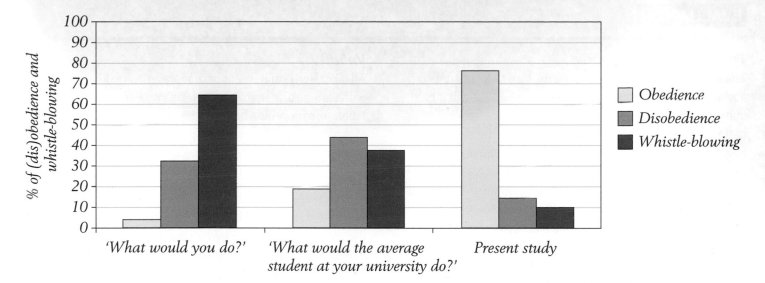

Dispositional factors

None of the six personality traits assessed was associated with levels of obedience, disobedience or whistle-blowing. Nor was social value orientation. With regard to religiosity, neither religious affiliation nor frequency of worship predicted behaviour. However there was a moderate relationship with depth of faith, with those expressing strong religious faith being slightly more likely to whistle-blow.

Figure 1.7
Estimates of obedience vs findings from the main procedure.

CONCLUSIONS

1   People are very obedient and whistle-blowing is uncommon.
2   People overestimate the tendency to blow the whistle and underestimate the likelihood of obedience.
3   There is little or no evidence to suggest that dispositional factors affect obedience or whistle-blowing.
4   On a theoretical level, results support the findings of previous research showing that we tend to see ourselves as 'special' and rate ourselves as less likely to follow destructive orders.
5   Results have implications for social psychology research. The inaccuracy of estimates of behaviour in this situation suggests that all scenario-based research lacks validity.

STRETCH & CHALLENGE

Compare the ethical issues raised in the studies by Milgram and Bocchiaro *et al*. In what ways did the researchers in the more recent study learn from Milgram's experiences?

EVALUATION

The research method

The study was a laboratory procedure. Like Milgram, the authors refer to it as an 'experimental' study, although it had only one condition. Laboratory studies such as these have particular strengths and limitations. Because the procedure takes place in a highly controlled environment it is possible to eliminate many extraneous variables and be reasonably confident that it is the independent variable we are interested in that is affecting the dependent variable. Laboratory procedures are straightforward to replicate, making them reliable. The potential weakness of laboratory studies lies in the realism of the environment and the participants' tasks. In this case the procedure was very lifelike because the situation being investigated was that of a psychologist carrying out a study, and this is exactly what happened – there was nothing artificial about the procedure.

Qualitative and quantitative data

The data gathered in this study was quantitative, in the form of percentages of participants displaying obedience, disobedience and whistle-blowing behaviour. This was a strength because the researchers were interested in making comparisons between rates of disobedience and whistle-blowing (by definition quantitative), and comparing these to estimates. This requires the use of quantitative data.

Ethical considerations

As a behavioural study of obedience, this study might have raised some of the same ethical issues as Milgram's study, however the researchers were clever in designing the study so as to minimise these problems. The situation was relatively low in stress because participants were not ordered to inflict direct harm, as Milgram's participants were. Also, they were left alone when deciding whether or not to obey, and were not 'prodded'. This is quite different from having to refuse to obey an experimenter face-to-face while being told that 'the experiment requires that you continue'. In addition, extensive piloting was carried out to establish that participants considered the procedure to be acceptable, and participants had the opportunity to withdraw their data if they were not satisfied with the ethical conduct of the study.

The design of the study necessarily involved deceit. This is an ethical issue, however deceit can be acceptable in research, provided that participants are informed of the true nature of the study as soon as possible and that they are happy about the study once they are aware of it. These conditions were met.

Validity

All laboratory studies set out to represent a real-life situation, with varying degrees of success. This was unusual for a laboratory procedure because the real-life situation it set out to represent was that of taking part in a laboratory study! Therefore, in spite of the artificial surroundings and unusual task, ecological validity was actually very good.

Reliability

Remember that reliability means consistency. A procedure has external reliability if we can precisely replicate it and consistently get the same results when we do so. Laboratory procedures such as that used in this study are generally easy to replicate. Such a study also has internal reliability if we can be reasonably sure that all participants have a similar experience. In this study conditions were well standardised, so it does seem that this study has good internal reliability.

Sampling bias

The sample in the main study was made up of 149 undergraduate students from a Dutch university. The sample size was large for a laboratory study – this is a strength as it reduces the probability that results are affected by extraneous participant variables. However, the sample characteristics and sampling method are less good. Volunteer sampling is good in terms of ethics but is unlikely to lead to a representative sample as most people do not volunteer. The population from which the sample is drawn – undergraduates at a Dutch university – may be unrepresentative of the general population, and may not generalise to other age groups and cultures.

Ethnocentrism

Although the researchers looked at a sample from a single population (students from a Dutch university), they did assess religious affiliation as one of the variables that might affect obedience. Religion is strongly associated with culture, and in this study no religious differences were found, for example between the behaviour of Christian and Muslim participants. There was therefore some account taken of culture. This was limited, however, so the study can still be said to be to some extent ethnocentric.

Practical applications

Whistle-blowing is under-researched and of great interest to people in many fields. There has, for example, been considerable publicity recently about whistle-blowing over poor-quality care provided in the health service.

COMPARISON OF STUDIES

Milgram's Study of Destructive Obedience **&** *Bocchiaro et al.'s Experiment into Disobedience Towards Unjust Authority*

THE TOPIC
Obedience

The studies by Milgram and Bocchiaro *et al.* are both about social psychology, specifically about obedience to orders or instructions to commit acts that go against the moral codes of the individuals receiving those orders or instructions. However, Milgram's study involved direct orders to commit an act of physical violence – administering painful and possibly dangerous electric shocks. This was based on an attempt to understand the role of destructive obedience during the Holocaust. On the other hand, Bocchiaro *et al.* were concerned with more everyday situations in which people comply with unethical instructions. Accordingly their study involved a more typical workplace situation: giving instructions to mislead people into taking part in a distressing procedure. Another difference was that Bocchiaro *et al.* were interested in whistle-blowing as a third option, in addition to the options of obedience and disobedience.

THE RESEARCH METHOD AND DESIGN
Laboratory procedures with a single condition

Both studies were described by the authors as experimental, although they had only a single condition. Both studies were carried out in a laboratory and both involved a situation where participants were aware that they were taking part in research but were not aware of the nature of the study. In both studies the procedure involved the experimenter giving the participant an instruction. However, a key difference was that Milgram's orders were to directly inflict pain on another person and put them in danger. In contrast, in the Bocchiaro *et al.* study, participants were ordered merely to write a message.

SAMPLE AND SAMPLING
Mixed-sex students vs male adults

Both of these studies employed a volunteer-sampling method involving responses to an advert. However, Milgram's advert

was placed in a newspaper, whereas that used by Bocchiaro *et al.* was placed in a student cafeteria. Milgram used an all-male sample, whereas Bocchiaro *et al.* used a mixed-sex sample.. The target population was different, however. Milgram used adults aged 20 to 50 and from a variety of occupations. Bocchiaro *et al.* studied just undergraduate students with a much younger mean age and a smaller age range.

EXPERIMENTAL MATERIAL AND MEASUREMENT OF THE DEPENDENT VARIABLE
Quantitative data on rates of obedience

The two studies used rates of obedience as the main dependent variable. For Milgram this was the number of people giving the full 450V shock. For Bocchiaro *et al.* it was the number of people writing the message to persuade other students to take part in sensory deprivation. Bocchiaro *et al.* also measured the frequency of whistle-blowing.

Both studies involved collecting quantitative data in the form of obedience rates. In addition to the headline obedience rates, Milgram also collected qualitative data in the form of transcripts of what participants said and observations of their behaviour. Bocchiaro *et al.* also collected additional information but this was quantitative, including personality traits and values orientations. There was thus a much greater emphasis on quantitative data in the Bocchiaro *et al.* study.

APPLICATIONS
Real-world atrocities vs whistle-blowing in the workplace

Both these studies have applications in understanding, predicting and tackling the tendency to obey orders that directly or indirectly lead to harm and suffering in others. Milgram's study is directly applicable to predicting atrocities, and is used for exactly this purpose by the International Criminal Court. Bocchiaro *et al*'s study is more relevant to understanding more everyday injustice, such as that in the workplace. In particular the low rates of whistle-blowing in this study help us to understand why it often takes so long for really bad practice at work to be identified and challenged.

KEY THEME: RESPONSES TO PEOPLE IN AUTHORITY

Milgram used a laboratory procedure to test destructive obedience, showing that people are surprisingly likely to obey orders to carry out immoral acts. Bocchario *et al.* used a similar laboratory procedure to show that people were also surprisingly likely to obey instructions to encourage people to take part in an unethical experiment. They also found that people rarely took the opportunity to blow the whistle on the experimenter.

KEY THEME

Responses to people in authority
Both studies found that participants were willing to act unethically when ordered to by people in authority.

Milgram
Ethically controversial study. All-male sample. Additional measures were qualitative, including observations and transcripts. Applicable to real-world atrocities.

Similarities
Investigated obedience to direct orders to harm others. Laboratory procedures with a single condition. Samples recruited using an advert. Collected quantitative data in the form of obedience rates.

Bocchiaro *et al.*
Researchers used elaborate ethical safeguards. Mixed-sex sample. Additional measures were quantitative. Applicable to whistle-blowing in the workplace.

PRACTICE QUESTIONS

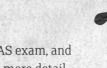

Here are some of the sorts of questions that you could be asked in Sections A and B of your AS exam, and some examples of successful and less successful answers. We look at Section B questions in more detail in Chapter 6, on pages 206–8 and 212–14.

SECTION A: CORE STUDIES

1 From the study by Milgram on obedience:
   (a) Describe the sample. [2]
   (b) Suggest **one** problem with generalising from this sample. [2]
2 Milgram claimed that his study of obedience produced two 'surprising findings'. Outline **both** of these findings. [4]
3 Milgram's study has been strongly criticised. Outline **one** reason why Milgram should have conducted his study. [2]
4 Outline **one** difference between Milgram's study of obedience and Bocchiaro et al.'s study of disobedience and whistle-blowing. [3]
5 Outline **one** similarity between Milgram's study of obedience and Bocchiaro et al.'s study of disobedience and whistle-blowing. [3]
6 From the study by Bocchiaro et al. into disobedience and whistle-blowing, explain what is meant by 'whistle-blowing'. [2]
7 (a) What is a pilot study? [2]
   (b) Give **two** reasons why Bocchiaro et al. conducted a pilot study. [2]
8 Explain what Bocchiaro et al. found about the relationship between dispositional factors and whistle-blowing. [2]

SECTION B: AREAS, PERSPECTIVES AND DEBATES

9 (a) Outline how social psychology explains behaviour. [2]
   (b) Suggest **one** strength of claiming that behaviour is only due to nurture. Support your answer with evidence from **one** appropriate core study. [3]
   (c) Suggest **one** weakness of claiming that behaviour is only due to nurture. Support your answer with evidence from **one** appropriate core study. [3]
   (d) Explain how any **one** core study can be considered to be located within the area of social psychology. [5]
   (e) Discuss the extent to which social psychology can be viewed as useful. Support your answer with evidence from core studies. [12]

SECTION A   4 Outline **one** difference between Milgram's study of obedience and Bocchiaro et al.'s study of disobedience and whistle-blowing. [3]

Rachel's answer:

The participants in Milgram's study had to give people electric shocks but the people in Bocchiaro's study had to write a letter.

Charlotte's answer:

One difference between the two studies is the way in which they gathered information estimating the behaviour of the participants. Before he conducted his study, Milgram asked psychology students to estimate how many people out of 100 would obey his orders to give electric shocks to another person.

We say: Rachel has given a key difference between the two studies: the behaviour chosen to measure obedience was very different in each study. However, she could have given more detail, e.g. she could have clarified that the difference she is outlining is the behaviour that was being observed in each study, or she could have expanded her descriptions of 'give people electric shocks' and 'write a letter' to demonstrate greater knowledge and understanding of the studies and how they differ. There are lots of differences between the two studies: the sample sizes were different, they were conducted in different countries, and it could be argued that they differ in terms of the ethical issues that they raise. Bocchiaro measured personality differences in his studies, where as Milgram did not.

In contrast to this, Bocchiaro asked a sample of participants (who were not taking part in the actual experiment) to read a detailed description of the study and to respond to two questions. The first was asking them what they would do and the second asked them to say what the average student at their university would do.

We say: This is a very good answer which gives a clear account of an interesting difference between the two studies. Charlotte starts by describing the difference (the way they collected information estimating the behaviour of the participant) and then goes on to give information about how this was done in both studies.

5 Outline **one** similarity between Milgram's study of obedience and Bocchiaro *et al.*'s study of disobedience and whistle-blowing. [3]

Rachel's answer:

They both showed that people obeyed.

We say: This is a correct statement but Rachel has not taken into account the command word 'outline', nor the fact that there are three marks available here. This answer needs some expansion. This could stay as the first sentence but would need to be followed by further sentences describing the obedience in each study.

Charlotte's answer:

Both studies demonstrate the power of authority. In Milgram's study around two-thirds of the participants continued to obey the instructions to give electric shocks to the learner right up until the 450 volt level. In Bocchiaro's study obedience was even higher, with three-quarters of participants completing the statement that they were asked to write.

We say: This is a much stronger answer and Charlotte has obviously taken note of the command word 'outline' and has not simply identified a similarity between the two studies but has provided some further information to back up the first sentence.

8 Explain what Bocchiaro *et al.* found about the relationship between dispositional factors and whistle-blowing. [2]

Rachel's answer:

There was no relationship.

We say: This is broadly correct and would gain credit although even a two-mark question requires some elaboration. Rachel really needs to expand this answer a little more and demonstrate that she does understand what was found.

Charlotte's answer:

There was no relationship between personality and whistle-blowing, which was a little bit surprising. There was a small relationship between depth of faith – the stronger your faith the more likely you were to whistle-blow.

We say: A very good answer from Charlotte. She is correct in stating that none of the personality variables showed any relationship with whistle-blowing and that depth of faith showed only a moderate relationship. The fact that Charlotte has gone on to explain the direction of this relationship is a further strength.

SECTION B 9 (b) Suggest **one** strength of claiming that behaviour is only due to nurture. Support your answer with evidence from one appropriate core study. [3]

Rachel's answer:

One strength is looking at the factors in the person's environment.

Charlotte's answer:

One strength is that it allows us to recognise that people are not always to blame for their negative behaviours. Milgram's study shows us that people gave electric shocks not because they were cruel sadistic people but because the social situation made it very difficult for them to behave otherwise.

We say: This is a very short answer which doesn't really make a clear point. Why is looking at the factors in the person's environment a strength? There is definitely the start of a valid point here but Rachel needs to make sure that she explains herself clearly to the examiner.

We say: This is much better. Charlotte has identified a clear and very interesting strength and has given evidence from one study to back up this point.

9 (c) Suggest **one** weakness of claiming that behaviour is only due to nurture. Support your answer with evidence from one appropriate core study. [3]

Rachel's answer:

One weakness is ignoring biological explanations.

Charlotte's answer:

One weakness is that it means that we might ignore individual personality or biological factors when trying to explain a behaviour. For example there might have been significant differences in biological measures such as anxiety between those who did help and those who didn't in the Piliavin study, but a focus solely on nurture would mean that the researcher would not be looking for this.

We say: Although this is as short as Rachel's previous answer, this is making a valid point. What is missing is the support from an appropriate core study, which has been explicitly asked for in the question.

We say: This is another clear answer from Charlotte. There is a clear point being made that is the same point that Rachel made in her answer. Charlotte has also responded to the second part of the question, which asks for support from an appropriate core study.

PILIAVIN *et al.*'s FIELD EXPERIMENT INTO BYSTANDER BEHAVIOUR

Piliavin, I.M., Rodin, J. and Piliavin, J.A. (1969) Good samaritanism: an underground phenomenon? *Journal of Personality & Social Psychology,* **13**: 289–299

IN BRIEF

Aim: To study the factors affecting whether people would help a collapsed man on the New York underground.

Method: Experimenters faked collapse on New York underground trains, and the number of people who helped and the time taken to help were recorded. The race, apparent responsibility of the victim (ill or drunk), the presence of a model helper, and the number of passengers present were varied.

Results: 79% of victims received help. Help was more likely if the victim appeared to be ill. There was some increased tendency for people to help those of their own race. The number of bystanders made little difference, and most people were helped before the model could initiate helping.

Conclusion: Provided people are in a closed environment where they cannot simply leave, they are likely to help someone in need. Helping is most likely when the victim is seen as not responsible for the situation and is the same race as helpers. The number of bystanders is not important in this situation.

KEY IDEAS

The word **'bystander'** is defined differently in different sources. We are using the term broadly to mean anyone who is present at an incident but not directly involved. The terms 'bystander effect' and 'bystander apathy' describe the behaviour of bystanders who do not assist those who need help in an emergency.

WEB WATCH

You can watch a report on the Genovese murder and some early research online. Go to YouTube and search for 'shocking bystander effect'.

You can also see an animation of the Piliavin study here: http://goanimate. com/movie/0CCb_m0Vk5uE/1?utm_ source=gigyabookmark.

CONTEXT

This study is concerned with **bystander** behaviour. Bystanders are people who witness events and have to choose whether to intervene or not. Recently there has been a lot of debate over 'have-a-go-heroes' who put themselves at risk to intervene and attempt to stop crimes taking place. Most of the time bystanders can help without putting themselves at risk. However, surprisingly often we choose not to act to help people in need.

The Kitty Genovese murder

Psychological research into bystander behaviour was triggered by a murder that took place in New York in 1964. Excerpts from the *New York Times* article describing the incident are shown opposite.

Some of the details of the story as it was reported at the time have since been challenged. Given the layout of the block, it would not have been possible for anyone to have seen the whole incident, so each person would have seen just fragments of the event. Also, the area was not actually as quiet as the article implies – one neighbour said that rows between couples leaving a local bar were common late at night. Given these facts, we cannot be sure that 38 people really saw, correctly interpreted, and chose to ignore the murder. However, the Genovese murder captured the public imagination and stimulated psychological research into bystander behaviour.

ACTIVITY ✳

THIRTY-EIGHT WHO SAW MURDER DIDN'T CALL THE POLICE

by Martin Gansberg

For more than half an hour 38 respectable, law-abiding citizens in Queens watched a killer stalk and stab a woman in three separate attacks in Kew Gardens. Twice their chatter and the sudden glow of their bedroom lights interrupted him and frightened him off. Each time he returned, sought her out, and stabbed her again. Not one person telephoned the police during the assault; one witness called after the woman was dead.

That was two weeks ago today. Still shocked is Assistant Chief Inspector Frederick M. Lussen, in charge of the borough's detectives and a veteran of 25 years of homicide investigations. He can give a matter-of-fact recitation on many murders. But the Kew Gardens slaying baffles him—not because it is a murder, but because the 'good people' failed to call the police.

This is what the police say happened at 3:20 A.M. in the staid, middle-class, tree-lined Austin Street area: Twenty-eight-year-old Catherine Genovese, who was called Kitty by almost everyone in the neighborhood, was returning home from her job as manager of a bar in Hollis. She parked her red Fiat in a lot adjacent to the Kew Gardens Long Island Railroad Station, facing Mowbray Place.

Miss Genovese noticed a man at the far end of the lot, near a seven-story apartment house at 82–40 Austin Street. She halted. Then, nervously, she headed up Austin Street toward Lefferts Boulevard, where there is a call box to the 102nd Police Precinct in nearby Richmond Hill. She got as far as a street light in front of a bookstore before the man grabbed her. She screamed. Lights went on in the 10-story apartment house at 82–67 Austin Street, which faces the bookstore. Windows slid open and voices punctuated the early-morning stillness.

Miss Genovese screamed: 'Oh, my God, he stabbed me! Please help me! Please help me!' From one of the upper windows in the apartment house, a man called down: 'Let that girl alone!' The assailant looked up at him, shrugged, and walked down Austin Street toward a white sedan parked a short distance away. Miss Genovese struggled to her feet. Lights went out. The killer returned to Miss Genovese, now trying to make her way around the side of the building by the parking lot to get to her apartment. The assailant stabbed her again. 'I'm dying!' she shrieked. 'I'm dying!'

Windows were opened again, and lights went on in many apartments. The assailant got into his car and drove away. Miss Genovese staggered to her feet. A city bus, 0-10, the Lefferts Boulevard line to Kennedy International Airport, passed. It was 3:35 A.M. The assailant returned. By then, Miss Genovese had crawled to the back of the building, where the freshly painted brown doors to the apartment house held out hope for safety. The killer tried the first door; she wasn't there. At the second door, 82–62 Austin Street, he saw her slumped on the floor at the foot of the stairs. He stabbed her a third time—fatally.

Source: **New York Times**, *March 27, 1964*

Figure 1.8 Kitty Genovese.

Q

1 How could you explain these events according to the individual and dispositional hypotheses?

2 What do you think you would have done?

KEY IDEAS

One early explanation for the bystander effect is **diffusion of responsibility** (Latane and Darley, 1968). This occurs when groups of people witness an emergency together and each individual only assumes a fraction of responsibility for helping. The larger the group the less responsibility placed on each individual and the less likely they are to help.

Diffusion of responsibility

Latané and Darley (1968) proposed that the key issue in deciding whether we help or not is whether we see it as our personal responsibility to do so. One reason why groups of people do not help individuals in need is that responsibility is shared equally among the group so that each person has only a small portion of responsibility. They called this idea **diffusion of responsibility**. In a series of lab experiments they demonstrated that the more people who are present in an emergency, the less likely people are to help.

AIM

Piliavin *et al.* wanted to extend early studies of bystander behaviour in several key ways. First, they wanted to study bystander behaviour outside the laboratory, in a realistic setting where participants would have a clear view of the victim. Second, they wanted to see whether helping behaviour was affected by four variables:

1 The victim's responsibility for being in a situation where they needed help
2 The race of the victim
3 The effect of modelling helping behaviour
4 The size of the group.

By observing variations in the size of the group, they were able to test whether diffusion of responsibility occurred.

METHOD

Participants

An estimated total of around 4,550 passengers travelled in the trains targeted by the researchers. These were all regarded by the researchers as 'unsolicited participants'. An average of 43 were present in each carriage in which the procedure was conducted, and a model average of eight were in the immediate or 'critical' area. The racial mix of passengers was estimated as 45% black and 55% white.

Design and procedure

The study was a field experiment carried out on trains on the New York subway. The procedure involved a male experimenter faking collapse on a train between stops, in order to see whether he was helped by other passengers. One particular stretch of track was targeted where there was a 7.5 minute gap between two stations.

Experimenters worked in teams of four, two females to record the results, and two males who would play the roles of victim and model helper. There were four teams, one containing a black male. Each male taking the role of victim took part in both drunk and ill conditions. Seventy seconds after the train left a station the victim would stagger and fall. He then lay still on his back with eyes open, not moving until helped. Between six and eight trials were run on a given day, between 11am and 3pm. Four independent variables were manipulated in the procedure:

1   Victim's responsibility: operationalised as carrying a cane (ill – low responsibility) or smelling of alcohol and carrying a bottle wrapped in a paper bag (drunk – high responsibility).

2   Victim's race: operationalised as black or white.

3   Presence of a model: operationalised as whether a male confederate; either close to or distant from the victim; helped after 70 or 150 seconds.

4   Number of bystanders: operationalised as however many people were present in the vicinity.

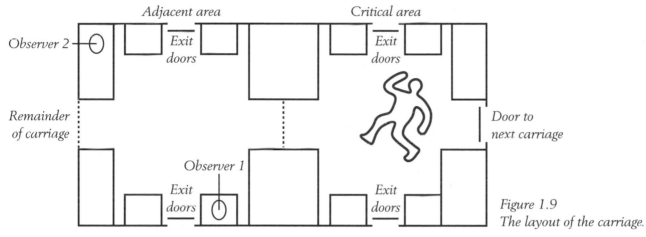

Figure 1.9
The layout of the carriage.

Four males, aged 24–29, and identically dressed in casual clothes, took the role of models of helping behaviour. Four model conditions were applied to both apparently drunk and ill victims:

• Model stood in the critical area and helped after 70 seconds
• Model stood in the critical area and helped after 150 seconds
• Model stood in the adjacent area and helped after 70 seconds
• Model stood in the adjacent area and helped after 150 seconds.

The dependent variable, helping, was measured in the following ways:

• Time taken for first passenger to help
• Total number of passengers who helped.

In addition the gender, race and position of each helper was noted. Qualitative data was also gathered in the form of comments from passengers.

RESULTS

Overall, a higher proportion of people helped than was the case in previous laboratory experiments: 79% of victims received spontaneous help from passengers, and in 60% of cases where the victim was helped it was by more than one person. Most helpers were male.

• ***Ill versus drunk conditions.*** In the cane condition, the victim received help 95% of the time without intervention from a model. In the drunk condition, this was reduced to 50%. People took longer to help the drunk victim than the ill one: over 70 seconds in 83% of the drunk trials, but in only 17% of the cane trials. However the proportion of cases in which more than one person helped was the same.

QUESTION SPOTLIGHT!

What potential extraneous variables might affect results, and what controls did the researchers put into place to counteract these?

Why was it important to fake the collapse in a long gap between stations?

What ethical issues are raised by this type of procedure? How could the researchers have responded to these issues?

Also make sure you know your IVs.

QUESTION SPOTLIGHT!

Most of the data gathered here is quantitative. However there is some qualitative data too. *Identify the qualitative data and suggest why it was useful.*

TABLE 1.3 RESPONSES TO AN ILL OR DRUNK PERSON		
	Cane condition	Drunk condition
% helped spontaneously	95	50
% helped in under 70s	83	17

- **Race of victim**. In the cane condition, black and white victims were equally likely to be helped. However, in the drunk condition, black victims were less likely to receive help. Also, in the drunk condition, there was a slight same-race effect – people were a little more likely to help a drunk of the same race as themselves. The proportion of cases in which help came from more than one person did not vary by race.
- **The effect of modelling**. The model intervening after 70 seconds was more likely to lead to help from other passengers (in nine cases) than the one intervening after 150 seconds (three cases). However, the researchers noted that because passengers helped spontaneously in the vast majority of trials, there were too few cases of helping after modelling to analyse in detail.
- **Number of bystanders**. There was no evidence for diffusion of responsibility. There was a mild effect in the opposite direction – when more passengers were present, people were slightly more likely to receive help.
- **Other observations**. In a significant minority of trials (21 of 103), some passengers moved away from the critical area. More comments were made in drunk trials, and more when no passenger spontaneously helped. The researchers interpreted this as meaning the comments were in response to passengers feeling uncomfortable about the situation.

CONCLUSIONS

Piliavin and his colleagues admitted that the situation they set up was unusual in that their participants were trapped in a carriage with a collapsed person and therefore could not simply walk away as they could normally. In this situation:
- An ill person is more likely to receive help than a drunk person.
- Men are more likely to help another man than women are.
- People are slightly more likely to help someone of their own ethnic group, especially when they appear drunk.
- There is no strong relationship between size of group and likelihood of helping. The small correlation between group size and helping behaviour is positive rather than negative. Therefore there is no support for diffusion of responsibility.
- The longer an incident goes on, the less likely people are to help (even if help is modelled), the more likely people are to leave the area, and the more likely they are to discuss the incident.

Explaining the findings

The researchers explained the findings in terms of arousal and the costs and rewards of alternative responses. Perceiving an emergency raises arousal levels. According to the situation, this can be interpreted either as sympathy or as fear and disgust. The closer one is to the emergency and the longer it continues, the more arousal increases. Arousal is also greatest when the bystander can empathise with the victim. The behaviour of bystanders aims to reduce the arousal level. This can be achieved in four ways:

1 helping directly
2 leaving to find help
3 leaving the area
4 dismissing the victim as unworthy of help.

Which of these options is chosen depends on the costs and benefits of helping or not helping. These are shown in Table 1.4. If the benefits of helping and the costs of not helping outweigh the costs of helping and the benefits of not helping, then help will be offered.

This model explains neatly the behaviour of participants. The drunk is helped less because there are greater costs in terms of fear and embarrassment. People help their own ethnic group more because they can feel more empathy with them. Late modelling has less effect than early modelling because people will have found another coping strategy by then.

TABLE 1.4 COSTS AND BENEFITS OF ALTERNATIVE RESPONSES

	Costs	Benefits
Helping	fear, embarrassment, effort, disgust	praise
Not helping	self-blame, blame from others	continuing activities

EVALUATION

The research method

The study was a field experiment, and field experiments are associated with particular strengths and weaknesses. The major strength is the natural environment in which it is conducted and the opportunity to create realistic situations. The weaknesses centre around the difficulty in controlling variables. In this case the researchers put into place a number of controls. The victims were the same age and sex, and dressed identically. They collapsed in the same way. The same stretch of track was used on each trial to ensure that there was always the same time available, and the timings before a model helped were kept the same. Nevertheless, not all conditions could be kept constant. The number and nature of the passengers boarding the particular carriage was unpredictable. Some might have seen the incident several times, and, if so, it is hard to predict how they might have responded to that.

Quantitative and qualitative data

Like Milgram, Piliavin *et al*. collected both quantitative and qualitative data. However, their emphasis was very much on the quantitative. This was appropriate, given the aims of the study. They were interested in how many people helped and how long it took them to do so under each condition. However, qualitative data in the form of what comments people made about victims collapsing was also useful as an indicator that people were responding to the emergency by justifying why they were not helping. This was important, as this became one of the strategies for reducing arousal levels in Piliavin *et al*.'s model of bystander behaviour.

Ethical considerations

Field experiments always raise ethical issues because they involve interfering with people going about their business who have not agreed to take part in the study. The following issues are particularly important in this case:

- **Harm and distress.** People observing the collapse felt some anxiety. Those who did not help might have suffered some guilt afterwards. It is also possible that someone might have injured themselves helping a victim up.
- **Consent.** People did not give consent to taking part in an experiment. Nor were they free to choose not to participate.
- **Deception.** People were deceived by the collapse of the actor. They were not informed later that he was an actor or that he was ok.
- **Withdrawal.** People could not ask to have their data removed from the analysis, as they did not know they had taken part in a study.
- **Debriefing.** Participants had no opportunity to be debriefed or de-hoaxed. They might have left the situation in distress and they certainly did not know they had taken part in an experiment.

Validity

The validity of the procedure is good. The behavioural measures of helping used in this study have much better validity than alternatives such as self-report measures because actual helping is recorded rather than estimates of helping. Ecological validity is also good. Remember that there are two aspects to ecological validity: the naturalness of the environment, and the realism of the task or situation. This study does well on both counts. People were in their natural environment on a train, and the situation of seeing an ill or drunk person collapse is an entirely normal one.

Reliability

Because the procedure was carried out in a natural setting the internal reliability of the study was poor. Not all participants had the same experience in the study because of factors like time of day and the purpose of their journey. In addition some participants may have ended up taking part more than once if they travelled that route regularly.

Sampling bias

The sample was large at around 4550. The proportion of black and white passengers was also representative of the local population. However, taking the sample from those travelling between 11am and 3pm might have left those at work or in education in the middle of the day under-represented. There was no control over who entered the target carriage or stood in the critical area, therefore the sampling method was opportunity sampling. This is unlikely to be representative.

Ethnocentrism

This study falls foul of the charge of ethnocentrism. It was conducted in a single city, and it was assumed that the findings could be generalised to other cultural contexts. In fact we know from the next study by Levine *et al.* that helping behaviour varies massively between different cities around the world. Although it is not entirely clear what cultural factors impact on helping behaviour it seems extremely likely that cultural factors do make a difference.

Practical applications

There are many situations in which people require help. Understanding when people are likely to actually receive this help can help to save lives. In particular you can apply the findings of this study to maximising the chances of receiving help if you ever need it yourself. Make sure you don't appear drunk. If you are male, appeal to other males for help. If you can, get to a place where people can't simply leave, in order to reduce their arousal levels. Oh, and get help immediately — the longer the emergency goes on, the less likely you are to receive help!

Figure 1.10
125th Street Station, *where the victim was helped off the train.*

STUDY 4

LEVINE *et al.*'s CROSS-CULTURAL COMPARISON OF HELPING BEHAVIOUR

Levine, R., Norenzayan, A. and Philbrick, K. (2001) Cross-cultural differences in helping strangers. *Journal of Cross-cultural Psychology,* **32** (5): 543–560.

IN BRIEF

Aim: To investigate differences in non-emergency helping behaviour towards strangers in a range of cultures and to understand differences in terms of cultural traditions and economic productivity.

Method: A total of 1198 participants in 23 countries were given the opportunity to help in one of three situations involving a dropped pen, someone with a bad leg struggling to pick up dropped magazines, or a blind person requiring help to cross the street.

Results: There were significant cultural differences in helping, ranging from 93% in Rio de Janeiro to 40% in Kuala Lumpur. People in countries with a cultural tradition of *simpatia* and low economic productivity were more helpful.

Conclusion: There are significant cultural differences in non-emergency helping behaviour. These are associated with both economic factors and cultural values.

CONTEXT

Levine *et al.* note that there is anecdotal evidence to suggest that strangers are much more likely to receive help in some cities than others. A range of explanations has been suggested for these variations, including the population size and rate of population change, economic factors, and cultural values. However, almost all previous research focused on population size, showing that the likelihood of receiving help declines with the size of a city's population. However, Levine *et al.* point out that cities vary in many ways apart from size. They suggest that every city can be seen as having a personality rather like that of an individual.

There were a number of other limitations in previous research. Most studies had used unrepresentative opportunity samples, making it hard to draw conclusions about cultural differences. Also, very few studies had taken place outside the USA, and most of those compared urban and rural areas in the same country. The idea behind the Levine *et al.* study was to compare behaviour in the largest city of different countries in order to understand the impact of economic and cultural differences between countries on helping behaviour.

The authors were particularly interested in three classes of factor influencing the helpfulness of people in a city towards strangers: economic, cultural and cognitive. The first class is economic factors. It has been suggested that within the USA there is a weak positive correlation between the economic wealth of a

Figure 1.11
Cities can be seen as having a personality. You may be more likely to receive help in some cities than others.

KEY IDEAS

Collectivist societies include many in the Far East and Africa. The cultural values of collectivist societies centre on obligations to a group rather than to the self, so individuals are obliged to put the needs of family, company or community ahead of their own.

Individualist societies, such as Britain, USA and – to a varying extent – Western European countries, place more emphasis on the rights and freedoms of the individual and their nuclear family.

Simpatia is a cultural value particularly associated with Spanish and Latin American societies. It is defined by a concern for the well-being of others, with an obligation to be friendly, polite and helpful.

city and people's helpfulness. On the other hand it has also been suggested that financially well-off societies require that individuals behave selfishly in order to generate wealth. If true, this would suggest that people in prosperous cities may be less, rather than more helpful.

The second class of factor is cultural. Triandis (1995) has suggested a distinction between **collectivist** societies and **individualist** societies. It may be that collectivist societies are more concerned with the welfare of others and are therefore more helpful. On the other hand collectivist societies tend to be mostly concerned with other members of the same community rather than strangers. A second cultural factor is *simpatia*, the cultural value of concern for others. ***Simpatia***-oriented societies may be particularly helpful towards strangers.

The third class of factor identified by Levine *et al.* is cognitive. Milgram (1970) suggested that the rapid pace of modern city life results in sensory overload. To cope with this, city-dwellers filter out non-essential information so they literally do not notice when someone needs help. There was little evidence for or against this idea prior to this study.

AIM

The aim of the study was to examine the tendency of people in the largest city of each of 23 countries to help a stranger in a non-emergency situation. Three more specific aims were investigated:

1 To establish if the tendency of people to help strangers is universal or dependent on the characteristics of a city.
2 To test whether the helping of strangers varies between cultures.
3 To investigate whether particular characteristics of a community, such as city size, are associated with the tendency to help strangers.

METHOD

Participants
Participants were from large cities in 23 countries: Austria (Vienna), Brazil (Rio de Janeiro), Bulgaria (Sofia), China (Shanghai), Costa Rica (San Jose), Czech Republic (Prague), Denmark (Copenhagen), El Salvador (San Salvador), Hungary (Budapest), India (Calcutta), Israel (Tel Aviv), Italy (Rome), Malawi (Lilongwe), Malaysia (Kuala Lampur), Mexico (Mexico City), the Netherlands (Amsterdam), Romania (Bucharest), Singapore (Singapore), Spain (Madrid), Sweden (Stockholm), Taiwan (Taipei), Thailand (Bangkok), and the United States (New York). The selection of countries and cities was influenced by available opportunities; the experimenters who volunteered were interested cross-cultural psychologists or travelling students. The total number of participants was 1,198. Individual participants were selected simply for being the second person to cross a certain line on a pavement. Children, older people and people with visible physical disabilities were excluded from selection.

Design and procedure

This was a cross-cultural study carried out in the field. Because the conditions involved comparing naturally occurring groups (the people in each city) the study should be described as a quasi-experiment rather than a true experiment. The procedure was carried out in two or more locations in city centres during office hours on summer days.

To minimise extraneous variables all experimenters were male and they did not speak to participants. To further standardise conditions experimenters were trained in exactly how to carry out the procedure. The reliability of experimenter behaviour was not tested in this study but it had been tested in a previous study using the same training procedures and found to be good.

Helping behaviour was tested in three non-emergency situations:

- Dropped pen: experimenters dropped a pen and appeared not to notice as they approached a participant.
- Hurt leg: experimenters walking with a limp and a leg brace dropped a pile of magazines and appeared to struggle to pick them up.
- Blind person crossing road: experimenters wearing dark glasses and with white canes stepped up to a crossing and held out their cane, signalling that they wanted help crossing the road.

In each case the participant was scored as helping if they chose to intervene in any way. So in the pen condition they were counted as helping if they just told the experimenter they had dropped it, and in the blind person condition they were counted as helping even if they just told the experimenter when it was safe to cross. Participants were not directly asked for help. The rate of helping for each country was obtained by averaging the rate of helping on the three measures.

Community variables (i.e. the characteristics of the cities and their inhabitants) were assessed as follows:

- Population size: taken from the United Nations Demographic Yearbook.
- Economic prosperity: taken from the Purchasing Power Parity (PPP) statistics published by the World Bank.
- Cultural values: six independent cross-cultural psychologists rated each country from 1 (very collectivist) to 10 (very individualistic), and their average ratings were used. Spanish and Latin American countries were all coded as *simpatia* and all others non-*simpatia*.
- Pace of life: measured by average observed walking speed. Speed was measured according to the time taken to walk 60 feet (18.3m) between two markers.

Figure 1.12
This study used a blind man needing help crossing the road as an example of a non-emergency helping situation.

QUESTION SPOTLIGHT!

This study makes use of primary data, for example in the form of the experimental measures of helping behaviour. It also uses secondary data, for example the measures of population size and economic prosperity.

1 Explain what is meant by primary and secondary data.
2 What is the advantage of using secondary data in this study?

RESULTS

Helpful and unhelpful cities

There were substantial differences between the likelihood of non-emergency helping in the different cities. The city where help was most likely was Rio de Janeiro, with a helping rate of 93%. Kuala Lumpur, Malaysia, came in last with help only being offered 40% of the time. Rank order and overall percentage of helping behaviour for each city are shown in Table 1.5 on the next page.

STRETCH & CHALLENGE

From a perspective of mainstream British cultural values some of the findings as regards the three measures of helping seem very odd. Why should people respond so much more positively to a blind person than to someone with a leg injury? Even stranger is the fact that in some cities people appeared to see the dropping of a pen as more of an emergency than the struggles of people with disabilities.

1 What cultural explanations can you think of for these anomalies?

2 What methodological issues might have produced these anomalies?

TABLE 1.5 OVERALL PERCENTAGES FOR HELPING IN THE 23 CITIES

City, Country	Rank	%
Rio de Janeiro, Brazil	1	93.99
San Jose, Costa Rica	2	91.33
Lilongwe, Malawi	3	86
Calcutta, India	4	82.67
Vienna, Austria	5	81
Madrid, Spain	6	79.33
Copenhagen, Denmark	7	77.67
Shanghai, China	8	76.67
Mexico City, Mexico	9	75.67
San Salvador, El Salvador	10	74.67
Prague, Czech Republic	11	75
Stockholm, Sweden	12	72
Budapest, Hungary	13	71
Bucharest, Romania	14	68.67
Tel Aviv, Israel	15	68
Rome, Italy	16	63.33
Bangkok, Thailand	17	61
Taipei, Taiwan	18	59
Sofia, Bulgaria	19	57
Amsterdam, Netherlands	20	53.67
Singapore, Singapore	21	48
New York City, United States	22	44.67
Kuala Lampur, Malaysia	23	40.33

The three measures of helping

Helping was fairly consistent across the three measures. Most of the time those cities where people tended to help in one situation were also where people tended to help in the others. However, there were some interesting anomalies. In New York 75% of participants helped the blind man cross the road but only 28% helped the man with the leg injury pick up his magazines. In Mexico City people were helpful to both the measures involving disability (92% for the blind man; 80% for the man with the bad leg) but much less so with the dropped pen (55%). In a minority of cities — including Vienna, Budapest and Copenhagen — people were most helpful in the dropped pen situation!

Relationships between helping and population variables

Correlations were calculated between helping behaviour and population variables. Results are shown in Table 1.6. Only economic prosperity was found to correlate significantly with helping, with a correlation of −0.43. The better off the residents of a city are, the less helpful they are. Helping was not related at all to population size or collectivism. The two least helpful cities – Kuala Lumpur and New York – differed substantially in both size and collectivism/individualism. Walking speed correlated weakly with helping behaviour.

TABLE 1.6 CORRELATION BETWEEN HELPING AND COMMUNITY VARIABLES				
Community characteristics	**Helping measures**			
	Overall helping	**Blind person**	**Hurt leg**	**Dropped pen**
Population size (city)	−.03 (23)	−.06 (23)	.22 (23)	−.21 (23)
Purchasing power parity (PPP)	−.43 (22)	−.42 (22)	−.21 (22)	−.32 (22)
Walking speed	.26 (20)	.06 (20)	.23 (20)	.24 (20)
Individualism/collectivism	−.17 (23)	−.09 (23)	−.21 (23)	−.07 (23)

The other significant finding was that people in countries with *simpatia* as a cultural value were significantly more helpful than others, all falling in the top half of the rank order. The mean rate of helping for *simpatia* countries was 82.87%, compared to 65.87% in non-*simpatia* countries.

CONCLUSIONS

1 Helping behaviour in non-emergency situations is not universal but varies between cities.

2 There are large variations in the likelihood of receiving help in non-emergency situations in different cultural contexts. There was however no relationship between helping and collectivism/individualism, although there was a significant difference between helping in *simpatia* and non-*simpatia* cultures.

3 The only characteristic of cities measured in this study that correlates with helping is economic prosperity: poorer cities tended to have higher rates of helping. Helping was not related to city size or pace.

MATHS MOMENT

The mean rate of helping in simpatia countries was 82.87% with a standard deviation of 8.84. The mean rate of helping in non-simpatia countries was 65.87% with a standard deviation of 13.41. The difference was statistically significant.

1 Explain what is meant by variance and standard deviation.

2 What does the larger standard deviation in non-simpatia countries show?

3 Explain what is meant by a significant difference.

4 Draw a bar chart to compare the two mean rates of helping.

EVALUATION

The research method

The study was a field experiment, and field experiments are associated with particular strengths and weaknesses. The major strength is the natural environment in which it is conducted and the opportunity to create realistic situations. The weaknesses centre around the difficulty in controlling variables. In this case the researchers put into place a number of controls to minimise extraneous variables. In particular the experimenters were highly trained so that as far as possible all participants had similar experiences.

Qualitative and quantitative data

Levine *et al.* collected quantitative data. This was appropriate given the aims of the study. They were interested in how many people helped. The other variables associated with helping were also quantified so that mathematical relationships with helping could be established.

Ethical considerations

In some ways this study raises the same issues as the Piliavin *et al* study. Field experiments always raise ethical issues because they involve interfering with people going about their business who have not agreed to take part in the study. The following issues are particularly important in this case:

- **Consent:** People did not give consent to taking part in an experiment. Nor were they free to choose not to participate.
- **Deception:** People were deceived by the actions of the experimenters. They were not informed later that he was an actor.
- **Withdrawal:** People could not ask to have their data removed from the analysis as they did not know they had taken part in a study.
- **Debriefing:** Participants had no opportunity to be debriefed or de-hoaxed. They are unlikely to have been distressed by the procedure but they certainly did not know they had taken part in an experiment.

Validity

The issues here are very similar to those of the Piliavin *et al.* study. There is a straightforward behavioural measure of helping – this has very good validity. People were unaware they were taking part in a study so their behaviour was unaffected by experimenter effects. Ecological validity is also very good because people were tested in the natural environment of their home city street and because the situation – of seeing a person drop a pen, or pick up magazines, or struggle to cross the road – was very true to life.

Reliability

Because the procedure was carried out in a natural setting the internal reliability of the study was poor. Not all participants had the same experience in the study because of factors such as time of day and the purpose of their journey. On the other hand the experimenters were highly trained to make sure they gave all participants as consistent an experience as possible.

Sampling bias

The sample was large at around 1200. Individual participants were chosen randomly, which is more likely to lead to a representative sample than the opportunity sample in the Piliavin *et al* study. There were reasonable controls in place to match the samples in the different cities being compared. District and time of day were matched. A strength of the sample was that it was drawn from a number of cultural contexts.

Practical applications

There is a practical application here for travellers! Whether for business or pleasure, many of us will visit a range of cities around the world. It is helpful to know at the outset where we are likely to receive help if we need it, and where we are not. Based on the findings of this study it might be wise to take particular care not ever to need help in New York or Kuala Lampur! This means planning one's trip to these cities very carefully indeed.

DO IT YOURSELF

You aren't in a position to explore national differences in helping behaviour, and looking at cultural differences locally may get you into hot water ethically. What you could do, if you have access to two communities of different size (e.g. a town and a city), is to compare helping rates there. You should be quite cautious about any helping behaviour practicals, but non-emergency helping raises fewer ethical issues than the kind of emergency helping used in the Piliavin *et al.* study. You could partially replicate the Levine *et al.* study but perhaps stick to the dropped pen condition as that puts the least social pressure on people who have not consented to take part.

COMPARISON OF STUDIES

Piliavin et al.'s Field Experiment into Bystander Behaviour **&** *Levine et al.'s Cross-cultural Comparison of Helping Behaviour*

THE TOPIC
Bystander behaviour *towards emergency and more everyday situations*

The studies by Piliavin *et al.* and Levine *et al.* are both about social psychology, specifically about bystander behaviour – the extent to which people will offer help to strangers in need. However, there were differences in the aims of the two studies. Piliavin *et al.* were concerned with helping in an emergency situation in which someone clearly needed urgent assistance. On the other hand Levine *et al.* were concerned with more everyday situations in which people were faced with non-emergency situations. In Levine *et al.*'s study participants encountered strangers who would clearly benefit from help but who were not in immediate danger. In addition Levine *et al.* were primarily interested in differences between cities and their populations, whereas Piliavin *et al.* were more interested in the nature of the emergency situation.

THE RESEARCH METHOD AND DESIGN
Both field experiments using independent measures designs

Both studies were experiments carried out in the field. Both studies were carried out in busy city environments, and both involved a situation where participants were unaware that they were taking part in research. In both studies participants were in familiar natural environments. Another similarity between the two studies was that both used an independent measures design. Different participants took part in each condition.

There was however a difference in the independent variables studied. Piliavin *et al.* studied the effects of four independent variables: the victim's race, the victim's responsibility for the situation, the presence of a model, and the number of bystanders. Levine *et al.* were interested in the effect of population differences between cities.

SAMPLE AND SAMPLING
Both used large samples of non-consenting participants

Both of these studies used very large samples. Piliavin *et al.* estimated that around 4550 people were present for their procedures although of course the majority did not get directly involved in the situation. For Levine *et al.*, the total sample size was just under 1200. In both studies participants had not volunteered to take part in a study, nor were they aware that they were participating.

The target populations were similar in the two studies, although Piliavin *et al.*'s study was located in a single city whereas Levine *et al.* were interested in 23 cities. Sampling in both cases had a systematic element. For Piliavin *et al.* this took the form of making sure a good range of train times were covered. For Levine *et al.* this meant that the largest city in each country was chosen and that individual participants were chosen according to who passed a point in the street at a particular time.

EXPERIMENTAL MATERIAL AND MEASUREMENT OF THE DEPENDENT VARIABLE
Quantitative and *qualitative data*

The two studies used rates of helping as the main dependent variable. For Piliavin *et al.* this meant how many people helped the victim and how long they took to do so. For Levine *et al.* it was the number of people helping or offering help to the person in need. In both cases, the DV was help offered without being asked.

Both studies involved collecting quantitative data in the form of helping rates. However, Piliavin *et al.* also collected some qualitative data in the form of passenger comments. Levine *et al.*'s data was entirely quantitative.

APPLICATIONS
Helping behaviour in the real world

Both these studies have applications in understanding and predicting helping behaviour in real life. From Piliavin *et al.* we can learn that if we are taken ill in a public place and need help, we need to make sure people realise that we are ill and not drunk. Levine *et al.*'s findings have important implications in terms of travelling – if we need help, we can expect it a lot more in some cities than in others.

KEY THEME: RESPONSES TO PEOPLE IN NEED

Piliavin *et al.* and Levine *et al.* used field experiments to investigate helping behaviour. Both found that overall most people in need did receive help. However they also found that key variables affect the likelihood of receiving help. These include the apparent responsibility of a victim for their situation and the city in which the emergency takes place.

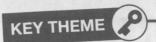

KEY THEME

Responses to people in need
Both studies looked at variables affecting helping behaviour towards strangers. Piliavin et al. looked at the nature of the situation. Levine *et al.*'s cross-cultural study identified different behaviours in different cities.

Piliavin *et al.*
Studied helping behaviour in an emergency situation in New York. Primarily concerned with overall rates of helping and how this was affected by the nature of the victim and the situation.

Similarities
Both were field studies testing helping behaviour in natural urban environments and independent measures designs. Both used non-consenting participants. Both used helping behaviour as the main dependent variable, and had good ecological validity.

Levine *et al.*
Studied helping behaviour in non-emergency situations in 23 cities around the world. Primarily concerned with the differences between helping rates in different cities. Large sample of 1200. Collected quantitative data.

PRACTICE QUESTIONS

Here are some of the sorts of questions that you could be asked in Sections A and B of your A level exam, and some examples of successful and less successful answers. We look at Section B and C questions in more detail in Chapter 6 on pages 206–18.

SECTION A: CORE STUDIES

1 The study by Piliavin *et al.* (subway Samaritans) was a field experiment.

  (a) Explain why a field experiment was used. [2]

  (b) Give **one** disadvantage of a field experiment for this investigation. [2]

2 Outline **one** ethical issue raised by the study by Piliavin *et al.* [2]

3 (a) Explain what is meant by diffusion of responsibility. [2]

  (b) Suggest why the study by Piliavin *et al.* did not provide evidence for diffusion of responsibility. [2]

4 Outline **one** difference between the study by Piliavin *et al.* into subway Samaritans and the study by Levine *et al.* into cross-cultural altruism. [3]

5 From the study by Levine *et al.* into cross-cultural altruism: Outline **one** way in which helping behaviour was measured. [2]

6 Levine *et al.* were particularly interested in three factors that might influence the helpfulness of people in cities.

  (a) Identify and describe **two** of these factors. [2]

  (b) Outline the results for **one** of the factors. [2]

7 Levine *et al.*'s study is cross-cultural. Outline **two** problems that might be encountered when conducting cross-cultural research. [4]

8 Outline **one** conclusion that can be drawn from Levine *et al.*'s study into cross-cultural altruism. [2]

SECTION B: AREAS, PERSPECTIVES AND DEBATES

12 (a) Describe the difference between a social explanation for behaviour and a cognitive explanation for behaviour. [4]

  (b) Explain how any **one** core study can be considered to be providing a social explanation for behaviour. [5]

  (c) Evaluate the problems of investigating social explanations for behaviour. Support your answer with evidence from **one** appropriate psychological study. [6]

  (d)* Identify and discuss the strengths and weaknesses of providing social explanations for behaviour. Support your answer with evidence from appropriate psychological studies. [20]

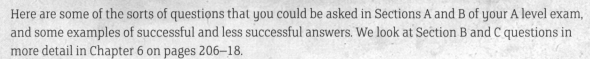

SECTION A   3 (a) Explain what is meant by diffusion of responsibility. [2]
(b) Suggest why the study by Piliavin *et al.* did not provide evidence for diffusion of responsibility. [2]

Liam's answer:

(a) When people don't feel that they have to help.

(b) Because people did help the victim

Rina's answer:

(a) Diffusion of responsibility is where the responsibility for acting in an emergency situation is shared out among all the people present. The more people that are present, the less likely any one individual is to help.

(b) Diffusion of responsibility may not have occurred because people were in a closed situation, a train carriage, and not able to leave the situation. So it was harder for them to think that someone else would do something because it was obvious that no-one was doing anything.

We say: Part (a) doesn't quite go far enough in explaining the concept. The key idea is that the more people there are present, the less individual responsibility a person feels for acting. For part (b), Liam hasn't quite understood the question. It is correct to say that people did help but the question is asking you to explain why they helped. There were lots of people there but diffusion of responsibility did not occur.

We say: A very good answer from Rina. These are nice clear explanations that demonstrate good understanding of the concept of diffusion of responsibility and of the findings of the study.

6 Levine *et al.* were particularly interested in three factors that might influence the helpfulness of people in cities. (a) Identify and describe two of these factors. [2] (b) Outline the results for one of the factors. [2]

Liam's answer:

(a) The factors were someone dropping a pen, someone with a bad leg and a blind person.

(b) People helped the blind person more than the drunk person.

Rina's answer:

(a) The three factors were economic, cultural and cognitive. Cultural was whether the society was collectivist or individualist. Cognitive was measures of pace of life and sensory overload.

(b) The study found that poorer cities had higher rates of helping. This means that there was a negative correlation between wealth and helpfulness.

We say: Liam has got himself a bit confused here! The answer he has given to part (a) is incorrect. These are the conditions that were tested in each of the different cultures. The three factors that Levine *et al.* were particularly interested in were economic, cultural and cognitive factors. Two of these needed to be named and briefly described. In part (b), Liam seems to have got this study and the study by Piliavin *et al.* confused. This is easy to do when studies are focusing on similar behaviours, so it is important to learn the names of the authors of the core studies as well as the studies themselves, as both these studies do discuss helpfulness.

We say: This is a very good answer. Although Rina has identified three factors in part (a), she has obviously read the command to describe two of these and has done this well. Her answer to part (b) is also well explained and shows good understanding.

7 Levine *et al.*'s study is cross-cultural. Outline two problems that might be encountered when conducting cross-cultural research. [4]

Liam's answer:

It might be really expensive to do cross-cultural research and there might be language problems.

Rina's answer:

One problem when conducting cross-cultural research may be practical problems such as language difficulties. Not fully understanding another language might mean that it is easy to misinterpret what is being said to you. The second problem is ethnocentrism. This is where researchers judge the behaviour they have observed by the standards of their own culture, and this often leads to researchers viewing their own culture as the norm and other cultures as somehow inferior to this. Lack of understanding of other cultures is at the root of this.

We say: This is another very brief answer from Liam. The expense of cross-cultural research is not necessarily a problem if researchers in different cultures collaborate with each other. The language problem is a valid point, although Liam needs to elaborate on this.

We say: This is a better answer from Rina. In particular, her discussion of ethnocentrism is excellent and shows good understanding of a concept that students often find difficult and confusing.

SECTION B 12 (a) Describe the difference between a social explanation for behaviour and a cognitive explanation for behaviour. [4]

Liam's answer:

Social psychology explains behaviour through obedience, conformity, disobedience and bystander behaviour.

We say: This does identify some of the aspects of behaviour that social psychology focuses on but is not answering the question that was asked. The question is asking for a difference between a social explanation and a cognitive explanation.

Rina's answer:

Social psychology explains behaviour though an examination of the individual in their social context. Social psychology claims that behaviour is influenced through the real or imagined presence of others and that the social context is more important than individual personality characteristics. Cognitive psychology explains behaviour through and examination of the internal cognitive processes that underlie the behaviour such as memory, thinking and decision making.

We say: This is better. Rina is focusing on the overall assumptions of the two explanations, that behaviour is determined by its social context or by its underlying cognitive processes.

12 (b) Explain how any **one** core study can be considered to be providing a social explanation for behaviour. [5]

Liam's answer:

The study by Milgram is social psychology because it looks at why people obey or disobey. The study by Bocchiaro *et al.* is also a social psychology study because it looks at whistle-blowing. The study by Piliavin *et al.* is a social psychology study because it looks at helping behaviours in a real-life situation.

We say: Although Liam has given quite a lot of information here, it is not clearly directed at the question. What this does is to describe the topic areas that three of the core studies examine, but the question clearly asks for just one. Further, this is more focused on the topic of the study rather than on the explanation that is being offered.

Rina's answer:

The study by Piliavin *et al.* is clearly within the area of social psychology as it looks for situational reasons to explain why someone will or won't help someone else. By varying the appearance of the 'victim', Piliavin *et al.* demonstrate that the reasons for the behaviour are located outside the person, in the social situation.

We say: Once again, Rina's answer contains more information and is more clearly focused on the question. However, there are five marks available for this question and Rina could have given more detail.

THE SOCIAL AREA OF PSYCHOLOGY

We have now looked in some detail at four social-psychological studies. Based on these studies let's see what we can tease out about the social area of psychology. We have already said that social psychology is concerned with how people interact with one another. Breaking that down a bit we can identify some assumptions underlying the area.

1 Human behaviour is influenced by the situation as well as individual characteristics

Common sense tells us that some people are more helpful, aggressive, obedient, etc. than others. In other words there are individual differences in our social behaviour. However, social psychologists have uncovered a lot of information about something less obvious: the ways in which our social behaviour is influenced by the situation. Take Milgram, for example. Although he started with the hypothesis that the Holocaust was the result of the German national character, he soon realised that in a situation where people are receiving direct orders from a person in a position of authority, the majority of us will obey those orders even though we may suffer distress if this means going against our individual beliefs. Behaviour in this situation was therefore affected by the situation. This does not mean that individual differences are irrelevant – Elms and Milgram (1966), for example, found that people with an authoritarian personality were particularly obedient in the Milgram procedure – but it does mean that we are all affected to some extent by the social situation.

2 We can understand human behaviour in terms of influence by individuals and groups

The most obvious example of individual influence in the studies we have looked at is in Milgram's study. Here, an individual who has the appearance of legitimate authority influences others by giving them direct orders. This influence is so powerful that the majority of participants obeyed his orders even though they did not want to do so and although doing so meant going against their own morals. Piliavin *et al.* also attempted to study the influence an individual can have on others by modelling helping behaviour. This is slightly different because we are talking about an individual influencing a group. Modelling works when one person (the model) demonstrates a behaviour for others to imitate. Modelling certainly can influence behaviour, as Bandura *et al.* showed in their study (see Chapter 3). In the Piliavin *et al.* study it didn't really work as planned because the vast majority of the passengers helped spontaneously before the model had a chance to model helping.

Humans are a social species and we spend much of our time in groups. Understanding how we behave in groups and are influenced by group membership is just as important to understanding our social behaviour as is understanding the influence of one individual on another. Piliavin *et al.*'s study is the only one here directly concerned with groups. One of their aims was to test the idea that people in groups diffuse responsibility for helping behaviour between all the members so that each member has relatively little responsibility and is unlikely to help. The Piliavin *et al.* study did not support the idea of diffusion of responsibility because larger groups were found to be slightly more likely to provide help than smaller groups (diffusion of responsibility would predict the opposite).

3 Research can help us understand social issues

All the researchers we have looked at in this chapter have been inspired by the wish to understand real-life social issues. For Milgram it was the idea that people commit atrocities and that one factor influencing atrocities seems to be obedience to orders. For Bocchiaro *et al.* the issue is disobedience in the face of unethical practice and whistle-blowing. These are highly topical social issues at the moment with many high profile cases in the news involving reporting or failure to report bad practice in the National Health Service, for example.

Inspired to explain events like the Kitty Genovese murder, Piliavin *et al.* aimed to explain why people are sometimes helpful to one another in an emergency and sometimes much less so. In similar vein Levine *et al.* looked at helping behaviour on a broader level, comparing cities with different cultural values and economic prosperity.

STRENGTHS AND WEAKNESSES OF THE SOCIAL AREA
Strengths

1   **Real-life relevance.** All the studies in this chapter are clearly relevant to understanding real-life social issues. Some psychological research has been accused of being of interest to only a small group of academics. This cannot be said about social psychology however. Everyone is affected by obedience, by tyranny and by helping behaviour.

2   **Good range of research methods.** All the studies we have looked at in this chapter test cause and effect relationships, so they are (broadly) experimental. Social psychologists have been imaginative however in the range of experimental methods they have used. Milgram and Bocchiaro *et al.* used highly controlled laboratory settings.

Piliavin *et al.* and Levine *et al.* preferred to conduct their experiments in the field. This range of methods is a strength of social psychology as it means that findings of controlled lab studies can be checked out in real-life settings and vice versa.

Weaknesses

1 **Social-psychological research often raises ethical issues.** Often it seems that the more relevant to real life a study is the more it raises ethical problems. All the studies we have looked at in this chapter raise serious ethical issues. Milgram deliberately deceived participants, caused them stress, and when they protested during the experiment they were prodded to continue despite their discomfort. Piliavin *et al.* involved large numbers of participants without consent or debriefing. In spite of extensive safeguards Bocchiaro *et al.* put people in a moderately stressful situation. This is not to say these studies should not have been carried out, just that we always have to weigh up the benefits of social research against the costs.

2 **Social determinism.** When reading about social psychology, you could be forgiven for thinking that all our behaviour is simply a product of the social situation and that therefore we have no individual responsibility for our actions. The 'I was just obeying orders' defence is a classic example of this type of thinking. Actually social situations influence us just as our biology, our development and our cognitive processes influence us – none of these excuse us when we behave badly, even though they help us make sense of good and bad behaviour.

C2
COGNITIVE
PSYCHOLOGY

This area of psychology considers the mental processing of information. In this chapter we will look four studies.

For AS we consider two studies that highlight the theme of memory:

1 Loftus and Palmer's (1974) experiments on eyewitness testimony. The aim was to investigate how the type of question asked affects memory by comparing the effects of different verbs and asking about an event that did not happen.

2 Grant *et al.*'s (1998) laboratory experiment looking at the effect of silent or noisy study and exam environments, specifically whether changing the environment affects performance.

For A level we additionally look at two studies paired around the theme of attention:

3 Moray's (1959) experiments on auditory attention. The aim was to test how much we are able to notice of a spoken message that we are not attending to.

4 Simons and Chabris's (1999) study of visual inattention. The research used a laboratory experiment to investigate the failure to notice an obvious event when attending to another task and the influence of unexpectedness and the complexity of the additional task.

We will look at these studies in detail, evaluating each one and exploring their applications. We also consider them in their pairs, using them to think about the key themes. Finally we will use them to explore issues in cognitive psychology, looking at the strengths and limitations of this area.

LOFTUS AND PALMER'S STUDY OF DISTORTION OF WITNESS MEMORY

Loftus, E.F. and Palmer, J.C. (1974) Reconstruction of automobile destruction: an example of the interaction between language and memory. *Journal of Verbal Learning & Verbal Behaviour*, **13**: 585–589

IN BRIEF

Aim: To investigate the effect of questioning on witness memory of a car accident.

Experiment 1: 45 students watched film of car crashes. They were then asked to estimate the cars' speeds, using different verbs to describe the crash. Estimated speed varied according to the verb used, with 'smashed' leading to the highest estimates.

Experiment 2: 150 students underwent a similar procedure but were asked about broken glass at the scene. When the word 'smashed' was used, participants still estimated a higher speed, but, in addition, they wrongly remembered seeing broken glass at the scene of the crash.

Conclusion: Wording of questions can alter witness memories of events.

CONTEXT

How well do you remember events you have seen? Psychologists are concerned with the accuracy of our memory of events. As far back as 1909, G.M. Whipple reviewed evidence and concluded that **eyewitnesses**' memory of events is considerably less accurate that we would like to believe. This may be particularly true when we are asked to recall numerical values, such as time, distance or speed. By the 1970s, several studies had shown that people tend to over-estimate the time and speed involved in complex events. In one study, Marshall (1969) asked Air Force personnel to estimate the speed of a car that they had been watching. Although the participants knew that they would be questioned, their responses varied wildly and were inaccurate (their estimates were between 10–50mph, whereas the actual speed was 12mph).

Fillmore (1971) suggested that one such factor might be the language used to describe the motion, and that using words such as 'smashed', rather than more neutral words, such as 'hit', could lead people to judge speed to be greater.

Loftus and Palmer subsequently proposed that: 'Given the inaccuracies in estimates of speed, it seems likely that there are variables which are potentially powerful in terms of influencing these estimates' (1974: 585). In other words, if we are poor at judging speed, then there must be factors other than the actual speed that affect our judgement.

The inaccuracy of **eyewitness memory**, and the potential for memories to be distorted by the use of language, have important practical applications. In particular, the police and the courts often rely on **eyewitness testimony** in

Figure 2.1
Elizabeth Loftus

WEB WATCH @

Test your own skill as an eyewitness. Go to www.youramazingbrain.org and click on 'Test yourself'.

STRETCH & CHALLENGE

Normally, more participant details are reported in psychological studies. Suggest a reason why this might be less important in cognitive psychology than in some other areas such as social psychology or individual differences.

 KEY IDEAS

An **eyewitness** is someone who sees an event such as a crime or an accident. Technically, someone who hears the incident is an 'earwitness' and someone who, for example, smells gas prior to an explosion would be a 'nosewitness'. This study is concerned with the accuracy of **eyewitness memory** and, by implication, the usefulness of **eyewitness testimony** – the accounts given by witnesses to the Police and in court.

Laboratory experiments take place under controlled conditions. They test cause and effect by comparing two or more conditions. The **independent variable** (IV) is the factor that is being investigated and differs between the conditions. The **dependent variable** (DV) is the thing that can change and is measured for the results.

Fillers are questions put into a questionnaire or interview to disguise the aim of the study by hiding the important questions amongst irrelevant ones. This means that the participants are less likely to alter their behaviour by working out what the researcher is looking for.

order to make decisions about what actually took place and who was responsible for what happened. By the time of Loftus and Palmer's study, there was concern in legal circles about the use of leading questions, and the likelihood that such questions can cause inaccurate eyewitness testimony. Loftus and Palmer define a leading question as 'one that, either by its form or content, suggests to the witness what answer is desired or leads him to the desired answer' (1974: 585). The present study is concerned with the effect on eyewitness memory of asking leading questions about the speed of a car.

GENERAL AIM

The overall aim of the study was to test whether the phrasing of questions about a car accident could alter participants' memory of an event.

EXPERIMENT 1

AIM

The aim of the first experiment was to see whether using different verbs to describe a collision between two cars would affect estimates of the speed at which they were travelling when the crash took place.

METHOD

Participants

Forty-five students took part in the first experiment. No details of age or gender were recorded.

Design and procedure

The study was a **laboratory experiment** using an independent measures design. Participants were shown seven films of car crashes, taken from training films used by the Seattle Police Department and the Evergreen Safety Council. In four of the films the speed of the car was known because the crashes were staged for training purposes. The speeds in these films were 20mph, 30mph, 40mph and 40mph. After watching the films, all participants were asked to write an account of the accident and then to answer a series of questions. All but one of the questions were **fillers**, designed to make it harder to work out the aim of the experiment. The other question was a *critical* question, meaning that it was closely concerned with the aim of the study. This question was: 'About how fast were the cars going when they hit each other?'

The **independent variable** was the verb used in the critical question. For one group this was 'hit'. The other groups received the same question but with the verb 'contacted', 'bumped', 'collided' or 'smashed' instead of 'hit'. The **dependent variable** was the mean estimated speed of the car.

RESULTS

Results were in the form of quantitative data. Participants' estimates of the speed at which the cars were travelling were not affected by the actual speed. The mean estimates for each of the crashes in which the speed was known are shown in Table 2.1. This shows that we are generally poor at estimating speed. However, estimates of the cars' speeds did vary according to the verb used in the critical question. These results are shown in Table 2.2.

TABLE 2.1 MEAN ESTIMATES AND ACTUAL SPEED IN FOUR CRASHES

Film number	Actual speed (mph)	Estimated speed (mph)
1	20	37.7
2	30	36.2
3	40	39.7
4	40	36.1

CONCLUSIONS

Participants' estimates of the speed at which the cars were travelling when the accident took place varied according to the verb used to describe the crash. There are two possible reasons for this:

1 *Response bias.* When a participant is unclear what speed to estimate, the verb gives them a clue as to whether they should estimate a high or low figure.

2 *Memory distortion.* The verb used in the question actually alters a participant's memory of the crash.

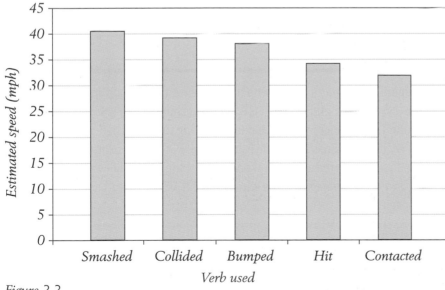

Figure 2.2
Loftus and Palmer's participants estimated different speeds according to the verb in the leading question

MATHS MOMENT

Draw a bar chart to illustrate the estimated speed data from Table 2.1.

MATHS MOMENT

Explain why a bar chart rather than a histogram has been used to illustrate the data from Table 2.2 in Figure 2.2.

TABLE 2.2 MEAN ESTIMATES OF SPEED IN ANSWER TO THE CRITICAL QUESTION

Verb used	Estimated speed (mph)
Smashed	40.5
Collided	39.3
Bumped	38.1
Hit	34.0
Contacted	31.8

QUESTION SPOTLIGHT!

The Loftus and Palmer procedure has been challenged because in some ways it is unrealistic. *Suggest two reasons why this might be an issue.*

Figure 2.3
We are generally poor at estimating the speed of cars in a crash

QUESTION SPOTLIGHT!

Experiment 2 was crucial to the conclusion drawn by Loftus and Palmer. *Explain the purpose of Experiment 2.*

EXPERIMENT 2

AIM

The aim here was to investigate whether the different speed estimates found in Experiment 1 were, in fact, the result of a distortion in memory. This was done by seeing whether participants who heard the words associated with high-speed estimates would be more likely to incorrectly remember broken glass at the crash site.

METHOD

Participants

One hundred and fifty students took part in the second experiment. No details of age or gender were recorded.

Design and procedure

As in the first experiment, the method was a laboratory experiment with an independent measures design. All participants watched a film of a car crash. The entire film lasted less than one minute, and the accident itself lasted four seconds. All participants were given a questionnaire that first asked them to describe the accident in their own words, and then to answer a series of questions. As in the first experiment, there was a critical question. The first 50 participants received the question: 'About how fast were the cars going when they smashed into each other?' Another 50 participants received the question: 'About how fast were the cars going when they hit each other?' Finally, a control group of 50 participants received questions that did not ask about the speed of the cars. A week later, the participants returned and answered a further 10 questions. The critical question among these was: 'Did you see any broken glass?'

RESULTS

As in Experiment 1, participants who heard the word 'smashed' in the critical question estimated a higher speed (10.46mph as opposed to 8.0mph in the 'hit' condition). The numbers of participants reporting that they had seen broken glass in each condition is shown in Table 2.3. More than twice as many people incorrectly remembered seeing broken glass having heard the word 'smashed' in the question compared to those who heard 'hit' or who heard no question about speed.

TABLE 2.3 NUMBERS OF PARTICIPANTS REPORTING SEEING BROKEN GLASS IN EACH VERB CONDITION

Response	'smashed'	'hit'	'control'
yes	16	7	6
no	34	43	44

CONCLUSIONS

The general conclusion from the two experiments is that the way in which questions about events are worded can affect the way in which those events are remembered. The results of Experiment 2 are important because they strongly suggest that this is not simply due to response bias. Instead it seems that post-event questions actually become part of the memory for that event. Therefore, the wording of questions can actually distort event memory.

STRETCH & CHALLENGE

Draw either a paired or a stacked bar chart for the results of Experiment 2.

QUESTION SPOTLIGHT!

If you offer an answer evaluating the research method for this study, make sure your answer makes reference to the study itself. A generic answer will gain limited credit.

EVALUATION

The research method

The study was a laboratory experiment. Because the procedure took place in a highly controlled environment, with precise timing of films, presentation of the question order, the inclusion of fillers, etc., it was possible to eliminate many extraneous variables. The researchers could therefore be reasonably confident that it was the independent variable of the verb that was affecting the dependent variables of speed and recall of broken glass. The potential weaknesses of laboratory studies such as that of Loftus and Palmer lie in the realism of the environment and the participants' tasks. It is hard to set up laboratory procedures in such a way as to ensure that people behave as they would in real life. In this case, watching a film is not the same experience as witnessing a real event. Actual car crash witnesses would be likely to experience much more intense feelings, such as fear or shock, and emotions are known to affect memory. Witnesses to a real crash would also have much more significant motives for accurate recall – their testimonies would have genuine consequences for convictions.

Qualitative and quantitative data

The data gathered in this study were quantitative. This is both a strength and a weakness. On the plus side, the statistics allow easy comparison of the conditions, clearly showing that memory is affected by the wording of questions. On the other hand, there was no opportunity for participants to comment either on what they remembered, or on their experience of being questioned in this way. Such qualitative data might have added to the completeness of the findings.

Ethical considerations

This is a straightforward laboratory experiment, with minimal ethical issues. One possible ethical issue might concern any participants who happened to have experienced real car crashes. As the participants were students, they might have felt obliged to participate even if their experiences meant that they didn't want to. If so, this would raise a question about whether their informed consent was genuine.

Validity

The high levels of control imposed by conducting the study in laboratory conditions ensured that few extraneous variables could influence the outcomes, for example the filler questions reduced the likelihood that the participants worked out the aim. Some of the films were of real accidents, so in this respect the context was realistic. These factors raise validity. However, the overall validity would be reduced both by the lack of realism, in terms of the artificiality of the remaining films and the context, and by the possibility that some participants might have worked out the aim of the experiment, especially in Experiment 2. These factors threaten the ecological validity of the study as both the environment and the task were quite artificial. Participants had a better view of the crash than is typical in real-life situations, but they were probably more relaxed and less motivated to remember details, given that they were in a familiar and safe situation and knew that they were taking part in a study. Remember that it can be quite upsetting to witness an accident in real life, and this emotional response can make the event more (or less) memorable. It is therefore possible that participants' memory was unrepresentative for these reasons.

Reliability

Laboratory procedures are highly standardised, for example the length of the films was specified, which makes them reliable. The standardisation also ensures that the procedure is replicable. In the case of Loftus and Palmer's study, it is interesting to note that very similar results were found for speed estimates with the verbs 'smashed' and 'hit' in Experiments 1 and 2. This suggests that the findings are reliable.

Sampling bias

The participants were all students, not chosen by any representative sampling method. This means that they were unlikely to be truly representative of the population. They are likely to have been predominantly white, middle-class and within a narrow age-range, and they all had the same occupation. This is important for the following reasons:

- Because the participants were students they could have been particularly vulnerable to demand characteristics. In other words, they might have been strongly influenced by cues suggesting what the researchers expected to find. However, the independent measures design would possibly have eliminated the worst of this problem.
- Because the participants were all students, they were very used to taking in information and being tested on it, so they might have been better able to recall accurately than most people.
- The participants were less likely to be drivers than the population as a whole, and their speed estimates might have been less accurate as a result of their lack of experience with cars.

These sample characteristics could mean that the results were partly a product of the sample.

Practical applications

Studies such as this are important in helping authorities to understand how to question witnesses to important events such as accidents and crimes. Following the work of Loftus and her colleagues, the use of leading questions – both by the police immediately after an event, and later in the courtroom – is now tightly controlled. This is likely to have improved the rate of successful criminal convictions.

STRETCH & CHALLENGE

Many aspects of cognition are assumed to be independent of culture. However, it is possible that there are cultural influences on the effects of leading questions. To be certain that Loftus and Palmer's conclusions about reconstructive memory are not ethnocentric, what would it be necessary to do?

Figure 2.4
Eyewitness testimony is important in many criminal cases

GRANT *et al.*'s STUDY OF CONTEXT-DEPENDENT MEMORY

Grant, H.M., Bredahl, L.C., Clay, J., Ferrie, J., Groves, J.E., McDorman, T.A. and Dark, V.J. (1998) Context-dependent memory for meaningful material: information for students. *Applied Cognitive Psychology,* **12**: 617–623.

IN BRIEF

Aim: To test for context-dependency effects caused by the presence or absence of noise during learning and retrieval of meaningful material.

Method: The research method was an experiment, using an independent measures design. Opportunity sampling was used to find 39 participants (aged 17–56 years, females and males). The independent variable was the matching or mismatching of study and test conditions. The study/test condition pairs were: matching (silent/silent and noisy/noisy) and mismatching (silent/noisy and noisy/silent). Participants always studied and retrieved while wearing headphones. In the noisy condition the recorded sound of a cafeteria was played. Participants read a short piece of meaningful material and were tested first on their recall using a short-answer test, and then on their recognition using a multiple-choice test.

Results: The presence of noise or silence during study or test conditions in itself had no effect. However, in both types of test, performance was better in matching conditions than non-matching ones, i.e. retrieval is improved when studying and testing are performed in similar environments.

Conclusion: Noise may not distract study, but as performance is worse when in mismatched conditions, and exams are held in silence, students would benefit from studying in quiet surroundings.

CONTEXT

Many studies have shown that **recall** is better when the participant is in the same environment during recall as they were when learning occurred, in situations as diverse as different classrooms, indoors or outdoors, on land or in water, and with a range of features to indicate contexts, such as colours, images or types of music. This effect was originally explained by the encoding specificity principle (Tulving, 1972) as the consequence of 'context-dependency effects'. This suggests that some aspects of the environment during learning are stored or 'encoded' with the to-be-remembered item and become part of the 'memory trace'. These extra pieces of information, or '**cues**', then help with retrieval of the learned items. Thus, when the environment at learning and recall 'matches', recall is better than when the two environments are mismatched.

The effect of context-dependency is less consistently found for **recognition** tests, i.e. where the participant has to identify previously learned material, rather than recalling it with minimal aid. For example, in a study using divers as participants, Godden and Baddeley (1975) showed that in contexts matched for encoding and retrieval (i.e. water/water or land/land) the effects of context were much greater than for mismatched environments (water/land or land/water).

KEY IDEAS

Cue dependency is the idea that when a to-be-remembered item is stored, other pieces of information present at the same time are stored with it. These extra pieces of information, from the context or the person's state, can later act as cues to aid recall. They provide a way to retrieve the to-be-remembered item itself if they are also present at the time of recall.

KEY IDEAS

There are several different ways to trigger memories. A key difference is between recall and recognition. **Recall** is the accessing of memories with very few prompts, such as when you write an essay and you have to remember lots of information with just a short title to help you. In **recognition**, we are required to decide which of two or more items we have seen before, such as when you answer a multiple-choice question by selecting the option that you have previously learned is correct. In recognition there are many more cues to assist with memory, so the task is easier.

Another important difference relates to the material used in memory studies. Many experiments use lists of nonsense syllables to overcome the risk, when using real words, that some items might have particular relevance to some participants and so would be more (or less) likely to be remembered. However, the reality is that we don't learn nonsense syllables in everyday life; we need to remember things that relate to our shopping, our courses or our jobs. These are described as **meaningful items** because they are understandable and we can relate to them.

Smith, Vela and Williamson (1988), however, found no context-dependency effects on recognition using different levels of processing (such as counting vowels, making rhymes or generating images) as contexts. This difference has been used to suggest that recall and retrieval rely on different processes. One explanation says that recognition tasks themselves act as strong retrieval cues, so any additional effects of context are minimal. If this were so, then even in recall tasks using **meaningful items** this 'outshining' of existing cues, in this case from meaningfulness, would prevent context-dependency effects appearing (Smith, 1986). Indeed, some recent evidence also supports the outshining hypothesis. For example, Isarida *et al.* (2012) tested undergraduates in a 'long study time' condition for words or non-words. When these were recalled in matching or non-matching environments, the context cue helped only in the non-word condition, i.e. when meaningfulness had not already provided sufficient information to cue recall.

The idea that salience (meaningfulness) matters to context-dependence is important as it is useful to know about the factors affecting memory for realistic material, such as the things that students have to learn on their courses. An interesting comparison by Smith (1988) looked at recall of meaningful items by reviewing studies of students' exam performance in which they had been tested in the same room as they had been taught, or a different one. The findings of these studies were mixed, although most found that there was no harm in changing rooms, i.e. that context-effects were absent even with meaningful material. However, you probably study in lots of different places — at home, in the library, at friends' houses, on the bus, etc. — so the material you learn might not have specific context-related cues that tie it to the classroom. Indeed, Smith reports one study which controlled for this, and still found a context-dependency effect.

In this study, Grant *et al.* suggest that perhaps an important difference between study environments and test environments was the amount of background noise. Think about the exam room — it's silent — whereas you might study while listening to background music, with the television on, or with people talking around you. Of course, people differ in the type of music they like, so rather than introduce a potential confounding variable, Grant *et al.* investigated the effect of general noise, in matching and mismatching learning and retrieval conditions, for both recall (short-answer questions) and retrieval (multiple-choice questions). To ensure that they were testing memory for meaning, rather than simple verbatim memory, they gave participants a comprehension task on new material which mimicked a typical classroom test.

AIM

The aim of the study was to test the effect of noise as a source of context on the studying and retrieval of meaningful material in an academic context. A focus on changing learning context was important as students can chose where to study but not where they are tested.

METHOD

The study was an experiment and the experimental design was independent measures.

Participants

The 39 participants were aged 17–56 years (17 females and 23 males). They were recruited by opportunity sampling: eight psychology students, acting as experimenters, each found five acquaintances who would be participants. (The result from one participant was excluded.)

Design and procedure

The independent variable was whether the study and test conditions were matching (the same) or mismatching (different). The experimental design was independent measures (between subjects), so each participant experienced just one of the four possible combinations:

Figure 2.5
How often do you study while listening to music?

matching	study context:	silent	study context:	noisy
	test context:	silent	test context:	noisy
mismatching	study context:	noisy	study context:	silent
	test context:	silent	test context:	noisy

The background noise for the noisy condition was a tape made in the university cafeteria at lunchtime, with the hum of conversation, occasional words or phrases but no audible sentences, and the sound of chairs and dishes. It was played moderately loudly through headphones (also worn by participants in the silent condition). The to-be-remembered material was a two-page article on psychoimmunology, which was interesting and understandable (but unfamiliar) to the participants. Each participant was asked to read the article through once, highlighting or underlining if they wanted to. Reading time was recorded but not controlled. During reading, all participants wore headphones (with the tape playing in the noisy condition). After a 2-minute break, they asked the participant to answer the two tests. The short-answer test was always given to participants first, to ensure that material was being recalled from the article itself rather than from information in the multiple-choice test. The dependent variable of retrieval was therefore measured in two ways (recall and recognition) for each participant:

- recall: a short-answer test of 10 questions (producing single-word or phrase answers)
- retrieval: a multiple-choice test of 16 questions.

MCQ

6. The article describes a study that looked for the common thread in the sudden deaths of 54 men. The common thread turned out to be:

   a. Depression   **b.** Age   **c.** Lack of exercise   **d.** Poor diet

7. The article describes a quote by the microbiologist Rene Dubois who examined the link between tuberculosis and a variety of factors. Dubois said that "as long as there is ____ there will be disease". What goes in the blank space?

   a. Medicine   **b.** Stupidity   **c.** Change   **d.** Poverty

SAQ

4. The article describes a study that looked for the common thread in the sudden deaths of 54 men. What did the common thread turn out to be?

5. The article describes a quote by the microbiologist Rene Dubois who examined the link between tuberculosis and a variety of factors. Dubois said that "as long as there is ____ there will be disease". What goes in the blank space?

Figure 2.6
Excerpts from the multiple-choice and short-answer questions

QUESTION SPOTLIGHT!

Look at Figure 2.6. Can you see how the multiple-choice questions (MCQs) could act as a cue for the short-answer questions (SAQs) if read first? *Using questions from the sample as examples, explain why the SAQ test was always given first.*

MATHS MOMENT

Look at the standard deviations in Table 2.4. Which condition shows:

a   the greatest spread
b   the smallest spread?

RESULTS

There were individual differences in reading time, but no consistent differences between noisy and silent study conditions or test (retrieval) conditions. An independent measures comparison of study and test conditions showed two interesting outcomes. First, there were no significant patterns for the individual variables, i.e. whether material was learned or retrieved in each of the environments made no difference to the short-answer question test or the multiple-choice question test results. However, there was an interaction between study and test conditions. For both the short-answer and multiple-choice tests, performance was significantly better in matching conditions than in non-matching ones (this pattern can be seen in Table 2.4 and Figure 2.7). This suggests that recall is better when studying and testing are performed in similar environments in terms of the noisiness of the surroundings.

TABLE 2.4 MEANS AND STANDARD DEVIATIONS FOR SHORT-ANSWER AND MULTIPLE-CHOICE TESTS				
	Study condition			
	silent		noisy	
Test condition	mean	standard deviation	mean	standard deviation
Short-answer test				
silent	6.7	1.22	5.4	1.9
noisy	4.6	1.17	6.2	2.2
Multiple-choice test				
silent	14.3	1.58	12.7	1.64
noisy	12.7	1.64	14.3	1.77

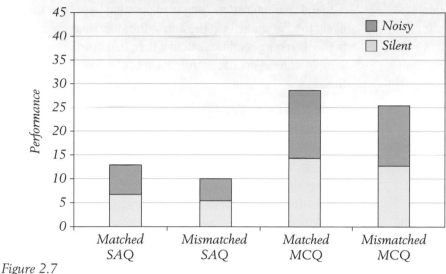

Figure 2.7
A comparison of scores for matching and non-matching study and test conditions

CONCLUSIONS

Grant *et al.* drew two main conclusions from this study:

1   As there was no independent effect of noise on performance, the claim made by many students – that noise does not affect their capacity to study – is supported.
2   However, as context-dependence affects retrieval in both SAQ and MCQ tests, students should study in quiet surroundings, as exams are typically held in silence.

STRETCH & CHALLENGE

In their review of classroom management around the world, Hayden, Levy and Thompson (2007) note that classrooms are remarkably similar across a wide range of cultures, with fairly consistent approaches to classroom management, although cultural differences were also found. Chiu and Chow (2011) reported cultural differences in classroom discipline in a cross-cultural study of 41 countries. In a cross-cultural study of students' study skills, some consistent differences have been found (Morena and di Vesta, 1991).

If cultural differences do exist, to what extent might this invalidate the generalisation of the findings of Grant *et al.* beyond the original cultural group tested?

EVALUATION

The research method

In experiments it is possible to control extraneous variables. In this case, the participants had the same silent or noisy conditions (using headphones and the tape) and were given the same instructions (e.g. to ignore the content of the tape). To ensure that retrieval was from long-term memory not from short-term memory, there was a timed two-minute break between studying and testing. Such controls raise validity and improve reliability. However, as it was an experiment, some variables could not be standardised so well, for example the amount of time given for the initial reading of the article was not controlled.

Qualitative and quantitative data

The data gathered in this study were quantitative. This is both a strength and a weakness. On the plus side, the statistics allow easy comparison of the conditions, clearly showing that although study and learning conditions independently do not affect retrieval, their match or mismatch does. On the other hand, there was no analysis of essay-style questions, which would have involved qualitative analysis to enable comparison, or of participants' views on what it felt like to study in silence. The conclusion suggests this is preferable, but if students feel unable to concentrate, or cannot work for as long without some additional source of stimulation, they may end up learning less. Either source of qualitative data might have added to the completeness of the findings.

Ethical considerations

Although this is an experiment, the participants were aware that they were participating and were not deceived and were debriefed after testing, so it raises few ethical issues.

Participants were given enough information to give informed consent (i.e. that the experiment would test their reading comprehension, they would wear headphones, and there would be a silent-study and a sound-study condition). They were asked if they had any questions and were given the right to withdraw at any point during the study.

Validity

As we have said, the controls and the use of realistic materials contribute towards making the findings of the study valid. However, although the findings suggest silent study is best, implementing such a strategy might be unwise. While the study used meaningful material, it was not relevant, i.e. it did not have the pertinence that students' own subjects would have. If the participants had been retrieving information within an existing framework of knowledge, the results might have been different. Furthermore, the silent condition in the experiment, which was only 30 minutes long overall, did have an effect but this may not generalise to longer periods of study, such as whole evenings or days. The negative effects of boredom, day-dreaming or lack of motivation, which could reduce the time spent studying or its effectiveness, may mitigate the benefit of matched environments, reducing the validity of the findings. Nevertheless, the experiment did represent the study and learning conditions for students reasonably well and the material used was more like course material than other items typically used in memory experiments, such as word lists or nonsense syllables.

Reliability

Several aspects of the study were standardised, such as the materials (headphones and tape) and procedure (the instructions to ignore the content of the tape), which ensured reliability of the procedure between participants and between conditions. They would also have allowed for replication. Furthermore, the similarity in the pattern of the results across test conditions also suggests the results are reliable. However, as eight different students acted as experimenters, the amount of time given for the initial reading of the article could not be controlled. This could have reduced reliability.

Sampling bias

As all the participants were chosen from the acquaintances of the experimenters (who were psychology students) they are unlikely to have formed a representative sample, although there was a good age spread and roughly equal numbers of males and females. Furthermore, their knowledge that their friends, the experimenters, were psychology students may have affected their approach to the study by introducing demand characteristics. They may possibly have been more likely to have worked out the aim of the study and tried harder in the matching conditions than if they had been drawn from a sample who did not necessarily have psychology students for friends.

Practical applications

This study is useful in its direct applicability to students' study habits. It provides a good foundation for at least suggesting to students that they should try studying in silence. In a sense, there is also evidence for the source monitoring hypothesis and its implications for eyewitness testimony. Johnson *et al.* (1993) suggest that, according to source monitoring, recalling the source of a memory matters. If factors such as leading questions distort eyewitnesses' ability to identify the source of their memory, worsening the accuracy of their testimony, context may, conversely, help to improve their accuracy.

Figure 2.8
As exam rooms are always silent, how would it be best to study?

COMPARISON OF STUDIES

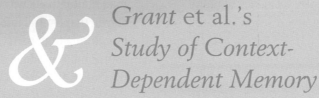

Loftus and Palmer's Study of Distortion of Memory **&** *Grant et al.'s Study of Context-Dependent Memory*

THE TOPIC
Effects between *versus* during *encoding and retrieval*

The studies by Loftus and Palmer and Grant *et al.* are both about cognitive psychology, specifically about the extent to which our memory produces an inevitable and accurate record of the material encoded: both found that it does not. However, Loftus and Palmer looked at the disrupting effect of information received *between* encoding and retrieval (in the form of leading questions), and Grant *et al.* looked at the disrupting (or enhancing) effects of the environment *during* the processes of encoding and retrieval (specifically if they matched or not).

THE RESEARCH METHOD AND DESIGN
Experiments using an independent measures design

Although both studies were experiments using an independent measures design there were some differences, for example in the level of control. In Loftus & Palmer's study the films were of fixed durations for all participants, whereas reading time could differ in the Grant *et al.* study. The two studies were similar in that manipulation of the IV was achieved at the testing stage, in Loftus and Palmer by asking leading or non-leading questions and in Grant *et al.* by testing in matching or mismatching environments. However, in Grant *et al.* the environment in which the participants were tested was not as well controlled, as although each student experimenter had an identical tape of the background noise, they played it to their participants through their own tape player and headset.

SAMPLING TECHNIQUE AND THE SAMPLE
Opportunity sampling and student participants

The sample sizes were similar (Loftus and Palmer: 45 in Experiment 1, 150 in Experiment 2; Grant *et al.*: 39) and were probably similar in composition, Loftus and Palmer having used all students, and Grant *et al.* having used acquaintances of students. Both therefore used opportunity sampling, a non-representative method, so the samples would, to an extent, have had limited generalisibility. However, cognitive processes such as memory are likely to be similar across a wide range of people.

EXPERIMENTAL MATERIALS AND MEASUREMENT OF THE DV
Ecological validity, mundane realism and quantitative data

For the main experimental stimuli, Loftus and Palmer used driver education films from the Seattle Police Department and Grant *et al.* used a published paper by Hales, both of which were real-world materials relevant to the study. The mundane realism of the studies was also similar in that both gathered data for the DV using simplistic questioning (short answer or closed questions) producing quantitative data, which only partly represents real-world questioning of witnesses and exam candidates. Overall, however, both studies lack ecological validity in some respects as the emotion and motivation of the participants would have been different from those experiencing real car crashes or sitting exams.

APPLICATIONS
Courtroom versus classroom

The topics of both studies have obvious applicability to real-world settings, in the courtroom and the classroom, both suggesting that traditionally accepted behaviour (the use of leading questions and revising in a noisy environment) could be improved. While Loftus and Palmer's findings have already made an impact on the judicial system, the more recent findings of Grant *et al.* have yet to have an influence. This may be in part because the consequences of this research are less important – it is not a social and moral question of the innocent being convicted or the guilty going free, but a matter of individual choice about study habits. Furthermore, there is no counterargument for any 'benefits' from the use of leading questions, whereas students might justifiably doubt how long they could motivate themselves to work in silence or the possibility of doing so in a noisy hall of residence or home.

KEY THEME: MEMORY

Prior to Loftus and Palmer's study, it was known that memories were imperfect – they could be influenced – but this study provided one of the earliest insights into the effects of post-event information. It showed, by the combination of experiments 1 and 2, that the changes in memory that occurred as a result of leading questions were due to the reconstruction of memory rather than any other process. This has led to not only a considerable field of research into eyewitness testimony but also to practical changes in the legal system.

Grant *et al.*'s study has explored a different area of memory, that of context-dependency, again an area that aims to explain why our memories are less accurate in some situations than others. Unlike Loftus and Palmer, prior research had demonstrated clearly some factors affecting cue dependency, and a range of theories had been proposed to explain these.

Grant *et al.*'s research differed because it explored the importance of the factor of meaningfulness, and did so in the realistic context of university study. Various aspects of the source-monitoring hypothesis suggest that meaningfulness may matter to eyewitnesses. For example, it has been shown that central information is better at directing source-monitoring than peripheral information, and that unfamiliar source information is more often misattributed. Such evidence implies that witnesses who comprehend the situation may be able to produce more accurate testimonies than those who are confused, e.g. because they do not know what is happening or are frightened.

KEY THEME 🔑

Loftus and Palmer showed eyewitness testimonies were less accurate if **leading questions** are used as memory is reconstructed. Grant *et al.*'s experiment on study habits demonstrated that **context** helps retrieval but also showed that **meaningfulness** matters; so eyewitnesses who are aware that a crime is happening should give more accurate testimonies than those who are not.

Loftus and Palmer
Laboratory experiment investigating effects between encoding and retrieval.

Similarities
Both experiments on memory using the same experimental design (independent measures) and the same non-representative sampling method.

Grant et al.
Experiment investigating effects during encoding and retrieval.

PRACTICE QUESTIONS

Here are some of the sorts of questions that you could be asked in Sections A and B of your AS exam, and some examples of successful and less successful answers. We look at Section B questions in more detail in Chapter 6 on pages 206–8 and 212–14.

SECTION A: CORE STUDIES

1 Describe the aim of the study into context-dependent memory conducted by Grant *et al.* [2]

2 Identify the two types of test undertaken by the participants in Grant *et al.*'s study into context-dependent memory. [2]

3 From Grant *et al.*'s study into context-dependent memory:
   (a) Describe how the sample was obtained in this study. [2]
   (b) Suggest **one** way in which this sample may be biased. [2]

4 Outline **two** conclusions that can be drawn from the study into context-dependent memory conducted by Grant *et al.* [4]

5 From Loftus and Palmer's study into eyewitness testimony: Identify the independent variable and the dependent variable in Study 1. [2]

6 From Loftus and Palmer's study into eyewitness testimony: Describe the two kinds of information that go into an individual's memory for a complex occurrence. [4]

7 From Loftus and Palmer's study into eyewitness testimony:
   (a) What is ecological validity? [2]

   (b) Outline **one** way in which Loftus and Palmer's study lacks ecological validity. [2]

8 Outline **one** difference between Loftus and Palmer's study into eyewitness testimony and Grant *et al.*'s study into context-dependent memory. [3]

SECTION B: AREAS, PERSPECTIVES AND DEBATES

9 **(a)** Outline the cognitive area of psychology. [2]

   (b) Suggest **one** strength of the cognitive area. Illustrate your answer with evidence from **one** appropriate core study. [3]

   (c) Suggest **one** weakness of the cognitive area. Illustrate your answer with evidence from **one** appropriate core study. [3]

   (d) Explain how any **one** core study can be considered to be located within the area of cognitive psychology. [5]

   (e) Discuss the extent to which psychology can be viewed as a science. Support your answer with evidence from core studies. [12]

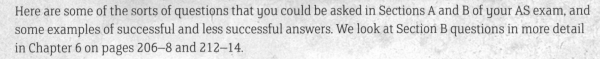

SECTION A   **3 From Grant *et al.*'s study into context-dependent memory:**

(a) Describe how the sample was obtained in this study. [2]

(b) Suggest one way in which this sample may be biased. [2]

Rachel's answer:

(a) opportunity

(b) it was biased because it was a small sample

Charlotte's answer:

(a) The sample was obtained through opportunity sampling where eight members of the class acted as experimenters and recruited five acquaintances to serve as participants.

(b) The sample was biased because the participants were all friends or acquaintances of the experimenters and so this is likely to mean that they share some characteristics and are unlikely to be representative of the general population.

We say: This is another very brief answer from Rachel. 'Opportunity' is correct although the examiners will be expecting a bit more information in response to a question that asks you to describe. Rachel also needs to expand her answer to part (b): a small sample is not necessarily a biased one and there are other reasons from this study that could have been offered.

We say: These are good answers which show a good understanding of the study. Charlotte has given just about the right amount of information for questions worth two marks.

6 From Loftus and Palmer's study into eyewitness testimony:

Describe the two kinds of information that go into an individual's memory for a complex occurrence. [4]

Rachel's answer:

Information obtained directly from the event and information obtained after the event.

Charlotte's answer:

One is the information that we obtain from directly experiencing the event, and the other is information that we get after the event, such as listening to other people talk about the event or information in leading questions.

We say: This is correct, although it would be advisable for Rachel to give a little more in the way of description here as this is a four-mark question. If the question had said 'Identify the two kinds of information that go into an individual's memory for a complex occurrence', this would have been an ideal answer.

We say: This is more detailed and is likely to be more what the examiners are looking for. Charlotte has described the 'after the event' information very well indeed.

8 Outline one difference between Loftus and Palmer's study into eyewitness testimony and Grant et al.'s study into context-dependent memory. [3]

Rachel's answer:

They both have practical applications: one to learning and one to eyewitness testimony.

Charlotte's answer:

Loftus and Palmer were investigating the effects of leading questions on the accuracy of memory specifically eyewitness testimony whereas Grant et al. were looking at the effects of learning and recall in matching or mismatching environments. These are very different aims and very different aspects of memory.

We say: Rachel has identified a difference in the way that each study can be applied but she has written this as if it were a similarity ('they both have'). It would be much clearer if she had started her answer with something like: 'One difference is the practical application of the study'.

We say: This is a clear answer that has focused on the difference between the specific aspect of memory under investigation.

SECTION B   9 (a) Outline the cognitive area of psychology. [2]

Rachel's answer:

This area studies cognition and cognitive processes.

Charlotte's answer:

ognitive psychology focuses on internal mental processes, such as memory, attention and thinking. We cannot see mental processes but we can infer them from people's behaviour. Cognitive psychology challenged behaviourism, saying that psychology should focus on internal mental processes rather than observable behaviour, but still use experimental methods.

We say: It is never a good idea to use the words in the question again in the answer! Rachel needs to make it clear to the examiner that she knows what the terms 'cognition' and 'cognitive processes' mean.

We say: This is better. Charlotte's answer explains cognitive psychology well and the comparison with behaviourism, although not explicitly asked for, adds to the evidence of her understanding.

9 (d) Explain how any one core study can be considered to be located within the area of cognitive psychology. [5]

Rachel's answer:

Grant et al. is from the area of cognitive psychology as it looks at memory. Grant studied the effect of noise on learning

Charlotte's answer:

Loftus and Palmer is a cognitive study as it looks at cognitive processes, language, memory and recall. It says memories are constructed from two types of information: what we obtain directly from observing or experiencing an event, and what we obtain after the event, in this case the leading questions which seemed to change the memory of the event. Even though we can't 'see' this process taking place, we can infer that it is taking place because of the participants' responses. Because Loftus and Palmer conducted Study 2, showing that more people said that they saw broken glass if they had heard the word 'smashed', we know that this was not just people giving the answers they thought the experimenters wanted.

We say: This is a very weak answer from Rachel. It is correct to identify the topic as memory and it is correct that this is a cognitive process (although Rachel has not explicitly made this point). To achieve marks here you would have to consider the assumptions of the cognitive area of psychology and the methodology typically used within it.

We say: This is a detailed and thoughtful answer to the question. There is also a very nice link between Charlotte's answer to the previous question and her answer to this one.

MORAY'S STUDY OF DICHOTIC LISTENING

Moray, N. (1959) Attention in dichotic listening: affective cues and the influence of instructions. *Quarterly Journal of Experimental Psychology*, **11** (1): 56–60.

IN BRIEF

Aim: To test factors that would enable an unattended, dichotically presented message to be noticed.

Method: The research method was a laboratory experiment with three studies: two with a repeated measures design and the last an independent measures design. The participants included both females and males. In Study 1 memory for words (the Dependent Variable) from the shadowed prose message, a repeated word list in the rejected message, and control words were compared (the Independent Variable). In study 2 instructions were either preceded or not by the participant's name (the IV) and whether or not the participant heard the instruction was the DV. In study 3 participants listened to passages with occasional numbers in and were either told they would be asked questions about the shadowed message or that they should remember all the numbers they could (the IV). The DV was the number of digits reported. Controls included matching the volume of the messages, ensuring the participant's name was not louder, and that the passages were read at a steady speed without expression.

Results: Study 1 showed that none of the content of the rejected message (the word list) could be remembered. Study 2 showed that affective instructions (using the participant's name) were sometimes heard, i.e. could break through the attentional barrier. Study 3 showed that numbers could not be made important enough to break through the attentional barrier and be noticed in the rejected message even when they were expected.

Conclusion: Directing attention away from the message in one ear blocks the verbal content of that message. One's own name can, at least sometimes, break through this attentional block. Neutral material (numbers) cannot be made important enough (using expectations) to break through the attentional barrier.

KEY IDEAS

Two messages played at once can either be arranged **binaurally**, i.e. both presented to both ears at the same time, or **dichotically**, i.e. with a different message in each ear. In a **shadowing task**, participants have to repeat one message as they hear it. This is much more difficult when two messages are presented binaurally than when they are presented dichotically.

Headphones send different messages to each ear

Rejected message

"Where will this end?" said the lady, speaking more to herself than to him. "I have grown so old in these last few hours ..."

Shadowed message

Ransom noted the exact make and pattern of the pack. It must have been from the same shop in London where he had bought his own …

Ransom noticed the exact make and pattern of the pack. It must have been from the same shop in London where he had bought his own …

Speech output

Figure 2.9 Dichotic listening task

CONTEXT

In a classic study, Cherry (1953) used the method of **'shadowing'** to test divided attention. Participants were required to repeat one of two messages as they were listening to them. The two messages were always presented simultaneously, either both played to both ears at the same time (**binaural task**), or one to each ear (**dichotic task**). He found that in binaural presentation it was very difficult to separate the messages. However, in dichotic presentation, not only could the participants separate the messages very effectively, but they were also almost entirely unaware of the content of the rejected (unattended) message. For example, they could not recall any words or phrases and did not notice if the language changed (from English to German). They were, however, aware of some changes, such as from speech to a tone or if the speaker's gender changed.

To explain such findings, various studies investigated how such selective blocking of information could occur. Peripheral blocks (producing rejection of the message at a structure in the ear, such as the cochlea, or in early processing in the brain, at the cochlear nucleus) were suggested (e.g. by Galambos, 1955). However, as these could only prevent responses in a limited way, such as blocking information from one ear, such explanations were unlikely to account for blocking or accepting particular *types* of stimuli. More complex processing was shown to occur only in the cortex, the outer layer of the brain which is used for tasks such as detecting patterns. For example, Sharpless and Jasper (1956) used cats to demonstrate the importance of the auditory cortex (for sound). Cats with a damaged auditory cortex could do simple tasks such as detecting differences in pitch (tone) and localisation (deciding where a stimulus has come from), but they could not perform more complex discriminations between sounds. This led Moray to suggest that the dichotic shadowing task uses a high level (cortical) mechanism.

Although most features of the rejected message are ignored, it seems that some break through the attentional barrier. Moray was interested in what kinds of stimuli and situations might lead to this, observing that mothers hear children crying and that a person at a cocktail party can respond when they hear their own name mentioned in another conversation. (The latter is often attributed to Cherry, since 'the Cherry cocktail party phenomenon' sounds much funnier.)

WEB WATCH @

Find a pair of stereo headphones and try out a dichotic listening task. Go to:

www.linguistics.ucla.edu/people/schuh/ lx001/Dichotic/dichotic.html or search on YouTube for 'dichotic listening task'

The iDichotic app, which allows you to test yourself on dichotic listening tasks, is free. Look at this website, which looks at worldwide patterns of selective attention: http://dichoticlistening.com

Figure 2.10
The cocktail party phenomenon: do you notice someone in another group saying your name?

KEY IDEAS

'**Affect**' refers to emotions or feelings. Personally relevant information is therefore described as having '**affective content**'. The idea of 'affect' in psychology is often used in comparison to 'behaviour' (actions which are done) and 'cognition' (thoughts and beliefs). Together, affect, behaviour and cognition (A, B, C) are key elements in the explanation of any human experience.

AIM

The aim of the study was to test Cherry's dichotic listening findings in relation to, firstly, the amount of information recognised in the rejected message; secondly, the effect of hearing one's own name in the unattended message; and thirdly, the effect of instructions to identify a specific target in the rejected message.

METHOD

The research method was a laboratory experiment, with three separate studies.

Participants
Study 2 had 12 participants and Study 3 had two groups of 14. The number for study 1 is not recorded. All participants were undergraduates or research workers and included females and males.

Design and procedure
All three studies used a dichotic listening task. The messages were recorded onto tape in the same male voice at rates of 130 or 150 words per minute. Two controls were that the rejected message was played at a volume that seemed to the individual participant to be the same as the shadowed message, and the two messages were always played through headphones directing the separate messages to each ear individually. Before each experiment, the participant had four practice prose passages to shadow.

Study 1: Participants heard a short list of simple words repeated 35 times in the unattended ear whilst they shadowed a prose message in the attended ear. The word list was faded in after shadowing began and faded out as the attended message ended. The experimental design was repeated measures. There were three conditions of the independent variable: the shadowed message, the rejected message and a control. The dependent variable was measured in two ways: the participant was asked to recall all they could from the unattended message and were then given a recognition test. The recognition test included words from the shadowed message, the rejected message and a control set of words that had not been present in either message.

Study 2: Participants shadowed ten short passages of light fiction, each being a different condition having a different set of instructions either at the start or within the passage (in two conditions participants were warned about this), or both. The participants were told that their responses would be recorded and that the object was 'to try to score as few mistakes as possible'. The ten sets of instructions are listed in Table 2.5. In three of the six conditions with instructions during the passage, the instruction began with the participant's own name, e.g. 'John Smith, you may stop now'. All participants experienced all of the ten conditions, i.e. the experimental design was repeated measures, and the four 'no instruction' conditions were interspersed randomly. Of the remaining pairs, the one without the individual's name (e.g. with the instruction 'You may stop now') was always presented before the same instruction with their name. The independent variable was whether the instructions in the message were

TABLE 2.5 EXPERIMENTAL CONDITIONS IN STUDY 2 (THE AFFECTIVE INSTRUCTIONS ARE HIGHLIGHTED)

Passage	Instruction at start of passage	Instructions within passage
I	Listen to your right ear	All right, you may stop now.
II	" " " " "	No instruction.
III	" " " " "	John Smith, you may stop now.
IV	" " " " "	No instruction.
V	" " " " "	Change to your other ear.
VI	" " " " "	No instruction.
VII	" " " " "	John Smith, change to your other ear.
VIII	Listen to your right ear: you will receive instructions to change ears.	Change to your other ear.
IX	Listen to your right ear.	No instruction.
X	Listen to your right ear: you will receive instructions to change ears.	John Smith, change to your other ear.

preceded by the participant's own name (**affective** instructions) or not (non-affective instructions). The dependent variable was the frequency with which the instruction was heard.

Study 3: Messages were constructed which had digits interspersed with the words towards the end of the passage (experimental). Similar messages had no digits (control). Participants heard either two experimental messages or one experimental and one control message. The experimental design was independent measures. The participants always shadowed an experimental message but one group was told beforehand that they would be asked questions about the content of the shadowed message and the other was told that they should remember all the numbers they could (the independent variable). The mean number of digits in the message and the mean number of digits reported were calculated (the dependent variable).

RESULTS

Study 1: The results showed no evidence of the words from the rejected message having been recognised, as the mean recognition rate was much lower than for the shadowed message and was even lower than that for words not present in either list (see Table 2.6).

TABLE 2.6 MEAN RECOGNITION OF WORDS (* SIGNIFICANT AT $p \leq 0.01$)

Previous appearance of words (independent variable)	Mean number of words recognised (out of 7)
In the shadowed message	4.9*
In the rejected message	1.9
New words (neither message)	2.6

QUESTION SPOTLIGHT!

1 Why do you think it was important that the word list in Study 1 was faded in after shadowing began?
2 In Study 2, the condition without the individual's name was conducted before the equivalent one with their name. *Explain why this was important.*

MATHS MOMENT

Calculate the mean percentage of words remembered from the shadowed and rejected messages in Study 1 using the data in Table 2.6.

Hint: because the results are the percentage of words remembered in each condition, they do not necessarily have to add up to 100.

QUESTION SPOTLIGHT!

Moray says that it was unlikely that the failure to remember words from the rejected message was because of the 30 second delay between the end of shadowing and recognition as words from early in the shadowed message were recalled. *Explain why this observation is important.*

MATHS MOMENT

Using the data from Study 2 given in Table 2.7 on page 66, calculate the percentage of presentations that were heard following the affective and non-affective instructions.

KEY IDEAS

The **t-test** is a parametric statistical test. You do not need to learn about it, but, like all other statistical tests, it produces an observed value. For the t-test this is called 't' (see page 305).

TABLE 2.7 FREQUENCY OF HEARING THE AFFECTIVE AND NON-AFFECTIVE INSTRUCTIONS IN THE REJECTED MESSAGE

	Affective instructions (preceded by name)	Non-affective instructions (not preceded by name)
number of times presented	39	36
number of times heard	20	4

TABLE 2.8 MEAN FREQUENCY OF HEARING DIFFERENT AFFECTIVE MESSAGES

Instruction given	Mean frequency per participant of hearing the affective instructions in the rejected message
'Own name', you may stop now	0.33
'Own name', change to your other ear	0.33
'Own name', change to your other ear (after pre-passage warning)	0.80

Study 2: Table 2.7 gives the number of times the instructions were presented and heard in the two levels of the independent variable (affective and non-affective instructions). A **t-test** showed that the difference between the affective and non-affective instruction conditions was highly significant (t=3.05, $p \leq 0.01$). The data indicate clearly that the presence of a name can cause the instruction to be heard, i.e. affective content in the rejected message is able to break through the attentional barrier.

(NB The data in Table 2.7 are from 12 participants, but as some heard the instruction to change ears and did so, there were more than 36 presentations of the affective instructions as the affective instruction intended for the shadowed message became an instruction in the rejected message). It was also more likely following pre-passage warning that there would be a message to change ears (see Table 2.8), although this difference was not significant.

Study 3: The mean number of digits reported when the participants had been told they would be asked about the content, and when told specifically to listen for digits was not significantly different (at $p \leq 0.05$). This shows that the participants could not be primed to respond to digits heard in the rejected message, unlike their spontaneous recognition of their own name in the rejected message seen in Study 2. Even when alerted to the possibility of hearing digits, this stimulus did not seem to be 'important' enough to break through the attentional barrier.

CONCLUSIONS

Moray observes that an 'identification paradox' exists: although the content of the rejected message is not attended to and is blocked from conscious perception, this block does not prevent a response to one's own name. In relation to this, he drew four conclusions from the study:

1   When the participant directs attention to the message in one ear, rejecting the message in the other ear, almost all of the verbal content of the rejected message is blocked.
2   This rejection is apparent even when the message is repeated many times: there is no trace of a short list of simple words presented many times being remembered.
3   Subjectively important messages, such as one's own name, can penetrate the block: so we may hear instructions containing our own name even in the rejected message.
4   It is very difficult (though perhaps not impossible) to make neutral material important enough to penetrate the block.

EVALUATION

The research method

In laboratory experiments it is possible to control extraneous variables leading to higher validity. In this case, the participants had the loudness in each ear individually matched to ensure that differences in the messages were not caused by differences in volume, and the messages were recorded to ensure that they were spoken at a constant speed and without expression. How loudly the participant's own name was spoken was checked, to be certain that it had not been stressed.

Qualitative and quantitative data

The data gathered in this study were quantitative. This is generally both a strength and a weakness. On the plus side, statistical analysis allowed easy comparison of the conditions, showing that although digits cannot be noticed, even when they are expected, one's own name can be detected at least some of the time in the rejected message when it is not expected. There was no analysis of qualitative data, although this would be difficult, as the process of detecting particular stimuli in the rejected message is unconscious so participants would be unable to give much indication of why they succeeded in detecting different types of stimuli or failed to do so.

Ethical considerations

As with Loftus and Palmer and Grant *et al*, this is a laboratory experiment that raises few ethical issues. Participants were students and research workers, and they had practice sessions, so they were aware of what was going to happen. The task, the materials and the findings were all unlikely to cause distress.

Validity

The level of control achieved ensured that any greater recall of the name than other words was the result of the IV (the affective nature of the stimulus) not to extraneous variables such as volume. However, the situation may not have been very realistic in the sense that we rarely need to continuously listen to and repeat a message. Nevertheless, the task tested by dichotic listening does represent the everyday situation of trying to follow one source of information, such as a conversation, while ignoring distracting noise, chatter or dialogue. Think about trying to hear an announcement on a crowded train station, or your phone in a busy street. The use of everyday materials (light fiction) and the individual's own name also helped to make the task realistic, raising ecological validity.

Reliability

Controlling variables such volume, and the use of headphones, raised reliability, and standardised the procedure between participants and between conditions to allow for replication. However, some differences in the participants' experiences did arise, for example only some heard and responded to the instruction to change cars, so the passage intended to be the 'shadowed' message then became the 'rejected' message, and one participant also spontaneously reverted to shadowing the original ear without noticing.

Sampling bias

The sampling method may have been non-representative, although there is no reason to suppose that students and research workers differ from the general population in relation to their selective attention skills. It was important that the sample included both male and female participants as it is possible that there is a gender difference in selective attention. Various studies have demonstrated that there are differences in processing of verbal material by men and women, and differences in lateralisation (i.e. the way in which information is processed by the left and right sides of the brain) between the sexes. Welsh and Elliot (2001) even suggested that there may be differences in the strategies used by men and women in dichotic listening tasks.

Figure 2.11
Selective attention to one ear
happens in everyday life

Ethnocentrism

It is possible that in different languages, words are processed in different ways. To what extent could Moray's conclusions therefore be considered to be ethnocentric? Ke (1992) found that, in a dichotic listening task, monolingual English, and bilingual English-Chinese speakers responded differently, with the monolingual English participants having a right-ear advantage, suggesting left hemisphere processing that was not evident in bilinguals. This suggests that the specific language, or certainly an additional language, alters the way in which English speakers use their brains in a dichotic listening task. Such effects may also arise in the real world, as Tabri et al. (2010) found that even highly competent (early acquisition) bi- and tri-lingual speakers found listening in noisy environments more difficult than monolinguals. However, bilinguals also show some advantages, with participants fluent in both Swedish and Finnish performing better in a dichotic listening task than monolinguals (Soveri et al., 2011). Given these differences between languages, wider generalisations may not be valid in some respects.

Practical applications

While the findings suggest that hearing our name can overcome the attentional blockade, this is only partial. Only some of the participants noticed their name some of the time. This finding has also been robustly replicated, thus, while we can generalise the conclusion that 'people often hear their own name when not paying attention', we cannot make the wider generalisation that 'people hear their own name when not paying attention', because often they do not.

The high validity and reliability of this study provided a strong scientific foundation. As a consequence, this study was central to many years of research into the process by which we can selectively attend to some inputs and the nature of stimuli that can overcome the attentional block. The topic of attention has led, ultimately, to useful research in areas such as driver safety (Moray, 1990). More recently, applications have included using directional attention to one's own name as a test of consciousness in long-term coma patients (Cheng et al, 2013) and using tests of the ability to switch attention between messages to understand children with listening, but not hearing, disorders (Dharmani et al., 2013).

STRETCH & CHALLENGE

1 Between studies 2 and 3, Moray compared the participant's own name with numbers to demonstrate the kinds of stimuli that could and could not break through the attentional barrier. Suggest a different pair of stimuli that could be tested, one with high affective valence, one without, and explain what difference you might expect to find in a similar study.

2 Consider whether there are any ethical issues with the study you have proposed.

SIMONS AND CHABRIS'S STUDY OF INATTENTIONAL BLINDNESS

Simons, D.J. and Chabris, C.F. (1999) Gorillas in our midst: sustained inattentional blindness for dynamic events. *Perception,* **28**: 1059–1074 .

IN BRIEF ❗

Aim: To investigate the effect of several factors on 'inattentional blindness'.

Method: The research method was a laboratory experiment using an independent measures design. Volunteer sampling was used to find 228 participants (mainly undergraduates).

Results: Approximately half of the participants failed to notice the unexpected event across all conditions. Participants were more likely to notice the unexpected event in the opaque condition than in the transparent condition. They were also more likely to detect the umbrella woman than the gorilla. When participants were attending to the black team they were much more likely to notice the gorilla than those participants attending to the white team.

Conclusion: A significant number of individuals are likely to fail to notice an ongoing, prominent but unexpected event when they are otherwise engaged in a primary monitoring task. The ability to detect such an event can be influenced by the complexity and nature of the monitoring task.

CONTEXT

Research into visual perception reveals that we are surprisingly unaware of the details of our environment from one view to the next. For instance, we often fail to notice significant changes to objects or scenes ('change blindness'). In a similar way, when we are attentive to another object or task, we often fail to perceive an unexpected object, even if it appears at the point of fixation. This phenomenon has been termed 'inattentional blindness' (Mack and Rock, 1998).

In a series of important but unpublished studies, Neisser *et al.* (1979) devised a divided-visual-attention task in which observers viewed superimposed videotapes of two teams playing a ball-passing game. Observers were asked to attend to one team of players, pressing a key whenever one of them made a pass, while ignoring the actions of the other team. After a short time, a woman carrying an open umbrella walked across the screen. The games then continued after she walked off. It was found that of 28 observers; only six reported the presence of the umbrella woman. However, when observers just watched the screen and did not perform any task, they always noticed the umbrella woman.

One explanation could be 'inattentional amnesia'. Wolfe (1999) proposed that the unexpected event (e.g. the umbrella woman) is being consciously perceived, but then immediately forgotten. If this is true, the reason observers do not report its appearance results from a failure of memory not a failure of perception. However, this theory has been brought into question by Becklen and Cervone (1983) who performed a similar divided-attention task but included a condition

WEB WATCH @

This website gives seven examples of change blindness images, and gives you the chance to time yourself at spotting the change:
www.gocognitive.net/demo/change-blindness

Figure 2.12
Vanishing act: Magicians commonly use misdirection to perform illusions. This relies on our inability to give equal attention to every detail within our visual field.

 **KEY IDEAS**

Superimposition is the placing or laying of one thing on top of something else. In this case it is used to refer to the placement of a video on top of an existing video. For Simons and Chabris this was relatively straightforward as they were able to superimpose moving images using digital editing software. However, Neisser *et al.* created their effect in the 1970s by showing both of the separately recorded videos on an angled, half-silvered mirror.

 QUESTION SPOTLIGHT!

Simons and Chabris used a volunteer sampling technique in their study. *Outline an alternative method for obtaining a random sample from a target population.*

in which the video was stopped immediately after the umbrella woman left the screen. They found no significant difference in reporting rates between the video being stopped immediately or being left to play, indicating that delay has no effect on recall of the unexpected event.

In the present study, Simons and Chabris reviewed the existing body of research into the phenomenon of inattentional blindness. They wanted to examine the variables that affect inattentional blindness in naturalistic, dynamic events. These included further investigation of Neisser's original experiments, looking at the role played by **superimposition** and the visual similarity of the unexpected object to the attended ones. Importantly they also sought to systematically consider the role of task difficulty in detection.

AIM

The aim of the study was to investigate the influence of several factors on inattentional blindness. One of these was looking at the effect of superimposition compared to live events within the video recording, another was measuring the impact of task difficulty, and a third considered whether the unusualness of the unexpected event had an impact on detection rates.

METHOD

The research method was a laboratory experiment. It had an independent measures design, with participants taking part in only one of 16 different conditions (see Table 2.9 on page 72, which has four conditions of the unexpected event and four possible combinations of easy/hard and white team/ black team, making 16 all together).

Participants

There were 228 participants in total, recruited using volunteer sampling. Most were undergraduate students who were offered a reward of a candy bar or a single fee for their participation in this and other unrelated studies.

Design and procedure

The researchers created four videotapes using the same camera, each lasting 75 seconds. Each tape showed two teams of three players, one team wearing white shirts and the other wearing black shirts. The members of each team moved randomly around a small space, passing an orange basketball to one another in a set order, either as an aerial pass or a pass with a bounce.

Twenty-one experimenters tested the participants individually. They used a standardised script to deliver instructions on the task, and carefully followed a written protocol outlining how and when to present the video and collect data for each trial. The videos were presented on a variety of television monitors ranging in size between 13 and 36 inches.

One independent variable was the two 5-second unexpected events, which appeared after 44–48 seconds into the videos. In one condition, known as the 'Umbrella Woman' condition, a tall woman holding an open umbrella walked across the picture from left to right, similar to the sequence used in Neisser's (1979) study. In the 'Gorilla' condition, a shorter woman wearing a full gorilla costume walked through the action in the same way.

The second independent variable was the two styles of video: in the 'Transparent' condition, each of the teams and the unexpected event were all filmed separately, made partially transparent, then superimposed on one another using digital techniques. In the 'Opaque' condition, all seven actors were filmed at the same time, which required careful rehearsal to avoid collisions.

The third independent variable was the team colour that the participants were asked to follow (Black or White). Participants were instructed to keep either a silent mental count of the number of passes made by the attended team (the Easy condition), or separate silent mental counts of the number of bounce passes and aerial passes made by the attended team (the Hard condition). The difficulty of the task (Easy or Hard) was the fourth and final independent variable.

After performing the task, observers were immediately asked to write down their count of passes, then verbally answered a surprise set of questions (see Figure 2.13).

Figure 2.13
List of questions used by experimenters following the visual attention task

> (i) While you were doing the counting, did you notice anything unusual on the video?
> (ii) Did you notice anything other than the six players?
> (iii) Did you see anyone else (besides the six players) appear on the video?
> (iv) Did you see a gorilla [woman carrying an umbrella] walk across the screen?

Details of any 'yes' responses were noted. Observers were then asked whether they had previously heard of or participated in an experiment such as this. Lastly, the participants were debriefed and were given the opportunity to re-watch the video.

RESULTS

For a number of reasons, some participant data had to be discarded, for example, because participants admitted to having heard of inattentional blindness, or that they had lost count of the number of passes. The remaining 192 participants were distributed equally across the 16 conditions of the $2 \times 2 \times 2 \times 2$ design (12 per condition).

Out of the 192 participants across all conditions, 54% noticed the unexpected event and 46% failed to notice the unexpected event. This key finding supports existing research findings, with participants demonstrating a substantial level of inattentional blindness for a dynamic event.

Participants were more likely to notice the unexpected event in the opaque condition (67%) compared to the transparent condition (42%). However, this still leaves a significant proportion of participants in the opaque condition who

Transparent Umbrella-Woman

Transparent Gorilla

Opaque Umbrella-Woman

Opaque Gorilla

Figure 2.14
Video stills illustrating the unexpected event across different conditions

WEB WATCH @

Attempt the inattention tasks here using the original versions from Simons and Chabris's study:
www.theinvisiblegorilla.com/videos.html

MATHS MOMENT

Simons and Chabris found that, overall, the Umbrella Woman was noticed more often than the Gorilla (65% versus 44%; $v^2 = 8.392$, $p<0.004$; n = 96 per condition). Identify the observed value from the details given here and name the statistical test used.

STRETCH & CHALLENGE ◎

The researchers in this study employed an independent measures design.

1 Why do you think this experimental design was chosen?

2 What are the drawbacks of using an independent measures design in this study?

failed to detect the event (see Table 2.9). As expected, more participants noticed the unexpected event in the Easy (64%) than in the Hard (45%) condition.

Perhaps surprisingly, more participants noticed the umbrella woman (65%) than the gorilla (44%). When participants were attending to the black team, they were, however, more likely to notice the gorilla than when attending to the white team: 58% vs 27% respectively. By contrast, there was little difference in how many participants noticed the umbrella woman (62% when monitoring the black team; 69% when monitoring the white team). Instead of the gorilla being noticed for standing out against the white team members, it appears that individuals are more likely to notice an unexpected event that shares basic visual features with the object they are observing (e.g. similar colours).

TABLE 2.9 PERCENTAGE OF PARTICIPANTS WHO NOTICED THE UNEXPECTED EVENT IN EACH CONDITION

	Easy task		Hard task	
	White team	Black team	White team	Black team
Transparent				
Umbrella woman	58	92	33	42
Gorilla	8	67	8	25
Opaque				
Umbrella woman	100	58	83	58
Gorilla	42	83	50	58

CONCLUSIONS

Simons and Chabris conclude that, overall, approximately half of observers will fail to detect an ongoing, unusual and unexpected event while engaged in a different task of visual attention. Furthermore their findings suggest that:

1 Inattentional blindness occurs more frequently in cases of superimposition as opposed to live action, but is still a feature of both.

2 The degree of inattentional blindness depends on the difficulty of the primary task, and is more likely when the primary task is hard.

3 Observers are more likely to notice unexpected events if these events are visually similar to the events they are paying attention to.

4 Objects can pass through the spatial area of attentional focus and still not be 'seen' if they are not specifically being attended to.

EVALUATION

The research method

There were a number of controls put in place to manage the influence of extraneous variables within this laboratory experiment. For example, the timings of the presentation of the video were identical for each participant, and the moves in the 'opaque' condition were carefully rehearsed so that the videos for the black and white teams were the same.

Qualitative and quantitative data

This experiment collects quantitative data in the form of 'yes/no' responses to the questions following the video. It provides information that is easy to analyse statistically and not open to interpretation. Although this method produces quite simplistic data, calculating the percentage who noticed the unexpected event means we can directly compare a number of conditions.

Ethical considerations

This study raises few ethical issues. Each individual's consent was obtained prior to their participation. Although the design of the experiment required that participants were not fully aware of the true aim of the task, the video and questioning were very unlikely to cause any distress. Also, participants were fully debriefed after completing the experiment and were allowed to view the video again. This is important as finding out there had been a gorilla/umbrella woman they had not seen might have been frustrating.

Validity

This study has low ecological validity because participants completed the attention task watching a video, within a controlled situation. In real life, even when we concentrate carefully on tasks requiring our attention there would be a number of other environmental distractions. Furthermore the task of counting ball passes does not in itself reflect our typical visual attention tasks. Note that surprising events do happen in real life, so the use of the gorilla or the umbrella woman are not aspects that have the ecological validity. Can you think of an unexpected event that you have seen that could be used in such a video?

Simons and Chabris's findings were consistent with previous research, including computerised trials of inattentional blindness, increasing the likelihood that we can generalise their findings to other situations. However, it is important to note that, overall, roughly half of participants still noticed the unexpected event. This means that inattentional blindness is not a universal visual experience.

Reliability

A large number of researchers were conducting the individual trials, which could potentially introduce issues of reliability. However, this was controlled for through the use of a standardised script to consistently brief and question participants. Nevertheless, because there were 21 different experimenters, a range of television screen sizes were used, from 13 to 36 inches, which could have introduced inconsistencies.

Sampling bias

The sampling method was volunteer sampling, and the sample consisted mainly of undergraduate students. This means it may be difficult to generalise, for example because they are likely to have been predominantly young people who could be more vigilant than average. However, the researchers controlled for participant variables such as knowledge of the phenomenon being investigated, which would have removed some bias from participants who were familiar with the type of task they were being asked to do.

Ethnocentrism

While assumptions are often made that basic cognitive processes are universal, that may not always be the case. A range of studies have demonstrated cultural differences in perception, such as those explaining why we see illusions, and how we see depth. A study by Masuda and Nesbitt (2006) demonstrated cultural differences in change blindness. They expected that there may be differences between East Asian and American participants because the cultures differ in their focus on central or peripheral aspects of a stimulus. They did indeed find a difference, with Asian participants being more likely to detect changes in the context than in the focal aspects of an image. This suggests that the findings of Simons and Chabris may be ethnocentric as the participants were all selected by student experimenters at Iowa State University in Midwest America.

Practical applications

The findings of Simons and Chabris's study are useful in explaining why we may fail to notice certain events in real-world situations when our attention is focused on a different goal. It can also be used to identify situations that may increase the likelihood of inattentional blindness, for example when undertaking a particularly challenging task. This research also leads us to question when such 'blindness' occurs. It could be either that we fail to perceive the unexpected event altogether, or that it is quickly forgotten due to its irrelevancy to our main task.

COMPARISON OF STUDIES

Moray's Study of Dichotic Listening **&** *Simons and Chabris's Study of Inattentional Blindness*

THE TOPIC
Attention and inattention in auditory versus visual stimuli

The studies by Moray and by Simons and Chabris are both about cognitive psychology, specifically about attention: both found that we fail to attend to some aspects of the perceptual environment that we might expect people to notice because they are pertinent or unusual. However, Moray was investigating auditory attention and found that we are not aware of obvious features of an unattended message, such as numbers, and even fail to notice our own name some of the time. Simons and Chabris were studying visual inattention and found that we tend to fail to notice an ongoing but unexpected event. An important similarity is that both studies were investigating a dynamic event, that is they used an ongoing, changing stimulus rather than a single, static one, so in this respect both were quite lifelike.

THE RESEARCH METHOD AND DESIGN
Laboratory experiments using different experimental designs

Although both studies were laboratory experiments, Moray used both repeated measures and independent measures designs whereas Simons and Chabris only used an independent measures design. So, in both studies there was control of variables, which increases validity and reliability. For example, the voice, volume and speed of speech were controlled in Moray's study and the moves for the video were rehearsed in the study by Simons and Chabris. However, they experienced different problems owing to the design. In Moray's study the use of a repeated measures design meant that it was possible that the participants could become aware of the aim, for example in Study 2 the various conditions were deliberately put in a specific order to minimise this risk. For Simons and Chabris, using an independent measures design, there was a risk of individual differences between the groups.

For example, participants in one condition may have been better at concentrating on a task, so were less likely to notice the distracter as they were focused on counting passes, or they may have actually supported a sports team who wore black or white shirts.

SAMPLING TECHNIQUE AND THE SAMPLE
Sample included undergraduates

In Moray's studies 2 and 3 there were 12 and 14 participants respectively, who were undergraduates and research workers, so it is likely that they were an opportunity sample. Simons and Chabris also used a sample of mainly undergraduate students, although the sample was larger (228 participants; 12 participants per condition across the whole of their study) and they were recruited by volunteer sampling. Although Moray specifies that both genders were used, Simons and Chabris do not. With non-representative sampling methods and unspecified gender ratios, the findings may have limited generalisibility. However, as we said of memory research, the cognitive processes of attention are likely to be similar across a wide range of people.

EXPERIMENTAL MATERIALS AND MEASUREMENT OF THE DV
Ecological validity, mundane realism and quantitative data

Both studies were laboratory experiments presenting dynamic material that bore some resemblance to real life, albeit using electronic equipment (audio and video recordings). In Moray's case there is a parallel to common experiences, such as being in an environment where there are two or more ongoing conversations, and in the study by Simons and Chabris there is the similarity to situations such as failing to notice friends waving at you in a theatre when you are focused on finding your seat. In terms of the task, Moray used text from a novel, lists of numbers and the participant's own name as experimental material, all of which are reasonably relevant given that it was a laboratory experiment. Simons and Chabris used a video of a basketball game as the familiar context and the deliberately unexpected events of a passing gorilla or a woman with an umbrella. Again, these are appropriate for a laboratory study. In both cases, the materials are more realistic than nonsense syllables or simple lists of words. Both the tasks were followed by simplistic questions, counting the number of times the participants noticed the intended change or unexpected event, producing quantitative data that allowed direct comparison of levels of attention.

APPLICATIONS
Explaining apparent lack of vigilance or concentration

The topics of both studies have applicability to real-world settings to help us to understand why people fail to notice key events, especially when their attention is focused elsewhere. For example, Moray's research has led to practical applications such as driver safety, as well as in both health and educational settings. The findings of Simons and Chabris help to explain situations such as when a police officer is in pursuit of a criminal but fails notice other important events, such as someone being assaulted (Chabris *et al.*, 2011), or when doctors miss important facts about patients when there are competing demands on their attention (Mohan *et al.*, 2014).

KEY THEME: ATTENTION

These studies have served to illustrate the extent to which we are selective in our attention. When focused on a task we become relatively unaware of many events in our environment which we would normally undoubtedly notice, whether they are auditory or visual.

KEY THEME

Attention

Moray showed that people almost entirely block an unattended auditory message, being unable to notice repeated words or numbers, and are even reasonably unlikely to notice their own name in the rejected message. Simons and Chabris's study demonstrated that we are also visually unaware: people often fail to notice unexpected events, especially when these are superimposed, contrasted against a difficult task, and similar to the event they are attending to, even when both are in the same spatial area.

Moray
A study of attention to dichotically presented auditory messages. The experimental design used both repeated measures and independent measures and the sampling method was non-representative.

Similarities
Both were laboratory experiments on attention with control of the IV and DV and some procedural controls, e.g. the video and audio recordings used as stimuli.

Simons and Chabris
A study of attention/inattention to visual stimuli. The experimental design was independent measures and the sampling method was volunteer sampling.

PRACTICE QUESTIONS

Here are some of the sorts of questions that you could be asked in Sections A and B of your A level exam, and some examples of successful and less successful answers. We look at Section B and C questions in more detail in Chapter 6 on pages 206–18.

SECTION A: CORE STUDIES

1 From the study by Moray into dichotic listening explain what a shadowing task is. [2]

2 Outline **one** control that was used in the study into dichotic listening conducted by Moray. [2]

3 Outline **two** conclusions that can be drawn from the study into dichotic listening conducted by Moray. [4]

4 Suggest **one** improvement that could be made to the study by Moray into dichotic listening. [3]

5 Describe the sample used in Simon and Chabris's study into visual inattention. [2]

6 Outline **one** conclusion that can be drawn in relation to visual inattention from Simons and Chabris's study. [2]

7 Suggest **one** weakness of the way that the study by Simon and Chabris into visual inattention was conducted. [3]

8 Outline **one** difference between the study conducted into visual inattention by Simon and Chabris and the study into dichotic listening conducted by Moray. [3]

SECTION B: AREAS, PERSPECTIVES AND DEBATES

12 (a) Describe the difference between an experimental and a non-experimental method. [4]

(b) Explain how **one** psychological study can be considered to be an experiment. [5]

(c) Evaluate the usefulness of using the experimental method in psychology. Support your answer with evidence from **one** appropriate psychological study. [6]

(d)* Discuss the strengths and weaknesses of collecting quantitative data. Support your answer with evidence from appropriate psychological studies. [20]

SECTION A   1 From the study by Moray into dichotic listening explain what a shadowing task is. [2]

Liam's answer:

Shadowing means paying attention to one message and not the other.

We say: Not quite. The result of being asked to do a shadowing task is likely to be that you pay attention to one message and not to the other, but the task is one in which you are asked to repeat one message as you hear it.

Rina's answer:

A shadowing task is where the participant can hear two different messages (one in each ear) and is asked to repeat one of the messages as they hear it.

We say: Rina has got this right and has explained this clearly.

2 Outline **one** control that was used in the study into dichotic listening conducted by Moray. [2]

Liam's answer:

Volume

We say: Liam has a tendency to give very short answers to questions and this is likely to lose him marks. This answer is partially correct but he needs to explain this in more detail. If he had said that the volume of both messages was similar, this would have given the examiner a little more detail.

Rina's answer:

The messages were always played through headphones which directed one message to each ear.

We say: Another correct answer from Rina and again an answer that gives a bit more detail than Liam's!

7 Suggest **one** weakness of the way that the study by Simon and Chabris into visual inattention was conducted. [3]

Liam's answer:

A volunteer sample is a weakness.

Rina's answer

Lots of different researchers were used to collect the data. Overall there were 21 different people collecting data. This means that it would be very hard to standardise all the aspects of the way this study was conducted. They did use a standardised script but they didn't control for the size of the screens and it may be easier to see the gorilla on a large screen than a small screen.

We say: There are three marks for this question and so the examiners are going to be looking for more detail than this. Liam could expand this answer by explaining clearly why a volunteer sample is a weakness. If he could put this into context (in other words, why is a volunteer sample a weakness for this study), then this would make his answer even better.

We say: Rina has written a much better answer. Although it could perhaps be improved further (it is a little repetitive to begin with and the point about the standardised script is more a strength than a weakness), it does contain a clear weakness which is well explained and contextualised.

SECTION B   12 (a) Describe the difference between an experimental and a non-experimental method. [4]

Liam's answer:

An experimental method is like an experiment and a non-experimental method is an observation or a questionnaire.

Rina's answer:

An experimental method is a method that manipulates an IV and measures the effect of this manipulation on the DV. For example, manipulating the temperature and measuring how much work people do. A non-experimental method does not manipulate an IV and uses methods like observation or self-report to investigate the topic. This means that non-experimental methods cannot draw cause-and-effect relationships and experimental methods can.

We say: Liam appears not to have read the question properly. He has given examples of methods in his answer but has not described the difference between an experimental and a non-experimental method as he has been asked to do. Remember that this is Section B and the questions are worth more marks!

We say: This is a very good answer. Although Rina could perhaps have mentioned control as another feature of experimental methods, the answer she has given is very detailed and shows a very good understanding of the difference.

SECTION B 12 (b) Explain how **one** psychological study can be considered to be an experiment. [5]

Liam's answer:

Moray's study is an experiment. Moray was investigating dichotic listening and he played messages to both ears and studied what people heard. He found that people heard their own name even when they weren't paying attention.

We say: Liam still isn't reading the questions! The question is not asking you to describe a study that is an experiment but to describe how (or why) the study can be considered to be an experiment. There is unfortunately nothing in Liam's answer that shows his understanding of this.

Rina's answer:

Simon and Chabris's study was an experiment as it had independent variables that were manipulated by the experimenters. These included two versions of an unexpected event (either a woman with an umbrella or a gorilla walking across the screen), whether the film was transparent or opaque and whether the task was easy or hard. Because these variables were all manipulated by the researchers, we can call this an experiment. It also used an independent measures design, which means that participants only took part in one condition, and it controlled factors such as the timing of the unexpected event so that this occurred at the same time for everyone.

We say: Once again, Rina has given us lots of detail and has clearly answered the question that was set. The detail about the independent variables is very good (perhaps she could have explained what 'transparent' and 'opaque' meant in the context of this study or what the task actually consisted of, but there is a lot of creditworthy material here). The sentence about the independent measures design needs a little more explanation, but the point about control is a good one.

THE COGNITIVE AREA OF PSYCHOLOGY

We have explored in detail four important studies from the cognitive area of psychology. Each pair of core studies has explored a key theme that helps us understand more about how human beings process information and the kinds of factors that improve, or worsen, our cognitive abilities. By considering these pieces of research we can outline some key assumptions:

1 Mental (cognitive) processes are key to understanding human behaviour

Cognitive psychology emphasises the importance of processes such as attention, perception, memory, language and thinking, which are important in all human activity. We feel and behave in particular ways because we perceive what is happening around us, attend to particular aspects of it, remember what has already happened, and think and talk about these things.

A We may feel that we are trying hard to attend to incoming information, such as when we are in a lesson, or driving a car. However, evidence from the studies by Moray and by Simons and Chabris show that we often fail to attend even to pertinent or unusual events. If we do not notice visual or auditory stimuli, we cannot possibly remember them.

Our memories are affected by the way we encode and retrieve information, which can be illustrated by the findings of two of the core studies. Loftus and Palmer showed that memories can be altered by questions asked after an event we have seen, which explains why witnesses' accounts of what they have seen can be altered by leading questions. Grant *et al.* showed that the match or mismatch between encoding and retrieval contexts affects recall. This relates to the common experience of failing to remember when in a different environment from the one in which we learned material, which is particularly important for students studying for exams.

2 We can understand the mind as an information processor

Before cognitive psychology, psychologists were much more likely to just look at a stimulus (an aspect of the environment that people respond to) and our response to it. This stimulus-response psychology was sometimes called the 'black-box approach', because it treated the mind as something we could not see into. By understanding mental processes, cognitive psychologists are opening up the black box.

We input information through the senses and make sense of it. Throughput involves paying attention to information, storing it, thinking about it and retrieving it. Output might be in the form of a behaviour, a decision or an emotional response.

Moray's study investigated what allows or blocks access to auditory attention, that is, how some aspects of an unattended message – which reaches our senses – fails to break through an attentional block. Simon and Chabris considered how we fail to pay attention to sensory information reaching our eyes. We 'see' the gorilla – in that its image reaches our retina – but we often do not attend to it so we do not store that information.

The Loftus and Palmer study is concerned with the effect of how later input of information about an event affects memory for that event. This alteration of the information in the mind affects output, in the form of decision-making about the speed at which cars were travelling and the presence of broken glass. The Grant *et al.* study reveals that the situation affects processes occurring both during input (studying) and during output (exam performance).

This way of looking at the human mind as an information processor makes use of the computer analogy. In other words we are looking at the mind as if it were a computer, which we understand in terms of input, throughput and output of information. This is not to say that cognitive psychologists believe that the mind works exactly like a computer, rather that computers provide a useful way of trying to understand what happens in the mind.

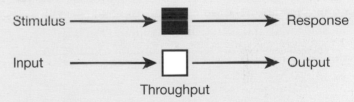

Figure 2.15
The black-box approach versus the cognitive approach

STRENGTHS AND WEAKNESSES OF THE COGNITIVE AREA OF PSYCHOLOGY
Strengths

1 **Good scientific status.** The cognitive area of psychology has many of the features of good science. Most research is experimental and takes place as far as possible in conditions where extraneous variables can be controlled. Theories and ideas are open to being tested by researchers. For example, in all the studies in this section it was possible to control other variables that might have affected performance, for example by ensuring that extraneous variables such as timings and ease of viewing or hearing were constant, e.g. by using recorded materials.

By conducting laboratory experiments, the researchers in each study could be sure that the IV was the cause of any changes in the DV. For example, in Loftus and Palmer's study they used the two experiments to distinguish between the direct effects of the verbs, which could cause a response bias and indirect memory distortion.

2   **Opening up the 'black box' has extended our understanding of people.** Before cognitive psychology existed, psychologists had some understanding of human behaviour and human emotion. However, how we attend, think, remember and make sense of the world around us are also essential aspects of human psychology, and without a cognitive approach it is very difficult to look at those. A cognitive understanding of psychology has opened up a range of practical applications. For example, there are now psychological therapies that work by altering how people think about things that are bothering them. Legal procedures involving witness testimony have evolved to incorporate a modern cognitive understanding of memory. Applications to safety, health and education have all evolved from research into attention.

Weaknesses

1   **The computer analogy breaks down.** Adopting an information-processing approach to psychology makes the assumption that the human mind processes information in the same way as a computer does. In some ways this is true: like a computer, we receive, recognise, store and retrieve information and we use language to make that information easier to work with. However, unlike a computer, we are emotional, intuitive and influenced by instinct as well as logic – that is, cognition is an active process dependent on a range of factors both internal and external. These things alter what happens to information in the mind. We are much slower than computers in our processing but we are much better at making use of mental short cuts. We are therefore only partly justified in treating the mind as an information-processing machine. Futhermore, while the processes occurring in a computer are known (they have been programmed so we understand them and they can therefore be measured directly), this is not so of cognition. The only way we can study cognitive processes is to observe the consequences of that cognition, i.e. the 'output' of behaviours such as our actions or speech.

2   **Cognitive reductionism.** When we focus on mental processes we ignore many other important aspects of human psychology. The mind is emotional and instinctive as well as logical, and it is influenced by unconscious factors that cannot easily be explained by a cognitive approach. Perhaps more importantly, as individuals, we never process information in isolation but always within a social context, influenced by the people around us. By focusing on a particular set of mental processes within the individual mind, the cognitive area of psychology can neglect these key parts of human psychology and so is guilty of reductionism.

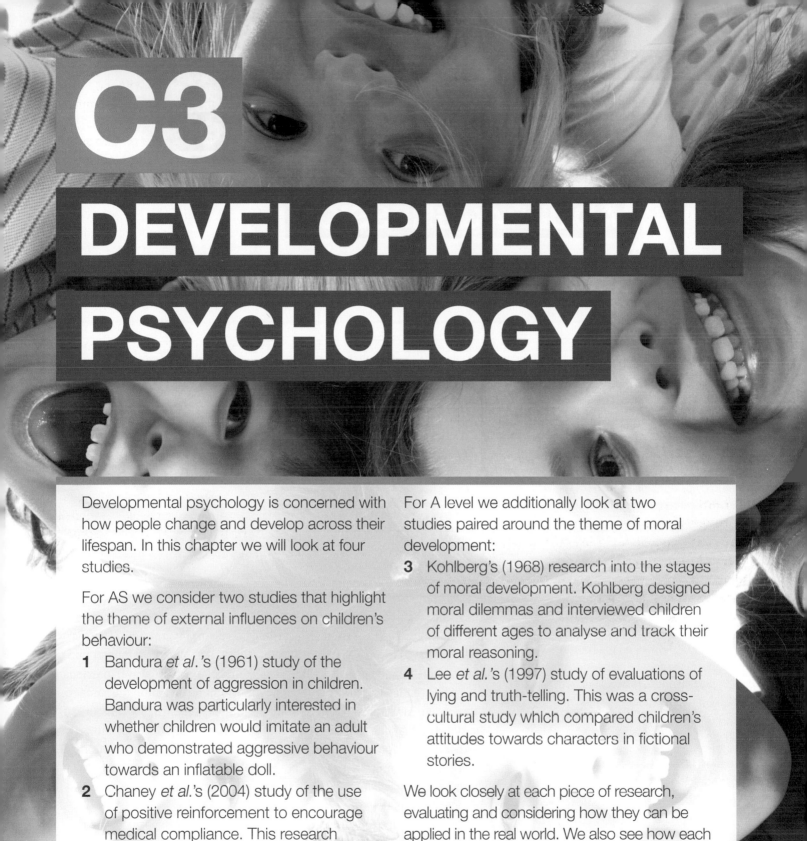

C3

DEVELOPMENTAL PSYCHOLOGY

Developmental psychology is concerned with how people change and develop across their lifespan. In this chapter we will look at four studies.

For AS we consider two studies that highlight the theme of external influences on children's behaviour:

1 Bandura *et al.*'s (1961) study of the development of aggression in children. Bandura was particularly interested in whether children would imitate an adult who demonstrated aggressive behaviour towards an inflatable doll.

2 Chaney *et al.*'s (2004) study of the use of positive reinforcement to encourage medical compliance. This research compares how effectively asthmatic children took medication using a standard inhaler with a novel, reward-giving device.

For A level we additionally look at two studies paired around the theme of moral development:

3 Kohlberg's (1968) research into the stages of moral development. Kohlberg designed moral dilemmas and interviewed children of different ages to analyse and track their moral reasoning.

4 Lee *et al.*'s (1997) study of evaluations of lying and truth-telling. This was a cross-cultural study which compared children's attitudes towards characters in fictional stories.

We look closely at each piece of research, evaluating and considering how they can be applied in the real world. We also see how each pair of studies can help us understand a key theme. Lastly we use them to explore issues within developmental psychology, looking at the strengths and limitations of this area.

BANDURA *et al.*'s STUDY OF CHILDREN'S IMITATION OF ADULT AGGRESSION

Bandura, A., Ross, D. and Ross, S.A. (1961) Transmission of aggression through immitation of aggressive models. *Journal of Abnormal & Social Psychology,* **63**: 575–582

IN BRIEF

Aim: To investigate the extent to which children would imitate aggression modelled by an adult, and to investigate the effects of gender on imitation.

Method: 72 children were divided into three groups. One group saw an adult attack an inflatable doll (a Bobo doll) in a play room. A second group saw an adult behave non-aggressively, and a third group did not see an adult playing. All the children were then frustrated by being banned from playing with attractive toys and left to play in a room containing a Bobo doll.

Results: Children who had witnessed the aggressive adult were more likely to play aggressively with the Bobo doll. Boys were more likely than girls to imitate physical aggression, especially from a male model.

Conclusion: Children can acquire aggression through observation of adults modelling aggression. They selectively imitate gender-specific behaviour and boys imitate male models, at least selectively.

KEY IDEAS

Observational learning is learning behaviour through observation of that behaviour in another individual, known as the **model**. Observational learning can be seen in many species. Albert Bandura and colleagues demonstrated observational learning in humans and built the idea into social learning theory.

Identification is another idea from social learning theory. We identify with a model when we adopt their behaviour in order to become like them.

CONTEXT

This study is concerned with the tendency of children to imitate adult social behaviour, specifically aggression. Learning behaviour by imitating others is called **observational learning**. Several studies had already demonstrated that children are influenced by witnessing adult behaviour. However, previous studies had tended to show children repeating adult behaviour in the same situation and in the presence of the adult that modelled the behaviour. Although this suggests that children **identify** with adult **models**, it does not show whether they will go on to repeat the observed behaviour in other situations and without the adult present. One purpose of the study, therefore, was to test whether children will reproduce observed behaviour in a new situation and in the absence of the model.

This study is also concerned with the learning of gender-specific behaviour. Previous studies had shown that children are sensitive to gender-specific behaviours. For example, children see their parents as preferring gender-stereotyped behaviour. Aggression is a good example of a gendered social behaviour, being associated with masculinity.

A further purpose of this study was to investigate whether boys were more likely to imitate aggression than girls, and whether they would be more likely to imitate male than female models.

AIMS AND HYPOTHESES

The overall aim of the study was to investigate observational learning of aggression. Specifically, the study aimed to see whether children would reproduce aggressive behaviour when the model was no longer present, and to look for gender differences in learning of aggression. Several hypotheses were tested:

1   Participants exposed to an aggressive model would be more likely to reproduce similar aggression than those exposed to a non-aggressive model and those who did not see a model at all.
2   Participants exposed to a non-aggressive model would be less aggressive than those not exposed to a model at all.
3   Participants would imitate aggression modelled by a same-sex adult more than that modelled by an opposite-sex adult.
4   Boys would be more inclined than girls to imitate aggression.

METHOD

Figure 3.1
Albert Bandura

Participants

There were a total of 72 participants: 36 male and 36 female. All were selected from the nursery school of Stanford University. Ages ranged from 37 months (just over three years) to 69 months (five-and-three-quarter years). The mean age was 52 months (four years and four months).

Design

This was a laboratory experiment, using an independent measures design. The effect of three independent variables was tested:
*   The behaviour of the model – aggressive or non-aggressive;
*   The sex of the model; and
*   The sex of the children.

There were eight conditions in all. The children in each condition were matched for their aggression levels, so that this did not become a confounding variable. This was achieved by the experimenter and a nursery teacher independently rating 51 of the children on a scale of 0 to 5. Very good agreement between the two raters was achieved (0.89). The conditions were as follows:

1   12 boys and 12 girls were exposed to an aggressive model. Six boys and six girls saw aggression modelled by a same-sex model, while the rest saw it modelled by an opposite-sex model.
2   12 boys and 12 girls were exposed to a non-aggressive model. Six boys and six girls saw non-aggression modelled by a same-sex model, while the rest saw it modelled by an opposite-sex model.
3   A control group of 12 boys and 12 girls did not see a model display any behaviour, aggressive or otherwise.

QUESTION SPOTLIGHT!

Be clear on the distinction between aims and hypotheses. *Outline one aim and one hypothesis from this study.*

QUESTION SPOTLIGHT!

Identify two controls in the design of the Bandura *et al.* study. *Explain how one of these controls is helpful in avoiding the effects of extraneous variables.*

Procedure

The procedure consisted of three stages.

1 **Modelling the behaviour**. Each child was brought individually into a play room and invited to join in a game. This lasted for 10 minutes. In the first two conditions there was also an additional adult present in the room. In the aggressive condition, this adult demonstrated aggression towards a 5-foot tall inflatable Bobo doll, kicking and hitting it, including with a hammer. They also said aggressive things, such as 'kick him ... pow ... sock him on the nose'. In the non-aggressive condition, the adult assembled toys and did not interact with the doll. In the control condition, there was no additional adult in the room.

2 **Aggression arousal.** In order to annoy the children and increase the chances of aggressive behaviour, all the children were then taken to a different play room with some very attractive toys. After being allowed to play with these for around two minutes, the participants were told they were not allowed to play with them any more as they were 'the very best' toys and they were going to be reserved for other children.

3 **Testing for delayed imitation**. Children were then observed playing for the next 20 minutes as the experimenter remained in the room but busied herself with paperwork. Two more observers watched through a one way mirror. The room contained a range of toys including a bob doll (smaller than the one seen earlier). During the observation, the observers were unaware which condition the child was in. This helped eliminate bias.

Three types of aggression were recorded by observers:

1 Imitative aggression – physical and verbal aggression identical to that modelled in stage 1;

2 Partially imitative aggression – similar behaviour to that carried out by the model;

3 Non-imitative aggression – new aggressive acts not demonstrated by the model.

DO IT YOURSELF

For ethical reasons you should not attempt to carry out any experimental research that looks at modelling of aggression. However there are other ways of investigating the link between modelled aggression and aggressive behaviour. You may wish to design questionnaires that measure how often participants watch violent films or play violent video games. Participants could then rate their own levels of aggression and you could look for a correlation between self-reported aggression and frequency of watching violent media.

Figure 3.2
Aggression is modelled
and imitated

RESULTS

Quantitative data was recorded. This showed significant differences in levels of imitative aggression between the group that witnessed aggression and the other two groups. This was true of physical and verbal aggression. To a lesser extent this was also true of partial imitation and non-imitative aggression. Significantly more non-aggressive play was recorded in the non-aggressive model condition. In terms of the hypotheses tested:

1 Children who had witnessed an aggressive model were significantly more aggressive themselves.
2 Overall, there was very little difference between aggression in the control group and that in the non-aggressive modelling condition.
3 Boys were significantly more likely to imitate aggressive male models. The difference for girls was much smaller.
4 Boys were significantly more physically aggressive than girls. Girls were more verbally aggressive than boys after observing a female model.

MATHS MOMENT

Look at Table 3.1. For the first row, male participants' imitative physical aggression:
1 Identify the ratio of aggressive behaviour following aggressive modelling by a male to that following aggressive modelling by a female.
2 What percentage of male imitative aggression followed an aggressive male model?
3 Express this as a fraction.

TABLE 3.1 AGGRESSION SCORES RECORDED BY OBSERVERS

Participant group	Aggressive male model	Aggressive female model	Non-aggressive male model	Non-aggressive female model	No model
Male imitative physical aggression	25.4	12.8	1.5	0.2	2.0
Female imitative physical aggression	7.2	5.5	0.0	2.5	1.2
Male imitative verbal aggression	12.7	4.3	0.0	1.1	1.7
Female imitative verbal aggression	2.0	13.7	0.0	0.3	0.7
Male non-imitative aggression	36.7	17.2	22.3	26.1	24.6
Female non-imitative aggression	8.4	21.3	1.4	7.2	6.1

CONCLUSIONS

1 Witnessing aggression in a model can be enough to produce aggression by an observer. This is important because it had been widely believed prior to this study that learning aggression was a more gradual process in which a learner experimented with aggression and was rewarded in some way for doing so.
2 Children selectively imitate gender-specific behaviour. Thus boys are more likely to imitate physical aggression than girls. Because boys but not girls were more likely to imitate aggression in a same-sex model, it could be concluded only cautiously that children selectively imitate same-sex models. It could not be ruled out that this process is specific to boys, as girls who witnessed a female model were more verbally aggressive than boys.

WEB WATCH

You can read the original research paper here:
http://psychclassics.yorku.ca/Bandura/Bobo.htm
You can also see footage of the study on YouTube.
Go to www.youtube.com and search for 'Bobo doll experiment'.

There is more than one possible explanation for these findings. One suggestion was that children were not *learning* aggression at all, but that they were just *disinhibited* by witnessing the adult aggression. In other words, they already knew how to act aggressively but it became okay when the adult did it. However, if this were true, we would expect that children would be aggressive to the doll in a wide range of ways. In fact, although there was non-imitative aggression, they tended to imitate exactly the style of aggression modelled by the adult. This suggests that they were actually learning the aggression.

EVALUATION

This is a classic example of a laboratory experiment, strong on experimental control but weaker on ecological validity.

The research method

This study was a classic laboratory experiment, with the strengths and weaknesses that typically go with laboratory experiments. On the positive side, there are many excellent controls that cut down the risk posed by extraneous variables. All participants had very much the same experience, with the same rooms and toys being used in all conditions. This is a particular strength of the design. However, like many laboratory experiments, this one lacks a degree of realism. Hitting a Bobo doll is very different from hitting a person, and we should be cautious about applying results obtained in this experimental situation to more lifelike situations.

Qualitative and quantitative data

Typically for a laboratory experiment, only quantitative data were gathered in this study. This is both a strength and a weakness. On the plus side, numbers allow us to easily compare the levels of aggression in each condition. As long as we are concerned with observable behaviour we are on safe ground in rating what we observe quantitatively. However, what we don't get from this data is much indication of what is happening in the minds of the children doing the imitating. If you watch the film of Bandura's participants, you can see that some seem to have quite powerful emotional responses to the situation. It would have been really interesting to have qualitative data about what they thought and felt when hitting the doll.

Ethical considerations

All studies making use of children raise additional ethical issues above and beyond those conducted on adults. This is because, unlike adults, children cannot really give informed consent to take part in studies, nor can they withdraw as easily. A typical response to these issues is to get parental permission. Although in their research paper Bandura *et al.* thank the head teacher of the nursery school, they do not make clear what steps they took to ensure parental permission. In this case, children were not doing anything substantially different from their everyday activities so there is little risk of real harm or serious distress, although they were deliberately annoyed by not being allowed to play with the nicest toys. Mild distress was therefore caused, and this is an ethical issue. A more serious issue would be any lasting change to the children's behaviour. However, the type and level of violence children witnessed here was similar to that which they would expect in cartoons, so it is highly unlikely that any child was left more aggressive by participating.

STRETCH & CHALLENGE

In groups, design a follow-up study to check for long-term increases in aggression for participants. Consider how long you would follow up participants and how you would measure long-term changes to aggression.

Validity

We have already said that realism is often a problem for laboratory experiments. This is for two reasons: first, the environment differs from real life; and second, the tasks carried out by participants tend to differ from those they carry out in real life. This study took place in two play rooms similar to those in which children played in other situations, so the fact that they were technically in a laboratory is not too much of a problem. However, being asked to play with a strange adult in an unfamiliar room is not a typical everyday task. More importantly, the experience of hitting a Bobo doll is very different from hitting a real person because the doll does not react. Understanding real-life violence is more complex, because our hitting a person has a range of consequences – both external (e.g. they might hit back, or cry) and internal (e.g. we feel some degree of empathy with the pain of being hit). Studying aggression against a doll lacks realism and so the procedure lacks ecological validity.

STRETCH & CHALLENGE

Bandura *et al.*'s study drew a sample of participants from a particular area in one country. It might be difficult to apply their conclusions to children in other cultures. Why might there be limitations to generalising about aggressive behaviour across different cultures?

Reliability

Reliability was excellent. Conditions were closely controlled and we can take it that all participants had very much the same experience. The most relevant participant variable – prior aggression – was also controlled, by assessing each child for aggression and matching the levels of aggression between the groups. The reliability of observers was assessed and found to be very good. Reliability was therefore a strength of the study.

Sampling bias

Sample size was quite large for a laboratory experiment. At first glance this appears to be a strength of the study. However, consider the number of conditions. By the time we get down to, say, boys imitating a male aggressive model, there are only six participants in that condition. That is quite a small group, and any confounding participant variables could have quite a large effect. A larger sample would have helped avoid this. Bandura *et al.* do not say how their sample was selected from the nursery school, but drawing a sample from a single nursery school is problematic in itself. The nursery used for this study was attended by the children of academics, who are not representative of the population at large. This means that there could be difficulties in generalising results.

Practical applications

This study has interesting applications in settings where we are concerned with children's learning of aggression. Child psychologists and social workers work with children who have witnessed domestic violence. This study informs this work by emphasising the likelihood of children imitating the sort of violence they observe in their parents. The study also has important implications for understanding the link between media violence and children's aggression, suggesting that children, particularly boys, are likely to imitate physical aggression when it is modelled by a male adult.

CHANEY *et al.*'s FUNHALER STUDY

Chaney, G., Clements, B., Landau, L., Bulsara, M. and Watt, P. (2004) A new asthma spacer device to improve compliance in children: a pilot study. *Respirology*, **9** (4): 499–506.

IN BRIEF ❗

Aim: To test whether an asthma spacer device known as a 'Funhaler' could provide positive reinforcement to improve adherence in child asthmatics compared to devices in current use.

Method: The research method was a field experiment using a repeated measures design. The independent variable was the type of device used: a standard spacer device (a 'Breath-a-Tech' or 'AeroChamber') or a novel device known as the 'Funhaler'. The dependent variable was the compliance level to the prescribed medical regime. The sample consisted of 32 children who were instructed to use a Funhaler instead of their normal pMDI (pressurised metered dose inhaler) and spacer inhaler to administer their medication. The Funhaler used a number of features to distract the attention of children from the drug delivery and to reinforce correct use of the device. Parents of participants then completed questionnaires after use of the standard inhaler and the Funhaler.

Results: The findings showed that compliance was higher when using the Funhaler, with children showing greater satisfaction and willingness to use the Funhaler compared to the standard inhaler. Parents' attitudes towards medicating their children were also more positive when using the novel device.

Conclusion: The Funhaler may be useful as a functional incentive device that could improve compliance to medical regimes in young asthmatics.

KEY IDEAS

The term **'compliance'** in this study means the extent to which a patient correctly 'complies' or follows a plan of medical treatment. In this study it refers to how closely young children with asthma and their parents administer asthma medication at the correct dosage and times recommended by their doctors. The words 'compliance' and 'adherence' are used interchangeably in this study. There is, however, some debate around describing a patient as 'non-compliant', as it seems to imply ignorance or deliberate defiance of medical advice. In fact, research shows there are many complex factors which reduce medical compliance, including the high costs of medication, negative side-effects, and poor communication between doctors and patients.

CONTEXT

Low rates of medical **compliance** are a current issue in the healthcare system. This is because it is linked to increased emergency hospital admissions and mortality rates for patients. For asthmatics this is particularly relevant as use of medication through traditional inhalers is designed to both prevent and relieve attacks.

Classic research has consistently shown that young children struggle to comply with doctors' instructions to take asthma medication as often as they should. Rates of compliance for offering medication regularly to asthmatic children range from 30 to 70% (Smith *et al.*, 1984). Additionally, Celano *et al.* (1998) found that children often find it difficult to master the deep breathing technique required to inhale the correct amount of their medication through normal inhalers and spacers. These two issues combined mean that a sizeable proportion of young children do not manage to inhale any medication at all.

Recent studies, such as that by Chapman *et al.* (2000), have identified various reasons why children are particularly poor at taking medication. These include ignorance, fear, boredom, forgetfulness and apathy. However, behaviour modification based on **operant conditioning** is one approach used by health practitioners and psychologists to improve compliance. Through use of rewards it might be possible to improve the way in which asthmatic children administer their medication. Chaney *et al.* proposed that children's sensitivity to positive reinforcement could be used to good effect in designing a new inhaler device. Researchers in this study wanted to analyse participants' attitudes and behaviour towards the new device; testing positive reinforcement could increase compliance.

AIM

The aim of this study was to test whether use of positive reinforcement via the Funhaler could improve medical compliance in young asthmatics, compared to use of a conventional asthma inhaler with no additional features.

METHOD

The research method was a field experiment which used a repeated measures design. The independent variable (IV) was the device used to administer the asthma drugs. The researchers compared standard small-volume spacer devices, including the 'Breath-a-Tech' and 'AeroChamber', with a novel device known as a 'Funhaler'. The dependent variable (DV) was how well participants complied with their prescribed medical regime, measured through parental responses to a self-report questionnaire.

Participants

The study involved 32 children: 22 male and 10 female. The age range was 1.5–6 years, with a mean age of 3.2 years and average duration of asthma of 2.2 years. The sampling technique was a random sample of asthmatic children who had been prescribed drugs delivered by pMDI and spacer (pressurised metered dose inhaler) and were recruited from clinics across a large geographical area.

Design and procedure

The study was undertaken in participants' homes over a two week period. The children's parents gave informed consent to take part and completed a structured, closed question questionnaire with an interviewer about their child's current asthma device. This included questions on both the parent's and child's attitudes towards medication and their compliance levels. Participants were then asked to use a Funhaler instead of their normal pMDI and spacer inhaler to administer their medication without further instructions on use, except that parental guidance was required. The 'Funhaler' incorporated the standard pMDI inhaler and spacer that you may be familiar with (see Figure 3.4 on page 91), along with an additional attachment. The attachment included incentive toys such as a spinning disc and whistle. These were designed to distract children from the drug delivery event itself and to encourage and reward deep breathing patterns required for effective delivery of medication. This was a form of operant conditioning that was known as 'self-reinforcement', as correct use of the device rewarded the user, requiring no external encouragement from a parent or doctor. After this time, parents completed a matched item questionnaire on the Funhaler to allow direct comparison with the standard device. Researchers also conducted one random check via telephone, checking on participant usage of the Funhaler on the previous day.

KEY IDEAS

Operant conditioning is a form of associative learning, whereby we learn by the consequences of our actions. We form new associations and connections between certain stimuli and responses. When we complete a behaviour that has a positive outcome, we are more likely to repeat that action. For example, parents might entice children to complete their homework by offering a tasty snack as a reward. When the child completes their work, they are then rewarded with the snack. This process is known as reinforcement. It can be a powerful strategy used to shape the behaviour of both humans and animals.

Figure 3.3
Failure to take asthma medication can in some cases lead to emergency hospital admissions

WEB WATCH @

Can you teach an old bird new tricks? For a simple, clear illustration of operant conditioning in practice, go to:

https://pantherfile.uwm.edu/johnchay/www/oc.htm

This link leads you to a simulation where you can use the principles of reinforcement to train a bird to perform movements.

MATHS MOMENT

1   The study uses a random sample of patients from seven local paediatrician or general practice (GP) clinics. Explain how a stratified technique could be used to obtain a more representative sample. (Read more about stratified sampling on page 271).

STRETCH & CHALLENGE

Read a short introduction to behavioural techniques such as operant and classical conditioning on page 197. Now research different ways in which these types of conditioning have been used in practice. Do you think the use of these techniques is justified?

DO IT YOURSELF

This study makes use of a sampling method called 'random sampling'. It means each person in the target population has an equal chance of being chosen. Try to find at least three methods to take a random selection of five members of your class and note down certain relevant characteristics. For example, this could include their gender, age and other subjects they are studying. Do you think your random sample is a good representation of the rest of the class or year group?

RESULTS

The survey showed that use of the Funhaler was associated with improved parental and child compliance. The researchers collected 27–32 valid responses to each pair of questions being collected. Fifty-nine per cent of parents were found to have medicated their children on the previous day when using their standard device compared to 81% when using the Funhaler. Researchers also found 50% of children took the four or more cycles per aerosol delivery or 'puffs' when they used the standard device, compared to 80% achieving this with the Funhaler. A number of problems when taking medication – such as screaming when the device was brought close to the child's face, unwillingness to breathe through the device, or unwillingness to breathe for a long time – were all significantly reduced when using the Funhaler. Sixty-eight per cent of children reported pleasure when using the Funhaler, whereas only 10% enjoyed using the standard device. Parents also reported improved satisfaction with the device (see Table 3.2).

TABLE 3.2 CHILD'S ATTITUDE TO USING THEIR DEVICE AND PARENTAL APPROACH TO MEDICATING THEIR CHILD (PERCENTAGE OF VALID CASES IS SHOWN IN BRACKETS)*

	Existing spacer devices	Funhaler
Child's attitude to using their device:		
Pleasure	3 (10%)	21 (68%)
Acceptance	18 (58%)	6 (19%)
No interest in device	1 (35%)	1 (3%)
Suspicion	0 (0%)	3 (10%)
Mild fear or dislike	4 (13%)	0 (0%)
Strong fear or dislike	6 (19%)	0 (0%)
Panic or phobia	2 (6%)	0 (0%)
Total number of valid cases	**31 (100%)**	**31 (100%)**
Parent's approach to medicating their child:		
Completely happy	3 (10%)	19 (61%)
Confident	10 (32%)	5 (16%)
Acceptance	12 (29%)	6 (19%)
Mild concern	2 (7%)	1 (3%)
Strong concern	4 (13%)	0 (0%)
Dislike	5 (16%)	0 (0%)
Total number of valid cases	**31 (100%)**	**31 (110%)**

* Some subjects gave more than one response.

Figure 3.4
Breath in, breath out: The Funhaler (left) used in Chaney et al.'s *study versus the Breath-a-Tech (right)*

CONCLUSIONS

Chaney *et al.* conclude that the Funhaler and its use of positive reinforcement techniques improved levels of medical compliance in young asthmatics. Specifically they argue:

1 The use of the Funhaler could possibly improve clinical outcomes, such as lowering rates of admissions to hospital for asthma attacks.
2 Devices that use self-reinforcement strategies can improve the overall health of children.

QUESTION SPOTLIGHT!

1 Explain what is meant by operant conditioning. Can you give one example of its use in shaping human behaviour?
2 Can you outline the procedure used by Chaney *et al.* in this study?

EVALUATION

The research method

The study is a field experiment and used controls to try to manage the influence of extraneous variables on the DV (which was compliance to medical regime). For example, the questionnaires used to assess each device contained matched questions to ensure the children's' responses were directly comparable. However, the study's findings rely on self-report, which is open to bias as participants might over-report use of the Funhaler in order to please the experimenters.

Qualitative and quantitative data

This study reports quantitative findings given in numerical form, such as the numbers of asthmatic children and their parents who administered medication on randomly checked days. It allowed the researchers to directly and objectively compare the use of each device. However, they did not report in this study any verbal or written feedback from children and parents. This lack of qualitative data means they have assumed and not demonstrated that the operant conditioning device known as the Funhaler is what encouraged better compliance.

Ethical considerations

This study is fairly ethically sound. Informed consent was obtained from the parents of the child participants, who were too young to give consent themselves. They were briefed as to the aims of the study and all data responses were anonymised, which ensured their privacy. As this study involved the use of drugs essential to children's health, care was taken to ensure that the experimental Funhaler device administered a satisfactory level of medication. This means that the children were protected from physical harm.

Validity

As a field experiment, this study could be considered to have high ecological validity. Even though participants were aware that they were part of the research, they were going about their everyday lives and using the devices in their own environments. On the other hand, the children had already had lots of experience using the standard device and knew that they were trying out a novel device. This could have biased their questionnaire responses and created an order effect, making participants more likely to report use of the Funhaler. The researchers tried to minimise any bias by not giving extra explanation or instructions on the Funhaler's usage. However, it could be that without monitoring by researchers, use of the Funhaler is more similar to that of the standard device.

Reliability

The procedure and materials for this study are standardised and it would be straightforward to carry out the test again. It has high levels of replicability, and as participants were all given the same instructions we could say the findings are fairly reliable.

Sampling bias

This study used a random sampling method which reduces bias and ensures a fairly representative sample. The sample included a fair number of families, from widely differing socioeconomic and geographical areas of Perth, Western Australia.. This means that the sample contained a very wide range of individuals from across a large area.

Ethnocentrism

Behaviourists believe that external factors, including complex cultural influences can play a part in reinforcing desirable behaviours. While the Funhaler's reinforcing features are used to influence children's behaviour regardless of location, there could be other social and cultural influences that affected the compliance rates in this study. These might relate to societal attitudes towards medical treatment (which vary cross-culturally), meaning Chaney *et al.*'s findings might not be applicable outside of Australia.

Practical applications

As discussed, correct compliance to a medical regime is important for asthma sufferers for whom prevention of an asthma attack is essential for their well-being. The consequences for children of forgetting or not wanting to use their inhaler regularly can be particularly serious. Chaney *et al.* have shown the use of a device that can self-reinforce the correct technique and dosage of medication in children. It does not rely on outside influences such as parental nagging or sticker charts, for example. The Funhaler device and other self-reinforcement devices and strategies could therefore be used to improve medical compliance in other age groups, if the reward mechanism is appropriately appealing.

STRETCH & CHALLENGE

The current UK government has put together something known as 'The Behavioural Insights Team', often called the 'Nudge Unit'. It applies insights from academic research in behavioural economics and psychology to public policy and services. Several of their key projects, such as reducing usage of plastic bags and use of prosocial media, rely on the operant conditioning principles of punishment and reinforcements.

You can read about their ongoing work on their research blog:
http://www.behaviouralinsights.co.uk/blog.xml
Could you identify and explain how one of these projects uses the principles of operant conditioning to change people's behaviour?

COMPARISON OF STUDIES

Bandura et al.'s *Study of Children's Imitation of Adult Aggression* & *Chaney* et al.'s *Funhaler Study*

THE TOPIC
Influence of social learning versus operant conditioning

The studies by Bandura *et al.* and Chaney *et al.* are both about developmental psychology, specifically about the ways in which external influences can influence behaviour. However, Bandura *et al.* looked at how children imitate aggressive behaviour they have observed in adult role models, and Chaney *et al.* looked at how children will increase desirable behaviour such as medical compliance when positively reinforced.

THE RESEARCH METHOD AND DESIGN
Laboratory experiment versus field experiment using independent groups design versus repeated measures design

Although both studies were experiments, Bandura *et al.* used a laboratory experiment and Chaney *et al.* used a field experiment. In both studies, therefore, there were attempts to control variables, which increases validity and reliability. The extent to which this was achieved was different Chaney *et al.*'s study experimenters could not control the many environmental factors that would have impacted on compliance. Additionally, Bandura *et al.* used an independent measures design, which meant participants viewed different behaviour from models, while Chaney *et al.*'s participants trialled both asthma devices, making the study a repeated measures design.

SAMPLING TECHNIQUE AND THE SAMPLE
Opportunity versus random sampling method; both used young children

Bandura *et al.* drew their participants from a local nursery, while Chaney *et al.* used a random sampling method to recruit children and their families through local paediatrician or GP clinics. Bandura *et al.*'s method is likely to be less representative overall, as the children have come from a smaller geographical area and are likely to share more characteristics than the diverse sample obtained by Chaney *et al.* Both studies used young children of a similar age, with the mean age of children being 4.3 years in Bandura *et al.*'s study, and 3.2 years in Chaney *et al.*'s sample.

EXPERIMENTAL MATERIALS AND MEASUREMENT OF THE DV
Both studies used tasks that lacked validity and collected mainly quantitative data

In the study by Bandura *et al.*, children were asked to play in the presence of strange adult in an unfamiliar room and then had their behaviour towards a Bobo doll observed. Neither of these tasks was particularly ecologically valid and may not represent how aggression is learned in real life. Similarly, children and families involved in Chaney *et al.*'s study might have behaved differently as they were monitored via self-report on use of the Funhaler.

Both studies collected primarily quantitative data. In the Bandura *et al.* study this consisted of the observers' recordings of the three types of aggression displayed by children. In the Chaney *et al.* study, researchers recorded compliance rates through random questioning and a formal matched item questionnaire. In both pieces of research, the use of quantitative data allowed a simple and direct comparison of the experimental and control conditions.

APPLICATIONS
Modifying children's behaviour

Bandura *et al.*'s study has many important applications when dealing with how individuals learn and express aggression in the real world. It can help psychologists and social workers understand the attitudes and behaviour of children from families who have witnessed physical and verbal aggression, for example. Chaney *et al.*'s study is also useful for those looking to modify children's behaviour, specifically through the use of positive reinforcement to encourage young people to follow treatment programmes in their home environments. Both of these studies support the development of strategies to improve children's safety and well-being.

KEY THEME: EXTERNAL INFLUENCES ON CHILDREN'S BEHAVIOUR

Bandura *et al.* make a major contribution to our understanding of how children acquire new behaviours. The study shows how the principles of observational learning – observation and imitation of an adult role model – can be used to explain aggressive behaviour. This contradicted the existing theories of the time, such as Freud's idea that watching aggression would actually lower one's own aggressive impulses. Importantly it also demonstrated that the characteristics of a role model might influence how likely they are to be imitated.

By contrast, Chaney *et al.* identified a particular issue in clinical practice: issues of non-compliance to medical regimes. The study is also significant on the grounds that it demonstrates how effective simple, low-cost operant conditioning strategies such as the Funhaler can be. This changes our understanding of how children's behaviour can be influenced by external forces. Instead of being an outdated, disused approach, operant conditioning is at the cutting-edge of behavioural modification, and can usefully be applied to real-world issues such as children's health.

KEY THEME

External influences on children's behaviour
Bandura *et al.* used a laboratory experiment to test the theory of observational learning, showing that children are likely to imitate aggressive role models. Chaney *et al.* tested the use of operant conditioning to improve medical compliance, and found that young asthmatics responded to the use of rewards.

Bandura et al.
Investigated aggression, using a laboratory experiment with an independent measures design. The study was highly controlled, but low in ecological validity and unethical.

Similarities
Both studies focus on helping us understand external influences on children's behaviour. They both used children of similar ages as participants, and collected mainly quantitative data. They can both be applied to modifying behaviour.

Chaney et al.
Investigated medical compliance using a field experiment with a repeated measures design. The study was ethically sound and ecologically valid, but had low control.

PRACTICE QUESTIONS

Here are some of the sorts of questions that you could be asked in Sections A and B of your AS exam, and some examples of successful and less successful answers. We look at Section B questions in more detail in Chapter 6 on pages 206–8 and 212–14.

SECTION A: CORE STUDIES

1 Describe the sample used in Bandura *et al.*'s study into the transmission of aggression. [3]

2 From Bandura *et al.*'s study into the transmission of aggression: Outline how the model displayed aggressive behaviour. [3]

3 Describe **two** findings from the study by Bandura *et al.* on the imitation of aggression. [4]

4 Describe **two** ethical issues raised in the study by Bandura *et al.* on the imitation of aggression. [4]

5 Chaney *et al.*'s Funhaler study was a pilot study:
   (a) Describe what a pilot study is. [2]
   (b) Suggest **one** reason why a pilot study might be conducted. [2]

6 Describe the sample used by Chaney *et al.* in their Funhaler study. [3]

7 Outline **two** conclusions given by Chaney *et al.* in their Funhaler study. [4]

8 Outline **one** similarity between the study by Bandura *et al.* into the transmission of aggression and the study by Chaney *et al.* into the use of Funhalers. [3]

SECTION B: AREAS, PERSPECTIVES AND DEBATES

9 **(a)** Outline how developmental psychology explains behaviour. [2]
   (b) Suggest **one** strength of investigating development. Support your answer with evidence from one appropriate core study. [3]
   (c) Suggest **one** problem when investigating development. Support your answer with evidence from **one** appropriate core study. [3]
   (d)* Explain how any **one** core study can be considered to be located within the area of developmental psychology. [5]
   (e) Discuss the problems of conducting research with children. Support your answer with evidence from core studies. [12]

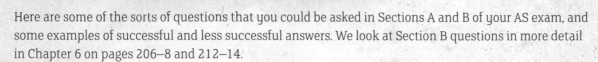

SECTION A   5 Chaney *et al.*'s Funhaler study was a pilot study:

(a) Describe what a pilot study is. [2]

(b) Suggest **one** reason why a pilot study might be conducted. [2]

Rachel's answer:

(a) A pilot study is conducted before the real study.

(b) It is quicker than a big study.

Charlotte's answer:

(a) A pilot study is a small-scale study conducted to pre-test a method before conducting a larger study.

(b) One reason why a pilot study might be conducted is so that the experimenters can identify any problems with the study, such as questions on a questionnaire that don't make sense and these problems can be resolved before the larger-scale study is conducted.

We say: Rachel has identified one aspect of a pilot study, although her answer is very vague. A pilot study is a study that is conducted before a larger study, usually to test the feasibility of the study or the validity of some aspect of the study. This needs to be explained in a little more detail. Rachel's answer to part (b) is also much too vague. This does not really identify a reason why a pilot study would be conducted. This answer needs to be explained further.

We say: Charlotte has provided two clear and concise answers to these questions. These both suggest a very good understanding of this research method.

4 Describe two ethical issues raised in the study by Bandura et al. on the imitation of aggression. [4]

Rachel's answer:

One ethical issue is the amount of distress that was caused to the children and the other ethical issue is the lack of consent from the children.

We say: Rachel has identified distress as her first point and although this is a correct answer there is no real description here. Rachel needs to elaborate on this answer and describe what it was that happened to the children that might have caused them distress. The second point that Rachel makes is suggesting that children should be able to give consent to participate in a study. This is not correct as consent for children to take part in a study would be the responsibility of their parents.

Charlotte's answer:

The first ethical issue is protection from harm. It is possible to argue that the study by Bandura et al. was unethical because it may have had long-term effects on the children who participated. They may have become more aggressive permanently as a result of their experiences of the study. The second ethical issue is that is unlikely that the children's parents gave fully informed consent. Although Bandura et al. thank the headteacher of the nursery school, they do not give details of asking for parental permission. Even if parents were asked if their children could take part it is highly unlikely that full details of the procedure would have been given, as most parents would probably have refused if they had been told exactly what was going to happen.

We say: This is a good answer from Charlotte. She has selected two appropriate points and has given plenty of description for each one. In fact the description of the second point has become a discussion and there is probably more here than was asked for.

6 Describe the sample used by Chaney et al. in their Funhaler study. [3]

Rachel's answer:

Boys and girls aged 5 and 6.

We say: Rachel needs to look at the mark allocation. If there are 3 marks for a question then you should try and give a little bit more information than this. Rachel is correct in stating that the sample contained both boys and girls but she is incorrect in terms of the age range. In fact the children's ages ranged from 18 months to 6 years.

Charlotte's answer:

There were 32 children. 10 male and 22 female. They were between 18 months old and 6 years old, and were from seven different clinics.

We say: Charlotte has provided more detail in her answer and all of these points are correct.

SECTION B 9 (b) Suggest **one** strength of investigating development.

Support your answer with evidence from **one** appropriate core study. [3]

Rachel's answer:

One strength of investigating development is that you can use longitudinal studies.

Charlotte's answer:

One strength of investigating development is that you can identify reasons for change and factors that influence development. For example, Bandura et al.'s study provides evidence that children learn behaviour from role models. The children who saw role models behave aggressively were more likely to behave aggressively themselves.

We say: Rachel's answer is the start of a good point. She is referring to a key technique in developmental psychology – the use of longitudinal studies – although she is not really saying very clearly what the strength is. She could go on to explain that longitudinal studies allow us to identify changes over time. There is also no supporting evidence from an appropriate core study. Make sure that you provide this if it is asked for, as you will not be able to achieve full marks if you do not answer all parts of a question.

We say: Charlotte has identified a good point as her strength, and has provided evidence from a core study.

9 (c) Suggest **one** problem when investigating development. Support your

answer with evidence from **one** appropriate core study. [3]

Rachel's answer:

One problem with investigating development is that longitudinal studies take a long time. For example, Freud's study of Little Hans took over two years.

Charlotte's answer:

One problem when investigating development is that human behaviour is so complex that it is almost impossible to isolate one variable in order to study it. For example, even though Bandura was able to provide evidence that children copied role models, he was not able to investigate all the other variables that might have been involved in determining a child's level of aggression.

We say: Rachel has identified a key problem although she could have given a little more information. The supporting evidence is appropriate (if brief) even though this is from the individual differences area. Section B questions will not necessarily focus on only one area and if you can make the evidence relate to the question then it will be accepted.

We say: This is a clear point and Charlotte has obviously chosen a point that she is able to illustrate from the core studies that she has covered. There is a very clear link between the point and the evidence.

KOHLBERG'S STAGES OF MORAL DEVELOPMENT

Kohlberg, L. (1968) The child as a moral philosopher. *Psychology Today*, **2**: 24–30.

IN BRIEF

Aim: To investigate moral development from age 10 to 28.

Method: The research method was a longitudinal study. 75 American boys aged 10–16 were followed up for 12 years. Every three years they were presented with moral dilemmas designed to measure specific moral variables such as motives for obedience and the value of human life. Moral dilemmas were also given to children in a range of cultures.

Results: Based on their responses to moral dilemmas moral development was divided into three broad levels of morality each of which contains two stages. Each stage is a distinct moral philosophy. There were differences in pace but not sequence of development across nationality, social class and religion.

Conclusion: There is a universal sequence of stages to moral development. Children in the same stage of moral development tend to reason in the same way.

KEY IDEAS

Stage theories are those theories that see psychological development as taking part in stages. Kohlberg defined a stage as an 'invariant developmental sequence' (1968: 27). This means that stages happen one at a time in the same order. Stages are associated roughly with ages but development through stages takes place at varying speeds and a child can spend time half way between stages.

CONTEXT

Kohlberg pointed out that adults do not usually listen to children's moral philosophies. As Kohlberg himself put it: 'If a child throws back a few adult clichés and behaves himself, most parents – and many anthropologists and psychologists as well – think the child has adopted or internalised the appropriate parental standards' (1968: 25).

Kohlberg was critical of most psychologists' assumptions about childhood morality. For example the behaviourists (see page 196 for a discussion) believed that moral behaviour was acquired through the learning processes of conditioning. Freudians (see page 198) on the other hand saw morality as developing through a good balance between love and authority in parenting. According to Kohlberg there was little evidence supporting either of these approaches.

Where psychologists had tried to investigate childhood morality, Kohlberg felt that they had often found very few positive results. For example no measurable personality traits were associated with words that we use in everyday life, such as honesty or self control. Tests of morality conducted in or based on one situation rarely predicted results in another. So, for example, someone who cheats in one situation is not a cheat per se because often, in other situations, they do not cheat. This means that morality is very difficult to pin down and carry out research on.

Kohlberg was inspired by the work of Jean Piaget, a Swiss psychologist and biologist. Piaget had proposed a theory of intellectual development in which children think and reason differently at different **stages** of development.

Piaget had applied his theory to moral development, proposing that children's moral reasoning develops through childhood, becoming complete by adolescence. However, Kohlberg disagreed with Piaget's view that moral reasoning was complete by early adolescence, and set out to explain how it continued to develop into young adulthood.

AIM

The aim of the study was to investigate development in moral reasoning throughout adolescence and early adulthood. A secondary aim was to assess the extent to which these changes hold true in a range of cultural contexts.

METHOD

The study was a **longitudinal** design in which data was gathered by means of interviews.

Participants

Seventy-five American boys took part in the study. At the start of the study they were aged between 10 and 16 years. At the end of the study they were aged 22–28 years.

Design and procedure

The design was longitudinal. Participants were followed from early adolescence for 12 years until early adulthood. Every three years each participant was interviewed individually. In the interviews each participant was presented with a series of moral dilemmas.

All the dilemmas were philosophical in nature and some were taken from medieval ethics literature. Between them the dilemmas were designed to measure 25 moral themes, for example the value of human life and reasons for obeying rules. Each dilemma involved options with different moral implications.

Once participants understood the dilemma they were asked what the character in the dilemma should do. For example, to assess development of understanding of the value of human life, questions included:

1 'Is it better to save the life of one important person or a lot of unimportant people?'
2 'Should the doctor mercy kill a fatally ill woman requesting death because of her pain?'

The same dilemmas were presented to young people in Taiwan and Mexico. The design was different however. There was no longitudinal follow up of these participants. The design was instead **cross-sectional**, with groups of Mexican and Taiwanese young people of different ages compared.

KEY IDEAS

There are two ways to study developmental changes. **Longitudinal studies** follow up the same participants over time as they change with age. **Cross-sectional studies**, by contrast, compare different groups of participants of different ages. Cross-sectional designs are quicker but validity may be affected by the extraneous variable of individual differences between the participants in each age group.

STRETCH & CHALLENGE

Why do you think Kohlberg used a cross-sectional design for cross-cultural comparison even though he preferred to use a longitudinal design to study his American sample?

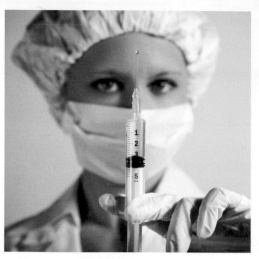

Figure 3.5
Mercy killing, used in Kohlberg's study,
remains an important dilemma today

RESULTS

Based on participants' responses to the moral dilemmas at different ages Kohlberg proposed that moral development went through a series of three levels and six stages. These are summarised in Table 3.3.

TABLE 3.3 KOHLBERG'S LEVELS AND STAGES OF MORAL DEVELOPMENT	
Level	**Stage**
Preconventional	1 Orientation towards punishment
	2 Orientation towards self-interest
Conventional	3 Good-boy-good-girl orientation
	4 Orientation towards authority
Postconventional	5 Social contract orientation
	6 Orientation towards conscience and ethical principles

Preconventional level

Stage 1: Orientation towards punishment and deference to power. Good and bad are defined purely in terms of consequences such as punishment. Those in power can punish therefore they can define what is morally right.

Stage 2: Orientation towards self-interest. Right is whatever suits one's own needs. Sharing and reciprocal helping take place but just on a 'you scratch my back, I'll scratch yours' basis.

Conventional level

Stage 3: Good-boy-good-girl orientation. Good behaviour is what pleases others and gains approval. This means there is considerable conformity.

Stage 4: Orientation towards authority. Rules and social order are paramount, so right consists of doing duty and showing respect for authority.

Postconventional level

Stage 5: Social contract orientation. Right is what has been agreed upon by a whole society, although there is room for personal opinion and values. Law is important but laws can be changed.

Stage 6: Orientation towards conscience and ethical principles. There are general ethical principles such as justice and equality, however they are not concrete rules and decisions are taken based on the circumstances of a case.

Kohlberg illustrated the six stages with the example of the value of human life.

Stage 1: Human life has the same value as that of any object so it is judged on its characteristics. So some human life is judged as more valuable, for example if people are stronger, cleverer, etc.

Stage 2: The value of any particular life is dependent on what that person can do for the individual.

Stage 3: The value of any particular life is based on the affection the individual and their family have for them.

Stage 4: Life is sacred because of religious or legal conventions

Stage 5: Life is valued as a universal human right and for what an individual can bring to their community.

Stage 6: Life is sacred because of the principle of respect for the individual.

Kohlberg believed that reasoning in different situations did not always fall rigidly into these stages. Each participant was seen as being in a particular stage when 50% of their responses to dilemmas fell neatly into that stage. Kohlberg was uncertain as to whether people generally went through stage 5 to get to stage 6, or whether stages 5 and 6 represented alternative mature orientations.

Kohlberg did not rigidly link stages to particular ages. With extracts from interviews, he illustrated how individuals at the same age could have quite different moral maturity. In response to the question 'should a doctor mercy kill a fatally ill woman requesting death because of her pain?' two 13 year olds answered as follows:

- Tommy: 'Maybe it would be good, to put her out of her pain, she'd be better off that way. But the husband wouldn't want it, it's not like an animal. If a pet dies you can get along without it – it isn't something you really need. Well, you can get a new wife, but it's not really the same.'
- Richard: 'If she requests it, it's really up to her. She is in such terrible pain, just the same as people are always putting animals out of their pain.'

Kohlberg interpreted these responses as meaning that Tommy is in stage 2 and Richard in stage 3.

CONCLUSIONS

1   Children, adolescents and young adults go through a series of stages in which their moral reasoning develops from the preconventional – based on self-interest; through conventional – based on rules and approval from others; to postconventional – based on respect for democratically agreed rules but also personal conscience.
2   Although there are variations in the rate of development, people growing up in a range of cultural contexts go through the same stages.

MATHS MOMENT

Kohlberg gathered qualitative data from his interviews.
1   Explain the difference between quantitative and qualitative data.
2   Outline one advantage of using qualitative data.

EVALUATION

The research method

The study used a longitudinal design to compare American young people's development at different ages. Longitudinal designs have the advantage over cross-sectional designs in that they eliminate individual differences as extraneous variables. Of course the cross-cultural data was cross-sectional, but this is understandable because of the practical difficulty in following up individuals around the world over several years.

Data was gathered by means of interviews, which are always limited by the extent to which respondents understand questions, are unaffected by the social desirability of responses, and choose to be honest. However, interviews allow participants to explore questions thoroughly.

Qualitative and quantitative data

This experiment collects qualitative data in the form of interview responses. This has the advantage that respondents to interviews could give full answers to questions rather than just select from a list of alternatives (which would have generated quantitative data). However, although qualitative interview data allows respondents to express their views fully, it is hard to draw conclusions from what they say.

Ethical considerations

This study raises very few ethical issues. It would be highly ironic if it had, given that the study was about people's understanding of moral issues! There was no deception or distress. Privacy was not invaded. As far as we can tell from the article, participants were not pressured into taking part.

Validity

This study has low ecological validity because the participants were asked about hypothetical moral dilemmas instead of being exposed to real ones. Most of the moral choices we make in everyday life are simpler than Kohlberg's dilemmas. The longitudinal design has good validity because it eliminates the extraneous variable of individual differences between participants at different ages.

Interviews have limited validity because of the extraneous variables that can influence responses. In addition Kohlberg's interpretation of participants' responses to questions was quite subjective. Look back to Tommy's and Richard's responses to the doctor's mercy-killing dilemma – the links between the two boys' responses and the stages Kohlberg allocated them to are not obvious. His questions therefore lack face validity.

Reliability

Kohlberg's procedure would be easy to replicate so in this sense it can be said to have good external reliability. However, its internal reliability is less good. Participants did not consistently give responses linked to a particular stage of development to different dilemmas.

Sampling bias

Kohlberg's sample in the longitudinal study was unrepresentative as all participants were American boys. This could be seen as ethnocentric. However, a strength of the study is that different social classes were sampled, and that additional samples were taken from a range of nationalities. The consistency of results across these groups suggests that the sampling bias in the main USA longitudinal study did not have a major impact on Kohlberg's findings.

Ethnocentrism

Kohlberg's sample in the longitudinal study was unrepresentative as all participants were American boys. This could be seen as ethnocentric. However, additional samples were taken from a range of nationalities. The consistency of results across these groups suggests that the sampling bias in the main USA longitudinal study did not have a major impact on Kohlberg's findings.

Practical applications

Kohlberg's use of moral dilemmas has been applied to a range of settings where ethical behaviour is considered important. These range from personal, social and health education (PHSE) at school to military training. In his Just Community Schools, Kohlberg (1975) applied the method to whole-school discipline. The idea is that if staff and students collaborate to put together a system of rules based on ethical principles there will be better student 'buy-in' and more willing co-operation.

STUDY 4

LEE *et al.*'s STUDY OF EVALUATIONS OF LYING AND TRUTH-TELLING

Lee, K., Cameron, C.A., Xu, F., Fu, G., and Board, J. (1997). Chinese and Canadian children's evaluations of lying and truth-telling. *Child Development,* **68**(5): 924–934.

 **IN BRIEF**

Aim: To compare cross-cultural evaluations of lying and truth-telling in situations involving prosocial and antisocial behaviours.

Method: The research method was cross-cultural study using a cross-sectional design. 228 Chinese and Canadian children aged 7, 9 or 11 took part in this study. Children were randomly assigned to one of two conditions: physical or social stories. The story was either prosocial or antisocial and contained either truth-telling or lying. Participants were read four stories and asked to rate each on how 'good' or 'naughty' the story's character was.

Results: Both cultures rated truth-telling in antisocial situations very positively and also gave similar ratings to lie-telling in antisocial behaviours. However, Chinese children rated truth-telling in prosocial situations less positively and lie-telling more positively in prosocial situations than Canadian children. This difference became greater with age and the comments of the Chinese children reflected their beliefs about being modest about one's good deeds and qualities.

Conclusion: Moral reasoning is shaped to an extent by cultural and social norms. The influence of these factors on moral evaluations increases with age.

CONTEXT

The development of moral reasoning has been a topic that has long held the interest of psychologists. As we have seen, both Jean Piaget and Lawrence Kohlberg proposed models of moral development that relied on a stage/age model. Piaget's work inspired the use of scenarios, stories and dilemmas in interviews with children of different ages as an important method for understanding reasoning. Piaget concluded that children younger than age 11 relied mainly on two factors to make moral judgements about lying: how 'big' the lie was (i.e. how much the lie that was told differed from the truth) and whether or not it was punished.

Further investigations have looked at the development of children's reasoning about intentions in lying and truth-telling at different ages. Piaget had concluded that young children did not use the motives of the characters in stories to inform moral judgements, but this view has now been challenged. Wimmer (1984) found that when the intention of the character was made clear, young children made similar judgements to those of older children about lying and truth-telling.

KEY IDEAS

Ethnocentrism is about seeing the world from the point of view of your own cultural group. It affects psychological studies as the individual researchers have their own ethnic and national group and, in most cases, conduct their research with participants from the same group. As a result, their findings and conclusions may be only generalised to specific cultural groups. For example, you may have noticed that many classic studies in psychology were conducted in American universities. They use participant samples of undergraduate students who were, in the main, white and middle-class, which cannot be truly representative.

Communism is the term used to describe an economic system where property (e.g. land, houses, transport systems, utilities) is owned collectively and labour is organised for the common benefit of all people. In practice, this theoretical system also involves a single-party, authoritarian government that plans, controls and enforces the collectivist policies. The country of China – or, to give it it's official title, 'The People's Republic of China' – is one of the few remaining nations to still describe itself as communist, and is a single-party state ruled by the Communist Party.

WEB WATCH @

Although much important psychological research continues to originate from American universities, some websites, such as Science Daily, offer a good way to increase awareness about studies going on all over the world.

Go to www.sciencedaily.com, select the 'Mind & Brain' menu and click on 'Psychology'. You can subscribe to their RSS feed or e-newsletter to get regular updates on new studies, including cross-cultural research projects.

Another challenge to prior research such as Kohlberg (1968) is the criticism that the moral dilemmas he used and the way in which the children's responses were evaluated and categorised is **ethnocentric**. Kohlberg's primary research was carried out in Western societies that emphasise values of individualism, self-promotion and competition. **Communist** societies, by contrast, teach values of patriotism, collectivism and modesty about individual achievements.

The present study sought to address these two issues with older research findings. Lee *et al.* used stories which made clear the intention of the main character as well as the facts of the situation. They also used a cross-cultural method to investigate cultural differences in judgements about right and wrong.

It is also worth noting that 'lying' and 'truth-telling' are arguably not objective acts. Factuality (whether a statement is true), intention (whether the speaker of the statement intends to be deceptive) and belief (whether the speaker believes what they are saying) are all parts of our social-cultural construction of 'lying'.

AIM

The aim was to investigate cross-cultural differences in children's understanding and moral valuations of lying. The study aimed to compare the responses of Chinese and Canadian participants to stories that involved lying and truth-telling, prosocial and antisocial situations.

METHOD

The research method used in this study was a cross-cultural method. Researchers conducted the test on each of the groups of participants, then compared their responses. This study had a cross-sectional design, meaning that participants in the different conditions were of different ages.

Participants

The participants in this study consisted of 120 Chinese children and 108 Canadian children.

TABLE 3.4 PARTICIPANTS IN THE STUDY OF EVALUATIONS OF LYING AND TRUTH-TELLING			
	7 years old	**9 years old**	**11 years old**
Chinese	40 (20 male, 20 female)	40 (20 male, 20 female)	40 (20 male, 20 female)
Canadian	36 (20 male, 16 female)	40 (24 male, 16 female)	32 (14 male, 18 female)

The Chinese children were recruited from elementary schools in Hangzhou, a medium-sized city in Zhejiang Province. No information exists in China to categorise families by their socio-economic status, whereas most of the Canadian children were from middle-class families. The Canadian sample was also recruited from elementary schools, but in a smaller city called Fredericton in New Brunswick.

Design and procedure

For each cultural group, half the participants were randomly assigned to a social story condition, and the other half to a physical story condition. The social stories involved the actions of the main child character affecting other people, whereas the physical stories involved only physical objects.

The participants were read aloud four different stories each. The stories were written to be familiar to schoolchildren in both cultures (see Figure 3.6). Two of the stories were known as 'prosocial' and involved a child intentionally carrying out a good deed. The other two stories were 'antisocial' and involved a child intentionally carrying out a bad deed. At the end of each of the four stories, the child character was asked by the teacher who had carried out the deed. In two stories the child character lied, and in the others they told the truth (see Figure 3.7).

Here is Alex. Alex's class had to stay inside at recess time because of bad weather, so Alex decided to tidy up the classroom for his teacher.
(Question 1: Is what Alex did good or naughty?)

So Alex cleaned the classroom, and when the teacher returned after recess, she said to her students, "Oh, I see that someone has cleaned the classroom for me." The teacher then asked Alex, "Do you know who cleaned the classroom?" Alex said to his teacher, "I did not do it."
(Question 1: Is what Alex said to his teacher good or naughty?)

Figure 3.6
Example of a physical, prosocial story of lying

The children were shown a seven-point rating chart which contained the following ratings: very, very good (three red stars), very good (two red stars), good (one red star), neither good nor naughty (blue circle), naughty (one black cross), very naughty (two black crosses), very very naughty (three black crosses). After explaining the chart, the stories were read aloud to individuals in a pre-arranged random order. They were read in the participant's own language and presented alongside illustrations. After the 'deed' section of the story was read aloud, the children were asked the question: 'Was what he (or she) did good or naughty'? The child could respond verbally or nonverbally or both using the rating scale. The question was repeated after the second part of the story (lie or truth-telling) was read. The interviewer systematically alternated the words 'good' and 'naughty' in the questions.

STRETCH & CHALLENGE

This study could also be seen as an experiment. What characteristics does it have that would make it a quasi-experiment? What experimental design is used in each condition?

Prosocial / lying	*Prosocial / truth-telling*
Antisocial / lying	*Antisocial / truth-telling*

Figure 3.7
Four types of stories

DO IT YOURSELF 🔍

This study makes use of moral stories to test children's reasoning about right and wrong. Have a go at writing two of your own short stories about situations involving lying in a prosocial and antisocial situation. Ask participants to read them both and make judgements about how good or naughty the character was using Lee *et al.*'s seven-point rating scale.

Do they refer to the intention of the characters? How about the scale of the lying? What differences do they identify between the prosocial and antisocial stories?

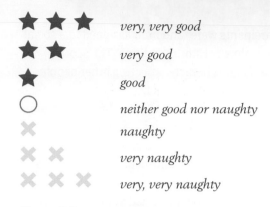

★ ★ ★   *very, very good*
★ ★   *very good*
★   *good*
◯   *neither good nor naughty*
✗   *naughty*
✗ ✗   *very naughty*
✗ ✗ ✗   *very, very naughty*

Figure 3.8
Lee *et al. used a simple picture chart like this to measure children's responses*

Figure 3.9
In this cross-cultural study, children were read each story aloud by the researchers

QUESTION SPOTLIGHT! ⭐

In this study, Lee *et al.* used specific measures such as randomising the order in which the stories were presented. *Can you explain why this is important?*

RESULTS

The children's responses were converted into points scores (e.g. 3 = very, very good; 0 = neither good nor naughty; −3 = very, very naughty). There were a number of similarities between the two groups, mainly in their similarly negative ratings of lying in antisocial situations and their positive ratings of truth-telling in those stories.

However, Chinese children differed from Canadian children in their evaluations of truth-telling and lying in prosocial situations. Overall, Chinese participants tended to rate truth-telling less positively than their Canadian counterparts. In fact, the Chinese children rated lying in prosocial situations, as demonstrated in the story in Figure 3.6, significantly more positively than the Canadian children. Perhaps most interestingly, these cultural distinctions became more obvious within older age groups, with children increasingly rating

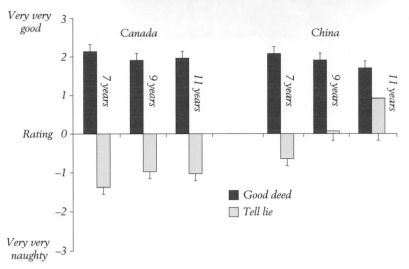

Figure 3.10
Chinese and Canadian children's ratings of lying in prosocial situations

lying more positively in prosocial situations. For example, 70% of Chinese 11 year olds rated lying positively in prosocial stories, compared to just 25% of Chinese 7 years olds.

Lee *et al.* suggest that this is because Chinese children are taught the values of self-effacement and modesty, and that this has an increasing impact on their moral reasoning as they age. In other words, through socialisation in school and through the media, children's judgements about right and wrong grow closer to society's expectations. To take one example, Chinese children explained their negative rating of truth-telling as 'naughty' in one story because it might seem as though the character was wanting or even begging for praise from a teacher, a practice explicitly discouraged in Chinese school children.

CONCLUSIONS

Lee *et al.* establish three main conclusions:

1 Moral reasoning can be influenced by our culture and the society in which we live.
2 The influence of socio-cultural factors becomes stronger as we age.
3 Some aspects of moral reasoning, such judging antisocial lying as bad, may be universal.

STRETCH & CHALLENGE

Visit the website of Dr Kang Lee: www.kangleelab.com

The website allows you to explore the ongoing research of Lee and his research team in Canada and internationally. There is a great page explaining myths and realities about lying in children under the section 'For Parents'. You can also read the examples of all the stories used in the study in the full test of the paper.

MATHS MOMENT

1 Using the data in Figure 3.10, outline one similarity between the ratings of Chinese and Canadian participants.
2 Now outline one key difference between the three different age groups of Chinese participants.

EVALUATION

The research method

The key strength of a cross-cultural study such as this is that the differences and similarities that were found point to a combination of universal and culturally specific causes. Lee *et al.* also tried to make measures appropriate and similar for both cultures, both through reading the stories aloud in the children's own language with illustrations and through the use of the visual rating scale.

Qualitative and quantitative data

Lee *et al.* collected mainly quantitative data. They used a seven-point scale which was then converted into a score for each story and participant. This was particularly appropriate for this study as it allowed a direct comparison between different cultural groups on a number of stories and factors. Researchers conducted limited post-test questioning about why children gave the good or naughty reasons. This qualitative data helped inform Lee *et al.*'s conclusions about the underlying reasons for differences in ratings within the prosocial situations. However, young children may not always express their reasoning clearly and, as the researchers point out themselves, some moral judgements may seem so culturally normal that children may not see the need to explain them.

Ethical considerations

Although the judgement task had potential to be morally harmful, in that it involved lying and truth-telling, the story content was age-appropriate and it is very unlikely that any children suffered any harm or distress.

Validity

This study has questionable ecological validity as the main task of judging a character's behaviour in a story is quite different to forming moral judgements in real life. On the other hand the stories were all designed to be easy for children to understand and they would also have been familiar with the scenarios, which improve the validity of the findings.

Another way in which the study had good validity was that researchers were careful to alternate use of the words 'good' and 'naughty' during questioning, and to also randomise the order in which the four stories were presented. This would have reduced the chance of leading the children towards specific answers, or of creating an order effect.

Reliability

The materials used in this study to measure moral judgements of lying and truth-telling were the same across all participants. Similarly, the instructions given to the children were identical, and they used a standard rating scale. These factors mean the study is highly replicable and the findings are likely to be quite reliable.

Sampling bias

The sample size was quite large in this study and covered a range of ages, and allowed cross-cultural comparisons to be made. Also, the study contained roughly equal numbers of males and females so it is possible to generalise the findings to both genders. One slight disadvantage perhaps is that not much was known about the backgrounds of the Chinese participants. Despite this, they were recruited from a city with similar demographics to the Canadian sample so are likely to be comparable.

STRETCH & CHALLENGE

This study is an important example of cross-cultural research that challenges ethnocentrism. In what way does it question what we might consider 'normal' or 'proper' moral development in children?

Practical applications

Importantly, this study shows us that moral development is not simply determined by age or level of cognitive development. Instead it is also influenced by the cultural norms of the society in which we live. This contradicts findings by Kohlberg about the universality of moral development, as it shows that children's reasoning is based on fundamentally different values that, if anything, strengthen and diverge further over time. Practically speaking, this highlights the difficulties with conducting cross-cultural psychological research and the pitfalls of mistakenly viewing other cultures as somehow 'under-developed'.

COMPARISON OF STUDIES

| Kohlberg's Stages of Moral Development | & | Lee et al.'s Study of Evaluations of Lying and Truth-telling |

THE TOPIC
Universal stages of moral development versus cultural differences in moral evaluations of lying and truth-telling

The studies by Kohlberg and Lee et al. are both about developmental psychology, specifically about development of morality. They both looked at how children make judgments about what is right and wrong in fictional scenarios. However, Kohlberg concluded that there is a universal sequence of moral development that all children naturally follow, and Lee et al. was concerned with establishing the influence of culture on children's moral development, particularly in relation to judgments about lying.

THE RESEARCH METHOD AND DESIGN
Longitudinal study versus cross-cultural study

The main difference between the two studies is that Kohlberg employed a longitudinal design which tracked the same participants over 12 years, whereas Lee et al. used a cross-cultural method. This produced a 'snapshot' of two groups of children in Canada and China, all of whom were either 7, 9, or 11 years of age. Although this meant Lee et al.'s study was much quicker to conduct, it still presented the challenge of working with participants from geographically distant locations. Also, it meant that individual differences could have affected Lee et al.'s results, as differences in scores between age groups might have been a result of individual factors. This was not a problem for Kohlberg as the same participants were tested as they reached different ages.

SAMPLING TECHNIQUE AND THE SAMPLE
Both use large samples from a range of different cultures; use of males versus mix of genders

Both studies used fairly large samples of participants which meant the findings were likely to be representative of their target populations. Kohlberg used an all male-sample of 75, whereas Lee et al. used a roughly equal mix of males and females in their sample of 228 schoolchildren. No information is provided in the studies about the way in which either sample was recruited. However, we do know that Kohlberg's main study was carried out on American males only and later with other cultural groups, whereas Lee et al. contrasted two very different cultural groups simultaneously. This is likely to have had an impact on how Kohlberg described his theory of moral stages and then measured the responses from children of other cultures against the stages.

EXPERIMENTAL MATERIALS AND MEASUREMENT OF THE DEPENDENT VARIABLE
Both studies used similar tasks that lacked validity; use of qualitative versus quantitative data

The use of moral stories or moral dilemmas was a similar strategy used in both these studies. One issue with the use of fictional accounts to investigate moral judgments is that they are not as realistic as real-life situations, where we must make ethical decisions ourselves. So the tasks used in both studies could be said to lack ecological validity.

Kohlberg's dilemmas were followed up by a series of questions from which he recorded participant's reasoned responses and later fitted them into appropriate categories of reasoning. This relied on his interpretation of the participant's response, which might have been biased. By contrast, Lee et al. used stories involving lying and truth-telling but measured participant responses using a seven-point rating scale. This produced a different sort of data, quantitative, which allowed a more straightforward and objective comparison.

APPLICATIONS
Moral development within educational settings

As discussed, Kohlberg's research has been particularly influential in the field of education, for example within discipline policies and in PHSE lessons.

Lee *et al.*'s contribution to this is very important, as they have challenged the assumption that all moral development follows the same sequence. What is true of children in one part of the world may not be true of others, and this research helps us to understand the limitations of universal approaches. For instance, some ideas and strategies for discipline in schools might work well for American or Canadian students, but be less appropriate for Chinese students.

KEY THEME: MORAL DEVELOPMENT

The studies by Kohlberg and Lee *et al.* were both concerned with moral development across the lifespan. Their findings are an example of a key debate in psychology: that of nature versus nurture. Kohlberg felt that human moral development is not affected by the wide range of cultural, religious or social backgrounds that exist. Furthermore he denied that children 'internalise' the moral values of their parents and society and asserted that the stages of moral development are a natural, universal phenomenon.

Lee *et al.*'s research directly contradicted this theory. In their study, it was found that Chinese and Canadian children had fundamentally different reasons underlying their judgments about lying and truth-telling. While there were some shared moral values (such as negative attitudes towards antisocial lying), some moral reasoning reflected contrasting cultural values, i.e. nurture. Chinese children favoured a more modest approach when doing good deeds, while Canadian children placed higher value on gaining individual recognition for doing the right thing. This contemporary study changes our understanding, as the influence of nurture makes us question the universality of stages of moral development.

KEY THEME 🔑

Moral development
Lee *et al.*'s study highlighted the influences of nurture, making us question Kohlberg's findings on the universality of stages of moral development.

Kohlberg
Investigated stages of moral development, using a longitudinal design. The findings were potentially ethnocentric and open to interpretation.

Similarities
Both studies focus on helping us understand moral development. They both used moral stories and questioning with participants, a method which is easy to replicate but may lack ecological validity.

Lee et al.
Investigated cross-cultural differences between two participant groups. The study used randomly assigned conditions to prevent bias and found evidence that moral development is not universal.

PRACTICE QUESTIONS

Here are some of the sorts of questions that you could be asked in Sections A and B of your A level exam, and some examples of successful and less successful answers. We look at Section B and C questions in more detail in Chapter 6 on pages 206–18.

SECTION A: CORE STUDIES

1   Describe the sample used in Kohlberg's study of moral development.   [3]

2   Discuss **two** weaknesses with the sample used in Kohlberg's theory of moral development.   [4]

3   Explain why Kohlberg's study can be described as a longitudinal study.   [2]

4   Describe what is meant by a 'moral dilemma'.   [2]

5   Explain why Lee *el al.*'s study of lying and truth-telling can be described as a cross-sectional study.   [2]

6   Describe the sample used in Lee *et al.*'s study of lying and truth-telling.   [3]

7   In Lee *et al.* study of lying and truth-telling, the experimenter varied the presentation of the words 'good' and 'naughty' in the questions. Give **one** reason why this would have been done.   [3]

8   Outline **one** difference between the study by Kohlberg of moral development and the study by Lee *et al.* into lying and truth-telling.   [3]

SECTION B: AREAS, PERSPECTIVES AND DEBATES

12 **(a)**   Describe the difference between a longitudinal and a cross-sectional approach in psychological research.   [4]

   (b)   Explain how **one** psychological study can be considered to be located within the area of developmental psychology.   [5]

   (c)   Evaluate the usefulness of collecting quantitative data in psychological research. Support your answer with evidence from **one** appropriate psychological study.   [6]

   (d)   Identify and discuss sources of bias in relation to the study of developmental psychology. Support your answer with evidence from appropriate psychological studies.   [20]

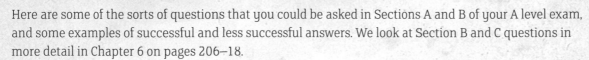

SECTION A   2 Discuss two weaknesses with the sample used in Kohlberg's theory of moral development. [4]

Liam's answer:

One weakness is that they were all boys and the other weakness is that they were all American.

We say: This answer identifies two weaknesses but does not really address the command to 'discuss'. The examiners will be expecting some expansion or explanation of the answers that you give.

Rina's answer:

One weakness is the sample was all boys. This is a problem because it is wrong to assume that the moral development of girls is going to be the same. The other weakness is that the sample is all American participants and again it is biased to assume that a small sample from one country can be used to represent people from all countries.

We say: Rina's answer is much better as she has first identified a weakness and has then explained this in a little more detail.

5 Explain why Lee *et al.*'s study of lying and truth-telling can be described as a cross-sectional study. [2]

Liam's answer:

Because they tested children of different ages.

We say: Liam, you need to give more information! This is the beginning of a good answer but you need to explain why this makes the study cross-sectional.

Rina's answer:

This was a cross-sectional study because the researchers tested the different age groups by selecting participants of all three ages at the same time, rather than following the same children from the ages of 7 to 11.

We say: Rina has explained this well. He has shown that she understands what a cross-sectional study is as well as showing that she understands why this study is cross-sectional.

7 In Lee *et al.*'s study of lying and truth-telling, the experimenter varied the presentation of the words 'good' and 'naughty' in the questions. Give one reason why this would have been done. [3]

Liam's answer:

Because otherwise children might have been influenced by the way that the question was asked.

We say: Liam, again, you need to give more information. This does suggest that there is some understanding; the form of the question could be an influence but you really need to spell this out fully. Don't ever assume that the examiner will work out what you mean – they can only mark what you have said.

Rina's answer:

The children had to respond to the question: 'Was what he (or she) did good or naughty?' By varying the question so that sometimes' good' was the first word and sometimes 'naughty' was the first word the question would not give the children cues to the response that the experimenter wanted.

We say: A good answer from Rina although even here there could be a little more explanation of the influence. What might happen if the word 'good' was always the first word in the question? Why would this be a problem?

SECTION B   12 (d) Identify and discuss sources of bias in relation to the study of developmental psychology. Support your answer with evidence from appropriate psychological studies. [20]

Liam's answer:

One source of bias is gender bias. Kohlberg only studied male participants and so his results only represent moral development in males. There is also ethnocentrism which is only studying one culture. Experimenter bias is when experimenters are biased in the way that they report their findings and sampling bias would be selecting a biased sample.

We say: There are 20 marks available here and this means that Liam should be writing a great deal more than this. Liam has identified gender bias, ethnocentrism, experimenter bias and sampling bias. He now needs to go further than this and explain first what each of these terms really means and then support his answer with examples from the core studies.

Rina's answer:

Four sources of bias are ethnocentrism, gender bias, experimenter/observer bias and social desirability bias.

Ethnocentrism is viewing everyone through the 'lens' of your own culture. This can mean that you assume that a sample from one culture can be used to represent all cultures or where you see your own culture as superior to all other cultures as you are assuming that your own culture is the norm against which all other cultures can be judged. Kohlberg's study focused on the development of American (male) participants and can be considered to be ethnocentric, although Lee et al.'s study compared children in Canada and China. Research is considered to show gender bias if it does not equally represent both males and females, either because it sampled only males and assumed that females would behave in a similar manner, or because the male results were used as the standard against which females were judged. For example, the study by Kohlberg has been criticised for only studying the development of boys and then using their results to develop a stage theory of moral development that was applied to both genders.

Experimenter/observer bias is where the assumptions and beliefs about the experiment or observation change the outcome. This is likely to be an unconscious bias on the part of the experimenter, perhaps by giving the participants subtle cues as to how to behave or, in an observation, by simply being present. Observer bias may have been present in the data collected by the observers in the study by Bandura et al.

Social desirability is where participants behave in the ways that they think they should behave, perhaps because they are responding to the cues of the experimenter and perhaps because they have preconceived ideas about how they should behave in an experiment or about what the researchers are looking for. This could have biased children's responses in the study of the Funhaler by Chaney et al.

We say: Rina has produced a good answer to this question. she has identified four sources of bias and has explained clearly what each one is. The links to the core studies are generally clear although some of them (particularly Bandura *et al.* and Chaney *et al.*) could be a little more detailed. However, there is no direct link made to the study of individual differences and although this may be implied, this answer would even be better if these links to developmental psychology were made explicitly.

THE DEVELOPMENTAL AREA OF PSYCHOLOGY

We have now looked in detail at four developmental studies. You can probably see from these that the developmental area of psychology is very wide-ranging. However, we can identify two shared assumptions of developmental psychologists:

1 People change and develop with age

Other areas of psychology focus on psychological processes in adults. Cognitive psychology looks at cognition taking place in the mind of the adult individual, and social psychology looks at processes taking place between adults. However, our everyday experience tells us that people change with age. What happens in the mind of a child is not entirely the same as what happens in the mind of an adult, and groups of young adults do not necessarily behave socially like groups of older adults. Two of the studies we have looked at in this chapter concern age specific-processes. Kohlberg and Lee *et al.* were both concerned with the development of moral reasoning in young children, and observed changes in this over time.

2 Human development is an interaction of the influences of nature and nurture

The other two studies focused on influences on children's development. Bandura *et al.* and Chaney *et al.* investigated the effect of observational learning and operant conditioning on children's behaviour. Bandura *et al.* found that the children who observed aggressive models were more likely to behave in an aggressive manner themselves, suggesting that how we are nurtured can shape our behaviour. However, he also found that boys were more likely to show physical aggression than girls, and this indicates that nature can play a role in children's development also. Research such as Lee *et al.*'s. also demonstrates the importance of cultural and social factors on human development.

STRENGTHS AND WEAKNESSES OF THE DEVELOPMENTAL AREA

Strengths

1   **Developmental psychology has improved our understanding of people at different ages and stages of development.** Understanding people are different at different ages has improved our understanding of human cognition, behaviour and emotion. This has changed our whole view as a society about, for example, what it means to be a child. Prior to theorists such as Kohlberg, who explored the development of moral

reasoning, children were largely thought of as little adults. Developmental psychologists have shown us that children, adolescents and adults each have their own psychological characteristics.

2   **Developmental research can help us positively influence children's behaviour.** As you will see from the studies contained in this chapter, they have some clear practical applications. For example, Bandura *et al.* demonstrate the influence of aggressive role models on children's behaviour. Understanding the influence of observational learning has led to measures such as film certifications, to reduce the negative impact of media violence on young audiences. Similarly, techniques such as positively reinforcing the correct use of asthma drugs as in the study by Chaney *et al.* has important health benefits for children.

Weaknesses

1   **Some aspects of development are hard to study scientifically.** One limitation in the developmental area is the difficulty psychologists face when attempting to measure children's thoughts and behaviour. We must therefore question how valid measurements of children's behaviour are, particularly when the tests are designed by adults! For example, Bandura *et al.*'s study has been criticised for assuming that the children's behaviour towards the Bobo doll was 'aggressive'. In actual fact it may be that the children interpreted their own behaviour as playful.

2   **There are many ethical issues in this area of psychology.** This area of psychology can pose some of the greatest difficulties in designing experimental procedures, materials and measurements that are appropriate for child participants. This is particularly true when studying behaviour such as aggression (e.g. Bandura *et al.*) or that can impact on children's health (e.g. Chaney *et al.*) as protecting children from physical or mental harm must be paramount. There are additional problems in collecting a participant sample, which requires informed parental consent, as well as briefing and debriefing young people in a way that makes sense to them.

C4

BIOLOGICAL
PSYCHOLOGY

Biological psychology is concerned with the action of genes, the nervous system and hormones on our behaviour, emotions and cognition.

For AS we consider two studies that explore the theme of regions of the brain:

1 Sperry's (1968) study of split-brain patients. This was a laboratory-based investigation, looking at participants who had all had an operation to separate the left and right halves of the brain. The aim was to see how this 'split-brain' procedure affected their cognition.

2 Casey et al.'s (2011) study of the neural correlates of delay gratification. This study compared brain activity in adults who had been good or poor at resisting temptation as children to identify different regions of brain activity during resistance to temptation.

For A level, we additionally look at two studies that highlight the theme of brain plasticity:

3 Blakemore and Cooper's (1970) study of the impact of early visual experience. This laboratory experiment compared kittens with different early visual deprivation experiences to see the effect on visually guided behaviour and on brain activity and cellular organisation in the visual cortex.

4 Maguire et al.'s (2000) study of taxi drivers' brains. This laboratory-based study investigated the role in navigation of a brain area called the hippocampus. The participants were taxi drivers who had been working for different lengths of time, whose brains were scanned to explore differences in hippocampal volume.

We will look at these studies in detail, evaluating each one and exploring their applications. We also consider them in their pairs, using them to think about the key themes. Finally we will use them to explore issues in biological psychology, looking at the strengths and limitations of this area.

SPERRY'S STUDY OF SPLIT-BRAIN PATIENTS

Sperry, R. (1968) Hemisphere deconnection and unity in consciousness. *American Psychologist.* **23**: 723–33.

IN BRIEF

Aim: To investigate the effects of hemispheric deconnection on perception and memory.

Method: Eleven patients who had had **commissurotomies** to separate the left and right hemispheres were tested in a laboratory using apparatus that could display stimuli independently to the left or right visual field. They were required to say, write or find what they had seen. Other tests used objects placed either separately or simultaneously in each hand, which participants had to find or name. Manual tests, such as copying hand positions, were also conducted.

Results: In split-brain patients, each hemisphere can perceive and remember information presented only to that hemisphere. Verbal responses were possible only when information was presented to the left hemisphere (e.g. though the right visual field or right hand).

Conclusion: Hemisphere deconnection causes the two hemispheres to operate independently, each having its own consciousness, including perception and memory. This produces a 'doubling' of conscious awareness, as each hemisphere is unaware of the other. The right hemisphere, although much less linguistic than the left, can use logic.

KEY IDEAS

Localisation means the limitation of a particular brain function to a particular structure. This is different from **lateralisation**, which limits a particular function to one side of the brain, i.e. to one hemisphere.

KEY IDEAS

Along the midline of the brain (in a vertical plane from front to back) there are several structures consisting of nerve fibres that join the left and right sides of the brain together. These are called **commissures**. They include the **corpus callosum**, the hippocampal commissure and the anterior commissure (see Figure 4.2). The cutting of such structures is called a **commissurotomy**.

CONTEXT

Historically, investigations looking at the anatomy of dead human or animal bodies, and, more recently, brain scanning, have told us about the structure of the brain. This has shown that the brain has clearly defined regions (see Figure 4.1). Other research has explored what the brain does – that is, it has investigated its functional roles. A key area of research is to link these two aspects together, to explore the **localisation** of function. This is the extent to which particular jobs are performed by particular parts of the brain. Some aspects of localisation link functions to specific structures, many of which are replicated in the left and right halves of the brain. In addition, some functions demonstrate lateralisation – that is, there is a difference between the roles of the left and right hemispheres. One example of **lateralisation** is our language function, which is restricted to the left side of the brain. Another example is the control of movement. Movement of each side of the body is largely controlled by the opposite side of the brain. This is called **contralateral control** (see p. 125).

Structural research shows that there are a number of structures which join the two halves of the brain – the right and left **hemispheres** (see Figure 4.2). This allows for the exchange of information across the brain. These include the **corpus callosum** (the largest), and the smaller anterior and hippocampal **commissures**. The particular focus of this study was to explore the effects when the two hemispheres are artificially separated (hemispheric separation). Earlier research into 'split brains' had been conducted by performing surgery on animals to deconnect the hemispheres by cutting through structures such as the **corpus callosum,** and had the effect of preventing 'cross-talk' between the hemispheres – that is, the animals appeared to be unable to exchange information from the left and right halves of their brains.

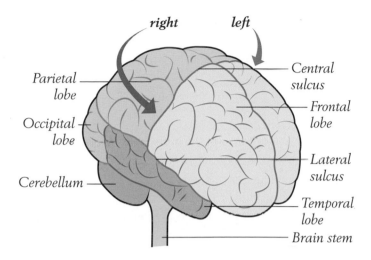

Figure 4.1
Investigations of brain structure show that it is divided into two 'halves' – the cerebral hemispheres – along the central line

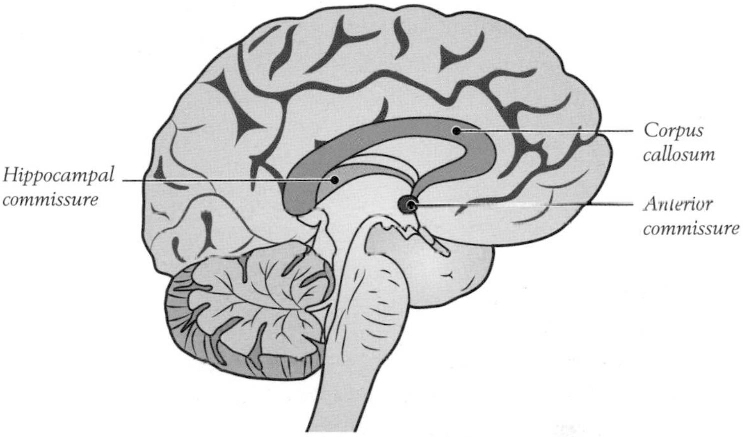

Figure 4.2
Investigations of brain structure show that internally it is divided into smaller structures

AIM

The aim of the study was to test the effects of hemispheric deconnection in humans. Specifically, to investigate whether cognition, including perception and memory, differs between the hemispheres, and the extent to which the hemispheres would normally interact to achieve these cognitive functions.

METHOD

Design

Sperry conducted his testing in a laboratory environment with control over specific variables. Some tests were conducted as comparisons between the left and right hemispheres. In essence, these were experimental in method, manipulating the independent variable of hemisphere, and measuring the effect on the individual's performance in tests of cognition (the dependent variable). As each participant could be tested on both the left and right hemisphere, these tests employed a repeated measures design. However, overall, the investigation more closely resembled a collection of case studies.

> **MATHS MOMENT**
>
> Assuming that only one of the participants was female, calculate the percentages of male and female participants in the sample.

KEY IDEAS

Each hemisphere receives input from the opposite visual field. It is important to understand that this is different from the view from each eye. Read and follow these instructions:

Shut one eye and stare at something small in front of you in the room, such as a mug or a door handle (this is your fixation point). Then, without moving your eye away from the object, decide what else you can see. You will be able to see a little either side of the object. The area to the left is in the **left visual field (LVF)** for the eye you have open. The area to the right is in the **right visual field (RVF)** for that eye. You can do the same for the other eye.

You will have demonstrated for yourself that what you can see to the left of a fixation point is in your left visual field, and what you can see to the right of a fixation point is in your right visual field.

In some of Sperry's experiments it was important to cover one eye, as an exchange of visual information between the left and right eyes occurs before it reaches the brain (at the optic chiasm). If both eyes are open (in normal people or in split-brain patients) information from the left visual fields of both the left and right eyes is passed to the right hemisphere. Similarly, the information from the right visual fields of both the left and right eyes is passed to the left hemisphere.

This transfer occurs across the optic chiasm. It is important to note that in Sperry's studies, the split-brain patients were typically exposed to stimuli presented to only one visual field (and only one eye), and thus only one hemisphere received information about the stimulus. This is illustrated in Figure 4.3.

Participants

The opportunity sample consisted of 11 patients with epilepsy (including at least one woman). They had all had an operation to divide the brain in half down the 'middle' (from front to back) along the corpus callosum to reduce the spread of epileptic seizures from one side to the other. They needed radical surgery as all had experienced severe symptoms such as seizures and convulsions, for a long time (e.g. over 10 years), and these symptoms could not be controlled with medication. They were evaluated at various times up to 5.5 years post-operatively. The surgery cut through the entire corpus callosum, the anterior commissure, hippocampal commissure and, in some patients, also the massa intermedia. The effect of this was to disconnect the two halves of the brain, thus preventing exchange of information between the left and right hemispheres.

Procedure

The general procedure was to expose one or both hemispheres to a stimulus and to elicit a response. Stimuli were visual, tactual (touch sense) or auditory (sound-based). Controls were employed to reduce input from extraneous variables. In visual tests, controls included covering the non-tested eye, and presenting stimuli to the **left visual field (LVF)** or the **right visual field (RVF)** separately. Each test began by fixing the gaze on the centre line of the screen and presenting stimuli for precisely measured durations (e.g. one-tenth of a second). This latter control was important to ensure that the time available would be insufficient for the participant's eye to move to view the stimulus in the 'other' visual field.

1   **Recognition of visual stimuli presented to the left and right hemispheres separately**

The visual stimulus of a picture of an object was presented to either the LVF or the RVF (i.e. to one side of the visual field of only one eye). The participant was then shown the same image again to either the same or the other visual field, and asked whether they recognised the object. For example, with the left eye closed, a picture of a ball would be flashed for one-tenth of a second to the left of the fixation point (so the image from the left visual field of the right eye would enter the right hemisphere). The participant would then see the same image flashed either to the left or to the right of the fixation point (so the image would reach the right or left hemisphere respectively).

2   **Responding with speech to visual stimuli presented to the left and right hemispheres separately**

A visual stimulus was presented to either the LVF or the RVF. The participant was then asked to describe the visual stimulus. For example, with the left eye closed, a picture of a spoon would be flashed to the left of the fixation point (so the image from the left visual field would enter the right hemisphere). Alternatively, with the left eye closed, a picture of a spoon would be flashed to the right of the fixation point (so the image from the right visual field would enter the left hemisphere).

3 Responding in writing to visual stimuli presented to the left and right hemispheres separately

This test was identical to the second test, except that the participant was required to write the name of the stimulus rather than say it. A visual stimulus was presented to either the LVF or the RVF. The participant was then asked to write down what the visual stimulus was. For example, with the right eye closed, a picture of a pear would be flashed to the left visual field and would enter the right hemisphere. Alternatively, a picture of a pear would be flashed to the right visual field and so would enter the left hemisphere.

4 Responding by pointing to visual stimuli presented to the left and right hemispheres separately

The test was also identical to the second test, except that the participant was required to point to the stimulus they had seen. A visual stimulus was presented to either the LVF or the RVF. The participant was then asked to point at the object they had seen, or at a picture of it, with either their left or right hand. For example, with the right eye closed, a picture of a pencil would be flashed to the right visual field of the left eye and would enter the left hemisphere. Such tests are described as cross modal, as they require the participant to receive information though one sense (mode) and respond through another.

5 Recognition of visual stimuli presented to the left and right hemispheres simultaneously

Two different figures were flashed simultaneously, one to the LVF, the other to the RVF. The participant was asked to draw with the left hand what had been seen. The drawing hand was hidden from the participant's visual field which had been used for that test. They then had to say what they had just drawn, still without looking. For example, the participant was shown a dollar sign in the left visual field and a question mark in the right visual field (Figure 4.4). They were then required to draw, out of sight, using their left hand, what they had seen, and finally to say what they had just drawn.

6 Recognition of pairs of related words presented visually and simultaneously to the left and right hemispheres

Words composed of two smaller words were presented to the participants such that half of the word fell in the LVF and half in the RVF. For example, the word 'keycase' was shown so that the LVF saw 'key' and the RVF saw 'case' (see Figure 4.5). There

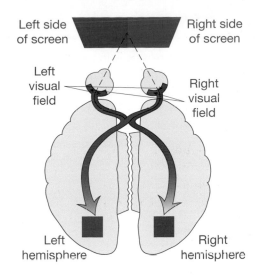

Figure 4.3
In a split-brain patient under experimental conditions, a stimulus presented to one visual field enters only the opposite hemisphere of the brain
Source: adapted from Sperry (1968), fig. 2, p. 725.

💡 KEY IDEAS

One example of lateralisation is in language. In typical right-handed people (and in the majority of left-handers too) language functions are largely restricted to the left hemisphere. Thus, we can talk or write only about things that have entered the left hemisphere.

WEB WATCH @

You can see animations and video of Sperry's experiments at www.nobelprize.org (enter 'split brain' into the search box) and http://www.youtube.com/watch?v=aCv4K5aStdU

Figure 4.4
Presenting with simultaneous stimuli to the left and right sides (test 5)

KEY IDEAS

Sperry uses several scientific terms. Although they are rather strange, it is helpful to understand them. **Stereognostic** refers to discovering the shape of something by touch. **Somesthetic** means 'the sense of the body', and refers to our ability to sense the position of our body parts. ('Soma' means 'body' and '…sthetic' refers to senses – think 'anae'-sthetic' – which blocks sensation.) **Topognosis** is the ability to identify where an object is on the skin.

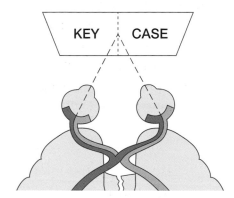

Figure 4.5
Presenting paired words to participants (test 6) Source: adapted from Sperry (1968), fig. 2, p. 725.

were the three possible ways to indicate recognition: the participant could use one hand to search through a selection of objects hidden from view for the one named by the word they had seen, they could say the name, or they could write the name.

7   Verbal identification of objects placed in the hand (stereognostic somesthetic discrimination)

The participant was prevented from seeing an object placed in either the left or the right hand. They were then asked to say or write the name of the object they had held or to retrieve the object they had held using either the left or the right hand. For example, a cup might be placed in the left hand and the participant asked to identify it by name (in speech or writing), or to find it from among other objects, once it had been taken away.

These tests are summarised, and some further tests conducted by Sperry (tests 8–12) are described, along with their results, in Table 4.1 (see pp. 122–4).

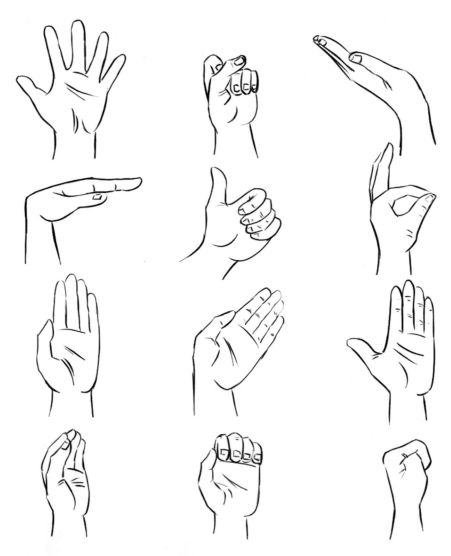

Figure 4.6
Hand positions for the symmetric hand-pose test (test 8)

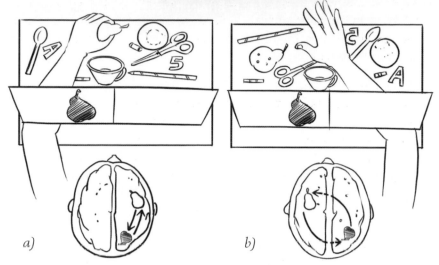

STRETCH & CHALLENGE

Emotionally, the right hemisphere responds like the left. For example, an image of a nude among other images elicits blushing or giggling. When asked to explain the emotional response, the participant – although aware of the arousal – cannot. Why not?

Similarly, when an incorrect verbal response is made by the left hemisphere (e.g. because the correct answer is known only to the right), annoyance is expressed by the right hemisphere through wincing, frowning and head shaking. Explain why.

Figure 4.7
An object felt by one hand will be recognised visually only by the corresponding (i.e. opposite) hemisphere. The pear can be found in (a) as the visual field, the hemisphere and the hand making the response all match. In (b), information from the left visual field enters the right hemisphere and cannot cross to the left hemisphere to instruct the right hand to find the pear.

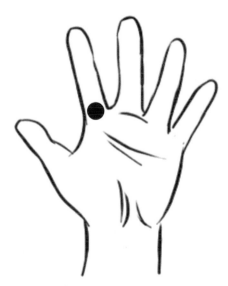

Figure 4.8
Presenting images of locations on hand to participants (test 10)

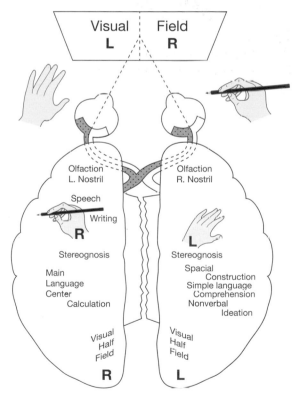

Figure 4.9
Functional lateralisation in split-brain patients
Source: Sperry (1968), fig. 3, p. 728.

TABLE 4.1: SUMMARY OF THE PROCEDURE AND RESULTS OF SPERRY'S SPLIT-BRAIN INVESTIGATIONS

		Procedure	Results	
			Description	Example
1	Recognition of visual stimuli presented to the left and right hemispheres separately	A picture was flashed to either the LVF or the RVF. The participant was shown the image again to either the same or the other visual field and asked whether they recognised the object.	Pictures of objects were recognised only if they were re-flashed to the same visual field.	The participant sees a picture of a ball in the LVF. They would recognise the ball only if it were presented again in the LVF. This is because memories about stimuli from one visual field cannot cross to the other hemisphere, so cannot be accessed in order to compare them to the stimulus when it is presented the second time, unless it is presented again to the same visual field.
2	Responding with speech to visual stimuli presented to the left and right hemispheres separately	A visual stimulus was flashed to either the LVF or the RVF, and the participant described it.	Participants could describe objects flashed to the RVF only.	A picture of a spoon flashed to the RVF could be named, but if shown to the LVF it could not be. This is because only stimuli presented to the RVF enter the 'speaking' left hemisphere. As speech is controlled only in the left hemisphere, stimuli in the right hemisphere cannot be named.
3	Responding in writing to visual stimuli presented to the left and right hemispheres separately	A visual stimulus was flashed to either the LVF or the RVF, and the participant wrote the name of it.	Participants could write down the name of objects presented to the RVF only.	A participant would be able to write 'pear' if a picture of a pear was flashed to the RVF, but they could not do so if it was shown to the LVF, as it would enter the right hemisphere. This is because writing is a language function so can be controlled only by the left hemisphere. To be able to write down what they have seen, the participant must view the object using the RVF.
4	Responding to visual stimuli by pointing	A visual stimulus was flashed to either the LVF or the RVF. The participant then pointed to that object.	Participants could correctly point to an object presented to the LVF or RVF.	If an image was flashed to the LVF, and hence to the right hemisphere, the participant could point to the object with their left hand (because the right hemisphere controls motor movement of the left side of the body). Likewise, if an image was flashed to the RVF, and hence the left hemisphere, the participant could point to the object with their right hand (because the left hemisphere controls motor movement of the right side of the body.
5	Recognition of visual stimuli presented to the left and right hemispheres simultaneously	Two different figures were flashed to the LVF and the RVF. The participant drew what they had seen with the left hand (hidden from view). They then said what they had drawn, without looking. (Figure 4.4.)	Participants could draw what they had seen in the LVF, but when asked what they had drawn said whatever had entered the RVF.	If shown a dollar sign on the left and a question mark on the right, participants draw a dollar sign but say 'question mark'. This happens because the dollar sign in the LVF goes to the right hemisphere (so can be drawn with the left hand using contralateral control), whereas the question mark, in the RVF, goes to the left hemisphere, so can be named.
6	Recognition of pairs of related words presented visually and simultaneously to the left and right hemispheres	Two small words which together made one were flashed so one fell in the LVF and the other in the RVF. Participants indicated recognition by: searching a hidden selection for the object, naming it, or writing the name. (Figure 4.5.)	Recognition of simultaneously presented stimuli differed according to the modality of the response.	If the word 'keycase' was shown so that 'key' reached the LVF and right hemisphere, a key would be selected by the left hand. The RVF would see 'case', so the left hemisphere would cause the participant to say or write that they had seen the word 'case'. Verbal responses are produced by the left hemisphere, so verbal recognition occurs only if stimuli are presented to the RVF. The left hand, controlled by the right hemisphere, will respond only to stimuli from the LVF.

7	**Verbal identification of objects placed in the hand**	The participant was asked to say or to write the name of an object they were holding or, to retrieve an object they had held.	Only objects held in the right hand can be named (in speech or writing). Objects held in either hand can be retrieved either immediately or after a delay, but only by the same hand.	If an apple is placed in the right hand, 'apple' can be said or written, but a verbal response could not be given if the apple was in the left hand. An apple could be found in a grab bag, or when among other objects, with either hand as long as it was the same hand that had originally held the object (i.e. there is no cross-retrieval). This happens because verbal functions are confined to the left hemisphere, so can only respond to stimuli in the RVF. Manual recognition can be controlled by either hemisphere, as long as it is the same one that made the initial identification.
8	**Symmetric hand-pose test**	The participant holds out both hands (where they cannot see them). One hand is put into a certain position and they have to imitate this position with the other hand (Figure 4.6).	Participants cannot imitate the position of one hand with the other hand unless it is very simple (e.g. a closed fist or a fully open hand).	A normal person asked to copy on their right a hand position with the first two fingers on their left hand crossed can do so, a split-brain patient cannot. This is because the information about the stimulus enters the opposite hemisphere from the hand moved by the researcher. As this is not the hemisphere controlling the other hand, a failure of cross-retrieval prevents access to the information.
9	**Crossed topognosis test and cross integration test**	Crossed topognosis: the participant holds their hands out of sight, palms up. The experimenter touches a point on a finger and the participant touches the same place with the thumb of the same hand. Cross integration: the participant touches the same place with the thumb of the other hand.	When asked to touch a point on the same hand as touched by the experimenter, participants can, but in the cross-integration test, split-brain participants typically fail.	The inability of most split-brain participants to achieve any cross-integration happens because the information about the touched hand enters the opposite hemisphere from the hand they must move, so they cannot access the necessary information to understand the movement required.
10	**Ipsilateral and homolateral manual visuognosis test**	An image of a black spot on a drawing of the hand is presented to either the LVF or RVF and the participant touches the same place with the thumb of either the left or the right hand (Figure 4.7).	Success depends on whether the visual field and hand making the response match. If the LVF sees the image, only the left hand can respond (and vice versa with the RVF).	An image shown to the RVF cannot be responded to by the left hand. This is because movement by each hand can be controlled only by the opposite hemisphere, and each hemisphere can receive instructions only from one visual field. When a visual field (e.g. the RVF and, therefore, the left hemisphere) is paired with the requirement for a response from the 'opposite' (e.g. left) hand, this cross-integration is impossible for a split-brain participant.
11	**Tactual recognition**	Simultaneous presentation: the participant holds out both hands and objects are put simultaneously in the left and right hands. They are removed and scrambled up with other objects. The participant uses both hands to search for the objects without looking. Cross-modal: the participant is shown a picture of an object in the LVF or the RVF, and searches for it with one hand.	Simultaneous presentation: the left and right hands search independently until each finds the object it had held. Cross-modal: the participant can find an object with a hand only if it was seen with the matching visual field.	Simultaneous presentation: if the left hand encounters the object held by the right hand, it will be unrecognised and rejected. This happens because the left and right hemisphere sensory functions, memory and motor control are independent in the split-brain patient. Cross-modal: if the participant sees a picture of a pear in the RVF they can find it with the right hand but not with the left (see Figure 4.8). This difference arises because the RVF, and hence left hemisphere, can control only the right hand.

| 12 | Tests of right hemisphere function | A range of tests similar to those above were conducted to investigate the range of functions in the right hemisphere. These included measures of cross-modal associations, reasoning, use of concepts, arithmetic, language comprehension and emotions. | The right hemisphere cannot perform complex verbal functions as this capacity is lateralised, i.e. it is limited to the left hemisphere. | If a clock is flashed to the LVF, and if the nearest item that can be found tactually by the left hand is a toy wrist watch, then subjects significantly select the watch. This demonstrates that the right hemisphere can understand the concept of 'timepiece' rather than just match shapes. Conceptual thinking by the right hemisphere is also shown by the ability of the left hand to sort objects into logical categories. With block numerals, pointing to answers or writing with the left hand, the right hemisphere can perform simple arithmetic and show simple language comprehension, e.g. being able to find by touch with the left hand an object named by the experimenter. |

MATHS MOMENT

Sperry reports that six participants were tested on adding numbers presented to the minor (right) hemisphere (test 12). Of these, four were able to correctly perform the arithmetic up to a product of about 20. Work out the percentage of participants who did and did not have this ability and present the results in a simple table with a title and headings. Draw a pie chart from your percentages.

KEY IDEAS

Aphasia is a disorder of language. For example, an aphasic individual might not recognise speech or words, or might know what they want to say but be unable to produce the words. The right hemisphere behaves in the same way, being unable to respond in speech or writing, unlike the left hemisphere.

RESULTS

Quantitative and qualitative data were gathered. Quantitative data were largely in the form of yes/no results – either the participants could perform a task or they could not. Qualitative data were typically descriptions of the participants' sensations and, in some cases, transcripts of their verbal responses.

1 Recognition of visual stimuli presented to the left and right hemispheres separately

Pictures of objects were recognised only if they were re-presented to the same visual field. This happens as memories about information from one visual field cannot cross the corpus callosum to the other hemisphere. Information therefore cannot be accessed for reference to check against when the stimulus is presented again, unless it is to the same visual field.

2 Responding with speech to visual stimuli presented to the left and right hemispheres separately

Participants could only describe objects presented to the right visual field. This happens because only the left hemisphere is used for speech (because it is a lateralised function), so only stimuli presented to the RVF can be named. The right hemisphere behaves as if it were **aphasic**.

3 Responding in writing to visual stimuli presented to the left and right hemispheres separately

This test was identical to the second test, except that it required writing (another verbal function) so the results were the same, in that participants could write down the name of objects presented to the right visual field only. So pictures shown to the right of the fixation point, in the right visual field, can be responded to in writing, but not those shown to the left visual field (as they enter the right hemisphere). The separation of responses from the left and right hemisphere is further supported by the qualitative data collected (see Box 4.1).

Box 4.1
Qualitative data
When asked to say or to write down the name of objects presented to the right visual field, participants could not do so. They would report having seen a flash of light. They behaved as though they were blind or 'agnostic', i.e. didn't believe that there had been a stimulus at all. But when asked to point to the same object they had denied the existence of, they could do so!

4 Responding by pointing to visual stimuli

This test was also identical to the second test, except that it required pointing (a non-verbal function). The results were therefore different. Participants could correctly point to an object presented to the LVF even though they would not be able to name it. So, if shown a picture in the left visual field (so the image would go to the right hemisphere) the participant could point correctly with their left hand. These results arise because hand movements such as pointing are controlled contralaterally (unlike lateralised language), so a response can be made to a stimulus reaching the right hemisphere.

5 Recognition of visual stimuli presented to the left and right hemispheres simultaneously

Participants appear to have two different streams of consciousness, one relating to the left hemisphere and the other to the right, so respond differently to stimuli presented simultaneously on the left and right. A participant will draw with the left hand what they have seen in the LVF (and entered the right hemisphere), but when questioned about what they have just drawn they describe what they saw with the RVF (which entered the left hemisphere). It is clear that the verbal left hemisphere remains unaware of the actions controlled by the right hemisphere (see Figure 4.10).

6 Recognition of pairs of related words presented visually and simultaneously to the left and right hemispheres

Simultaneously presented stimuli are responded to in different ways, depending on whether the response required is verbal or manual. Either hand can find an object seen by the appropriate hemisphere (e.g. LVF, right hemisphere, left hand). However, only the left hemisphere (from the RVF) can respond in speech or writing (see Figure 4.11). If these two tasks occur simultaneously, the two streams of consciousness operate independently and produce entirely separate responses. This is further supported by the qualitative data collected (see Box 4.2).

Box 4.2
Qualitative data
When asked to say or write down the word they had seen when exposed to the 'keycase' stimulus, participants responded with 'case'. When asked what kind of 'case' they had in mind, replies included: 'in case of fire', 'the case of the missing corpse' or 'a case of beer'. These indicate that the presence of the whole word 'keycase' did not influence the participants' thinking.

KEY IDEAS

Movement, or 'motor function', for each side of the body is controlled by the opposite hemisphere. This is called **contralateral** control. This means that each hemisphere can control pointing only by the opposite hand. If Sperry had asked participants to respond by pointing with their left hand to an object that had been seen using the RVF (and so had entered the left hemisphere), they would have been unable to do so, as this hemisphere can control only the right hand. Nerve fibres that stay on the same side of the body are called **homolateral** fibres. Those that (would) cross to the other side are called **ipsilateral** fibres. Contralateral control is governed by ipsilateral fibres. Note that the contralateral control is perfectly normal and is neither a consequence of, nor affected by, split-brain surgery.

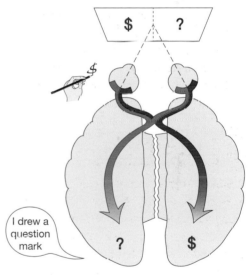

Figure 4.10
Each hemisphere appears to be unaware of the response made by the other hemisphere: the participant would draw a dollar sign (with the left hand) but say they had drawn a question mark

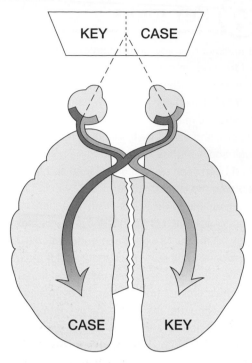

Figure 4.11
The verbal left hemisphere appears to be unaware of the word perceived by the right hemisphere

7 Verbal identification of objects placed in the hand

Objects placed in the right hand can be identified using words through speech or writing. The names of the same objects placed in the left hand cannot be said or written. However, the object can be retrieved from a grab bag or when scrambled among dozens of other objects, using touch alone. Although this is the case for both immediate recognition and following a delay, it can be successfully done only if the same hand (and therefore hemisphere) is used to retrieve the object as was used for initial identification. There is no cross-retrieval – that is, the participant cannot identify the object with one hand and then subsequently recognise it with the other. This inability of information about the stimulus to cross from one hemisphere to the other, which means it cannot be accessed, is called a failure of cross-retrieval. When given both manual and verbal tests, participants experience a contradiction in their ability. The explanations given in these situations are illustrated in Box 4.3.

> Box 4.3
> **Qualitative data**
> When first asked to make a spoken or written response to objects in the left hand, participants say that they can't 'work with that hand', that it is 'numb' or that they 'just can't feel anything or can't do anything with it' (although, of course, they can when they are not required to respond verbally). A particularly insightful response was that they 'don't get the message from that hand'. When, in subsequent tests, such individuals correctly retrieve objects that they had said they couldn't feel, they explain the contradiction by saying 'well, I was just guessing', or 'well, I must have done it unconsciously'.

The results of tests 8–12 are described, along with their procedures, in Table 4.1 (see pp. 122–4).

CONCLUSIONS

In relation to the specific aims of the study, Sperry drew two main conclusions:
1. In split-brain patients, perception in each hemisphere is independent. Information from one visual field or hand passes to only one hemisphere and is not available to the other hemisphere. If the information passes only to the right hemisphere, the individual cannot respond in speech or writing.
2. In split-brain patients, memory in each hemisphere is independent. Information from one visual field or hand is remembered only by that hemisphere and cannot be accessed by the other.

In addition, Sperry came to some general conclusions. In day-to-day life, split-brain patients are not obviously impaired. Although the streams of consciousness in their left and right hemispheres are independent, the sensory input is typically the same for both, so the individual is unaware of any difference in experience. Thus, they can interact, watch television and read a newspaper without difficulty. Furthermore, if given two simple, simultaneous tasks, each of which is controlled by a single hemisphere, a split-brain patient will perform at a better-than-normal speed. This is because interference normally caused by trying to attend to both left and right inputs together is eliminated.

Importantly, his findings led him to the overall conclusion that the non-dominant (right) hemisphere has a true stream of consciousness (like that of the left), which includes emotional reactions, and can perform both perceptual and motor functions.

EVALUATION

The research method

The study was a laboratory procedure, referred to as an experiment, although only some parts were truly experimental. Where two conditions (levels of the independent variable) were directly compared – such as when the participants' responses to LVF versus RVF stimuli were tested, or when left- versus right-hand responses were compared – these were experimental. Many comparisons were to non-split-brain people, although these individuals were not part of the sample included in this study. For this study, a control group of non-commissurotomised epileptics would have provided a better comparison.

Quantitative and qualitative data

A strength of Sperry's study was the depth and detail of the data he collected, which included both quantitative and qualitative data. It therefore has the strengths of both types of data (see p. 282 for a discussion). In this case, having both types of data was useful in interpreting the findings. For example, the qualitative data supporting tests six and seven help to show that the understanding of the effect of hemispheric deconnection is correct.

Ethical considerations

Although there were considerable ethical issues involved in the surgery itself, these are not issues in terms of the research conducted by Sperry. Indeed, understanding the reasons for their mental tiredness, and discovering that there are ways in which split-brain patients outcompete normal people, may have gone some small way towards helping the patients to make progress.

Validity

The procedures took place in a highly controlled environment, so it was possible to eliminate many extraneous variables and be reasonably confident that any independent variable being tested was affecting the dependent variable. For example, the visual restrictions imposed ensured that differences between responses to left and right visual field presentations were definitely caused by the failure of communication between the two hemispheres. For example, the non-tested eye was covered and participants were unable to see their own hands in the tactile tests. Furthermore, stimuli were displayed for a very short time. This ensured that it was not possible for the participant to glance away from the fixation point and view the stimulus through the other eye.

A key potential weaknesses with laboratory studies is the (lack of) realism of the environment and the participants' tasks, i.e. low ecological validity because the findings may not generalise beyond the laboratory setting. It is hard to set up laboratory procedures in which people behave as they would in real life, and Sperry's procedures are clearly utterly unlike real life. The findings therefore reflect this lack of realism and, although Sperry's study was concerned with discovering their problems rather than helping them in the real world, he did note that in day-to-day life, split-brain patients experience little impairment. They use both eyes simultaneously so both hemispheres will receive the same stimuli and the left hemisphere can 'speak out loud' to inform the right hemisphere about its thoughts. As a result, they demonstrate no indication of their two independent, parallel streams of consciousness.

Reliability

Remember that reliability means consistency. A procedure is reliable if we can precisely replicate it and consistently get the same results. Laboratory experiments are generally easy to replicate, and Sperry's procedure has been replicated. Although considerable variability between patients has been found (as it was by Sperry), his results have, in general, been supported. However, further evidence of the language ability

STRETCH & CHALLENGE

Even if human brains function independently of cultural influences, it is possible that Sperry's conclusions could be ethnocentric. If the study were used in exactly the same form on participants from other cultures, however, this would be inappropriate (you will understand why if you have already looked at Gould's study). Explain why the stimuli used by Sperry might lead to biased conclusions if used with non-American participants and suggest how these problems could be overcome.

of the right hemisphere presents some concern. Specifically, damage to the left hemisphere caused by early epilepsy might cause compensation, so that there is some reorganisation of language function to the right hemisphere (Zaidel, 1978). This would make the epileptic sample unrepresentative, and this pattern has been seen in recent brain-scanning studies (Thompson, 2000). Such acquisition might arise in split-brain patients as a consequence of their hemispheric deconnection. Baynes, Eliassen and Gazzaniga (1997) reported a case of a split-brain patient who, 12 years post-surgery, developed the ability to respond verbally to stimuli presented to the left visual field. Again, this would make Sperry's findings based on the testing of patients a decade post-operatively less generalisible.

Ethnocentrism

As we noted on page 116, there is some evidence for differences in lateralisation between people using different languages. If, for example, some cultures were less lateralised in their speech function, individuals from such cultures who underwent split-brain operations might produce rather different results. This would suggest that Sperry's results may only apply to cultures sharing the same lateralisation patterns as are found for English speakers.

Sampling bias

The sample was made up of 11 men and women who had undergone commissurotomies for intractable epilepsy. Although 11 sounds like a small sample, it is quite impressive given the rarity of such patients and the depth to which they were studied, so, overall, it is neither a particular strength nor weakness. Of course, because the participants were all patients suffering from epilepsy it is a restricted sample. Generalisation to the whole population might therefore be invalid, especially as epilepsy is a brain disorder and the findings relate to brain function.

The extent of the deconnection varied between patients, so there were likely to be differences between them. Although Sperry deliberately selected only patients who had had their surgery more than 4 years prior to testing, there were still differences in the duration of individuals' rehabilitation time, which again could have led to variation. In addition, although we know that both men and women were used, the number of each is not known, and there are gender differences in lateralisation of function (especially in terms of language), which would be important in terms of generalisibility.

Practical applications

The main practical implications of Sperry's work are the demonstration of hemispheric lateralisation and the findings that there are so few debilitating effects of the surgery. This provides an indication for surgical safety: patients receiving even extensive commissurotomies are unlikely to suffer noticeable cognitive effects (although subsequently some side effects on memory have been identified). In contrast, it also offers a warning: that unilateral damage could have profound effects, such as the implications of left-hemisphere surgery on speech.

QUESTION SPOTLIGHT!

It could be argued that Sperry's study is a quasi-experiment. *Explain why*.

CASEY *et al.*'s STUDY OF GRATIFICATION DELAY

Casey, B.J., Somerville, L.H., Gotlib, I.H., Ayduk, O., Franklin, N.T., Askren, M.K., Jonides, J., Berman, M.G., Wilson, N.L., Teslovich, T., Glover, G., Zayas, V., Mischel, W. and Shoda,Y. (2011) Behavioural and neural correlates of delay of gratification 40 years later. *Proceedings of the National Academy of Sciences,* **108** (36): 14998–15003.

IN BRIEF

Aim: To test whether delay of gratification in childhood predicts impulse self-control abilities in adulthood.

Method: The research method was a natural/quasi-experiment. As a longitudinal study composed of two experiments it used both an independent measures and repeated measures design. Participants were 562 individuals who had completed a gratification delay task at the age of 4. Experiment 1 was a behavioural task that tested whether individuals who were less able to delay gratification as children (low delayers) would, as adults, show less impulse control in suppressing responses to 'hot' cues relative to 'cool' cues. In Experiment 2, researchers used fMRI to examine neural correlates of delay of gratification in a task requiring responses to happy or fearful facial expressions.

Results: Participants identified as 'low delayers' as children had greater difficulty suppressing responses to 'hot' cues compared to those identified as 'high delayers'. Experimenters identified the right inferior frontal gyrus as a key region of the brain used in withholding responses, with low delayers showing reduced activity in this region during the 'no-go' trials. During the trials involving the most alluring stimuli, part of the limbic system known as the ventral striatum was more active in low delayers compared to that in high delayers.

Conclusion: The ability to resist temptation differs between individuals and is associated with varying levels of activity within the inferior frontal gyrus and ventral striatum. These individual differences do persist with age, but can also be influenced by contextual cues.

CONTEXT

Research has shown that there are individual differences in our capacity to resist temptation. Our ability to resist or delay immediate gratification is challenged by such factors as how alluring a stimulus is (Hare *et al.*, 2005). To test this idea, psychologists such as Shoda and Rodriguez (1989) developed delay-of-gratification tasks to measure how long young children can resist an immediate reward (e.g. a cookie) in order to receive a comparatively better but delayed reward (e.g. two cookies).

Psychologists believe we use 'cognitive control' to create strategies to delay gratification and prevent us from immediately acting on our impulses (Eigsti *et al.*, 2006). Cognitive control works by suppressing inappropriate thoughts or actions (e.g. immediately eating the cookie) which interfere with appropriate ones (e.g. waiting to receive several cookies). Eigsti *et al.* (2006) found that young children who focus only on the rewarding aspects of the alluring situation found it harder to suppress inappropriate actions in tasks of cognitive control.

Figure 4.12
Totally irresistible? Cookies are one example of alluring stimuli that have been used in delay-of-gratification tasks.

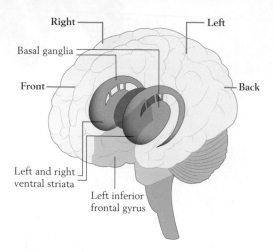

Figure 4.13
The inferior frontal gyrus and ventral striatum/basal ganglia

KEY IDEAS

The **inferior frontal gyrus** is a region of the brain situated in the frontal lobe. The right inferior frontal gyrus (RIFG) is implicated in go/no-go tasks, meaning that it is involved in the cognitive control process that helps us to inhibit or delay responses. By contrast, the **ventral striatum** is an area of the basal ganglia neural circuit located deep within the cerebral hemispheres of the brain. It receives input from many other brain areas, including the RIFG.

KEY IDEAS

An attractive stimulus or situation has two kinds of features or cues: **hot or cool cues**. The hot cues are those aspects that make it attractive, such as the nice taste of a biscuit. The cool cues are other aspects, that are not appealing, such as the shape of a biscuit. A cognitive strategy that helps people to resist temptation is to focus on the cool cues.

One explanation for how individuals manage to delay gratification is a cognitive strategy known as 'cooling'. This involves directing one's attention away from 'hot' or appealing features of the stimuli, such as its sweet taste, while focusing on the 'cool' or cognitive ones, such as its shape or weight. When prompted to use such strategies within experiments, participants in the 'cool' condition were able to resist tempting stimuli much more effectively than those directed to consider 'hot' features.

Furthermore, individuals appear naturally to exhibit differences in their use of strategies, even without experimenter prompting (Eigsti *et al.*, 2006). These differences could explain why some people seem naturally more able to resist temptation in everyday situations. Not contacting a potential girlfriend or boyfriend too soon after a first date might be an example of resisting a strong impulse; we even call these sophisticated social strategies 'playing it cool'.

A study by Metcalfe and Mischel *et al.* (1999) suggests that 'cool' and 'hot' patterns of thought each involve their own neurocognitive system; the 'cool' system based on cognitive control and the 'hot' system relating to desires and emotions. Psychologists can now use brain-imaging techniques to further investigate how biological systems may be implicated in self-control strategies. Casey *et al.* (2002) showed that cognitive control that aids in gratification delay may be linked to the **inferior frontal gyrus** in the brain, located within the prefrontal cortex. By contrast, limbic or emotional brain regions, such as the **ventral striatum**, are related to 'hot' situations involving immediate rewards (Somerville *et al.*, 2011).

In the present study, Casey *et al.* (2011), sought to investigate the hypothesis that the performance of young children in classic delay-of-gratification tasks may predict the capacity for self-control in adulthood. They recognised that as we age, our self-control may be challenged by stimuli of a changing nature. Rather than being tempted by sweet treats, complex needs, such as desire for social acceptance, may create more alluring situations for us as adults.

Their investigation focused on the involvement of the brain's inferior frontal gyrus because of its association with tasks requiring cognitive control. It was also chosen owing to its involvement in the interpretation and management of our responses to facial expressions, which are important in successful social interaction. Another area in the brain of interest to the researchers was the ventral striatum, which, as well as being associated with rewards, is known to play a role in inhibiting behaviour in complex social interactions.

AIM

In this study, researchers considered the extent to which the ability to resist temptation at preschool age affected the same participants in adulthood. Control over impulses and sensitivity to social cues at the behavioural and neural level were examined.

METHOD

The study was longitudinal, tracking the same participants from age 4 until they reached their forties. It was composed of two natural or quasi-experiments, as the independent variable (IV) was naturally occurring. The individual participants' ability to delay gratification was the IV; operationalised as 'high delayers' or 'low delayers'.

Participants

The sample was drawn from an initial cohort of 562 pupils aged 4 who had attended Stanford's Bing Nursery School and completed the original delay-of-gratification task during the late 1960s and early 1970s. From this original group, 155 then completed a self-control scale in their twenties, reducing to 135 participants who undertook the same measure in their thirties. Of those with scores either above or below average in terms of delay-of-gratification and self-control across all previous tests, 117 were contacted. Then 59 participants (23 males, 36 females) consented to take part in Experiment 1 and, of these, 27 (13 males, 14 females) also took part in Experiment 2. The researchers excluded one male participant's results from Experiment 2 owing to poor performance on the behavioural task.

Design and procedure

EXPERIMENT 1

The sample for this experiment was divided into 32 high delayers (12 male, 20 female) and 27 low delayers (11 male, 16 female). They had given their consent to take part in a behavioural version of a 'hot' and 'cool' impulse control task. The experiment was completed in participants' own homes via pre-programmed laptops. Participants completed two versions of what the researchers termed a 'go/no-go' task, in which participants were instructed to either press a button (go) or withhold a button press (no-go). The 'cool' version of the task included the presentation of male and female faces with neutral expressions; one sex was the go stimulus, and the other sex the no-go stimulus. The faces were drawn from the NimStim set of facial expressions (see Figure 4.14), a standard set of stimuli used by psychologists.

Prior to the start of the task, participants read on-screen instructions which told them to respond as quickly and accurately as possible. The screen also indicated which stimulus category (sex) served as the 'go' stimulus for each trial. Each face appeared for 500 milliseconds, followed by a 1-second interval between faces. In total, 160 trials were presented per run in pseudo-randomised order (120 go, 40 no-go). The task could therefore be described as a 2 (trial type: go, no-go) × 2 (stimulus sex: male, female) design (see Table 4.2). The accuracy and reaction times were acquired in four runs representing each combination of stimulus sex (male, female) and trial type (go, no-go). The '**hot**' and '**cool**' versions were chosen to explore the influence of alluring social **cues**. These two versions differed only in the use of happy expressions or neutral/fearful expressions respectively.

Figure 4.14
Participants viewed both happy and fearful faces similar to these

TABLE 4.2 EXPERIMENT 1: GRID TO SHOW THE 2×2 FACTORIAL DESIGN USED IN THE PRESENTATION OF FACIAL STIMULI TO PARTICIPANTS		
	Go	**No-Go**
Stimulus sex — Male	Male/Go	Male/No-go
Stimulus sex — Female	Female/Go	Female/No-go

EXPERIMENT 2

The sample contained 15 high delayers (5 male, 10 female) and 11 low delayers (7 male, 4 female). Participants were scanned with a functional magnetic resonance imaging (fMRI) scanner while completing a 'hot' version of the go/no-go task similar to that used in Experiment 1. The set-up enabled them to view the task via a rear projection screen. An electronic response pad was used to record responses to facial stimuli and reaction times. Forty-eight trials were presented per run (35 go, 13 no-go). Each face stimulus was presented for 500 milliseconds, followed by intervals ranging from 2 seconds to 14.5 seconds. Researchers collected imaging data for 26 no-go trials and 70 go trials per expression.

RESULTS

EXPERIMENT 1

Overall, both groups were highly accurate in their correct responses to go trials in both 'cool' and 'hot' conditions (99.8% and 99.5% correct, respectively). Low delayers were slightly more likely to respond mistakenly in no-go trials and performed slightly worse than high delayers in the 'hot' version of the task, however. Low delayers identified at 4 years of age showed greater difficulty suppressing their responses to happy faces than high delayers.

EXPERIMENT 2

Experimenters found no significant difference between the two delay groups on reaction times in correct go trials. Accuracy across both groups was very high for go trials, as in Experiment 1. Similarly, low delayers had higher false-alarm rates in no-go trials (14.5% false-alarm rate; see Figure 4.15).

As expected, the right inferior frontal gyrus appeared to be critical in withholding responses, with low delayers showing reduced activity in this region during the key no-go trials, as compared to high delayers or during go trials. There were high levels of activity in the reward-related region (the ventral striatum) for low delayers compared to the high-delay participants. This was most prominent during happy no-go trials for the low delayers (see Figure 4.16).

MATHS MOMENT 🖩

In experiment 1, low-delay participants committed more false alarms than high-delay participants (low delayers, 14.5%; high delayers, 10.9%). Draw and label a bar chart to illustrate this finding.

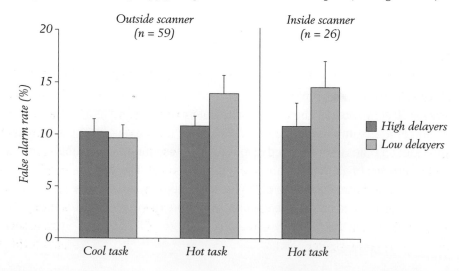

Figure 4.15
Results of Experiment 1 (outside scanner) and Experiment 2 (inside scanner) showing key differences in false-alarm rate on the 'hot' task between high and low delayers

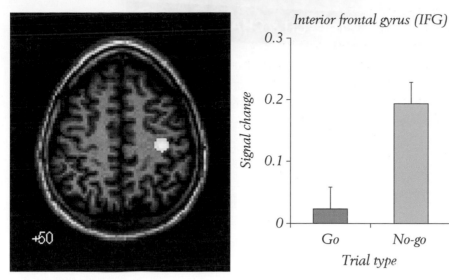

MATHS MOMENT 🖩

Casey *et al.* refer to a *p*-value of <0.05. Explain the difference between the 0.05 and 0.01 levels of significance.

Figure 4.16
Right: The right inferior frontal cortex was associated with correct inhibition of a response (no-go) relative to making a correct response (go)
Left: Activation map depicting right inferior frontal gyrus activation, significant at p<0.05

CONCLUSIONS

Casey *et al.* assert that there are three main conclusions from this study:

1 Resistance to temptation appears to be a relatively stable characteristic of an individual over time.

2 Cognitive control can be strongly influenced by contextual factors (e.g. 'hot' cues) in alluring situations.

3 Ventral frontostriatal circuitry supports resistance to temptation, with a combination of lowered activity in the inferior frontal gyrus and increased activity in the ventral striatum in low delayers.

EVALUATION

The research method

Experiment 2 took place under laboratory conditions and so it was possible to control extraneous variables. Experiment 1 used a carefully standardised programme to present stimuli and recorded participant responses with a high level of reliability and accuracy, thus avoiding human error. However, participants performed the behavioural task from Experiment 1 within their own homes, so there was a greater possibility of distractions in the environment.

Qualitative and quantitative data

The data gathered in this study were quantitative. The strength of this type of data is that it allows for direct comparison of conditions. In this case it showed that young children who performed poorly on the original delay-of-gratification task later showed diminished cognitive control in alluring situations as adults. However, this omits qualitative details such as analysis of the cognitive strategies employed by individual participants when approaching such situations.

Researchers were able to observe the differences between low and high delayers, but obtained no information about why their brains and behaviour varied significantly.

Ethical considerations

Informed consent was obtained from participants for both experiments. As a brain-imaging technique, fMRI is considered low risk, and the protection of participants from harm was assured.

Validity

The ecological validity of this study can be considered to be a key weakness. The nature and presentation of the go/no-go task was artificial and different from how we normally encounter and respond to facial expressions. Also, the use of fMRI scanning during the task may have had an impact on the way in which participants responded to stimuli. It is likely that genuine social interactions are more complex and may cause our brains to behave differently from how they behave under artificial conditions.

STRETCH & CHALLENGE

1 What practical issues might researchers face when collecting data using fMRI scanners?
2 In what way could these challenges impact on the sample of participants?

Reliability

Owing to the level of control involved in laboratory experiments, the method used in this study is fairly reliable. Casey *et al.* used an fMRI scanner to examine their results, and it is highly likely that if the experiment were to be repeated using the same equipment it would yield similar results.

Sampling bias

Although initially drawn from a large pool of 562 participants, this sample is limited to individuals who attended one nursery during a specific time period. This means the findings of the study are geographically limited and may only represent people from similar family backgrounds. Furthermore, not all the children from the original delay-of-gratification task took part, and within individual conditions there were much smaller numbers of participants.

STRETCH & CHALLENGE

Mischel (1961) demonstrated cross-cultural differences in delay gratification in young children when fathers were absent and, more recently, Kidd, Palmeri and Aslin (2013) have considered the idea of 'rational snacking' as an explanation for why some children might appear to be better or worse at resisting temptation. In their introduction, Kidd, *et al* say: 'Consider the mindset of a 4-year-old living in a crowded shelter, surrounded by older children with little adult supervision. For a child accustomed to stolen possessions and broken promises, the only guaranteed treats are the ones you have already swallowed.' Think about how such situations might lead to cultural differences in delay gratification. To what extent would this affect how ethnocentric Casey *et al.*'s conclusions are?

Ethnocentrism

As in Sperry (1968), this study also looks at brain function independent of cultural influences. Therefore it is unlikely that the findings of this study are ethnocentric. However, it might be that impulse control is nurtured differently in different societies, which might mean cross-cultural differences could be noted.

Practical applications

This study is useful in that it has provided further evidence about the localisation of neural function for tasks involving rewards and resisting temptation. It also found that our ability to exercise self-control is influenced greatly by contextual cues. The ability to delay immediate gratification in favour of long-term goals is useful for an individual's personal and social well-being, and this study shows us how both individual and situational factors can influence self-control.

COMPARISON OF STUDIES

Sperry's Split Brain Study & *Casey et al.'s Study of Gratification Delay*

THE TOPIC
Regions of the brain involved in perception and delay gratification

The studies by Sperry and Casey *et al.* are about biological psychology, specifically the role of different regions of the brain: both considered specific brain structures and their functions. Sperry was investigating the consequences on perception and memory of split-brain operations: the impact of severing the corpus callosum which links the left and right hemispheres. Casey *et al.* were studying the differences in areas of brain activity that could be linked to being able to delay gratification. Whereas Sperry aimed to demonstrate similarities in the way that all the split-brain patients' perceptual abilities differed from normal, Casey *et al.* aimed to demonstrate differences in activity in brain regions according to the individual's impulse control level.

THE RESEARCH METHOD AND DESIGN
Laboratory-based studies: single participant experiments and longitudinal studies

Although both studies were conducted in laboratories, they were quite different. Sperry tested several individual split-brain patients on a range of measures intended to investigate the effects of being unable to send neural messages between the cerebral hemispheres. Casey *et al.* compared one group of participants as children and then as adults, looking for differences in brain activity in between those having relatively high or low impulse control when young, and in response to more or less tempting cues.

SAMPLING TECHNIQUE AND THE SAMPLE
Restricted samples

Sperry's participants were an opportunity or volunteer sample but were restricted in that all had undergone a split-brain operation. Casey *et al.*'s participants were also a restricted sample, chosen for their scores (either consistently high or consistently low) on tests of delay gratification conducted when they were aged 4, and then in adulthood. In both cases, the specific selection of participants was necessary for the aims of the study, but such narrow samples may have other variables in common that limit the generalisability of the findings – although this is unlikely. For example, patients who require a split-brain operation may differ from the general population in some aspects of their perceptual processing prior to the operation.

EXPERIMENTAL MATERIALS AND MEASUREMENT OF THE DV
Quantitative data

Both experiments were conducted in laboratories, and this may reduce ecological validity. In Sperry's studies, laboratory facilities were essential for presenting the stimuli to a single visual field. The data collected, based on the participants' responses, which were often single words or pointing to an object, were quantitative. In Casey *et al.*'s study, part of the investigation was carried out in the participants' own homes (on a laptop) and the other in an fMRI scanner. Both produced quantitative data, the former about delay gratification and the latter about activity in the prefrontal cortex and ventral striatum. The tasks required of the participants in Sperry's study were relatively artificial, in that we never normally use a single visual field. In comparison the delay gratification choices used in Casey *et al.*'s study were more realistic: we do have to choose between 'less now or more later' in day-to-day life. However, the scanner environment was unfamiliar to the participants, so might have affected their behaviour, although this is unlikely as the pattern of responses was the same in and out of the scanner.

APPLICATIONS
Understanding the role of different brain areas

Both studies have contributed to our knowledge of the localisation of brain functions, which is useful in general to understand the specific problems that arise from brain damage affecting different areas of the brain. For example, Sperry's work reassuringly indicates the limited dangers of split-brain operations in terms of cognitive function but also confirms that unilateral damage could have severe effects. Casey *et al.*'s findings suggest that not only are differences in brain areas important to the capacity to resist temptation in order to gain longer-term rewards, but that contextual cues also affect our capacity to delay gratification.

KEY THEME: REGIONS OF THE BRAIN

These studies have illustrated that different brain areas perform different roles, this is the concept of localisation of function. However, in the nervous system, different functions are performed both by different areas of brain tissue and by the interconnecting networks between areas. These studies have also demonstrated the role of interconnections in the brain. Sperry's study does so by illustrating the key role of the corpus callosum and other structures of the central commissures in providing a communication channel between the hemispheres, without which the two halves of the brain have independent streams of consciousness. Casey *et al.*'s study showed that more than one area is involved in delay gratification so, like many behavioural functions, there is not a simple 'area for doing behaviour X' but that a behaviour is the product of many interacting brain areas.

KEY THEME 🔑

Regions of the brain
Sperry showed that the corpus callosum serves to unite the streams of conscious thought in the left and right hemispheres and these areas have some specialisation of function. Casey *et al.*'s study demonstrated that two brain areas, the prefrontal cortex and ventral striatum, are important in resisting temptation. These findings support the ideas of localisation of function and that behaviours are controlled by a network of brain areas.

Sperry
Single participant experiments investigating memory and perception in split-brain patients.

Similarities
Both were laboratory-based studies collecting quantitative data about regions of the brain. Limiting the visual field and using preloaded tests on laptops were ways to impose controls.

Casey *et al.*
A longitudinal study investigating delay gratification.

PRACTICE QUESTIONS

Here are some of the sorts of questions that you could be asked in Sections A and B of your AS exam, and some examples of successful and less successful answers. We look at Section B questions in more detail in Chapter 6 on pages 206–8 and 212–14.

SECTION A: CORE STUDIES

1 Give **one** reason why the patients had undergone an operation to deconnect the two hemispheres of the brain. [2]

2 The study by Sperry investigated the effects of hemisphere deconnection in split-brain patients. Describe how split-brain patients responded to visual material presented to their right visual field. [2]

3 Outline **one** problem with generalising from the sample used in this study. [2]

4 Describe **one** similarity between Sperry's split-brain study and Casey et al.'s study of neural correlates of delay of gratification. [3]

5 What was the aim of Casey et al.'s study of neural correlates of delay of gratification? [2]

6 The study by Casey et al. of neural correlates of delay of gratification was a longitudinal study:

(a) Describe what a longitudinal study is. [2]

(b) Suggest **one** weakness of using a longitudinal study. [2]

7 Briefly describe the procedure of Casey et al.'s study of neural correlates of delay of gratification. [4]

8 From the study by Casey et al. of neural correlates of delay of gratification:

(a) Describe the quantitative data collected. [2]

(b) Suggest **one** strength of quantitative data. [2]

SECTION B: AREAS, PERSPECTIVES AND DEBATES

9 (a) Outline how biological psychology explains behaviour. [2]

(b) Suggest **one** strength of claiming that behaviour is only due to nature. Support your answer with evidence from **one** appropriate core study. [3]

(c) Suggest **one** weakness of claiming that behaviour is only due to nature. Support your answer with evidence from one appropriate core study. [3]

(d) Explain how **one** psychological study can be considered as providing a biological explanation for behaviour. [5]

(e) Discuss the extent to which biological psychology can be seen as reductionist. Support your answer with evidence from core studies. [12]

SECTION A   1 Give **one** reason why the patients had undergone an operation to deconnect the two hemispheres of the brain. [2]

Rachel's answer:

They had an operation to deconnect the two hemispheres so that information could not be passed from one to another.

We say: This is only a partial answer to the question. Rachel clearly understands that this procedure prevented information from travelling across the corpus callosum from one hemisphere to another, but she has not explained why this was necessary. The 11 individuals that Sperry was able to test had all had this operation as a drastic measure for controlling epilepsy.

Charlotte's answer:

Because they had severe epilepsy and this treatment was a last resort after other treatments had failed. It didn't cure their epilepsy but it prevented the seizure from spreading across the corpus callosum to the other hemisphere so reduced the severity of the seizures.

We say: Well done, Charlotte. This is a very clear answer to the question. Well written and concise, this demonstrates an excellent understanding of the background to the study.

3 Outline one problem with generalising from the sample used in this study. [2]

Rachel's answer:

This was a very small sample of people from one country so it is not possible to generalise to people all over the world.

Charlotte's answer:

Sperry is using this study to try and draw conclusions about the working of 'normal' brains. It may be likely that the 11 participants here had differences in their brains apart from the deconnection due to the severity of their epilepsy. Therefore it may not be possible to draw conclusions about brain functioning in anyone other than an individual with a 'deconnected' brain.

We say: This answer suggests that Rachel perhaps doesn't understand this concept very well. Large samples don't necessarily mean that generalisation is easier. If thousands of 16 and 17 year olds were given a memory test, it would not be possible to generalise the test results to 70 year olds, and testing more and more 16 and 17 year olds wouldn't help. There are better answers that could be given.

We say: This is very well understood and is specific to the study. It really focuses on the fact that generalisation is the extent to which the participants in the study can represent or 'stand for' other participants and obviously in this study these participants can only represent a very tiny proportion of the population.

6 The study by Casey et al. of neural correlates of delay of gratification was a longitudinal study:

(a) Describe what a longitudinal study is. [2]

(b) Suggest one weakness of using a longitudinal study. [2]

Rachel's answer:

(a) It is a study that takes place over a long period of time.

(b) A weakness of a longitudinal study is that it takes a very long time before you get any results.

Charlotte's answer

(a) A longitudinal study is one that measures change over time by following a group of participants over a period of time and collecting data from them at regular intervals.

(b) A weakness of a longitudinal study is participant attrition. This is when participants drop out of the study or can't be contacted for various reasons. This has the effect of making the sample smaller at each data-collecting point. In this study the original sample of around 500 dropped down to around 130 when they were retested in their thirties.

We say: These are very basic responses; considerably more information is needed. It may be correct that a longitudinal study takes place over a long period of time but there is more to a longitudinal study than this. The important feature is that development or change is being measured by looking at the same participants at various times. The fact that you might have to wait for the results is a weakness, but one that is probably more than compensated for by the quality and usefulness of the results when the study is completed. Rachel still needs to develop her answers and give more detail (while taking into account the numbers of marks available).

We say: This is an excellent set of answers to the question. Charlotte shows a very good understanding of longitudinal research and has selected a weakness that is specific to this kind of study. The example from the specific core study is additional detail. It is always worth including a few words that put your answer in the context of the core study as this will show better understanding.

SECTION B 9 (e) Discuss the extent to which biological psychology can be seen as reductionist. Support your answer with evidence from core studies. [12]

Rachel's answer:

Reductionism means looking at only one factor and not others. The study by Sperry is reductionist as it only looks at the functioning of the hemispheres and doesn't look at the influence of any other factors. The study by Casey only looks at delay of gratification in terms of some tasks and not a whole range of things.

Charlotte's answer:

Reductionism refers to the level of explanation that is offered. A reductionist explanation is one that reduces explanation to the simplest level, therefore social explanations are more complex (less reductionist) than biological explanations (more reductionist). In this sense, any study offering only a biological explanation for behaviour is reductionist. However the focus of the study by Sperry is looking specifically at a biological process (the functioning of the hemispheres independently of each other) and so it is appropriate to be offering just biological explanations of these findings so although these are reductionist explanations, this is not necessarily a weakness. In the study by Casey there are likely to be environmental or social factors that also contribute to the ability someone has to delay gratification and so in this case the reductionist explanation may be missing the contributions of other important (non-biological) variables. Therefore it may be a weakness to offer biological or reductionist explanations of some behaviours but it depends on the behaviour.

We say: Rachel has misunderstood the concept of reductionism. This is something that students find quite complex and it is worth spending a few moments making sure that you understand this. Reductionism is not simply looking at one factor rather than a range of factors. Reductionism is about the level of explanation: social factors are reduced to individual factors which are reduced to biological factors. The biological explanation is the most reductionist level of explanation in psychology and depending on the behaviour being explained is likely to be missing a number of important social and environmental variables that may be required to gain a full understanding of the behaviour. Unfortunately Rachel's answer would not gain any credit and this question is worth 12 marks.

We say: Excellent. This is a very difficult concept and many students misunderstand reductionism to mean focusing on one variable. This would be incorrect and Charlotte has explained reductionism very well indeed. Her evaluation is also impressive and demonstrates an understanding that reductionism is a feature of explanations for behaviour rather than a feature of individual studies.

BLAKEMORE AND COOPER'S STUDY OF THE IMPACT OF EARLY VISUAL EXPERIENCE

Blakemore, C. and Cooper, G.F. (1970) Development of the brain depends on the visual environment. *Nature*, **228**: 477–8.

IN BRIEF

Aim: To test whether kittens raised in an environment of vertical or horizontal stripes would develop normal vision.

Method: The research method was a laboratory experiment, using an independent measures design. Kittens spent time in a striped cylinder apparatus from 2 weeks to 5 months and were tested on their visual perception. The independent variable was the visual orientation of the rearing environment (horizontal or vertical stripes). The dependent variable was measured in two ways: their behaviour in a normal environment and a physiological investigation of the direction of orientation of neurons in the visual cortex. Controls included being reared in darkness, the absence of contours in the cylinder apparatus and being prevented from seeing their own limbs.

Results: The kittens' eyes developed normally, but their behaviour and brains did not. Even after time in the light the kittens had poor visual tracking skills and depth perception. Different environments produced specific problems: the kittens failed to respond to objects in the orientation opposite to that which they had seen, e.g. a vertical-stripe reared cat did not chase a horizontally moving rod. Neurons in the brains of these kittens were also different, each lacking cells responding to the orientation of line that they had not experienced. Most neurons were, however, binocular, like those of a normal cat.

Conclusion: The changes in neurons in the visual cortex were the result not of degeneration but of brain plasticity, as neurons matched their sensitivity to the stimulation they received.

KEY IDEAS

Visual tracking is the ability to follow the path of a moving object. This is normally a smooth and accurate progression with the eyes or head.

Depth perception is the ability to judge the position of an object in space, e.g. to decide how far away it is. This is partly due to stereopsis, the ability of the brain to compare the view of the left and right eye. When an object is close, the two eyes see quite different views, when an object is far away, the left and right eye view are much more similar.

CONTEXT

Prior to Blakemore and Cooper's study, Hubel and Wiesel (1962) had shown that in normal cats, neurons in the visual cortex respond not just to light, but to specific features of the visual world. One type of neuron is orientation-specific, that is, each one responds to lines in a different direction, as though there were different neurons to detect the minute hand of a clock pointing to each of the minutes in an hour. Many of these neurons are activated by stimulation of either eye, i.e. they are **binocular**. In a later study, Hubel and Wiesel (1970) also demonstrated that total visual deprivation in kittens, such as when they are reared in continuous darkness, causes neurons in the brain that should be associated with the deprived eye(s) to decline in number. Susceptibility to this effect is greatest when kittens are between 4 and 8 weeks of age.

Later, Hirsch and Spinelli (1970) investigated the effect on neurons of the visual cortex in cats when their early visual experience is controlled. When the kittens were raised wearing a mask so that one eye saw only vertical stripes and the other only horizontal stripes, the normal cortical organisation changed. The kittens'

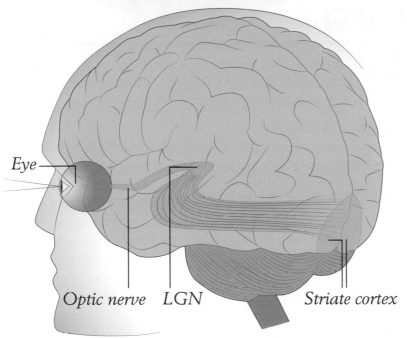

Figure 4.17
Area 17 of the primary visual cortex is also called the striate cortex because it is has a layered appearance in which neurons with similar stimulus properties are stacked in columns. For example, neurons that normally respond to a certain visual angle lie adjacent to ones orientated to a slightly different angle.

early experience caused most of the orientation-specific neurons of the visual cortex to become exclusive to either vertical or horizontal lines, depending on the stimulus the eye had received. In addition, these neurons could be activated only by that particular eye, i.e. they had become **monocular**. This illustrates the plasticity of the brain.

One problem with Hirsch and Spinelli's method was that the striped environment was fixed inside the animal's goggles, so it could not even see stripes in the real world. In a different kind of experiment, Held and Hein (1963) had shown that active interaction with the visual world is important for the development of normal visual responses in kittens. In their test, two kittens were reared with identical visual experience inside a vertically striped environment, but only one was free to move itself. The vision of the kitten that could not guide its own movement did not develop normally. As Held and Hein's evidence showed that independent movement was important, Blakemore and Cooper used a different method from that of Hirsch and Spinelli, allowing the kittens free movement and **binocular** vision, but still restricting the kittens' visual experience to either vertical or horizontal stripes.

AIM

The aim of the study was to investigate the effect on kittens' visual development of a restricted visual environment, consisting of either vertical stripes only or horizontal stripes only, in which the animal could move freely.

ACTIVITY ✳

Hold something thin (e.g. a mobile phone) with the narrow edge vertically against your nose. Shut one eye then the other. Because the phone is close, your eyes see very different views. Now ask someone to hold the phone three or more metres away. Now closing each eye makes very little difference – both eyes have similar views. This is the basis of detecting depth by stereopsis and relies on neurons in your visual cortex having a binocular input.

KEY IDEAS

The term **monocular** means 'one eye' (mono = one, ocular = of the eyes). It can be used to refer to vision itself, you are engaging in monocular vision if you close one eye, or to properties, such as cells that are monocular, i.e. that respond to input from only one of the two eyes. In contrast, **binocular** refers to both eyes – if you have both eyes open you are using binocular vision to read this.

WEB WATCH @

Look at the method used by Held and Hein. Their paired kittens received the same visual experience but differed in their ability to control their interaction with the visual environment.

http://ucalgary.ca/pip369/mod9/vision/vs

and http://embodiedknowledge. blogspot.co.uk/2011/12/classic-experiment-by-held-and-hein.html

These are summaries of the study, with illustrations.

STRETCH & CHALLENGE

You can watch a student video that describes the entire Held and Hein study, here:
www.youtube.com/
watch?v=wDri4u8MvYQ
Make a similar video for Blakemore and Cooper's study.

Figure 4.18
The visual display apparatus, with the cover and spotlight removed, showing vertical stripes

QUESTION SPOTLIGHT!

Explain why Blakemore and Cooper used a round tube rather than a square tube for the visual display apparatus.

METHOD

Participants

The participants were laboratory-raised kittens that were housed in complete darkness until 2 weeks of age.

Design and procedure

This study was a laboratory experiment with an independent measures design. The kittens were kept in the dark unless they were in the visual display apparatus or were being tested.

From 2 weeks of age until 5 months, each kitten spent an average of 5 hours a day in a visual display apparatus (see Figure 4.17). This was a vertical cylinder, 46cm in diameter, with a Perspex floor half way up, on which the kitten could move at will. The kittens saw no corners, there was no edge to the floor and, as the cylinder was 2 metres long, the laboratory floor and ceiling were a long way away. The entire inner wall of the cylinder was covered with high-contrast black and white stripes. For half of the kittens these stripes were vertical, and for the others they were horizontal. This difference in pattern was the independent variable.

Although Blakemore and Cooper did not raise control kittens (ones that were not exposed to an environment with limited visual stimulation), the findings were also compared to the previously established standard of brain development in the normal cat.

The dependent variables, i.e. the effects of this rearing, were measured in several ways. When the kittens were removed from the apparatus at 5 weeks of age they spent several hours each week in a small well-lit room containing chairs and tables, where their visual reactions were observed. Observations were made of their ability to move around and respond to objects, to jump from a chair to the floor, to follow a moving object, to judge the distance of objects to touch them, their startle responses and visual placing, as well as their responses to a rod held vertically or horizontally. Also, from 7.5 months, biological studies were conducted of individual neurons in the primary visual cortex of the kittens to investigate how they responded to lines in terms of orientation and whether they were monocular or binocular. This was done by anaesthetising the cat (which kept its eyes open) and presenting bright slits or edges of light while recording from individual neurons. Recordings were taken from 125 neurons from two kittens (one horizontally reared and one vertically reared).

Controls ensured that the kittens had identical visual environments, apart from their experience of vertical or horizontal lines. For example the cylinders were the same diameter and length, were illuminated from above by a spotlight, and had the same floor and cover. The kittens spent the same length of time in the apparatus, the remainder being in the dark, wore a collar to prevent them from seeing their own paws, and were allowed normal binocular vision.

RESULTS

Although the kittens' pupils responded in the normal way to a bright light, in terms of their behaviour they were unlike normal animals regardless of the orientation of the stripes in their rearing environment. They moved around mainly by touch rather than sight, they failed to stretch their paws out when they were held and brought down towards a table top (visual placing), and showed no startle response when an object was moved quickly towards them. They also appeared to be frightened when they reached the edge of the surface on which they were standing. These deficiencies, however, were overcome within about 10 hours of normal visual experience in the light, suggesting that they were the result of problems such as those described by Held and Hein (1963), caused by the absence of an opportunity to link vision with movement. For example, they soon showed normal startle and visual placing responses and could jump safely from a chair to the floor.

Some of the kittens' visual defects were, however, permanent. They bumped into stationary objects, followed moving objects clumsily – making jerky rather than smooth head movements – and were poor at judging the distance of objects in order to touch them, often reaching for objects beyond their grasp. There were also enduring differences between the kittens reared in different environments. When tested for their startle response to a Perspex sheet with black stripes on, a kitten responded only if it was presented with the stripes in the same orientation that they had grown up with. For example, a kitten raised in a horizontally striped environment would show a startle response if the sheet was brought towards them with the stripes in a horizontal orientation, but would not respond if it was turned around so that the stripes ran vertically. Similarly, when shown a rod held and moved vertically, a kitten raised in vertically striped cylinder would follow its movement with its head, chase it and play with it. A kitten raised in a horizontally striped cylinder in contrast would show no interest.

Figure 4.19
A kitten that has experienced a horizontally striped environment can follow and catch a stick held horizontally, but ignores a vertical one

KEY IDEAS

The **primary visual cortex** is part of the occipital lobe, an area at the back of the brain, on both sides. The primary visual cortex produces a detailed 'map' of the visual image we see. It has regions devoted to different aspects of the stimulus, such as its source (from the left or right eye), its colour, and individual features of its shape. The arrangement of the neurons is highly organised, with columns of adjacent cells responding to similar but slightly different features.

KEY IDEAS

Even though individual nerve cells (neurons) are incredibly small, it is possible to measure the activity of a single neuron, using a **micropipette**. This is a very fine tube filled with a solution of ions (molecules carrying a positive or negative charge). These micropipettes respond to the electrical activity inside a neuron that occurs when an impulse is generated, and this is displayed on a screen. This technique is known as **single-cell recording**.

WEB WATCH @

Listen to Colin Blakemore talking about visual deprivation in kittens in general and the method and results of this study in particular:

www.youtube.com/
watch?v=QzkMo45pcUo

This video shows a single-cell recording of orientation-specific cells in the visual cortex and of a kitten in a horizontally striped cylinder, and a second kitten in a vertically striped cylinder.

QUESTION SPOTLIGHT!

Blakemore and Cooper tested the reaction of the kittens' pupils to light. *Explain why it was important to the experiment that these responses were normal.*

In the physiological investigation of neurons in the cortex, differences were again found. Of all the units studied, only one was found not to be orientation specific. Although 75% of the neurons in both cats were binocular, as they would be in a normal cat, their orientation sensitivities were entirely different and abnormal. In each cat, no neurons had a preferred orientation within 20 degrees of the opposite orientation to lines in their rearing environment, and only 12 were within 45 degrees. In other words, for a horizontally reared cat, most of the neurons respond around the vertical axis and vice versa. In a chi-squared test, this pattern was highly significant ($p<0.00001$). Note that these neurons responded differently from normal, rather than being inactive or absent altogether.

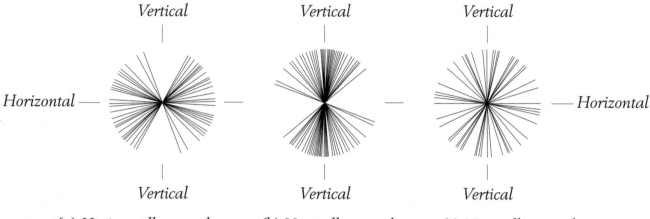

(a) *Horizontally reared cat* (b) *Vertically reared cat* (c) *Normally reared cat*

Figure 4.20
Polar histograms for the distribution of neurons with specific orientations in the brains of kittens with different rearing experiences

MATHS MOMENT 🖩

Draw a pie chart with two segments to show the proportion of the cortical neurons in Blakemore and Cooper's kittens that were monocular and binocular.

MATHS MOMENT 🖩

As an alternative to the polar histograms, Blakemore and Cooper could have represented their results using a histogram. The x-axis would show the difference in degrees from the lines in the rearing environment, and the y-axis would show the frequency of lines at each orientation. Sketch a rough graph to show the general pattern of a histogram for a horizontally reared cat.

CONCLUSIONS

Blakemore and Cooper drew two main conclusions from this study:

1 As there was no evidence that areas of the cortex were 'silent', or that areas of cortical cells were missing, this suggests that the changes are not the consequence of degeneration.
2 The difference between the differently reared kittens suggests that neurons change their preferred orientation according to the stimulation they receive, matching the ability of the brain to respond to the features in its visual input.

EVALUATION

The research method

The study was a laboratory experiment so scientific equipment was available. The researchers used a specially designed environment – the visual apparatus – as well as having access to equipment for recording the activity of single brain cells. A controlled environment is typical of laboratory experiments, and the degree of control that can be maintained over animals is much greater than for human participants. The kittens' exposure to the visual apparatus was precisely timed and they were kept in the dark otherwise, thus eliminating many extraneous variables. The researchers could therefore be reasonably confident that it was the independent variable of the direction of the stripes in the environment that was affecting the dependent variables of behaviour and neuronal activity.

One potential weakness of laboratory studies using animals is the generalisability of the findings to humans. Although there is no doubt that there are enormous differences in both the behaviours and brains of cats and humans, it is highly likely that they share a common organisation of neurons in the visual cortex. Cats, like humans, are mammals; we have evolved from the same evolutionary ancestors, albeit a very long time ago. Furthermore, cats, like us, have stereoscopic colour vision, that is they can point both eyes at the same object in order to determine depth and can distinguish a range of different wavelengths of light. Finally, their visual acuity is good, that is, they can see clearly. Thus it seems likely that these functions are controlled in the same way in their brains as in ours, so generalisations should be valid.

Qualitative and quantitative data

The data gathered in this study were qualitative and quantitative, which is a strength. On the one hand, statistical testing of quantitative data allows easy comparison of the conditions, clearly showing that the rearing condition affected the development of the kittens' visual cortex. On the other hand, there was qualitative data about the appearance of the kitten's behaviour, which provides a more detailed description of the effects illustrating the consequences of the reported changes to neurons in the visual cortex.

Ethical considerations

As this is a laboratory experiment using animals, the ethical issues raised are different from those in all the other core studies. When thinking about ethics with regard to animals, psychologists are bound not only by ethical guidelines, but

Figure 4.21
Is animal research justified?

also by laws in place to protect animals. In this section we will briefly consider some of these issues.

Non-human animals can, like us, experience pain and distress, and experimenters must consider this. In an experiment where it is likely that the animal will have some unpleasant experience, the experimenters must aim to limit the amount pain or distress caused, its duration, and the number of animals that suffer. The latter should be achieved without compromising the validity of the findings, by using the best designs and procedures possible. Similarly, experiments should be conducted in such a way as to minimise the time an animal spends in pain or distress, and if this is severe and prolonged it should be put down. Furthermore, experiments should be conducted on animals only if no suitable alternative is possible, such as a simulation or a test on non-living tissue. When animal studies are done, an appropriate species judged to suffer the least should be used. Finally, one way in which decisions can be made about whether an experiment on animals should be conducted is to visualise it within Bateson's Cube (Bateson, 1986), see Figure 4.22. This suggests that any animal research should be conducted only if it can be justified in terms of a balance between (high) certainty of benefit (low) suffering and (high) quality of research.

The animals in Blakemore and Cooper's study would have suffered some pain and distress from the invasive physiological procedures. In addition, it is possible that they were distressed by being separated from their mother while in the visual apparatus and being tested, although it was noted that the kittens did not seem to be upset by the monotony of their surroundings, so this may not have been the case.

Furthermore, this study reports only on the results of two animals, and no fewer could possibly have been used in this study. In terms of the quality of research, the rigour of the procedures and controls used means that the research was high in quality, helping to justify the use of the animals.

That animals were used at all has to be considered. Research such as this could not have been conducted on humans, it is too damaging, and to have used species less likely to suffer would have made generalising the findings to people more difficult. As neither the area of neurons affected, nor the response of those cells to deprivation, was already known, the study could not have been achieved though simulation.

Although there have been many positive applications of Blakemore and Cooper's research, this could not have been predicted at the time, so there would have been low certainty that the kittens' suffering would reap benefits. Therefore, on balance, the study had potentially low certainty of medical benefit, high quality of research and some animal suffering.

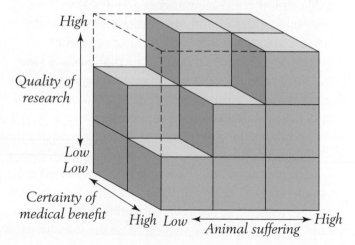

Figure 4.22
Bateson's Cube. This is used as a visual aid to judge the ethics of animal research. Ethically sound studies fall into the clear part of the cube.

QUESTION SPOTLIGHT!

Where would you put Blakemore and Cooper's study on Bateson's Cube?

Validity

The high levels of control imposed by conducting the study in laboratory conditions, and on animals, ensured that few extraneous variables could influence the outcomes, for example, the timing of exposure to the visual apparatus and keeping the kittens in the dark during the remaining time to ensure

that they had no experience of the opposite orientation lines. Procedures such as the collar they wore, and aspects of the apparatus, such as its length and clear floor, also contributed. As these all increased validity, the experimenters could be sure that it was the IV of exposure to stripes in one direction that was affecting the dependent variables of poor visually guided behaviour and absence of opposite-orientation neurons.

With respect to animal experiments, ecological validity is only indirectly relevant. A kitten in a plain striped environment is nothing like the life of a human, but if we consider what ecological validity really is, the question becomes more interesting. Ecological validity relates to the extent to which findings from one setting apply to another. So, do findings from cats apply to us? In some respects, yes: although their brains are much smaller, their visual cortex is likely to be very similar (see above). Are findings from a visually restricted environment such as the visual apparatus likely to apply to real life? The temptation is to say 'no', because our world is much more complex, but an experiment aims to remove extraneous variables to test just one factor. If all the variables apart from 'horizontal things' were removed from where you are sitting now, you would probably be left with a horizontal table top (with no legs), window ledges and a door frame (with no sides), etc. – in other words, lots of horizontal lines. The only way in which this differs from the kittens' situation is that your lines would have colour, texture and a range of thicknesses and distances.

Reliability

Laboratory procedures are typically highly standardised, and this is particularly so for studies on animals. It is possible to standardise aspects of an animal's environment and routine that it would not be possible to impose on people. For example, the kittens were always housed in the dark whenever they were not being used. Standardisation also ensures that the procedure is replicable. In the case of Blakemore and Cooper's study, it is interesting to note that almost every neuron tested showed the same pattern, of an orientation-specific response, and these were never closer than 20 degrees to the opposite orientation to the one they had seen. This suggests that the findings are reliable. Only two kittens were fully tested, however, which limits reliability, but this may not be particularly important in the context of this type of study.

Sampling bias

The participants were kittens, of which two were studied in full and provided the results of the physiological part of the study. Although this was only a preliminary investigation, and samples are always small in pilot studies, two is a very small

QUESTION SPOTLIGHT!

Figure 4.23
Human and cat visual cortex compared

Identify one similarity and one difference between a cat's brain and a human brain.

sample. Nevertheless, at least in the physiological part of the study, there is no reason to believe that all cats' brains would not work in the same way. Nevertheless, there is a possibility that one (or both) of the kittens was unusual and that other cats would not have developed in the same way.

Practical applications

Studies such as this are important in understanding the effects of visual deprivation in growing children. For example, if visual impairments are not detected or corrected early enough, these findings suggest that potentially long-term damage may be done to the cortical areas associated with the particular types of stimuli that cannot be seen. This is known to be the case with squint and with astigmatism. A person with a squint cannot make both eyes point in the same direction, and as a consequence depth perception is difficult as the field of view of the two eyes does not overlap sufficiently. One consequence of this is a decline in the number of binocular cells. Similarly, with astigmatism, a condition in which the eyeball is not perfectly round, lines in some orientations are not seen clearly. If detected and corrected early, this causes no problems, but if undetected, the neurons associated with the orientation of the defective sight will be understimulated and so will decline in number.

One further implication of Blakemore and Cooper's findings relates to the usefulness of laboratory animal studies in general. Benefiel and Greenough (1998) considered the welfare issues caused by the very limited environments experienced by laboratory animals and the effects this potentially has on their brain development. They observe that, as well as ethical problems, the abnormal brain development resulting from impoverished stimulation raises questions about the validity of generalisations to normal development. If animals are raised in normal laboratory cages, which themselves lack the richness of stimulation associated with living in the natural habitat, it is possible that any research done on them may under-represent their abilities and so give rise to potentially misleading results.

STRETCH & CHALLENGE

Use the Internet to find out about the research of G.M. Stratton and of Theodor Erismann and Ivo Kohler on adapting to inverted images. These studies demonstrated brain plasticity in humans. To what extent do their findings therefore suggest that it is valid to generalise from animal studies such as Blakemore and Cooper's, to humans?

WEB WATCH @

You can watch Erismann and Kohler's original film on YouTube. Search for 'Erismann and Kohler inversion goggles'.

STUDY 4

MAGUIRE *et al.*'s STUDY OF TAXI DRIVERS' BRAINS

Maguire, E.A., Gadian, D.G., Johnsrude, I.S., Good, C.D., Ashburner, J., Frackowiak, R.S.J., and Frith, C.D. (2000) Navigation-related structural change in the hippocampi of taxi drivers. *Proceedings of the National Academy of Science, USA.* **97**: 4398–4403R.

IN BRIEF

Aim: To investigate whether doing a job that demands navigational experience, and spending more years in that job, affect the volume of the hippocampus.

Method: The experimental analysis compared 16 right-handed male taxi drivers and 50 non-taxi-driving controls (IV), matched for gender, handedness and age range. The DV was hippocampal volume, measured with an MRI scan.
The correlational analysis explored a relationship between the measured variables of time spent as a taxi driver (between 1.5 and 28 years) and hippocampal volume, using 15 of the 16 taxi drivers, excluding the oldest.

Results: The posterior region (i.e. the back) of the hippocampus was larger in volume in taxi drivers, and the anterior region was larger in volume in non-taxi drivers. For the taxi drivers, the correlation between hippocampal volume and number of years spent driving a taxi was positive for the posterior region, and negative for the anterior region.

Conclusion: The distribution of grey matter in the hippocampus changes with use. The posterior hippocampus appears to store spatial information about the environment and to grow larger when used more.

KEY IDEAS

Localisation refers to the restriction of a particular brain function to a particular structure. **Plasticity** refers to the brain's ability to change in response to use.

Figure 4.24
The hippocampal volume of the black-capped chickadee increases during the food-storing season

CONTEXT

The concept of **localisation** of function is central to this study, as it illustrates a role of the hippocampus in navigation. The hippocampus appears to provide a 'cognitive map' – that is, a mental representation of spatial relationships. This role is well documented in previous research both on humans and on animals, as is the change in volume of the hippocampus with use. This is neural **plasticity**, the idea that brain structure and function can change with experience. In a review of research into hippocampal variations in nature, Lee *et al.* (1998) found that the hippocampus in birds and mammals, unlike most brain tissue, retains its ability to make new cells. So, when seasonal behaviours occur that use the hippocampus, such as homing or caching food, the hippocampus changes – growing more cells and increasing in volume. For example, Smulders *et al.* (1995) found that in birds such as the black-capped chickadee, which bury their excess food in the autumn and then retrieve it in winter, the hippocampus increases in volume during the period when they are learning food-store locations. Such evidence suggests that people who make greater use of their navigational skills might also develop hippocampi with a larger volume.

ACTIVITY ✳

BRAIN STRUCTURE SNAPSHOTS REVEAL SCIENCE BEHIND WHY ONLY HALF OF LONDON TAXI TRAINEES PASS THE KNOWLEDGE TEST

Scientists followed a group of 79 trainee drivers and a 'control group' of 31 non-taxi drivers. Magnetic Resonance Imaging (MRI) scans were used to take brain structure 'snapshots' of the volunteers, who were also given certain memory tasks.

At the start of the study, there were no obvious differences between participants' brains. Three to four years later, significant differences were seen. The 39 trainees who qualified had greater volumes of grey matter in their posterior hippocampus than the 40 who failed, or the non-taxi drivers.

In memory tasks, both qualified and non-qualified trainees performed better in tests involving London landmarks than non-taxi drivers. However, the qualified trainees – but not those who failed to qualify – were worse at other tasks, such as recalling complex visual information, than the controls. This suggests there might be a price to pay for the extra effort involved in acquiring the Knowledge, said the researchers.

They speculate that the findings may reflect an increase in the rate at which new neurons are generated and survive when faced with a significant mental challenge. The hippocampus is one of the few brain areas where new neurons continue to be born in adults.

Prof Maguire said: 'What is not clear is whether those trainees who became fully-fledged taxi drivers had some biological advantage over those who failed. Could it be, for example, that they have a genetic predisposition towards having a more adaptable "plastic" brain? In other words, the perennial question of "nature versus nurture" is still open.'
Source: The Mirror, 8 December 2011

Figure 4.25
Only around half of trainees finally make the grade as London taxi drivers by passing the Knowledge test

Q

1 Explain the finding that the trainees who qualified had greater volumes of grey matter in the posterior hippocampus than either those who did not qualify, or the control group.
2 What does Maguire mean by 'plastic' brains?
3 Why does she say that the 'perennial question of "nature versus nurture" is still open'?

AIM

The aim of the study was to investigate whether there was a difference in hippocampal volume between individuals who did, or did not, have extensive navigational experience.

WEB WATCH @

You can find out about the Knowledge here:
www.taxiknowledge.co.uk
and do a mock test here:
www.the-knowledge.org.uk

STRETCH & CHALLENGE

Maguire *et al.* (2000) refer to an earlier review article (Maguire *et al.*, 1999) which discusses issues in navigation research, including human and animal studies, sex differences and the use of different methodologies e.g. virtual reality and brain scanning. A free full-text copy is available at: http://wexler. free.fr (Click on 'library', scroll down and click on 'Maguire 1999: Human spatial navigation'.)

Read the article and produce a poster to illustrate one aspect of the review, explaining how it relates to the present study.

KEY IDEAS

In a **Magnetic Resonance Imaging** (MRI) scanner, a powerful magnetic field affects water molecules, and the changes in these molecules, which are detected by the scanner, produce a very detailed image that presents different brain areas in shades of black, grey and white. The technique of **voxel-based morphometry (VBM)** takes images in 1.5×1.5×1.5 mm 'blocks' (called voxels). This allows the volume of grey matter in small brain areas to be measured precisely. **Pixel counting** is an image analysis technique in which the number of pixels in a known area occupied by a particular tissue type (in this case hippocampal tissue) are counted and converted into a volume.

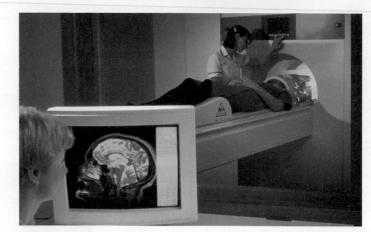

Figure 4.26 A Magnetic Resonance Imaging (MRI) scanner uses a powerful magnet to produce images of the brain

METHOD

Design

Although this study was based in a laboratory setting, the method used was a natural or 'quasi' experiment, because the participants already belonged to the existing groups of 'taxi drivers' and 'controls' – that is, they could not be allocated to the conditions by the researchers. A correlational analysis was also conducted, which considered the variables of hippocampal volume and time spent as a taxi driver.

Participants

The experimental group consisted of 16 right-handed male taxi drivers with a mean age of 44 years (range 32–62 years). Their experience as licensed London taxi drivers varied between 1.5 and 42 years (mean 14.3 years). Their training (i.e. time on 'the Knowledge') had taken an average 2 years (range 10 months–3.5 years, some part-, some full-time). All were medically, neurologically and psychiatrically healthy. The matched control group consisted of people on the **MRI-scan** database held at the unit where the experimental participants were scanned. From this group, females, left-handed males, those under 32 or over 62, and those with health problems, were excluded. This left scans of 50 people, which were used as the non-taxi-driving controls. The experimental and control groups did not differ in mean or range of age, and the spread of ages in each decade of life was similar in both groups.

Procedure

In the experimental part of the study an independent measures design was used. The independent variable was whether the individuals were London taxi drivers or were non-taxi drivers. Taxi drivers were chosen as their job demands a dependence on navigational skill and they are required to demonstrate a very high level of spatial understanding of locations and routes in London (the Knowledge). The dependent variable was the volume of the hippocampus (on the left and right side). This was assessed using measurements from MRI scans. There were several controls, which included:
* matching the samples in terms of age, gender and handedness;

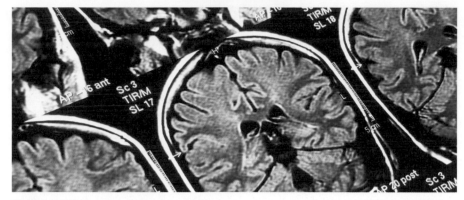

Figure 4.27
MRI scans are detailed images of brain structure

💡 **KEY IDEAS**

A researcher is described as working **blind** when they do not know which level of the IV a participant they are testing belongs to. This arrangement, called a 'single blind procedure', helps to avoid experimenter bias.

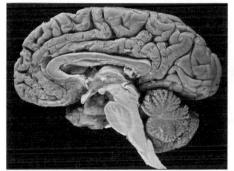

(a) sagittal plane

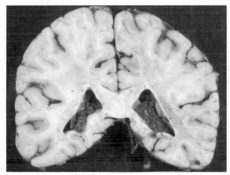

(b) coronal plane

Figure 4.28
Brain sections

- measurements of brain volume being done by one experienced individual who, in order to ensure that the assessments were consistent, was unaware of each participants' condition (i.e. they were working '**blind**'); and
- both experimental and control participants being scanned in the same MRI scanner unit.

The scans from 13 of the control group were used to produce an image 'template' against which all scans were judged using a technique called **voxel-based morphometry (VBM)**. These measures were used to calculate the volume of grey matter in different regions of the brain.

An image-analysis technique called **pixel counting** was used to compare 16 taxi drivers with 16 precisely age-matched controls. The total hippocampal volume on the left and right was measured using three-dimensional information from at least 26 visual 'slices' of each hippocampus, taken at 1.5mm intervals (therefore covering a total length of about 4cm). These slices were taken in 'cross sections' of the hippocampus on a coronal plane – that is, at right angles to the longest length of the hippocampus (Figure 4.28b). The images were analysed by counting the number of pixels occupied by hippocampal tissue, which was then converted into a volume. This volume was corrected for total intracranial volume – the size of the person's brain – (based on measurements from slices on

QUESTION SPOTLIGHT! ⭐

This study used a detailed matching procedure. Make sure you could answer a question asking for the ways in which the groups were matched.

QUESTION SPOTLIGHT! ⭐

Can you explain why it was important that the researcher assessing the scans was 'blind' to the group to which each participant belonged?

MATHS MOMENT 🖩

Which correlation between time spent as a taxi driver and right posterior hippocampal volume is stronger – the one based on VBM or the one based on pixel counting? Explain your answer.

STRETCH & CHALLENGE ◎

Maguire *et al.* (2003) tested navigation in an unfamiliar virtual environment and found better navigators did not have greater hippocampal volume. This supports the idea that level of navigational experience and the consequent brain changes, rather than innate navigational skill due to brain differences at birth, account for the navigational ability of taxi drivers. Explain why.

You can read more about this study here:

http://cream.fil.ion.ucl.ac.uk/Maguire/ Maguire2003.pdf

TABLE 4.3 PIXEL-COUNTING ESTIMATES OF HIPPOCAMPAL VOLUME

Side of brain	Intracranial volume correction	Taxi drivers	Controls
Right	Corrected	4159	4080
	Uncorrected	4300	4280
Left	Corrected	3977	3918
	Uncorrected	4155	4092

a sagittal plane – Figure 4.28a) to make all participants' data comparable. The same experienced researcher counted the pixels on all scans (both experimental and control) but was 'blind' to each participant's condition.

In the correlational analysis, a possible link between the two variables of time spent as a taxi driver (both in training on the Knowledge, and subsequently) and hippocampal volume was explored. One participant was excluded from this analysis as he had been a taxi driver for much longer than all the others (42 years, compared to 28 years for the next nearest participant).

RESULTS

This study collected only quantitative data. From the experimental investigation, the VBM data showed that the only brain areas with a significant difference between taxi drivers and the control group were the left and right hippocampi. The difference demonstrated by this technique was significant for the left and right posterior hippocampus (the back part), but not the left and right anterior hippocampus (the front part). The amount of grey matter in the hippocampus of taxi drivers was significantly different from that of non-taxi drivers.

The total hippocampal volumes measured by pixel counting were smaller on every measure for the controls, but the differences were not significant (see Table 4.3). Further statistical analysis, however, found differences between specific hippocampal areas and the left and right sides between taxi drivers and the controls. These differences were similar to those in Table 4.3, but were significant (see Figure 4.29).

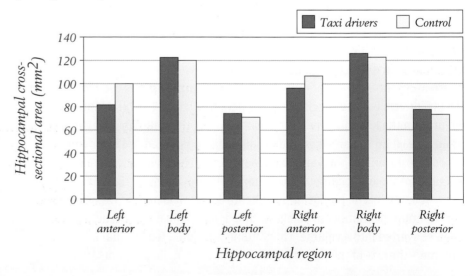

Figure 4.29
Comparison of hippocampal regions using data from pixel counting

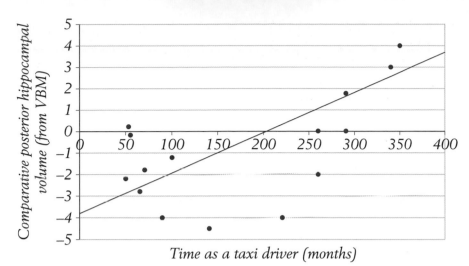

Figure 4.30
Positive correlation between time spent taxi-driving and posterior hippocampal volume.
Source: Maguire et al. (2000), fig. 3b, p.4401

MATHS MOMENT 🖩

Use the scatter diagram in Figure 4.30 to read off the time each participant had been a taxi driver. Use these figures to work out the median time spent taxi driving.

Figure 4.29 shows several differences that were significant:
- Controls had greater anterior hippocampal volume than taxi drivers.
- For both groups, the right hippocampal volume was greater than the left.
- The posterior hippocampal volume of taxi drivers was significantly greater in volume.

However posterior hippocampal volume did not differ between the left and right sides.

In the correlational investigation, a significant relationship was found between time spent as a taxi driver and right-posterior hippocampal volume. Correlation coefficients of r = 0.6 (based on VBM) and r = 0.5 (based on pixel counting) both indicated a positive correlation (see Figure 4.30). The pixel-counting data also revealed a correlation between anterior hippocampal volume and time spent working as a taxi driver. Here, the correlation coefficient of r = −0.6 indicated a negative correlation. The data from the driver whose scores were omitted from this analysis also conformed to the pattern: with 42 years' experience, his VBM measure was 13.7.

CONCLUSIONS

The results suggest that the distribution of grey matter in the hippocampus changes with use because the posterior hippocampus stores information about spatial relations in the environment, so its volume increases in response to demand for navigational skills. This explanation is more likely than the idea that people with a large posterior hippocampus choose to be taxi drivers. This is because the correlational data show that, as taxi drivers developed a better understanding of routes and locations, improving their cognitive maps over time, the volume of the posterior hippocampus increased.

EVALUATION

The research method

This research was a laboratory-based study, so many of the typical strengths and limitations apply (see p. 225). The scanning procedure took place in a highly controlled environment, and the sample was carefully selected. This eliminated many extraneous variables, such as the possibility that the hippocampal volume gets bigger (or smaller) with age, or that any differences in the volume of the left and right hippocampi were a function of handedness. Maguire *et al.* could therefore be reasonably confident that it was the independent variable (navigational experience) that was affecting the dependent variable (hippocampal volume). Laboratory procedures are generally straightforward to replicate, as the controls and standardised procedures make them reliable.

Quantitative data

A strength of Maguire *et al.*'s study was the use of quantitative data that could be analysed statistically, allowing the researchers to be more certain about their conclusions. Measurements of length and volume are highly objective, assuming the individual applying the criteria for measurement is reliable and independent of experimenter bias (see above).

Ethical considerations

The ethical issues of informed consent and competence were important in relation to the taxi drivers. Although MRI scanning is not in itself dangerous, it does carry risks for some individuals. An MRI scanner generates a powerful magnetic field, so it is therefore dangerous for people with metal implants, such as pacemakers or pinned bones. It would have been important for the ethical conduct of the study to ensure that the taxi drivers were not putting themselves at any greater risk than in their normal lives by offering to be scanned. Also, an MRI scanner is a confined space and it is noisy. Some people find this unpleasant or frightening. The participants would need to have been given sufficient details of the intended procedure to be 'informed', and given the option to be included in the study or not, i.e. to 'consent'. The control participants were not given unnecessary brain scans as their data were retrieved from an existing store, thereby avoiding the potential for additional distress in this group.

Validity

The validity of the comparison of taxi drivers and a separate control group could be questioned. As the occupations and interests of the control group were not considered, it is possible that this group included individuals with other reasons for a high demand on navigational skills – such as people who go orienteering, or happened to drive to lots of different places for their work. In fact, it is unlikely that this was a problem, as the correlational analysis demonstrated an increase in hippocampal volume with experience.

A potential weakness in laboratory experiments is often a lack of ecological validity, but the realism of the environment and task are not at issue here. The participants did not have to perform a task and, although the scanner is clearly a highly artificial environment, this cannot affect the volume of a brain area – that is, the participants cannot have responded to demand characteristics. In addition, the researcher assessing the scans was unaware of the participants' condition, thus increasing the validity of the measure of the DV, as they were less likely to be biased.

Reliability

Reliability means consistency, so a procedure is reliable if it can be precisely replicated and always produces the same results. To achieve consistency in the way in which the hippocampal volumes were recorded from the brain scans, one experienced individual assessed all of the images.

QUESTION SPOTLIGHT!

Sketch the graph in Figure 4.30 onto graph paper with an extended scale to cover the omitted taxi driver, and include these data. *Can you explain how these data support the general pattern?*

QUESTION SPOTLIGHT!

Maguire *et al.* studied only taxi drivers. Munte *et al.* (2002) and Gaser and Schlaug (2003) found that musicians' brains changed in response to experiences, and Dragnaski *et al.* (2004) found brain differences in jugglers undergoing training.

Could you explain what these studies show about the generalisibility of Maguire et al.'s findings?

Sampling bias

The experimental sample of 16 taxi drivers was quite large given that they had to be willing to undergo MRI scanning. As they were all London taxi drivers, they all lived in the same area, although there is no reason to suppose that men from any other city would differ.

As the sample was all male right handers, this might limit the generalisability of the findings, as navigation by females, or left-handed people, may differ. However, the age spread, the range and the nature of training (full-time or part-time), and time in the job all contributed to a varied sample. The matching of experimental to control participants used several important criteria (age, gender and handedness).

Practical applications

The identification of brain plasticity in human adults has important implications for hopes of rehabiliting people with brain damage. Although this study only shows that the hippocampus can alter its neuronal circuitry in adulthood, it suggests that other brain areas could too. This has the potential to lead to advances in diagnosis and treatment, identifying deterioration that could put people at risk, and using environmental demand to encourage the redevelopment of brain tissue. For example, Griffith *et al.* (2013) tested older patients with mild Alzheimer's disease and found that those with greater hippocampal damage also had poorer lane control when driving.

STRETCH & CHALLENGE

Why might Maguire *et al.*'s findings be unlikely to generalise to females? Search the internet for scientific evidence for gender differences in navigational ability.

STRETCH & CHALLENGE

While we may be confident that brains function independently of cultural influences, it might be possible to argue that the tasks expected of London taxi drivers differ from those in other major cities. For example, look up a map of central New York. How does the structure and naming of the streets differ from that of an English city? Search for a map of another city, such Venice. To what extent might geographical differences, or differences in the training of taxi drivers, mean that the conclusions of Maguire's study were ethnocentric?

COMPARISON OF STUDIES

Blakemore and Cooper's Study of the Impact of Early Visual Experience *Maguire et al.'s Study of Taxi Drivers' Brains*

THE TOPIC
Brain plasticity in the visual cortex versus the hippocampus

The studies by Blakemore and Cooper and Maguire *et al.* are about biological psychology, specifically about brain plasticity: both found that the brain adapts to experience with the environment. However, Blakemore and Cooper were investigating changes at the level of individual neurons and showed that, in the visual cortex, orientation-specific cells can change the kind of stimulus they respond to according the animal's early visual environment. Maguire *et al.* in contrast, were studying effect of taxi driving on the size of the hippocampus and found that with time spent taxi-driving, the posterior hippocampus increased in volume (and the anterior hippocampus decreased). An important similarity is that both studies found that the overall volume or number of cells did not appear to change, only their function or distribution.

THE RESEARCH METHOD AND DESIGN
Both experiments use an independent measures design, laboratory or quasi

Although both studies were conducted in laboratories and used an independent measures design, they were different types of experiments, and Maguire *et al.* also used a correlation. Blakemore and Cooper used a laboratory experiment to compare kittens raised with vertical or horizontal stripes, i.e. the environment could be controlled and the kittens could be randomly allocated to the levels of the IV. Maguire *et al.* had to use a quasi-experiment, because the participants in the two levels of the IV, taxi-drivers and non-taxi drivers, could not be randomly allocated. In addition, the time spent driving could not be controlled. In both cases rigorous controls over testing could be imposed, increasing validity; for example in the kittens' environment and the way that hippocampal volume was sampled.

An important consequence of using a quasi-experiment for Maguire *et al.* is that there may have been uncontrolled differences between the participants which affected the IV. Although they could be fairly sure that people who chose to be taxi drivers do not have larger posterior hippocampal volume to start with — as the correlation showed it increased with time driving — it may be the case that the hippocampi in such people respond more readily to environmental input about navigation. If so, the findings may not generalise beyond those who chose professions requiring navigational skills.

SAMPLING TECHNIQUE AND THE SAMPLE
Human versus animal participants

In the physiological part of Blakemore and Cooper's study there were only two participants, one in each condition. Although this is a very small sample, this is less important in physiological studies as it is likely that brains respond in consistent ways. However, as the sample was kittens, there is some question as to whether the findings would generalise to humans. In fact, the findings of Maguire *et al.* confirm that the human brain, even in adulthood, when less sensitivity to environmental input would be expected, is able to change in response to demands. Brain plasticity therefore appears to be a feature of animal and human brains and, at least in people, over much of the lifespan.

EXPERIMENTAL MATERIALS AND MEASUREMENT OF THE DV
Ecological validity and quantitative data

Both experiments were conducted in laboratories, and this may reduce ecological validity. Neither experiment could have been conducted in the field, and both used scientific equipment to measure the DV. In Blakemore and Cooper's study, microelectrodes were used to measure the activity of individual neurons and Maguire *et al.* used MRI scans to measure hippocampal volume. Both produced reliable, objective, quantitative data. This allowed both studies to use statistical testing. Importantly, although the measurements were taken in artificial situations (during surgery or in a brain scanner) this is not important as it could not have affected the participants performance because expectations cannot affect neuronal activity or brain size. A small amount of qualitative data were also recorded by Blakemore and Cooper in their descriptions of the kittens in the more everyday situation of a typical furnished room. These showed the same kind of effects as the more rigorous behavioural and physiological tests, suggesting that the kittens' deficits demonstrated in the quantitative measures were representative of behaviour in everyday situations.

APPLICATIONS
Understanding the effects of the environment and experience on brain development, in early life and adulthood
The topics of both studies have applicability to real world settings to help us to understand that the brain is capable of undergoing structural change in response to experience. This could be used to help to avoid damage to the brain and to facilitate brain development. Blakemore and Cooper's research can help us to identify the risks associated with uncorrected visual problems and Maguire *et al.'s* findings have implications for the detection and rehabilitation of people who have suffered brain damage from injury or disease.

KEY THEME: BRAIN PLASTICITY

These studies have illustrated that the brains of both young animals and human adults can change. Alteration at a cellular level allowed the individuals to perform better given the environmental demands they experienced, either visually or with regard to finding routes through London. In Blakemore and Cooper's study individual neurons became finely tuned to the orientation of lines experienced by the kittens and in Maguire *et al.*'s study, the taxi drivers' posterior hippocampi, performing key roles in navigation, increased in volume.

KEY THEME 🔑

Brain plasticity
Both studies show that experience matters; at a cellular level, the brain can respond to the **environment** and change its capacity to respond to those demands.

Blakemore and Cooper
Laboratory experiment on the effect of a controlled experience (line orientation) on the visual cortex using two young kittens.

Similarities
Both were experiments on brain plasticity with control of the IV and some procedural controls, e.g. keeping the kittens in the dark and matching the taxi drivers and controls. Both used the same experimental design (independent measures) and collected quantitative data.

Maguire *et al.*
Quasi-experiment investigating the effects of naturally gained navigational experience on hippocampal volume of adult humans.

PRACTICE QUESTIONS

Here are some of the sorts of questions that you could be asked in Sections A and B of your A level exam, and some examples of successful and less successful answers. We look at Section B questions in more detail in Chapter 6 on pages 206–18.

SECTION A: CORE STUDIES

1 What was the aim of the study by Blakemore and Cooper? [2]

2 From the study by Blakemore and Cooper:
   (a) What is a laboratory experiment? [2]
   (b) Explain why the study by Blakemore and Cooper is a laboratory experiment. [2]

3 Describe **two** controls used in the study by Blakemore and Cooper. [2]

4 Outline **one** reason why the study by Blakemore and Cooper can be considered unethical. [2]

5 From the study by Maguire *et al.* of taxi drivers' brains: Explain what an MRI scan measures. [2]

6 Outline **one** piece of evidence that suggests that the brains of taxi drivers are different from the brains of non-taxi drivers. [2]

7 Suggest **one** application of the findings from the study of taxi drivers' brains by Maguire *et al.* [2]

8 From Maguire *et al.*'s study of taxi drivers' brains:
   (a) Suggest the purpose of using a correlation in this study. [2]
   (b) Describe what the correlation indicated in this study. [2]

SECTION B: AREAS, PERSPECTIVES AND DEBATES

12 (a) Describe the difference between a biological explanation for behaviour and a social explanation for behaviour. [4]

   (b) Explain how **one** psychological study can be considered as providing a biological explanation for behaviour. [5]

   (c) Evaluate the usefulness of providing a biological explanation for behaviour. Support your answer with evidence from **one** appropriate psychological study. [6]

   (d) Identify and discuss ethical considerations in relation to biological psychology. Support your answer with evidence from appropriate psychological studies. [20]

SECTION A   3 Describe **two** controls used in the study by Blakemore and Cooper. [2]

Liam's answer:

One control was vertical stripes and one was horizontal stripes.

We say: Unfortunately Liam has given an incorrect answer to this question. He has given details about the two conditions of the independent variable rather than two controls. This sort of mistake is easy to make if you don't read the questions carefully!

Rina's answer:

Blakemore and Cooper controlled the environment that the kittens were raised in several ways. One control was that all the kittens in the experimental conditions were reared in complete darkness for the first two weeks of their lives and another was that they all wore a collar to prevent them from seeing their own bodies.

We say: Excellent. These are definitely controls and not variables and Rina has explained them very well indeed.

4 Outline one reason why the study by Blakemore and Cooper can be considered unethical. [2]

Liam's answer:

The kittens were not able to give consent.

Rina's answer:

It could be argued that the kittens would have experienced pain and distress as a result of the procedures that they were subjected to and the fact that they were removed from their mothers at birth.

We say: This would not gain any credit. There are different ethical guidelines for research with animals and consent is not part of this. (For details about these guidelines, see page 145.)

We say: This is a good answer to the question. The question only asked for an outline of one reason why this study could be considered unethical and this does this very well.

7 Suggest one application of the findings from the study of taxi drivers' brains by Maguire et al. [2]

Liam's answer:

This study could help us determine who would be a good taxi driver.

Rina's answer:

This study suggests that our brains have plasticity. This would suggest that structural change is possible and may even mean that treatments are possible for those who experience brain damage or deterioration of functioning such as Alzheimer's disease.

We say: This is not the case. These findings suggest that the differences between the brains of taxi drivers and the controls are likely to be the result of the years they have spent driving taxis rather than differences that existed beforehand.

We say: Another excellent answer from Rina. This shows very good understanding of a complex idea. The use of the word 'suggest' is particularly appropriate in this answer.

SECTION B   12 (a) Describe the difference between a biological explanation for behaviour and a social explanation for behaviour. [4]

Liam's answer:

A biological explanation looks at biological factors and a social explanation looks at social factors. Biological factors are internal to the person, like the functions of the brain and the nervous system, and social factors are external to the person, like the social environment and other people.

We say: The first sentence of this answer doesn't really tell us anything at all but the second does show some understanding of the difference between the two explanations. A little more information might help here.

Rina's answer:

In some ways this is related to the nature–nurture debate. Biological explanations tend to be nature explanations and social explanations tend to be nurture explanations (although this is a little simplistic). For example, a biological explanation for aggression would focus on the functioning of the brain and the nervous system and might explain aggression as the result of hormones or even brain damage. A social explanation might look at factors in the environment such as the presence of aggressive cues, aggressive models or crowds. However they can overlap because experience may have an effect on the biology of someone, such as the changes to the taxi drivers' brains shown by Maguire et al. or the fact that external stress can cause biological symptoms.

We say: Rina has put a lot of very good detail into this answer but this answer does lack a little bit of focus. The examples are great and the links to the core study by Maguire *et al.* is a useful one even though this was not explicitly asked for. It is possible that Rina is giving more information than is required here as this is only a four-mark question. The final point about the fact that the explanations are not totally different is an excellent one but probably not necessary in response to this question. Take care when answering questions that you check how many marks are available. You don't want to waste time giving too much information.

We say: A really interesting and well-written answer from Rina which demonstrates excellent understanding of the study and of the biological area. The links to debates such as free will and determinism are excellent as are the examples from the core study. One criticism that could be made of this answer is that it seems to focus on the core study almost entirely whereas the question asks for the usefulness of providing a biological explanation for behaviour in general and for this answer to be illustrated with examples from one core study. Flipping the answer around and starting with the points in the final sentence might produce an answer slightly more focused on the question.

12 (c) Evaluate the usefulness of providing a biological explanation for behaviour. Support your answer with evidence from one appropriate psychological study. [6]

Liam's answer:

The study by Sperry was a useful study because it showed us what each hemisphere does. It showed us that information from the right visual field goes to the left hemisphere and that information from the left visual field goes to the right hemisphere. It showed us that people who had their hemispheres deconnected didn't know what was in the other hemisphere.

We say: Liam has not grasped what the question is asking for. His answer is not focusing on the usefulness of providing a biological explanation – it is simply telling us what Sperry found.

Rina's answer:

The study by Casey offers a biological explanation for the ability to resist temptation, suggesting that there are differences in activity in the inferior frontal gyrus that are maintained through childhood and into adulthood. This is useful because it suggests that such differences are innate and even though Casey et al. showed that contextual cues are important, it is still suggesting that some of this type of behaviour is biologically determined. This might have links to free will and the ability to hold someone responsible for their behaviour or not. The more understanding we have of the extent to which biology determines our behaviour the less likely we are to hold someone responsible for behaviour that is outside of their control.

THE BIOLOGICAL AREA OF PSYCHOLOGY

1 We can understand differences in cognition and behaviour in terms of brain differences and changes

The brain is the most complex structure within the nervous system. The human brain is also more complex and, relative-to-body size, bigger than that of any other animal. This makes it important, but also difficult, to study. Although the nervous system is ultimately responsible for all of our emotions, cognitions and behaviours, the brain is in turn affected by other factors, such as our experiences. Blakemore and Cooper's study showing adaptation of individual brain cells to experience used an animal to investigate deprivation effects that could not be tested using humans, although the findings are likely to generalise to humans. This is possible because the brain of a cat, particularly the visual system, is so similar to our own. Maguire *et al.*'s study also illustrated brain plasticity and the complexity of the brain – how even two small areas, those of the anterior and posterior hippocampus, serve somewhat different functions. It specifically demonstrated how the brain determines behaviour through cognition, by providing evidence for the role of the hippocampus in navigational ability. Furthermore, this study clearly showed how experience affects the brain as more navigational experience leads to an increase in hippocampal volume.

Sperry's study served to show how the complex structure of the brain is related to its function, with the corpus callosum integrating the simultaneous streams of consciousness from the left and right hemispheres. Casey *et al.'s* study also supported the idea of localisation, with two areas being associated with delay gratification.

2 Differences in emotion, cognition and behaviour are genetically controlled

Maguire *et al.*'s study is one of many that expose or explore a key question in biological psychology: the extent to which any characteristic is determined by genetics versus the environment. In the case of Maguire *et al.*'s study, they demonstrated that there were changes in the hippocampus due to the environment, here provided by the Knowledge and subsequent taxi driving. This is an example of the nature-nurture debate, which is central to the biological area: nature representing the biological influences, and nurture the environmental ones. It is possible, of course, that some underlying genetic factor predisposed the individuals who became taxi drivers to do so precisely because they were able to learn navigational information. Teasing out the relative importance of the two influences is a central issue for biological psychology. The same could not be said of Blakemore and Cooper's findings, these were purely due to nurture, although the capacity of neurons to change their orientation specificity is an example of nature. Casey *et al.*'s study suggested that there may have been underlying differences in the brains of 4-year-olds as those with persisting high- or low-impulse control had differences in brain function as adults.

3 Brain activity can be studied and related to observable, measureable changes

Until electrical measures were developed in the early 20th century, the only way to study brain activity was by lesioning. This could provide some evidence for brain function as the absence of a behaviour or ability when a brain area was damaged implied that the damaged area was important for that function. However, as we can see from Sperry's study, the absence of the corpus callosum might prevent an individual from saying the answer to a question, even though the corpus callosum is not, itself, required for deciding upon or producing verbal response. Sperry's study showed how the absence of the corpus callosum led to a range of clearly observable cognitive deficits in a laboratory setting. Maguire *et al.* conversely showed that cognitive differences (in navigational skill) were linked to changes in brain structure. Casey *et al.* used fMRI to measure brain activity in regions associated with delay gratification and Blakemore and Cooper used single-cell recording to measure the activity of neurons in the visual cortex. These two studies illustrated how biological activity in the brain (which could not previously have been investigated) related to qualitative reports and quantitative measures of both the kittens' behaviour in relation to objects and lines and the ability of children and adults to resist temptation.

STRENGTHS AND WEAKNESSES OF THE BIOLOGICAL AREA
Strengths

1   **Scientific research methods.** All the studies in this chapter have used rigorous procedures. Laboratory experiments are typical of the biological area, as is the use of precise, scientific apparatus. Equipment such as that used by Sperry allows researchers to impose stringent controls so that they can be certain that extraneous variables are not responsible for any effects they observe.

This helps to ensure that the studies are valid. Techniques such as single-cell recording, MRI and fMRI are reliable tools for measurement.

2 **Leads to advances in understanding and practical applications.** By providing an understanding of the biological principles underlying the function of the nervous system, biological psychology offers a wealth of information that helps us to understand human responses. Furthermore, this can help us to understand what can go wrong with emotional, cognitive and behavioural control, and thus potentially help us to alleviate mental disorders or damage caused by illness or injury. Investigative techniques (such as MRI), drug treatments and some rehabilitation techniques rely on the findings of biological research.

Weaknesses

1 **Lack of ecological validity.** A common criticism of biological psychology – precisely because it uses highly controlled laboratory procedures – is that its findings may not relate well to real life. Maguire *et al.* studied brain activity in a small sample of people based on recordings taken inside a brain scanner, yet drew conclusions relating to navigational ability – a particularly 'real-world' behaviour. Sperry explored the cognition of people who had undergone an unusual operation and

therefore exhibited an unusual set of observable deficits. In contrast, in the 'real world', these people demonstrated few problems. Blakemore and Cooper studied visual development in kittens in an artificial environment. Casey *et al.* tested temptation in contrived experimental settings. These factors mean that the participants were unlikely to respond in entirely normal ways. Such criticisms illustrate the way in which biological studies might be divorced from the tasks of day-to-day life (a lack of mundane realism) and so might not generalise to the experiences of people outside the specific and contrived setting in which they were obtained (a lack of ecological validity). However, biological recordings are unlikely to be affected in the way that overt behaviour might be.

2 Reductionism. It is often argued that the biological approach is reductionist – because it attempts to explain complex behaviour in terms of genes, brain structure and chemicals. In reality, modern biological psychologists are exploring the extent to which such factors are important, rather than studying them to the exclusion of other factors. Nevertheless, the biological approach does not explore, and therefore cannot necessarily explain, how complex systems interact.

C5

INDIVIDUAL

DIFFERENCES

This area of psychology considers that there are many differences between individuals, as well as similarities. In this chapter we will look four studies.

For AS we consider two studies that highlight the theme of understanding disorders:

1 Freud's (1909) case study of a young boy experiencing the Oedipus Complex. The aim was to document and interpret the dreams, fantasies, anxieties and behaviour of Little Hans throughout a period of his psychosexual development.

2 Baron-Cohen *et al.'s* (1997) experiment looking at theory of mind in high-functioning adults with autism. They investigated this disorder using a specially designed task known as 'reading the eyes in the mind'.

For A level we additionally look at two studies paired around the theme of measuring differences:

3 Gould's (1982) review of the use of IQ testing. Gould demonstrates how early research involving mass mental testing has been used to support racist arguments of white superiority.

4 Hancock *et al.'s* (2011) study of the language of psychopathic murderers. The research uses interviews and statistical techniques to directly compare psychopathic and non-psychopathic offenders' accounts of crime narratives.

We will look at these studies in detail, evaluating and exploring applications of each. We also consider them in their pairs, using them to think about the key themes. Finally we will use them to explore issues of individual differences in psychology, looking at the strengths and limitations of this area.

FREUD'S CASE STUDY OF LITTLE HANS

Freud, S. (1909) Analysis of a phobia in a five-year-old boy. In The Pelican Freud Library (1997) Vol. **8**, *Case Histories*, pp. 169–306.

IN BRIEF

Aim: To record a case of the Oedipus Complex.

Method: A boy was followed through the course of a phobia of horses, to the end of the phobia. His dreams, anxieties and fantasies were recorded by his father and passed on to Freud, who interpreted them in line with his idea of the Oedipus Complex.

Results: Hans' fear of horses was interpreted as anxiety caused by a threat to castrate him in the context of his father banning him from his parents' bed. Dreams and fantasies were interpreted in the light of this theoretical position.

Conclusion: Hans experienced castration anxiety and the Oedipus Complex, but resolved this through his fantasies.

STRETCH & CHALLENGE

Of all Freud's ideas the **Oedipus Complex** is perhaps the most controversial. Freud's evidence came from self-analysis, the Little Hans case study and an analysis of literature in which Freud believed the Oedipus Complex cropped up fairly often. Consider these sources of evidence. What are the problems with using self-analysis and clinical case studies as evidence? Elements of the Oedipus Complex can be still be seen in modern films ranging from Star Wars to Back to the Future, but is this evidence?

CONTEXT

Sigmund Freud remains the world's most famous psychologist, even more than 70 years after his death. Freud wrote from the 1890s until the 1930s. His approach to psychological theory and therapy – called psychoanalysis – forms the basis of the psychodynamic area of psychology. Freud had a number of important ideas, some more controversial than others. Most controversially of all he proposed that childhood can be seen as a series of psychosexual stages. Each stage is characterised by a fixation on an area of the body and a distinct pattern of relationships to parents.

The oral stage takes place in the first year of life. The mouth is the main focus of pleasure at this stage, as the child is suckling and weaning. At this stage, they are totally dependent on their main carer, and they acquire the ability to accept nurture and have close relationships. From around one to three years of age, the child goes through the anal stage. Here the focus of pleasure is the anus, as the child learns to retain and expel faeces at will. This is also the time at which the parents start to exert control over the child's behaviour by potty-training them, and this is when the child acquires a pattern of relating to authority.

The third and most crucial Freudian stage of development is the phallic stage (from the word phallus, meaning penis), which lasts from around three to six years of age. In the phallic stage, boys go through the Oedipus Complex. This involves the development of a strong attachment to the opposite-sex parent, and a sense of the same-sex parent as a rival for their affection. Freud came to this conclusion after a period of self-analysis. He revealed his own **Oedipus Complex** in a letter to a friend: 'I have found in my own case too being in love with my mother and jealous of my father, and now I consider it a universal event in early childhood.'

One of Freud's most famous cases is that of Little Hans, whom Freud believed to be going through the Oedipus Complex.

AIM

To give an account of a boy who was suffering from a phobia of horses and a range of other symptoms, and to use this case to illustrate the existence of the Oedipus Complex.

METHOD

Participant

The participant was a Jewish boy from Vienna, Austria. He was five years old at the start of the study, although some events were recorded from a couple of years earlier. He was called Little Hans in the study, however his real name, Herbert Graf, was well known. Little Hans was suffering from a phobia of horses. His father, a fan of Freud's work, referred the case to Freud and went on to provide much of the case information.

Design

The design was a clinical case study. This means that the participant is a patient undergoing therapy. In this case, Freud's direct input in the therapy was very limited. Accounts of how often Freud saw Little Hans vary a little, but it almost certainly was not more than twice. Hans' father conducted regular discussions with Hans and passed these on to Freud, who analysed them in line with his theory. The results consist of Freud's analysis.

Case history

From around three years of age, Hans developed a great interest in his penis – his 'widdler' as he called it – and it was reported that he played with it regularly. Eventually, his mother became so cross that she threatened to send for a doctor to have it cut off if he didn't stop. Hans was very disturbed by this and developed a fear of castration. At around the same time, Hans saw a horse collapse and die in the street, and he was very upset as a result. When Hans was three-and-a-half years old his baby sister was born.

Shortly after this, when Hans was four years old, he developed a phobia of horses. Specifically, he was afraid that a white horse would bite him. When reporting this to Freud, Hans' father noted that the fear of horses seemed to relate to their large penises that reminded him of his dissatisfaction with the size of his own penis. At around the same time as the phobia of horses developed, a conflict developed between Hans and his father. Hans had been in the habit for some time of getting into his parents' bed in the morning and cuddling his mother. However, his father began to object to this. Hans' phobia worsened to the extent that he would not leave the family house. At this point, he also suffered attacks of generalised anxiety.

By the age of five Hans' phobia lessened, initially becoming limited to white horses, with thick pieces of harness (what we would now call a noseband) and blinkers in front of their eyes – which were likened by Freud to Hans' father's

KEY IDEAS

The **Oedipus Complex** is Freud's term to describe the three-way relationship dynamic between a child and the two parents, in which the child attaches strongly to the opposite-sex parent, and starts to see the same-sex parent as a rival. The name 'Oedipus' comes from Sophocles' play, *Oedipus Rex*, which was itself based on a Greek legend. In this play, Laius of Thebes is told he will one day be killed by his son, Oedipus, so he abandons him. However, Oedipus survives, and, as an adult, ends up killing his father and marrying his mother, unaware of who they are. Freud believed that we all react powerfully to this story because it triggers memories of our own Oedipus Complex.

 KEY IDEAS

Hans reported a fantasy to his father. Hans dreamed that there were two giraffes in his room at night. One was large and the other 'crumpled.' Hans took the crumpled giraffe away from the large one, which cried out. He then sat on the crumpled giraffe.

Figure 5.1
Hans dreamed of two giraffes in his room at night.

DO IT YOURSELF

Freud interpreted the giraffe fantasy as an expression of the Oedipus Complex. Have a go for yourself at dream interpretation. You will need one or more volunteers to keep a dream diary for a few days. This is kept by the participants' bed and is filled in immediately on waking. Participants bring their dream diaries for analysis. There are important ethical considerations here; participants must be fully aware that interpretations may be sexual in nature and they must have the right to withdraw from the study or withhold particular dreams from analysis. Participants' dreams should be treated as confidential; in fact we advise anonymising the dreams so that the group does not know who dreamed any particular dream. Then have a go at interpreting the dreams bearing in mind Freud's ideas. It's as simple as that! Obviously interpretations will vary and you have no way of testing their validity but hey ho! That's dream interpretation for you!

MATHS MOMENT

The data collected in the Little Hans case were qualitative.

1   Explain what is meant by the term 'qualitative' and how this type of data differs from quantitative data.

2   Explain one way in which qualitative data collected in the Little Hans case study could be converted to quantitative data.

QUESTION SPOTLIGHT!

You should be able to outline one dream, fantasy or phobia experienced by Little Hans. When talking about dreams, be clear that the giraffe dream is a true dream. Day-dreams such as the plumber are fantasies, not dreams.

moustache and glasses – and then disappearing altogether. The end of the phobia was marked by two fantasies:

- Hans fantasised that he had several children. When his father asked who their mother was Hans replied 'Why Mummy, and you're the Granddaddy'.
- The next day, Hans fantasised that a plumber had come and removed his bottom and penis, replacing them with new and larger ones.

RESULTS

Freud interpreted the case as an example of the Oedipus Complex. Specifically:

- Horses represented Hans' father.
- Horses made good father symbols because they have large penises.
- The anxiety Hans felt was really castration anxiety triggered by his mother's threat to cut off his 'widdler' and fear of his father caused by his banishing Hans from the parental bed.
- The giraffes in Hans' fantasy represent his parents. The large giraffe that cried out represented Hans' father objecting to Hans. The crumpled giraffe represented Hans' mother, the crumpling representing her genitals. The large giraffe, with its erect neck could have been a penis symbol.
- The children fantasy represents a relatively friendly resolution of the Oedipus Complex in which Hans replaces his father as his mother's main love object, but the father still has a role as grandfather.
- The plumber fantasy represents identification with the father. By this we mean that Hans could see himself growing a large penis like his father's and becoming like him.

Figure 5.2
Hans particularly feared white horses

CONCLUSIONS

Hans suffered a phobia of horses because he was suffering from castration anxiety and going through the Oedipus Complex. Dreams and fantasies helped express this conflict and eventually he resolved his Oedipus Complex by fantasising himself taking on his father's role and placing his father in the role of grandfather.

EVALUATION

The research method and sampling bias

Throughout this book we consider sampling and the general issues with the research method separately. In this case, the sampling is the problem with the method! That is, case studies such as this have a particular problem with their sample. By definition, they use very small numbers of participants, and, almost by definition, these participants are unusual enough to be sufficiently interesting to be worth writing about. Small samples of unusual people are a problem in psychology because it is hard to generalise from them to the population as a whole. Even if we accept that Little Hans had a full-blown Oedipus Complex, this does not mean that everyone has one, which is Freud's claim.

Qualitative and quantitative data

The data analysed in this study were exclusively qualitative, and the study has the strengths associated with qualitative data. There is a large volume of rich information in Freud's account of the Little Hans case. Freud meticulously recorded very detailed information, and this has allowed later researchers to offer alternative interpretations of the case. However, compared to the use of quantitative data, this method gives us very little concrete information about Hans.

Ethical considerations

There was no deceit in the case study. Although Hans did not give formal consent to take part in a study, his father did, and parental consent is quite normal for participants of Hans' age. Hans was not put through any experimental procedure that might cause harm or distress. There are issues however around confidentiality and privacy. Although Freud used the name Little Hans, the boy's real identity was well known in Vienna, where he and Freud lived. Hans' real name was Herbert Graf, and he went on to be a successful operatic director. It is not known whether being the subject of Freud's study ever caused him later problems, but we might regard it as questionable that his identity is public knowledge when he was linked to something as socially sensitive as the Oedipus Complex.

Validity

The Little Hans study raises particular problems of validity. First, the way the data was collected could have affected validity. Hans' father was a fan of Freud's work, and it is hard to know if this distorted his perception of the events he passed on to Freud. A further validity issue concerns making theoretical interpretations. Interpretation, by definition, involves going way beyond the information available to an observer. This is subjective, and good science requires an attempt at objectivity.

Reliability

Reliability is always a problem for clinical case studies because they are one-offs and cannot be replicated. Without replication we cannot assess test-retest reliability (see page 250) because by definition that requires an assessment to be carried out more than once. Nor can we really assess inter-rater reliability (see page 250) because Freud carried out his analysis alone, and clearly we cannot put ourselves in the shoes of multiple Freuds over a century later!

Ethocentrism

Ethnocentrism is a serious problem with the study. In fact this study is a classic illustration of ethnocentrism. Freud was looking at a single child from a very particular cultural context – middle-class Austrian society. From this he generalised the concept of the Oedipus Complex to the development of all boys in a wide range of cultural contexts. This is not simply a question of sampling bias; parenting practices and the cultural meanings of child–parent interaction vary massively between people living in different cultural contexts. Freud ignored this and proposed a universal phenomenon of the Oedipus Complex based purely on a European interpretation of events. This is highly ethnocentric.

Practical applications

As an illustration of the Oedipus Complex, the Little Hans case has been extensively used by psychotherapists for training purposes. An important aspect of such training is in-depth study of cases. This means that the study has an important practical application. A related strength of the study is its theoretical importance. It is hard to study the Oedipus Complex, but this case gives some evidence, however imperfect. It therefore has good theoretical importance.

BARON-COHEN *et al.*'s STUDY OF ADVANCED THEORY OF MIND

Baron-Cohen, S., Joliffe, T., Mortimore, C. and Robertson, M. (1997) Another advanced test of theory of mind: evidence from very high functioning adults with autism or Asperger Syndrome. *Journal of Child Psychology & Psychiatry,* **38**, 813–822.

IN BRIEF !

Aim: To test whether high-functioning adults with autistic spectrum disorders struggle to identify emotions from photographs of eyes (the Eyes Task).

Method: 16 adult volunteers with an autistic spectrum disorder were shown 25 photographs of pairs of eyes, and were asked to identify the emotions in them. Control groups of 50 adults with no diagnosis, and 10 adults with Tourette's Syndrome, carried out the same task.

Results: The autism group did significantly worse than the control groups in identifying the emotions.

Conclusion: Even high-functioning adults with autism struggle to recognise mental states in others.

Figure 5.3
Autism researcher Simon Baron-Cohen

CONTEXT

This study is concerned with the autistic spectrum. Autism is a life-long disorder usually diagnosed in childhood. A diagnosis of an autistic spectrum disorder requires that a person has difficulties in communication, relationships with other people and imagination. Children on the autistic spectrum struggle to understand other people's behaviour, and this in turn leads to difficulties in forming friendships and getting on with peers. Usually there is some degree of language delay, and because they lack imagination, they can fail to appreciate hazards and put themselves in dangerous situations.

Because individuals vary so much in their symptoms, it is usual now to refer to the 'autistic spectrum' rather than to 'autism'. Most people with autistic spectrum disorders are below average in intelligence, but this is not always the case. There are some people on the spectrum who have a small number of well-developed cognitive abilities, who are known as 'savants', and others with a range of well-developed abilities, who are known as 'high-functioning' individuals. This study is concerned with individuals on the spectrum who are said to be 'high-functioning', and those with Asperger Syndrome, a particular autistic spectrum disorder in which language development is mildly or not at all affected, yet the individual is still impaired in their social development.

Among autism researchers there is some debate as to what exactly causes autism. Simon Baron-Cohen *et al.* have suggested that a problem in 'theory of mind' – i.e. the ability to perceive mental states in other people – underlies difficulties in communication and social development. Baron-Cohen points out that if we cannot read other people's minds, we cannot have meaningful interactions with them, and without such interaction we cannot expect to develop normal language or form friendships.

There is considerable evidence to suggest that people on the autistic spectrum struggle with theory of mind tasks. However, this has been challenged by other researchers who have found that high-functioning adults with autism and Asperger Syndrome can usually succeed in standard theory of mind tasks. Baron-Cohen *et al.* answered this by suggesting that the standard theory of mind tests are too easy for high-functioning adults, and that if a more difficult test for theory of mind could be devised, then they would still be able to demonstrate a deficit in theory of mind when compared with adults who have no clinical condition, and adults with a different developmental problem. This is the idea underlying the current study.

AIM

The aim of the study was to test whether high-functioning adults with autism and Asperger Syndrome would struggle with a new and more difficult test for theory of mind. This new test, known as the 'Eyes Task,' involves reading emotion from photographs of eyes. In order to see whether this difficult test for theory of mind was particularly hard for people on the autistic spectrum, their results were compared with those of two matched groups, one no clinical condition, and one with a different disorder, **Tourette's Syndrome**.

METHOD

Participants

The autism group consisted of 13 men and three women of normal intelligence and with a diagnosis of high-functioning autism or Asperger Syndrome. They were a volunteer sample recruited through their doctors and in response to an advert in the National Autistic Society's magazine.

The control group was made up of 25 men and 25 women with no autism diagnosis. There was no test of IQ, but it was assumed that all were of normal intelligence. In addition, eight men and two women with Tourette's Syndrome

KEY IDEAS

Tourette's Syndrome is a condition that, like autism, is usually diagnosed in childhood, and can cause severe disruption to education and peer relations. The main symptom is tics or involuntary movements. These can include vocal tics in which the patient involuntarily says socially inappropriate things.

DO IT YOURSELF

You can download the Eyes Task from www.autismresearchcentre.com (click on 'Tests'), or run a version online at: www.questionwritertracker.com/quiz/61/Z4MK3TKB.html. You should not carry out research using participants on the autistic spectrum or any other developmental condition. However, you could practice using the Eyes Task to assess mind-reading in boys and girls. It is widely believed that girls are better than boys at this kind of task, but as scientists we should not just accept that, but should try to find out for ourselves.

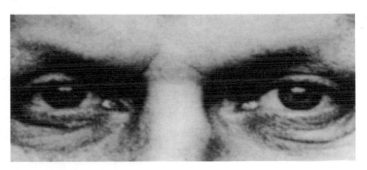

Figure 5.4
Examples of items from the Eyes Task (from Baron-Cohen et al.'s original paper)

QUESTION SPOTLIGHT!

Make sure you can explain clearly the purpose of both the 'normal' and Tourette's conditions.

took part in the study as a second control group. This was important because Tourette's has several key elements in common with autism. It exists in childhood and causes disruption to schooling and peer relations. Like autism, it is also believed to be associated with a biological problem in the frontal lobes of the brain. If theory of mind deficit is specifically a problem with autism, as opposed to being simply the result of a childhood disrupted by a psychological condition, the autism group would be expected to do worse on the Eyes Task than the Tourette's group.

Design and procedure

Participants were shown 25 black-and-white photographs of eyes for three seconds each, and asked to choose between two mental states represented by

No.	Target term	Foil
	TABLE 5.1 THE PAIRS OF CHOICES IN THE EYE TASK	
1	Concerned	Unconcerned
2	Noticing you	Ignoring you
3	Attraction	Repulsion
4	Relaxed	Worried
5	Serious message	Playful message
6	Interested	Disinterested
7	Friendly	Hostile
8	Sad reflection	Happy reflection
9	Sad thought	Happy thought
10	Certain	Uncertain
11	Far away focus	Near focus
12	Reflective	Unreflective
13	Reflective	Unreflective
14	Cautious about something over there	Relaxed about something over there
15	Noticing someone else	Noticing you
16	Calm	Anxious
17	Dominant	Submissive
18	Fantasising	Noticing
19	Observing	Daydreaming
20	Desire for you	Desire for someone else
21	Ignoring you	Noticing you
22	Nervous about you	Interested in you
23	Flirtatious	Disinterested
24	Sympathetic	Unsympathetic
25	Decisive	Indecisive

STRETCH & CHALLENGE

You are aware now of Baron-Cohen's Eyes Test and Happe's Strange Stories. Consider the characteristics of Autistic Spectrum Disorder and try to come up with additional ideas for tasks to assess autism.

the photographs. Some of these mental states were basic emotions, such as 'sad' or 'afraid'. Others were more complex, such as 'fantasising or noticing'. The list of choices is shown in Table 5.1.

Control tasks

In order to eliminate the possibility that the autism group simply had a visual problem that meant that they could not process the photographs, all participants were also asked to complete the two control tasks: a gender recognition task, in which participants had to identify the gender of the eyes, and a basic emotion recognition task, in which participants had to identify basic emotions shown in photographs of whole faces.

Validation of the Eyes Task

It was believed that the Eyes Task actually measures theory of mind ability. However, as it was a new test it was important to test this idea. In order to do this, participants in the autism and Tourette's groups also took another quite difficult test, **Happe's Strange Stories**. If the Eyes Task really measures theory of mind ability, then those who struggle with it should also score less well in the Strange Stories test.

RESULTS

On the control tasks, all groups performed normally on the tasks they completed. However, in the Eyes Task, the autism group did significantly worse than the two control groups. This is shown in Table 5.2. Although 16.3 out of 25 might appear to be a reasonable score, bear in mind that the participants had a 50% chance of guessing each emotion correctly. A result of 16.3 out of 25 is barely above what we would expect from chance.

No participants in the Tourette's group were incorrect in any of their Strange Stories responses, but the autism group struggled. The fact that the same participants struggled with the Eyes Task and the Strange Stories is evidence for the validity of the Eyes Task.

CONCLUSIONS

There are two main conclusions that can be drawn from the study.

1   Even high-functioning adults with autism, including those with Asperger Syndrome, have a significant problem with their theory of mind. In other words, they find it hard to read mental states in other people. This supports the idea that theory of mind deficit is central to understanding autism, and might even directly cause its main symptoms.
2   The Eyes Task is a valid test of theory of mind suitable for high-functioning adults with autism.

KEY IDEAS

Happe's Strange Stories is a fairly advanced test for theory of mind, aimed at older children. It involves asking children questions about the emotions and intentions of characters in unfamiliar stories.

TABLE 5.2 SCORES IN THE EYES TASK		
Condition	**Mean score out of 25**	**Range of scores**
Autism	16.3	13–23
None	20.3	16–25
Tourette's	20.4	16–25

MATHS MOMENT

Table 5.2 shows means and ranges.
1   Distinguish between the mean, median and mode.
2   Explain why the standard deviation might be a more useful measure of dispersion than the range.
3   Draw a bar chart representing the means in the three conditions.

QUESTION SPOTLIGHT!

If you offer an answer evaluating the research method for this study, make sure your answer makes reference to the study itself.

EVALUATION

The research method

The study was carried out in a controlled setting, so environmental conditions were well controlled, which is a strength. On the other hand, the ecological validity is poor because the situation was so different from an everyday real-life social situation and because the experience of looking at the Eyes Task is so different to that of judging emotion in faces in real life. A further problem is that this is a quasi-experiment, not a true experiment, because three naturally occurring groups were being compared. This means that the groups might not have been well-matched for all the relevant variables. This is made worse by the fact that the control group without a diagnosis were not rigorously tested to make sure they were comparable with the autism and Tourette's groups.

Qualitative and quantitative data

The data gathered in this study were quantitative. This is both a strength and a weakness. On the plus side, the numbers allow easy comparison of the conditions, clearly showing that theory of mind is worse in the autism group. On the other hand, there was no opportunity for participants to comment on what they experienced when they looked at the eyes, or on what they found difficult about the task. Such qualitative data might have added to the completeness of the findings.

Ethical considerations

Studies such as this have to meet very high ethical standards because of the use of vulnerable adults as participants. The participants were volunteers, they were not deceived, and they experienced no distress beyond that which they could expect in their daily lives.

Validity

This can be seen as a weakness of the study. The Eyes Task is carried out under controlled conditions, and the experience of judging emotion by looking at an isolated pair of eyes is very different from the real-life experience of judging emotions in whole moving faces with additional information such as body language and speech. On the other hand, the researchers did include a test for validity when they gave participants the Strange Stories task, and this supported the validity of the Eyes Task. Including such a test of validity is a strength of the study.

Reliability

Participants were shown the same pictures of the same size (15 × 10cm) for the same time (exactly three seconds) under the same conditions, with standard instructions. They therefore had a consistent experience, meaning that the internal reliability of the procedure was good. This procedure is straightforward to replicate, meaning that external reliability should also be good. However, no testing of external reliability was reported in the paper.

Sampling bias

The sample of adults on the autistic spectrum was quite small, at 16, and only three of these were female. This small sample size makes it hard to assume that this was a representative group of high-functioning adults with autism. Generalisability is therefore a problem. This is made worse by the fact that they were a volunteer sample, generally one of the less representative sampling methods. The sample of Tourette's participants was even smaller, at 10. This means that the sample and sampling method are weaknesses of the study.

Practical applications

If we accept that this study, in spite of its methodological limitations, demonstrates that even high-functioning adults with autism have problems when it comes to reading emotions in faces, then this could open up practical ways forward in helping high-functioning people with autism to manage their condition. For example, it might be possible to teach people on the spectrum to make use of different visual cues to judge emotion, or to teach those interacting with people on the spectrum to give very clear visual and verbal cues to signal what they are feeling.

COMPARISON OF STUDIES

Freud's Case Study of Little Hans & Baron-Cohen *et al.*'s Study of Advanced Theory of Mind

THE TOPIC
Understanding disorders

The studies by Freud and Baron-Cohen *et al.* are both concerned with individual differences, specifically in relation to psychological disorders. Freud's case study focused on the Oedipus Complex of Little Hans, while Baron-Cohen *et al.* investigated theory of mind in high-functioning adults with autism and Asperger Syndrome.

THE RESEARCH METHOD AND DESIGN
Case study versus quasi-experiment using independent groups design

The two studies used different research methods to collect data. Freud wrote a clinical case study about a five-year-old boy whom he had collected information about over a number of years. This means that he was able to give an in-depth, detailed account of Little Hans' dreams, phobias and conscious behaviour in relationship to his parents.

Alternatively, Baron-Cohen *et al.* carried out a quasi-experiment involving three participant groups who were tested under controlled conditions. Autism, Asperger Syndrome and Tourette's Syndrome are naturally occurring disorders. This means that participants cannot be randomly assigned to different conditions, which dictated the independent measures design of the experiment. The IV in this study was the three groups (high-functioning adults with autism, adults with Tourette's, and a control group with no diagnoses).

SAMPLING TECHNIQUE AND THE SAMPLE
Single male sample versus mixed sample

The sample in the Oedipus Complex study consisted of one five-year-old boy whose father was a fan of Freud's work. Case studies by their nature are highly unrepresentative and it would be unwise to attempt to generalise the findings of this study to other children. By contrast, Baron-Cohen *et al.* employed several techniques to gain their participant sample. The group of high-functioning adults with autism was

recruited as a volunteer sample through an advertisement, the Tourette's group was recruited directly from a referral centre, and the control group with no diagnoses was approached randomly from a university participant pool. The sample size overall amounted to 76 participants, and by comparison the sample size and technique used by Baron-Cohen *et al.* was likely to be more representative than in Freud's study.

EXPERIMENTAL MATERIALS AND MEASUREMENT OF THE DEPENDENT VARIABLE
Researcher bias versus standardised procedure; quantitative versus qualitative data

In general, case studies might be considered to have a good level of validity as the researcher often gets to know the participant(s) well, establishing rapport and using a variety of methods to collect a detailed picture of their experiences. In the case of Little Hans, however, this validity was somewhat compromised as Freud obtained his information secondhand through Hans' father, which may have introduced bias. However, Hans was a young child who was naïve to the study and likely to have behaved naturally. Still, it is a unique case study and would be difficult to replicate, therefore lowering its reliability.

On the other hand, Baron-Cohen *et al.* conducted their experiment under laboratory conditions, controlling for participant variables such as intelligence and gender, as well as establishing a standardised procedure for presenting the photographic stimuli. The nature of the Eyes task was, however, highly artificial, as were the surroundings in which the experiment took place, which reduced the ecological validity of the study.

Freud's study of Little Hans collected purely qualitative data. This consisted of Hans' father's recorded events, including details of his phobia, dreams and fantasies that were interpreted by Freud. Unlike case studies, experiments measure specific dependent variables. In Baron-Cohen *et al.'s* experiment, the DV was performance on a theory of mind task. This was operationalised as an individual score out of 25 on a task involving judging emotions from looking at photographs of eyes. This meant the study produced quantitative data, which enabled the researchers to calculate and directly compare the mean scores for the three different participant groups.

APPLICATIONS
Both used in theoretical and practical training methods

Freud's ground-breaking clinical case study of Little Hans has been used in the training of psychotherapists. Part of its significance is that it is a good example of in-depth qualitative research that has given insight into the Oedipus Complex, which would be very hard to study using alternative methods.

Baron-Cohen *et al.'s* study can be applied more directly to the practice of supporting high-functioning adults with autism or Asperger Syndrome to manage their condition. This includes offering visual cues to help individuals learn to judge the emotions of others.

KEY THEME: UNDERSTANDING DISORDERS

The case study of Little Hans is a fairly unique example of how a psychoanalyst has offered a detailed interpretation of a rarely studied childhood disorder. Furthermore, use of this methodology by Freud has shown that building up a

lengthy, detailed case history can help to fully understand how an individual experiences a disorder such as the Oedipus Complex. Both Freud's theory of psychosexual development and the methodology which he used to investigate it were ground-breaking and have influenced everyone who has studied psychological disorders since – whether they agree with Freud's approach or have set out to disprove his ideas!

On the other hand, Baron-Cohen *et al.'s* study is useful in helping us to understand a different sort of disorder. Results of this study offer strong evidence to support the theory that those with autistic spectrum disorders experience difficulty with social impairment. Importantly, this conclusion was arrived at through the creation of a valid assessment tool (the Eyes Test), which is one of the first of its kind for adults. In contrast to Freud's clinical case study, Baron-Cohen *et al.'s* research offers the possibility that we can measure and quantify disorders using objective tools, rather than through subjective interpretation by psychoanalysts.

KEY THEME

Understanding disorders
Both studies help us understand disorders. Baron-Cohen *et al.* showed that we can measure disorders using objectives tools, rather than the subjective interpretation used by Freud.

Freud
Used a case study of one boy. In some ways the study has low validity and reliability. It produced a lot of qualitative data.

Similarities
Both studies focus on helping us understand disorders. They are both useful in training therapists in theoretical and practical ways.

Baron-Cohen *et al.*
Used a highly controlled quasi-experiment. and a range of sampling methods to study both males and females. Produced quantitative data.

PRACTICE QUESTIONS

Here are some of the sorts of questions that you could be asked in Sections A and B of your AS exam, and some examples of successful and less successful answers. We look at Section B questions in more detail in Chapter 6 on pages 206–8 and 212–14.

SECTION A: CORE STUDIES

1 Describe **one** weakness of the study of Little Hans conducted by Freud. [2]

2 Describe **one** strength of the study of Little Hans conducted by Freud. [2]

3 From the core study by Freud, outline **one** piece of evidence that suggests Hans was nearing the resolution of the Oedipus complex. [2]

4 In Freud's study of Little Hans, Hans is described as having a phobia of horses.
   (a) Describe the explanation that Freud gives for this phobia. [2]
   (b) Describe an alternative explanation for this phobia. [2]

5 From the study by Baron-Cohen et al. on autism:
   (a) Identify **two** groups of participants used in this study. [2]
   (b) Explain why **one** of the groups of participants was used in this study. [2]

6 From the study by Baron-Cohen et al. on autism:
   Outline **two** of the ways the participants were tested. [4]

7 Baron-Cohen et al.'s study on autism in adults gathered quantitative data.

Explain **one** strength of gathering this type of data in this study. [2]

8 Describe **one** difference between Freud's study of Little Hans and Baron-Cohen et al.'s study of autism. [3]

SECTION B: AREAS, PERSPECTIVES AND DEBATES

9 **(a)** Outline the individual differences area of psychology. [2]
   (b) Suggest **one** strength of claiming that behaviour is only due to nature. Support your answer with evidence from **one** appropriate core study. [3]
   (c) Suggest **one** weakness of claiming that behaviour is only due to nature. Support your answer with evidence from one appropriate core study. [3]
   (d) Explain how any **one** core study can be considered to be located within the area of individual differences. [5]
   (e) Discuss the problems encountered when attempting to conduct useful research. Support your answer with evidence from core studies. [12]

SECTION A   1 Describe **one** weakness of the study of Little Hans conducted by Freud. [2]

Rachel's answer:
One weakness is that it was a case study.

We say: This is not a description of a weakness of this study. Although there are weaknesses associated with case studies (and with every other method), this answer has not told us anything about these weaknesses. Rachel could have said that the study was a case study of one individual (Little Hans) and so it would be very difficult to generalise the results of this study to anyone else.

Charlotte's answer:
One weakness of this study is that Hans' father collated the information about his son and sent it to Freud. This could have produced several sources of bias. Hans' father was also a follower of Freud's theories and so could have unconsciously manipulated the information that he chose to include or exclude from his reports in line with what he thought Freud would want to hear.

We say: This is a well-chosen weakness that Charlotte has described in plenty of detail.

4 In Freud's study of Little Hans, Hans is described as having a phobia of horses.

(a) Describe the explanation that Freud gives for this phobia. [2]

(b) Describe an alternative explanation for this phobia. [2]

Rachel's answer:

(a) Freud thought that Hans was afraid of his father because he thought his father would castrate him.

(b) Because he could just be afraid of all animals.

Charlotte's answer:

(a) Freud said that Hans' fear of horses represented his fear of his father. He pointed to the fact that Hans was especially afraid of white horses with black nosebands as these were most like a face with a black moustache. Hans had displaced his fear of his father onto a fear of horses.

(b) An alternative explanation would be a behaviourist explanation. Hans' father did report that Hans had been distressed after seeing a horse fall in the street and this could be explained through association: Hans had associated the horse with the distressing incident and reacted with anxiety every time he saw a horse.

We say: These answers are too brief and too vague. There is a hint of the correct answer in part (a), as Freud did say that Hans was afraid of his father, but Rachel really needs to go further than this to explain that Freud believed the fear of horses could be interpreted as representing a fear of his father. Rachel's answer to part (b) is incorrect. While it is possible that Hans could have been afraid of all animals, this is not an explanation.

We say: Charlotte has given two very clear answers to the questions. In part (a) Charlotte has given a clear and concise answer in the first sentence and has then gone on to elaborate on this answer in the next sentences. Taken as a whole, this provides excellent evidence of understanding. Charlotte's answer to part (b) is also very good and a particular strength of this answer is the use of psychological terminology (e.g. 'behaviourist' and 'association') and the clarity of the explanation.

5 From the study by Baron-Cohen *et al.* on autism:

(a) Identify two groups of participants used in this study. [2]

(b) Explain why one of the groups of participants was used in this study. [2]

Charlotte's answer:

(a) One group was the experimental group made up of people with diagnoses of autism or Asperger's syndrome. Then there were two control groups. One was a group of people with Tourette's syndrome.

(b) The group of people with Tourette's syndrome was used to allow the researchers to check that the lack of theory of mind is specific to autism rather than existing in a range of psychological conditions that disrupt childhood and relationships.

We say: Good answers again from Charlotte, who definitely knows these studies very well indeed. A nice concise identification of the groups in part (a) and a clear explanation in part (b).

SECTION B 9 (e) Discuss the problems encountered when attempting to conduct useful research. Support your answer with evidence from core studies. [12]

Rachel's answer:

If research is going to be useful it is important to study lots of people. This would make the core study by Freud not a useful study as he only studied little Hans. If research is going to be useful it needs to be up to date and Freud's study is really old so that means it is not useful any more.

Charlotte's answer:

If a researcher is trying to make their research useful then one thing that would be important would be to ensure that the research had high ecological validity. As little Hans did not know he was being studied and was being observed in his normal environment, it could be argued that this study does have high ecological validity. On the other hand, Baron-Cohen et al. asked participants to judge emotions shown in a still photograph of eyes. This is not high in ecological validity as this is not how we interpret emotions in everyday life. Although the researchers claim useful findings, this criticism could reduce the usefulness of their research.

   Research is only really ever going to be useful to those to whom the results will generalise. This means that research conducted at one time or in one place may not be useful years later or in a very different context. This does not mean that the research is not useful at the time but it would be very difficult to conduct research that would not date. This would reduce the usefulness of Freud's study.

   Finally, if research is going to be useful then it should have large representative samples. The study by Freud studies only one child whereas the study by Baron-Cohen et al. studied a larger sample.

We say: Rachel isn't reading the questions properly. This is not a question about whether the studies are useful or not but a question about what problems are encountered when trying to conduct useful research. Perhaps Rachel should consider underlining the key words in the questions to make sure that she is responding correctly. Obviously this is a short answer to a 12-mark question, but it also has another problem. The question asks you to support your answer with evidence from core studies, but Rachel has used only one study.

We say: Some good points here and Charlotte has clearly read the question carefully and is responding appropriately. The first two paragraphs are detailed and thoughtful answers to the questions although the final point in the last paragraph could be elaborated further.

GOULD'S STUDY OF BIAS IN IQ TESTING

Gould, S. J. (1982) A nation of morons. *New Scientist*, **6**: 349–352.

IN BRIEF

Aim: To highlight fundamental issues with intelligence testing, specifically in research carried out by psychologist Robert Yerkes (1921).

Method: The research method used by Yerkes within Gould's article was psychometric testing. 1.75 million US army recruits underwent mental testing during the First World War. Participants took one of three tests: Army Alpha (written test), Army Beta (pictorial test) or Individual Examination (spoken test). Each recruit was graded A–E and the scores used to determine placement in military ranks. Gould reviews and critiques Yerkes' methodology in his article.

Results: Yerkes found the average mental age of white American adults to be 13. Black men scored lower on average than white men. Fairer people of Northern and Western Europe had higher scores than darker people of Southern Europe and the Slavs of Eastern Europe. Gould finds systematic errors in the content, design and administration of such tests.

Conclusion: Yerkes' data showed that the average man could be considered a 'moron'. He also concluded that it is possible to grade individuals on intelligence by the colour of their skin. Gould concludes that intelligence testing of this kind is highly susceptible to bias and leads to racial discrimination.

KEY IDEAS

Hereditarians hold the belief that heredity is more important than factors such as environment in determining intelligence and behaviour. Heredity is the passing of traits from parents to offspring. In human beings this occurs through genetic inheritance. Modern techniques have allowed scientists to identify a number of physical and mental characteristics that have a certain genetic basis, for example, eye colour or particular blood disorders. However, there remain an enormous number of traits that we may be predisposed to, but not determined to inherit, or indeed traits for which we have yet to determine any genetic basis whatsoever.

CONTEXT

The idea that intelligence is a quality that can be measured is a controversial idea. It is complicated by arguments around what actually constitutes intelligence, and how it can be accurately tested. One important question to consider is whether the differences between individuals can be explained by genetic or environmental causes – the so-called 'nature–nurture' debate.

Early attempts to devise intelligence tests included that of Alfred Binet, who created the Binet-Simon Test in 1905 with another French psychologist, Théodore Simon. The purpose of their research was to use the test to help identify children who required special education, and the tests would produce a mental age score (Binet and Simon, 1913). For example, a 10 year old who was able to complete all the tasks a 7 year old could be expected to do would have a mental age of 7, and thus be identified as requiring additional help.

Importantly, Binet believed that intelligence was not a fixed characteristic and could be improved with appropriate support. He understood that there were limitations to this sort of testing and his work lead to our modern-day understanding of IQ, or intelligence quotient.

An alternative view holds that intelligence is a fixed characteristic: an individual difference owing to genetic factors. This **hereditarian** position has lead to the idea that intelligence testing could be used to identify and breed a superior group of people. Known as 'eugenics', this philosophy involves methods to encourage the reproduction of superior individuals or groups while inhibiting the growth of those groups considered inferior. During the early 20th century, eugenics was popular in both theory and practice, in forms such as birth control, racial segregation and, perhaps more notably, in genocide. One of the most notorious examples of this would be the eugenics-based ideology of Adolf Hitler and the Nazis in 1930s' and 1940s' Germany. This led to the systematic destruction of what were labelled 'inferior races', such as Jews, compulsory sterilisation of people with physical or mental disabilities, and policies to increase the birth rate among members of the so-called 'Aryan race'.

In the present study, evolutionary biologist Stephen Jay Gould examined the influential work of American psychologist Robert Yerkes as he carried out one of the largest tests of intelligence in history. The study summarises an article written by Gould who explores the methodology used by Yerkes (1921) as well as the implications for his research.

Figure 5.5
Just your 'Average Joe'? Yerkes' participant sample consisted of US army soldiers during the First World War

AIM

The aim of Gould's article was to reveal basic problems in attempts to measure intelligence. The aim of Yerkes' study (which Gould describes in detail) was to devise a scientific way to test the natural trait of intelligence on a mass scale.

METHOD

The research method used by Yerkes is large-scale **psychometric testing**, as outlined in Gould's article.

Participants

Yerkes administered his test to an opportunity sample of 1.75 million army recruits situated in training camps. These would have included adult men of different ages and from a range of backgrounds and regions across the USA.

Design and procedure

Yerkes wished to establish psychology as a serious science, and believed undertaking a systematic, large-scale mental testing programme could achieve this. Along with his assistant and psychologist E.G. Boring, he was granted permission by government officials to administer the mental tests to US Army recruits during the First World War. Yerkes collaborated with other hereditarian colleagues to create the army mental tests. In 1917, they had devised three types of tests:

- **Army Alpha** – This was a written test for literate recruits. It consisted of eight sections, with tasks such as filling in the missing number in a sequence, reordering words in a sentence and completing analogies.
- **Army Beta** – This was a pictorial test for men who were illiterate or who had failed the Army Alpha. It had seven parts, including completing a maze, number tasks and the complete-a-picture task (see Figure 5.6).
- **Individual Examination** – This was an individual spoken test for participants who had failed the Army Beta.

Figure 5.6
What is missing? Part six of the Army Beta Test

💡 KEY IDEAS

The theory and practice of psychological measurement is known as psychometrics. **Psychometric** researchers seek to achieve valid assessments that provide numerical measures of human personality traits, attitudes and abilities. Such tools may take the form of tests, questionnaires and interviews. An IQ test is a typical example of a psychometric test.

WEB WATCH @

Visit MENSA's website to find out more about contemporary IQ testing: www.mensa.org

MENSA is an organisation whose members have very high IQ scores. You can complete their just-for-fun test to get an idea of the types of questions you would find on a standard IQ test, and also browse the diverse list of MENSA members. You might be surprised who you find there! The website also contains some information on the challenges of creating unbiased intelligence measures.

The paper-based tests each took less than an hour to complete and were individually undertaken in supervised groups, often in very rushed and intimidating conditions. It was difficult to finish most parts of the tests in the time allowed, but participants were not warned of this.

Gould is highly critical of the materials used by Yerkes and his associates. While Yerkes asserted that he was measuring 'native intellectual ability', Gould argues that much of the test content relied heavily on cultural knowledge and access to formal schooling. This means that the tests were more likely to be assessing environmental influence than natural ability (see Figure 5.7). Furthermore, practices for administering the tests were discriminatory, with blacks being less likely to be called for recall to a Beta test.

Additionally, Gould explores issues with the procedure used to administer the mental tests. However, owing to the enormity of the task, there were inconsistencies between camps where the tests were undertaken. For example, all men, by either lack of schooling or foreign birth, were supposed to take Army Beta. This did not always happen, as administrators used different criteria for illiteracy. Perhaps most crucially, many men who scored nothing or next to nothing on the Army Alpha, and who should therefore have been given the Army Beta, were not given the chance to take it through lack of time or opportunity. These inconsistencies disproportionately affected men who were black or had recently immigrated. It was a systematic bias reflecting their lower levels of literacy and lack of access to education.

RESULTS

According to Yerkes, the results of the mental tests revealed the average mental age of white American men to be around 13 years old. Previous research had set the standard of adult mental age at 16 years, thus Gould called his article 'A Nation of Morons', as 13 was just above the edge of moronity.

Black Americans scored on average significantly worse than their white counterparts, with a mean mental age of 10.4 years. Yerkes also graded European immigrants according to their country of origin. His findings showed that the average man of many countries would be classed as a moron. Notably, differences were matched with fairness of skin, with Northern and Western Europeans scoring higher than Slavic people of Eastern Europe and darker-skinned immigrants from Southern Europe (see Table 5.3).

The results of the mental tests were also graded and thus influenced the assignment of different military roles. Under Yerkes' advisement, recruits with a score of C should be marked as 'low average intelligence – ordinary private'. Men who scored D and E could not be expected 'to read and understand written directions'.

Gould is highly critical of these 'findings', identifying a number of flaws which are explored in detail in the evaluation of this study below (see pages 182–3).

Crisco is a: patent medicine, disinfectant, toothpaste, food product

The number of a Kaffir's legs is: 2, 4, 6, 8

Christy Mathewson is famous as a: writer, artist, baseball player, comedian

Figure 5.7
Are you smarter than a 13 year old? Example questions from the Army Alpha Test

QUESTION SPOTLIGHT!

1 Read and answer the example questions in Figure 5.7. Do you agree that these questions are valid questions for measuring natural intelligence?
2 What are the implications of using materials to test intelligence that are low in validity?

TABLE 5.3 CHART SHOWING THE FINDINGS OF THE ARMY RECRUIT STUDY

Group	Mean mental age
White (American)	13.04
Black (American)	10.41
Russian (immigrant)	11.34
Italian (immigrant)	11.01
Polish (immigrant)	10.74

MATHS MOMENT

1 Using the data in Table 5.3, calculate the range of the mean mental ages across all groups.
2 Calculate the mean mental age for all groups given in Table 5.3.

CONCLUSIONS

Yerkes and his associates concluded that:
1 Intelligence is an innate quality with a hereditary basis. It is possible to grade individuals by the colour of their skin.
2 The average man of most nations could be considered a 'moron'.
3 Mental testing of this kind is a valid, scientific technique with wider implications for society.

However, Gould asserts that the internal contradictions and systematic prejudice of the materials and methodology thoroughly invalidated the conclusions drawn by Yerkes. It may be hard for us today to fully comprehend the extent of discrimination blacks, immigrants, poorer and less-educated Americans would have been subject to. As Gould points out, the army mental tests were a product of their time and the results were used to further support racist beliefs and practices.

EVALUATION

The research method

The research method used by Yerkes was standardised psychometric testing. One strength is that it was an attempt to objectively and scientifically measure levels of intelligence. It was also simple to administer and score the Alpha and Beta tests, allowing for a huge amount of data to be collected.

However, psychometric testing of this kind assumes that intelligence is fixed and unchanging over time and across different circumstances. Other research has shown that this is not always the case. Furthermore, Yerkes was also working on the assumption that intelligence was a distinct and measureable concept; again others would argue that it does not exist as a single, definable quality.

Qualitative and quantitative data

Psychometric testing of this kind produces only quantitative data. This means a person's intelligence is expressed numerically, in the form of an overall intelligence score. It enables straightforward comparison with other people and also allows us to establish a group 'norm'.

In theory it can detect abnormally low scores, which could help identify individuals who need additional support. However, in the case of the Army Recruit study, it was used as a political tool to further racist ideas and control immigration. Only focusing on quantifying intelligence via fixed-choice questions may also fail to capture a true picture of an individual's intellect. For example, counting an answer as simply 'wrong' on the test might ignore valid and sound reasoning.

Ethical considerations

For some of the participants, taking an examination was a totally novel experience that would have been quite daunting. Some of the recruits had never even held a pencil before, and were given little warning or instruction prior to the testing. There is no mention of obtaining consent or allowing recruits the right to withdraw from testing in the study. As Gould reports them, the conditions appeared stressful and would have breached the ethical guideline of preventing psychological harm to participants. It also means the men were denied a briefing beforehand, and were thus unaware what the test results would have meant for their futures.

Validity

Gould describes Yerkes' assertion that the mental tests were a true test of natural intelligence as 'ludicrous'. Yerkes' results did not take into account cultural biases in the tests, which advantaged middle-class whites and drastically reduced any claim to validity. Instead of purely measuring intelligence, the tests systematically advantaged those who were most literate, had spent longest in school, and were familiar with test-taking and using a pencil.

Recruits who had been in the USA for less time (e.g. recent immigrants) were also at a major disadvantage, as some test items relied entirely on knowledge specific to contemporary American culture (see Figure 5.7 for examples). Later research, showing that intelligence-test scores of immigrants positively correlated over time with length of time spent in America (and presumably increased cultural familiarity, education and literacy), strongly contradicts the validity of Yerkes' findings.

Reliability

The mental tests used by Yerkes in the Army Recruit study were standardised in their presentation and used a detailed mark scheme to be consistent in assessing each completed test. This means it was a fairly reliable method. If participants sat the test again they would be likely to answer similarly and receive similar scores.

One weakness in terms of reliability would be that there were differences in the conditions under which men sat the tests, depending on what camp they were in. Also, there were issues highlighted by Gould around the inconsistency in selection procedures for Alpha or Beta tests. This systematically disadvantaged black American and recently immigrated recruits, further lowering the reliability of the results.

Sampling bias

The sample used by Yerkes was truly impressive in scale, meaning his findings were likely to be highly representative. Perhaps more importantly, the participants had not volunteered or been specially selected for the mental tests, meaning that the sample included recruits from a wide range of ages, backgrounds and localities across the USA.

Ethnocentrism

Yerkes' mental tests would be considered to be highly ethnocentric methods of measuring intelligence. As Gould has shown, the results of the mass testing revealed heavy bias, as the tests relied on culturally specific knowledge and were not pure measures of intelligence. Later research has highlighted issues with IQ testing which should make us question whether it can ever avoid charges of ethnocentrism.

Practical applications

The work of Yerkes and his contemporaries had a significant impact, both in the field of psychometric testing, and within different social and political contexts. Some of the sections used on the Army Alpha include components now essential in modern IQ tests. The findings of Yerkes' study received huge public attention and the mental tests were revised and marketed to different sectors, most notably for use in education. IQ tests have considerable practical application in schools, and are used to identify and support those with additional needs as well as the academically gifted.

Instead of creating a valid mass-assessment tool, Gould suggests the study should teach psychologists to exercise scepticism around attempts at measuring intelligence. Yerkes intended to bring scientific credibility to psychometrics, but in doing so failed to acknowledge the serious flaws in design and administration of his test which render it invalid. Instead, he produced highly biased results that had a profound and negative impact on social policy. As Gould reports, the findings of the study were continually invoked in legal measures to restrict immigration to the USA on the grounds of eugenics. These arguments were persuasive to the US Congress, and restrictive immigration quotas barred an estimated 6 million Europeans between 1924 and 1939 from seeking refuge from persecution in their home countries.

DO IT YOURSELF

One important problem faced by researchers using psychometric testing today is that of constructing a valid and reliable measurement tool. Have a go at designing your own five-item 'intelligence test'. Then pair up with someone else who has attempted to do the same. Ask 10–15 participants to complete your test, and then your partner's test. Did you find that participants scored similarly on both tests?

HANCOCK *et al.*'s STUDY OF THE LANGUAGE OF PSYCHOPATHS

Hancock, J.T., Woodworth, M.T. & Porter, S. (2011) Hungry like the wolf: a word-pattern analysis of the language of psychopaths. *Legal and Criminological Psychology*, **18**(1): 102–114.

IN BRIEF

Aim: To examine how features of language are used in crime narratives by psychopaths.

Method: The research method was self-report. Researchers analysed transcripts of interviews using statistical text analysis. Participants were 52 male murderers recruited through a volunteer-sampling technique who were classified as psychopaths or non-psychopaths (control group).

Results: The study showed that psychopaths were more likely to describe cause-and-effect relationships when describing their crime. They also used twice as much language relating to basic physiological and self-preservation needs, while the control group used language relating to social needs. Also, psychopaths used language that framed their murder as more in the past, and in more psychologically distant ways than the control group.

Conclusion: Psychopaths use language in a fundamentally different way from non-psychopaths, with less focus on emotion and greater emphasis on meeting their basic needs.

KEY IDEAS

The term '**psychopath**' is used to describe individuals with a distinctive combination of cognitive, social and emotional characteristics. For example, they exhibit a reduced capacity for moral responsibility and may act extremely selfishly compared to the general population. Brain-imaging studies suggest a biological explanation for such differences (Raine *et al.*, 2004). Psychopaths are thought to comprise about one per cent of the general population, and may often find success as business people, politicians and cult leaders (Hare, 2006).

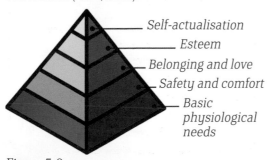

Figure 5.8
Maslow's hierarchy of needs

CONTEXT

Research has shown that language can provide useful insight into our underlying cognitive and emotional processes. This is because many aspects of the ways in which we express ourselves are unconscious and automatic. Features of language such as disfluencies (saying 'um' and 'ah'), how emotionally coloured our speech is, and even the use of past or present tense can reveal a lot about our personalities. These features can be used by researchers and clinicians to identify patterns that might indicate abnormality. This has been achieved with high levels of accuracy in identifying disorders such as depression and paranoia. In one study, statistical speech analysis was shown to be more accurate than a clinician's diagnosis (Oxman *et al.*, 1988).

Researchers have also recorded the narratives of psychopathic offenders to establish and compare detailed verbal accounts of their crimes. **Psychopaths** are individuals who exhibit abnormally high levels of selfishness and seemingly lack a conscience. There is a popular notion portrayed in the media that psychopaths are skilled conversationalists, verbally gifted in their ability to lie and manipulate (see Figure 5.9). One study that supports this idea is Porter *et al.* (2009), who found that psychopathic offenders in the Canadian penal system were approximately 2.5 times more likely than non-psychopaths to be successful in their parole applications, despite being far more likely to reoffend. However, conflicting research indicates psychopathic language might actually be less cohesive and more incoherent than that of non-psychopaths (Williamson, 1993). To examine the specific qualities of psychopathic language, Hancock *et al.* carried out a sophisticated statistical text analysis of two groups of convicted murderers.

AIM

The aim of the study was to test how crime narratives differ between psychopaths and non-psychopathic murderers. Psychopathic speech was analysed for indications of an instrumental or predatory world view, unique socio-emotional needs, and a poverty of affect (see p.64).

METHOD

A self-report method was used which involved face-to-face individual interviews.

PARTICIPANTS

The sample consisted of 14 psychopathic and 38 non-psychopathic male murderers (the control group) who were imprisoned in Canadian correctional facilities. All of the 52 participants had admitted their crime and volunteered for the study. The two groups did not differ on age, and their overall mean age at the time of their current homicide was 28.9 years (range of 14–50 years). A similar mean amount of time had elapsed since their crime across the two groups (psychopaths had a mean length of time since their crime of 11.87 years, non-psychopaths 9.82 years).

TABLE 5.4 TYPE OF CRIME COMMITTED BY PARTICIPANTS ACROSS BOTH GROUPS

Type of crime	Number of convictions
First-degree murder	8
Second-degree murder	32
Manslaughter	10
Not specified in study	2
Total	52

Design and procedure

The Psychopathy Checklist-Revised (PCL-R) was used to assess the participants against 20 different criteria. This clinical diagnostic tool measured affective traits and impulsive/antisocial traits to give individual scores out of 40 (30 or above is the cut-off for diagnosing psychopathy). The assessments were carried out by trained prison psychologists and researchers experienced in coding the test. An inter-rater reliability check was conducted on the PCL-R scores by having a trained graduate student re-code 10 randomly selected case files.

Figure 5.9
Fictional serial killer and cannibal Hannibal Lecter as portrayed by Anthony Hopkins in the 1991 film Silence of the Lambs.

KEY IDEAS

The **hierarchy of needs** is a theory outlined by Abraham Maslow (1943), who identified basic types of motivation and the order in which each must be met. While we do experience more than one need at a time, Maslow suggests that a certain need might dominate in various instances. Psychopaths appear to focus on basic needs, such as food, sex and shelter, while higher-level needs, such as spirituality, self-esteem and respect, seem to attract little interest.

MATHS MOMENT

1 Table 5.4 shows the breakdown of crimes committed by the participants. Convert the number of convictions into percentages.
2 Draw and label a simple pie chart to illustrate the crime data shown in Table 5.4.

WEB WATCH

Download or stream the TED talk video of humourist and author Jon Ronson entitled 'Strange Answers to the Psychopath Test'. Ronson discusses the traits of a psychopath, his encounters with psychopaths in the real world, and the extent to which many of us display psychopathic characteristics:

Go to www.ted.com/talks and search for 'Jon Ronson'.

STRETCH & CHALLENGE ◎

This study could be also seen as a quasi-experiment. What characteristics does it have that would make it a quasi-experiment?

QUESTION SPOTLIGHT!

1 Can you explain two ways in which the Hancock *et al.* study controlled extraneous variables?
2 After the PCL-R assessment was carried out, there was a random check on 10 of the tests. Why was this important?

At the start of each interview, participants were verbally briefed on the aims and procedure of the study. The offenders were asked to describe their offence in as much detail as possible while being audio taped. The interviews were carried out individually and lasted approximately 25 minutes each. Participants were prompted by interviewers using a standardised procedure known as the 'Step-Wise Interview', which facilitates open-ended questioning. The interviewers were two psychology graduates and one research assistant, who were all 'blind' to the psychopathy scores of the participants.

Each interview was then transcribed verbatim and analysed using two text-analysis tools. The first was known as Wmatrix, a programme that was used to analyse parts of speech and semantics contained in the 'copora' or whole body of the two groups of transcripts. The second tool was the Dictionary of Affect in Language (DAL) software programme, which specifically analysed emotional properties of language such as positivity, intensity and imagery.

RESULTS

The interviews of the psychopaths and control group produced a total 127,376 words. The results showed no significant difference in the average number of words produced by psychopaths and the control group. Instrumental language analysis showed that psychopaths were more likely to describe their homicide using subordinating conjunctions (1.82% of words in the psychopath corpora compared to 1.54% of words in the control corpora). These include words that show cause and effect, such as *'because'*, *'since'*, *'as'* and *'so that'*.

As the researchers had expected, the crime narratives of the psychopaths emphasised more basic needs, including food, sex and shelter, while on the other hand, the controls focused more on higher-level social needs, such as meaningful relationships and spirituality. Overall, psychopaths referred to basic physiological needs far more as often in comparison to the control group when describing their homicide.

Finally, emotional expression in language was analysed and compared. Psychopathic offenders were found to have used more past-tense forms of verbs (e.g. 'stabbed') and fewer present-tense forms of verbs (e.g. 'stab') than controls. Psychopaths' language also involved more concrete nouns. This data suggests that psychopaths viewed their crime as more in the past and more psychologically distant than did non-psychopaths. In terms of the content, psychopaths generally used less positive or emotionally intense language. There were more instances of callousness and lack of empathy in their narratives:

'...I just turned around and looked at him and I just stabbed him and I said, "None of your f***ing business".'

Their language was also significantly less fluent than controls, with 33% more disfluencies (such as 'um' and 'uh'):

'We got *uh*, we got high, and had a few beer, I like whiskey so I bought some whiskey, we had some of that, and then we *uh*, went for a swim.'

CONCLUSIONS

Hancock *et al.* conclude that psychopaths describe powerful emotional events in a rational but more primitive way compared to others. Their analysis suggests that, compared to non-psychopaths, psychopaths:

1 tend to view their crimes as the logical outcome of a plan
2 are more likely to focus on their own basic physiological needs
3 overall, are less emotional and less positive in their speech
4 are more emotionally detached from their crimes.

STRETCH & CHALLENGE

Hancock *et al.* identified a unique problem with the use of crime narratives for linguistic analysis. This was that there was the potential for participants to lie about details of their homicide, either to exaggerate for effect or to downplay their guilt. Consider how this could be avoided and outline a different task to enable a less biased analysis.

MATHS MOMENT

1 Identify whether the data used in Hancock *et al.'s* study is primary or secondary.
2 What are the implications for the validity of this study when using this type of data?

EVALUATION

The research method

The study used the self-report method of interviews to compare psychopaths' and non-psychopaths' crime narratives. Interviews have the advantage over questionnaires that they gather large amounts of detail and in-depth data about individuals. However, owing to how time-intensive they are compared to questionnaires, they tend to gather data across fewer participants.

Qualitative and quantitative data

Large amounts of qualitative data in this study were produced from individual interview recordings. This captured the richness of language used to describe each homicide, allowing the researchers to study the differences between psychopaths and non-psychopaths in great depth. However, in its raw form the audio-taped narratives were too detailed and varied to allow direct comparison. Each interview was subsequently transcribed and analysed, producing quantitative data that could be more easily assessed. This allowed researchers an overall view of differences in language between the two groups.

Ethical considerations

Standards of privacy and confidentiality were maintained as participants remained unidentified within the study.

Researchers took care to gain fully informed consent from participants, using a volunteer-sampling method. This took into consideration the circumstances of participants' imprisonment, and how it might affect their abilities to freely consent to contribute to the study. Participants were also given a full verbal brief at the outset of each interview.

Validity

The study has good ecological validity because participants were interviewed about their own real-life crimes, during which they provided detailed, in-depth accounts. Furthermore, the interviewing technique was designed specifically to avoid leading participants towards particular responses and to allow them to speak freely. However, in some cases participants were interviewed more than a decade after their crimes. Social desirability bias might have reduced the validity of the responses as participants might have wanted to appear remorseful.

Highly valid measures were used to determine psychopathy (the PCL-R). The linguistic analysis tools (Wmatrix and DAL) had been tested for validity and were being used extensively across other research, providing concurrent validity.

Reliability

Overall this study was very reliable. The interview procedure was capable of replication, as was the linguistic analysis. Additionally, there were random checks by another researcher, which confirmed a high level of inter-rater reliability.

Sampling bias

Hancock *et al.'s* sample was unrepresentative, as all participants were Canadian prisoners, which makes the study ethnocentric. Furthermore, all the participants were male, making it difficult to accurately generalise to a female population. The participants were recruited as volunteers, and this may also have introduced bias to the research as the sample is unlikely to represent murderers in the prison who chose not to participate. However, a strength of the sample is that a relatively large number of prisoners were interviewed, considering the time-consuming nature of this research method. This produced huge amounts of data for statistical analysis, which improves the representativeness of the research.

Practical applications

Understanding the language of psychopaths in turn reveals personality and behavioural traits that set them apart from the general population. It has the potential to help identify psychopaths and deal with them effectively. For example, as Hancock *et al.'s* study shows, psychopaths reveal an emotional distance from their crimes and motivations linked to basic needs. These key differences can be considered by those working in the criminal justice system, for example in developing appropriate ways to rehabilitating psychopathic criminals.

STRETCH & CHALLENGE ◎

Different languages use sentence structure and vocabulary in diverse ways. To what extent could Hancock *et al.'s* conclusions be considered to be ethnocentric in this respect?

Figure 5.10
Behind bars: convicted murderers diagnosed as 'psychopaths' may require different strategies to reduce the likelihood of reoffending

DO IT YOURSELF 🔍

Hancock *et al.* categorised specific words used in the crime narratives in terms of different levels of human needs. Write a brief fictional account of a petty crime (e.g. shoplifting or graffiti). Ask 10 people to explain what they think the motives of the offender in your story are. You could collect this data in the form of a short written or verbal questionnaire. Use Maslow's hierarchy of needs to identify and categorise their responses.

COMPARISON OF STUDIES

Gould's Study of Bias in IQ Testing & Hancock et al.'s Study of the Language of Psychopaths

THE TOPIC
Measuring differences

The studies by Gould and Hancock et al. are both concerned with individual differences, specifically about how we can measure and compare features such as intelligence and the use of language. Gould's article focused on the difficulties associated with creating a valid and reliable tool to measure intelligence, whereas Hancock et al. compared the language of psychopaths and non-psychopaths.

THE RESEARCH METHOD AND DESIGN
Psychometric testing versus interviews

The two studies were different in the way in which they collected their data. Gould explains how psychometric testing was conducted en masse through standardised tests, administered to large groups in across a number of training camps. The tests themselves were designed specifically to act as a valid and reliable tool to assess intelligence. In contrast, Hancock et al. conducted individual interviews with participants in prisons to gain detailed accounts of their specific crimes. Interviewers employed an open-ended questioning technique with participants, which produced diverse and in-depth narratives that were later transcribed for analysis.

SAMPLING TECHNIQUE AND THE SAMPLE
Army recruits versus psychopaths; opportunity versus volunteer-sampling

There were vast differences in the samples used in both these studies. Gould quotes Yerkes as having administered tests to 1.75 million army recruits from across the USA, while in total Hancock et al. obtained their data from just 52 offenders. An opportunity-sampling technique was used to conduct the mental tests, but in the language study participants volunteered to take part. Arguably the study of intelligence could be considered to be more representative owing to its sheer scale. However, Hancock et al. still achieved a fairly representative sample considering the time and effort involved in conducting individual interviews.

EXPERIMENTAL MATERIALS AND MEASUREMENT OF THE DV
Both had issues with valid measurement; both used quantitative data

There were serious flaws in both the validity and reliability of intelligence testing, as explained by Gould. The mental tests were systematically racially biased owing to their design and the way in which they were given to participants. Gould contests whether the tests can be considered in any way a valid measure of intelligence and argues that their findings should be discounted. Hancock et al. faced validity issues as well, such as the risk of offenders wishing to exaggerate their crimes or appear socially acceptable. Overall the psychopathic language study ensured much higher levels of validity and reliability with the use of a standardised procedure and careful measures, which avoided the use of leading questions.

Both studies relied on the use of quantitative data. For example, in Gould's article, he reports how Yerkes and colleagues used their Army mental tests to produce intelligence scores for each individual. By contrast, Hancock et al. used sophisticated software programs to analyse and compare transcripts of crime narratives. This meant that in both studies the researchers were able to easily compare their findings across different groups.

APPLICATIONS
Measuring intelligence versus identifying psychopathic offenders

The research conducted by Yerkes and others in Gould's article had a significant impact on the participants themselves as well as on many others. The results were used to influence selection procedures for army officers. The findings also drew the attention of those in the educational sector, who bought versions of the mental tests to administer to students to enable intelligence testing within schools. In addition, it had a considerable impact on immigration policy, providing 'evidence' for use by the eugenics movement.

Hancock et al.'s analysis identified key differences in the use of language between psychopathic offenders and

189

non-psychopathic offenders. There is scope for applying word-pattern analysis to criminals in order to calculate the likelihood that the individual is psychopathic. This in turn has practical applications for those working to rehabilitate offenders to better understand their motivations and attitudes.

KEY THEME: MEASURING DIFFERENCES

Gould's contribution to the theme of measuring difference in the area of individual differences is significant. He critiques early attempts to measure intelligence as a single, quantifiable trait. Yerkes' errors show us that constructing valid and reliable tests is very difficult and that the implications of getting it wrong in his case amounted to scientific racism. Nonetheless, intelligence testing and psychometrics as popularised by Yerkes and other hereditarians remains popular today.

By contrast, Hancock *et al.'s* study focused on a specific group of individuals who would be considered abnormal in our society. The study is significant on the grounds that it is able to transform the detail and nuance contained in individual crime narratives into comparable quantitative data. Significantly, Hancock *et al.* and other researchers now place greater emphasis on valid and reliable materials and methods in psychological research. They recognise the need to be discerning about how we measure differences, as well as the consequence of not doing so.

We have explored in detail four important studies from within the individual differences area of psychology. Each pair of core studies has explored a key theme that helps us understand more about how human beings differ from one another. By considering these pieces of research we can outline the following key assumptions.

KEY THEME

Measuring differences
Both studies were concerned with measuring individual differences. Gould highlighted the flaws in Yerkes' attempts to quantify intelligence. Hancock *et al.* sought to analyse language in a quantitative way to identify psychopathy.

Gould
Described work carried out to measure intelligence using psychometric tests. This work used an opportunity-sampling method to test army recruits.

Similarities
Both studies focus on measuring individual differences. They both collected quantitative data which allowed for comparisons between groups to be made. They each had difficulties with valid measurement of difference.

Hancock *et al.*
Investigated psychopathic language using individual interviews. A volunteer-sampling method was employed to study convicted murderers.

PRACTICE QUESTIONS

Here are some of the sorts of questions that you could be asked in Sections A and B of your A level exam, and some examples of successful and less successful answers. We look at Section B questions in more detail in Chapter 6 on pages 206–18.

SECTION A: CORE STUDIES

1 Gould conducted a review of IQ testing.
   (a) Explain what a review is. [2]
   (b) Outline **one** strength of a review. [2]
2 From Gould's study into bias in IQ testing:
   Outline **two** problems with the way the IQ tests used by Yerkes were administered. [4]
3 Describe **one** piece of quantitative data and one piece of qualitative data from Gould's review. [4]
4 Outline **one** conclusion that can be drawn from the review by Gould of intelligence testing. [2]
5 What was the aim of the study by Hancock *et al.*? [2]
6 Describe the method used by Hancock *et al.* [4]
7 From the study by Hancock *et al.*, describe what is meant by the term 'psychopath'. [2]
8 Describe the sample used in the study by Hancock *et al.* [3]

SECTION B: AREAS, PERSPECTIVES AND DEBATES

12 **(a)** Describe the difference between an individual explanation for behaviour and a situational explanation for behaviour. [4]
   (b) Explain how **one** psychological study can be considered as providing an individual explanation for behaviour. [5]
   (c) Evaluate the usefulness of providing a situational explanation for behaviour. Support your answer with evidence from **one** appropriate psychological study. [6]
   (d) Discuss the problems encountered when attempting to conduct useful research. Support your answer with evidence from core studies. [20]

Section A 2 From Gould's study into bias in IQ testing:

Outline **two** problems with the way the IQ tests used by Yerkes were administered. [4]

Liam's answer:

One problem was that the tests were biased and the other problem was that white Americans had an average mental age of a 13 year old.

Rina's answer:

One problem was that different army bases used different criteria to determine whether someone was literate or illiterate. This meant that the tests were not administered in the same way for all the recruits. Another problem was that lots of recruits scored practically nothing on the Alpha test and were not given the opportunity to sit the Beta test, reducing the validity of the scores.

We say: Liam has misinterpreted this question. The information that he has given is correct information from the study but it is not the correct answer to this question. This question is asking very specifically about the way that the tests were administered and not about anything else at all. The first point Liam has made is about the questions included in the test and the second point he has made is one of the findings.

We say: A clear and well-explained answer from Rina which shows good understanding of two of the problems in the administration of the tests. There is a nice style here with an identification of the problem followed by just a little bit of elaboration.

7 From the study by Hancock *et al.*, describe what is meant by the term 'psychopath'. [2]

Liam's answer:

Psychopaths are dangerous aggressive criminals.

Rina's answer:

A psychopath is someone with no capacity for empathy and who appears to lack a conscience. They are extremely selfish and often able to manipulate other people.

We say: No, this is incorrect. Psychopathy refers to a very specific set of characteristics to do with empathy and conscience. It is important to give a focused response rather than a general statement that could apply to a number of different things.

We say: This is a much better answer. Rina has identified several key characteristics of psychopaths and has simply listed them.

8 Describe the sample used in the study by Hancock *et al.* [3]

Liam's answer:

They were all murderers and some of them were psychopaths.

Rina's answer:

There were 52 male participants. There were 14 psychopaths and 38 non-psychopaths. All were convicted murderers and between 14 and 50 years old.

We say: This is broadly correct but could be described more clearly. All the participants were murderers but there were two groups: one group of psychopaths and one group of non-psychopaths. It might also be useful to give details, such as numbers of participants and ages/sex.

We say: Correct. This is plenty of detail and shows very good exam preparation. There is no need to elaborate on this kind of answer – simply give the answer that you have been asked for.

SECTION B 12 (a) Describe the difference between an individual explanation for behaviour and a situational explanation for behaviour. [4]

Liam's answer:

The difference is whether the explanation looks at things to do with the person or whether the explanation is to do with the situation the person is in.

We say: Liam has started well with his description of the individual explanation as 'things to do with the person', although examples would help here. The second part is weaker, though, as he uses the term 'situation' to describe 'situational', which is not very effective.

Rina's answer:

Individual explanations assume that the cause of the behaviour can be identified within the person, usually in terms of personality characteristics or similar measurable variables. In contrast, situational explanations look outside the person, at variables in the environment or the social situation.

We say: Rina's answer is better and the examples help a lot in demonstrating an understanding of the explanations and the difference between them.

12 (b) Explain how one psychological study can be considered as providing an individual explanation for behaviour. [5]

Liam's answer:

Hancock *et al.* is an individual study because it is looking at differences between people. Hancock et al. argued that there were differences in the way that psychopaths and non-psychopaths used language.

We say: Liam needs to give more information here. He is right to select Hancock *et al.* as one of the studies from the individual differences area but he needs to show how this relates to providing an individual explanation for behaviour.

Rina's answer:

Gould conducted a review of intelligence testing around about 100 years ago. Intelligence is an individual difference and so Yerkes was assuming that this was a measurable variable that would allow us to compare people. However Gould shows us that the early attempts to measure IQ were extremely biased and unreliable.

We say: Rina's answer is better than Liam's, as she has at least mentioned the feature of measurement and the ability to draw comparisons between people, which is a key feature in the individual differences area. However, this is still quite a brief answer which could be developed further. How would you develop this answer further to gain full marks?

THE INDIVIDUAL DIFFERENCES AREA OF PSYCHOLOGY

1 Individuals differ in their personality, thinking and behaviour

In many ways individual differences is a unique branch of psychology. The key assumption is that in order to understand the complexity of human behaviour and experiences it is better to focus on the differences between people. Unlike other approaches that assume humans are all pretty much the same, researchers in this area contrast aspects of thinking and behaviour. They are interested in a range of differences, including the study of developmental disorders such as autism and the Oedipus Complex, as well as how to measure personality traits such as psychopathy and intelligence. An example from one of the studies we have looked at is Baron-Cohen *et al.*'s study of high-functioning adults with autism. In this study, Baron-Cohen *et al.* focused on collecting data that could directly compare the ability to read emotions in the eyes of three groups of adults. Their findings illustrated that there are key differences in the processing of emotions between those with autistic disorders and those without.

2 It is possible to measure and study individual differences.

Researchers in this area assume that it is possible to form hypotheses, measure and collect data about the nature of individual differences in human behaviour. They also try to draw meaningful conclusions about aspects of behaviour that can vary from person to person. An area of the psychology of individual differences that continues to attract attention is research into intelligence. This is one of many factors that has traditionally been measured using standardised testing known as psychometrics. In the article by Stephen Jay Gould, he reports on early attempts to implement standardised mental testing as a forerunner to modern Intelligence Quotient (IQ) tests. This assumes that intelligence is a quality that is unique to each person and can be quantified in a way that allows us to compare individuals, thus establishing a normal range of intelligence.

3 We can understand human behaviour in terms of dispositional factors.

Dispositional factors in psychology refer to the idea that a person's behaviour could be explained by their personality or disposition rather than as a result of the situation that the person is in. The area of psychology concerned with individual differences explores this in different ways throughout the studies in this chapter. In one example,

Hancock *et al.* consider how the unique features of psychopathic language vary from that of non-psychopaths. They build on existing research to show that differences in word-pattern analysis are a result of personality differences not linked to situational factors.

Strengths and weaknesses of the individual differences area

Strengths

1 **Research has practical applications**. All the studies in this chapter are highly relevant to improving how we measure differences and understand disorders. Baron-Cohen *et al.*'s findings suggest that those with autism and Asperger Syndrome experience difficulties in recognising emotional expressions in others. Their research has aided developments in techniques and resources designed to help those affected overcome these difficulties and help improve their ability to interact socially.

2 **Different types of data used**. The studies we have looked at in this chapter use quantitative and qualitative data to achieve different outcomes. Hancock *et al.* collected a large body of qualitative data in the form of interview transcripts. This data was then changed into numerical form through computerised statistical analysis software, while still preserving examples of different language features. Using both types of data gives researchers the advantage of obtaining comparable, measurable results as well as exploring the meaning of certain aspects of their enquiry.

Weaknesses

1 **Methodology is sometimes subjective**. Some of the techniques used in studies in this area are not fully objective and may be open to bias. This is not to say that these techniques should not be used in psychology; in fact they may be the only methods available for studying some forms of individual difference. The case study of Little Hans highlights this issue well, as it provided an account of a phenomenon that is hard to study otherwise. However, it is really Freud's interpretations of Hans' father's interpretation of his son's experience. This means that the account is likely to be biased towards Freud's existing theories and assumptions.

2 **Ethical issues in this area**. A range of ethical issues have been raised by these four studies. When measuring individual differences or studying disorders, researchers may be working with vulnerable groups and need to consider issues of social sensitivity. In his article, Gould effectively criticises the Army Recruit tests on ethical and moral grounds. These include causing psychological distress to participants and a lack of informed consent. Importantly, he argues that measuring differences in psychology can be used for highly unethical purposes, such as to support discriminatory social policies.

C6 AREAS, PERSPECTIVES AND DEBATES

As well as the five approaches or areas of psychology you also need to know about two perspectives. Each area is concerned with particular aspects of psychology, so developmental psychology is about how we change with age, and individual differences is about the ways in which people vary from one another. Perspectives are different because they are theoretical ways to understanding human psychology. In this chapter we consider two perspectives: behavioural and psychodynamic.

We also look at some key debates that run throughout the different areas and perspectives:

- Nature–nurture
- Free will/determinism
- Reductionism/holism
- Individual explanations
- Usefulness of research
- Ethical considerations
- Conducting socially sensitive research
- Psychology as a science

PERSPECTIVES ON PSYCHOLOGY

THE BEHAVIOURAL PERSPECTIVE

Core studies that can be understood from the behavioural perspective include the following:

- **Bandura *et al.* (1961)** (p. 82). Bandura *et al.* explained the results of his study in terms of observational learning. Children learned aggression towards the Bobo doll by imitating the model.

- **Chaney *et al.* (2004)** (p. 88). Chaney *et al.* explained the results in terms of operant conditioning. In other words, children received reinforcement for correct use of the Funhaler in the form of an incentive toy that could whistle and whirl.

This approach dominated psychology for the first half of the 20th century. More than anyone else it was the behaviourists that established psychology as a scientific discipline. Few psychologists describe themselves as behaviourists nowadays; however the influence of behaviourism remains strong because behaviourists made many discoveries that still hold true. The following are some of the main assumptions of the behavioural perspective.

1. The proper subject matter of psychology is observable behaviour

The early behaviourists were determined to make psychology a respectable science. One way in which they tried to do this was to ignore the mind and focus on behaviour. This is because we cannot see directly into the mind, and the behaviourists believed that good science required that psychologists should study only what could be seen. Behaviourism is sometimes called 'black box' psychology, because it treats the mind as a closed box that we cannot see into. Instead, what is studied is stimulus and response. A stimulus is anything in the environment that is detected by one of the senses. A response is the behaviour that results from detecting the stimulus. We can show this in the form of a diagram – see Figure 6.1.

Stimulus ⟶ ⬛ ⟶ Response

Figure 6.1
The 'black box' model of behaviourism

2. We are products of our environment

In the nature–nurture debate, behaviourists fall on the side of nurture. In fact, the early behaviourists believed that human behaviour was entirely a product of environmental influences. John Watson, the founder of behaviourism, once said:

> Give me a dozen healthy infants, well-formed, and my own specified world to bring them up in and I'll guarantee to take any one at random and train him to become any type of specialist I might select—doctor, lawyer, artist, merchant-chief and, yes, even beggar-man and thief, regardless of his talents, penchants, tendencies, abilities, vocations, and race of his ancestors.
> *Watson, J.B. (1930)* Behaviourism. *University of Chicago Press*

By this, Watson meant that we are entirely products of environment and that if we can control someone's environment we can control their development. Modern behaviourists take a slightly less extreme view. For example, behaviourists studying the learning of phobias have identified the phenomenon of preparedness – we seem to be hard-wired to learn fear of some things but not others. We can easily acquire phobias of snakes and spiders, but not of cars or guns, which are actually much more dangerous. However, behaviourists are still concerned with the influence of the environment on behaviour.

3. We acquire our behaviour through learning

According to the behaviourists we learn our behaviour. In particular, behaviourists are concerned with three types of learning.

- **Classical conditioning**. Learning to associate a stimulus that already triggers a response (called an unconditioned stimulus) with another stimulus (a neutral stimulus), so that the latter comes to trigger the same response. For example, we might fear muggers but have no feeling about bus stops. If we are mugged at a bus stop we are likely to associate the bus stop with the mugging and learn to be wary of bus stops. Classical conditioning can explain how some simple responses – fear, salivation, sexual arousal, etc. – are learned.

- **Operant conditioning**. This is learning by the consequences of our actions. When we perform a behaviour and this has a good consequence we become more likely to repeat that behaviour. This is called reinforcement. Similarly, when something we do has a bad consequence we are less likely to do it again. This is called punishment. Operant conditioning can explain the development of quite complex behaviours, but not necessarily where the behaviour originated – remember that we have to try a behaviour for the first time before it can be reinforced or punished.

- **Observational learning**. This is a much more recently discovered type of learning than the previous two, and takes place when an observer imitates behaviour modelled by another individual. Observational or social learning is sometimes described as 'neo-behaviourist' rather than behaviourist, because the theory makes reference to cognitive processes. For observational learning to take place, the observer must attend to the behaviour being demonstrated and retain it in their memory. Attention and memory are cognitive processes and a true behaviourist would probably not place so much emphasis on this type of process.

STRENGTHS AND WEAKNESSES OF THE BEHAVIOURIST PERSPECTIVE
Strengths

- **Scientific status**. The kinds of research carried out by behaviourists conform closely to the standards of good science. Most studies, such as Bandura *et al.* (1961), are experimental and carried out under laboratory conditions. They are therefore highly reliable. Behavioural ideas are easily testable because they concern easily observed behaviour and there is an absolute minimum of inferring what is happening in the mind from behaviour that can be observed.

- **Practical applications**. Behaviourism has many practical applications in the real world. Understanding the role of observational learning in developing aggression has informed the debate about violence in the media, and the intervention in families where children observe domestic violence (see p. 87). Classical and operant conditioning also have important applications. We can for example use classical conditioning therapies to understand and treat mental disorders. Operant conditioning can be used to modify behaviour in a range of situations, including improving compliance to following medical recommendations (see p. 88).

Weaknesses

- **It is reductionist**. Reductionism takes place when we look at something complex and reduce it to something much simpler in order to be able to study and explain it. By ignoring most mental processes and focusing instead on just stimulus and response, behavioural theories are generally guilty of reductionism. Even social learning explanations of aggression are reductionist. There are many aspects to human aggression, including biological (hormones, evolution), cognitive (perception of the situation) and social (group membership, culture). In the light of this complexity it is very reductionist to look at aggression simply as a learned response.

- **It raises ethical issues**. Behavioural techniques are extremely powerful in altering human behaviour and this means that they give some people tremendous power over the behaviour of others. While this makes behaviourism very useful, it also raises ethical issues. Under what circumstances is it okay to forcibly alter behaviour? This may not seem controversial when encouraging children to better manage health conditions such as asthma. However, the use of punishment to shape the behaviour of humans and animals raises serious ethical issues. For example, early therapeutic techniques used to treat autism used shouting, striking and even electrical shocks to discourage unwanted behaviour such as self-harm.

THE PSYCHODYNAMIC PERSPECTIVE

Core studies that can be understood from the psychodynamic perspective include the following:

- **Freud (1909)** (p. 164). Freud explained Hans' phobia as the result of anxiety from the Oedipus Complex, and the end of the phobia as the resolution of the Oedipus Complex.

A
- **Kohlberg (1968)** (p. 98). Kohlberg used moral dilemmas to test children of different ages and establish universal stages of development.

- **Hancock et al. (2011)** (p. 184). Hancock *et al.*'s study of offenders relied on the assumption that our use of language is partially unconscious and can reveal features of our personality.

Like the behavioural perspective, the psychodynamic perspective is one of the older ways of thinking about psychology. However, in every other way it could not be more different! Where the behavioural perspective is highly scientific and helped establish psychology as a science, the psychodynamic perspective uses very different methods and is much more theoretical. As a result, it has never been accepted as part of mainstream psychology. The psychodynamic perspective has the following assumptions:

1. We are strongly influenced by the structure and drives of our unconscious mind

The 'unconscious mind' is the aspects of the mind that we are not consciously aware of. According to the psychodynamic perspective we are constantly affected by unconscious mental processes. Freud's later work introduced the theory that the human psyche is composed of three distinct parts: the Id, Ego and Super-ego (see Figure 6.2). The Id is entirely unconscious and contains the most basic human instincts, seeking immediate gratification and pleasure. The Super-ego, however, is our moral centre, which has internalised cultural rules as taught by our parents and other role models. Finally, the Ego is the rational element of personality, seeking to find socially acceptable ways to satisfy the demands of the Id. These concepts have influenced the work of theorists such as Kohlberg (whose stages of moral development parallel this model), or Hancock *et al.*'s in their study of psychopaths (who are dominated by desires to satisfy their most basic, primitive needs).

2. Our development is affected by early relationships

According to Freud and other psychodynamic theorists, the most crucial factor affecting our psychological development is our early experiences, and the most important early experiences centre around the quality of relationships with parents. In Freudian theory the most important aspect of parental relationships is the Oedipus Complex, as illustrated by the Little Hans case. In the Oedipus Complex, children attach strongly to the opposite-sex parent and see the same-sex parent as a rival for their affection. How parents handle this situation has an impact on the child's later development. According to Freud, a badly handled Oedipus Complex can leave a child sexually over- or under-confident, or with a too strict or too lax sense of morality.

3. Important information about the unconscious can be found in how we express ourselves outwardly

The psychodynamic perspective stands aside from the rest of psychology in terms of its approach to research. Where other perspectives try to be as scientific as they can, this is not possible for those working in a psychodynamic way. This is because the focus is the unconscious mind, which is extremely difficult to study scientifically. Instead, psychodynamic psychologists look for clues in dreams, therapy and slips of the tongue about what is happening in the person's unconscious. This can be seen in studies such as Hancock *et al.*, where the researchers assume that the choice of language used by murderers to describe their crime is not consciously controlled, and can therefore reveal key information about the personality of psychopaths.

STRENGHS AND WEAKNESSES OF THE PSYCHODYNAMIC PERSPECTIVE
Strengths

- **Explanatory power**. The psychodynamic perspective can be used to explain a wide variety of behaviours, including the more bizarre ones, such as multiple personalities, dreams of crumpling giraffes, and day-dreams of being fitted with big penises by a plumber! This is a serious point, because all these things are very difficult to explain using other perspectives or approaches. One contemporary application of Freudian theory is in understanding adult baby syndrome, in which adults take on infant behaviours, dressing in nappies and sometimes paying specialist prostitutes to feed and change them. In Freudian terms, this is straightforward to explain – the adult babies are regressing to an early stage of development at which their development stalled owing to something going wrong with their key relationships. There is no other explanation for adult baby syndrome that so neatly explains the phenomenon.

- **Occupies the middle ground on key debates**. Unlike behaviourism, which can be thought of as reductionist, determinist and taking an extreme nurture view in the nature–nurture debate, the psychodynamic perspective takes account of both innate instincts (nature) and environment too, in the form of parenting (nurture). This means that it allows for the influence of both nature and nurture, and it is not too reductionist because it looks at more than one aspect of our psychological functioning. As regards determinism, the psychodynamic perspective explains that we are strongly influenced by unconscious factors, *but* that once we become aware of these – e.g. through therapy or rehabilitation – we can exert our free will.

Weaknesses

- **Poor research methodology**. The kind of research carried out in the psychodynamic perspective often fails to live up to the standards of good science. By definition, case studies involve very small samples. To make this worse, the samples are always unrepresentative because they involve patients in psychological distress who have undertaken psychotherapy. Most people don't have therapy, so generalising from those who do to the whole population is difficult. Case studies cannot be replicated, so they lack reliability. Actually, some of Freud's ideas came not from case studies but from self-analysis. This is an even more questionable method. For example, the idea of the Oedipus Complex came from an intensive period of reflection on Freud's own childhood. Essentially he was saying that he had been through the Oedipus Complex, and therefore everyone else must have done. The Little Hans case was meant to illustrate this.

- **Theoretical ideas are sometimes vague and hard to test**. Two of the 'gold standards' of a sound scientific theory are that it has clear concepts, and that it can be scientifically tested. Ideas such as the unconscious and the Oedipus Complex are very hard to pin down precisely or to measure. It is also nearly impossible to design a study to test whether such things really exist. There is some supporting evidence, such as Freud's in-depth case study of Little Hans and Kohlberg's attempts to construct a valid test to measure stages of moral development. Compared to other psychological areas and perspectives, however, the psychodynamic perspective is weak on precision and testability.

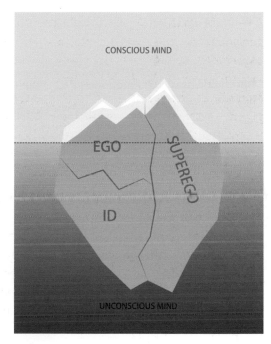

Figure 6.2
Freud's structural model of the human psyche: Freud proposes that, just like an iceberg, only a small amount of the mind is 'visible' to our consciousness

DEBATES IN PSYCHOLOGY

Name of debate	Principles and concepts		Examples of research	
Nature/ nurture	**Nature**	Sees genetic, biological factors as the explanation for thinking and behaviour.	Baron-Cohen *et al*. (1997)	
	Nurture	Sees behaviour as learned or acquired through experiences in the environment.	Chaney *et al* (2004)	
	Interactionist	Accepts that both nature and nurture factors are interconnected and human behaviour is a product of both.	Ⓐ Blakemore and Cooper (1970)	
Freewill/ determinism	**Freewill**	Some argue that human beings are entirely free to act as they chose and bear responsibility for the outcome of their behaviour.	Kohlberg (1968)	
	Determinism	Suggests we lack control of our behaviour and are controlled by our genes or past experiences.	Simons and Chabris (1999)	
Reductionism/ holism	**Reductionism**	Attempts to break down behaviour into its constituent parts and using single factors such as individual genes or particular hormones to account for a given action.	Maguire et al. (2000); Sperry (1968)	
	Holism	A holist approach sees human behaviour as too complex to be reduced to single explanations. Human beings are seen as more than the sum of their individual parts.	Lee *et al*. (1997)	
Individual/ situational explanations	**Individual**	Individual explanations look to the person as the cause of behaviour, specifically their personalities or dispositions.	Baron-Cohen *et al*. (1997); Hancock *et al*. (2011)	
	Situational	Situational explanations draw on circumstances around individuals; for example their group membership or the environmental context.	Milgram (1963); Moray (1959)	
	Situational versus individual		Bocchiaro *et al*. (2012)	

WORTHING COLLEGE LIBRARY

Applications of different positions	Comparison with other debates
Baron-Cohen *et al.*'s findings about people with autism indicate the role of nature, which has implications for the workplace, since their social ability would be hard to change so their differences must be accommodated. In contrast, the work of Chaney et al. suggests that in practical terms, the effects of reinforcements can influence children's health behaviours, an illustration of nurture.	Links to **determinism** – if our thinking and behaviour are entirely determined by our environment, where is the role for freewill? Links to **reductionism** – for example, the belief that a particular aspect of human behaviour could be explained entirely by genes.
The work of Simons and Chabris takes a relatively deterministic viewpoint, and related studies suggest that problems with doctors' diagnoses are possibly inevitable in the light of inattention to the unexpected. In contrast, the findings of Casey *et al.*'s work could suggest either a deterministic viewpoint – since early behaviour seems to predict adulthood ability to resist temptation – or a freewill perspective that everyone has a choice of resisting temptation or not. In practical terms, it is important to focus on the freewill perspective, so that people can be encouraged to take responsibility for their own actions, for example by negotiating rules.	Links to the **nature–nurture** debate (see above) Links to the **reductionism and holism** debate (see below)
The reductionist perspectives of studies such as Maguire *et al.* and Sperry are useful as they provide evidence of underlying causes. Brain structures (or their absence) have direct consequences on cognition and behaviour. Such studies can lead to an understanding of what is going wrong when people suffer from brain damage or disorders and, perhaps ultimately, how such problems might be avoided or improved through rehabilitation. A holist position is taken by Lee *et al.*, considering the diversity of influences on children's behaviour worldwide, showing that in terms of practical generalisations, for example to school discipline, a single explanation or approach is not sufficient.	Links to the **nature–nurture** debate (see above) Links to the **reductionism and holism** debate as reductionists look to one single cause of behaviour, meaning their explanations may remove the influence of freewill.
The work of both Milgram and of Moray have important implications for the prevention of air and road accidents. In Milgram's case there are situational factors of the role of the authority figure, but also individual ones, since we know that people differ in their obedience or resistance to authority (Elms and Milgram,1966). In Moray's case, situational factors include the source and pertinence of a signal. Again, there are individual factors, for example men and women may differ in aspects of attention. In the Bocchiaro *et al.* study, the situation led a surprising number of participants to obey. No personality traits predicted obedience or whistle-blowing, although those expressing deep religious faith were somewhat more likely to blow the whistle.	Links to **freewill and determinism** (see above) in cases where our behaviour is directed by group pressures which may alter our individual patterns of behaviour Links to the **nature–nurture debate**, as it highlights that both contribute to disposition not situation; therefore we should not expect nature and nurture individually to provide a complete explanation for behaviour.

Name of debate	Principles and concepts		Examples of research
Usefulness/ research	Useful	Research that adds to our knowledge and can be applied to real-world situations.	Loftus and Palmer (1974)
	Limited usefulness	Research that may lack credibility or be difficult to apply outside of the research setting.	Ⓐ Gould (1982)
Ethical considerations	Respect	Valuing the dignity and worth of all individuals. This includes awareness of how psychologists may influence people and appear to have authority, and of people's rights to privacy and self determination. Of particular importance are the standards of informed consent, right to withdraw and confidentiality.	
	Informed consent	Having sufficient knowledge about a study to know whether you want to agree to participate.	
	Right to withdraw	A participant should be aware that they can remove themselves, and their data, from the study at any time.	
	Confidentiality	Individuals' results and personal information should be kept safely and not released to anyone outside the study.	
	Competence	Valuing continuing development as a psychologist and the maintenance of high standards of work. This includes functioning optimally and within the limits of one's own knowledge, skill, training, education and experience.	
	Responsibility	Valuing the responsibilities of being a psychologist – to clients, the public, and the profession and science of psychology. This includes the avoidance of harm and the prevention of misuse or abuse of one's contributions to society. Of particular importance are the standards of protection of participants and the role of the debrief.	
	Protection of participants	Participants should not be put at any greater physical or psychological risk than they would expect in their day-to-day lives.	
	Debrief	Full explanation of aims and potential consequences of a study given to participants after participation to ensure that they leave in at least as positive a condition as they arrived.	
	Integrity	Valuing honesty, accuracy, clarity, and fairness in interactions and seeking to promote these in scientific and professional work as a psychologist. Of particular importance is adherence to the standard relating to deception.	
	Deception	Participants should not be deliberately misinformed (lied to) about the aim or procedure of the study. Where this is unavoidable, steps should be taken beforehand to ensure that they are unlikely to be distressed, and afterwards to ensure that they are not.	

Applications of different positions	Comparison with other debates
Loftus et al.'s study into the reliability of eyewitness testimony is useful research because the findings of the experiment are relevant to different contexts, such as in improving police interview techniques. Research such as the mass IQ testing outlined in Gould's article highlights the limited usefulness of some studies. In this case there were issues of credibility with methods and materials, meaning the findings were less valuable.	Links to the debate about **psychology as a science**. It could be argued that research that lacks credibility or a sound method is unscientific and that this also limits its usefulness.
Milgram: MINUS: deception over aim, roles, electric shocks, protection, participants' distress and physical injuries PLUS: competence regarding asking colleagues beforehand Sperry: PLUS: consent – the participants knew about the kinds of tests they would do Bandura et al.: MINUS: protection – the children may have suffered distress, for example from the frustration of being taken aware from the room of nice toys, or harm from learning aggression Freud: MINUS: right to withdraw PLUS: Little Hans recovered from his phobia so ultimately benefitted in terms of reduction of distress Piliavin et al.: MINUS: consent – the participants did not know they were in an experiment; protection – they could have been distressed by the behaviour of the victims PLUS: right to withdraw – the passengers could have moved to a different subway car, and seeing drunk or ill people on the underground is not unlike day-to-day stressors	

Name of debate	Principles and concepts		Examples of research	
Conducting socially sensitive research	Stigma	Psychologists should be aware that individuals or groups may experience feelings of shame and exclusion due to sensitive issues explored in research, such as gender, culture or illness.	**A** Gould (1982): Hancock *et al.* (2011)	
	Political consequences	In some circumstances the outcome of research may have implications for government policy and change the lives of people involved with or affected by the research.		
	Harm	Some issues may be controversial as they are too private or cause distress.	Freud (1909)	
Psychology as a science	The study of cause and effect	The investigation of a causal relationship, i.e. the search for a link between two variables such that a change in one variable can be demonstrated to be responsible for changes in another variable, as is seen in experiments in which the IV causes changes in the DV.	Cause and effect, e.g. Blakemore and Cooper (1970) – line orientation caused perceptual problems Lack of cause and effect, e.g. Freud (1909) – there may have been other reasons why Little Hans's phobia disappeared Replicability, e.g. Baron-Cohen *et al.* (1997) – Eyes Test, details of samples Lack of replicability, e.g. Freud (1909) – unlikely to find another child with similar symptoms and circumstances Control of variables, e.g. Moray (1959) – tone and speed of speech in the passages was constant, and all participants wore headphones Lack of control of variables, e.g. Sperry (1968) – there were differences between participants in the time post-operation and in the extent of their hemispheric deconnection Standardisation, e.g. Bandura *et al.* (1961) – the sequence of events, the model's behaviour, and the rewarding of the child's behaviour were all the same for every participant Lack of standardisation, e.g. Grant *et al.* (1998) – there were some differences in procedural detail between the eight experimenters Quantifiable measurements, e.g. Maguire *et al.* (2000) MRI Lack of quantifiable measurements, e.g. Freud (1909)	
	Falsification	Being able to demonstrate that something is not the case, i.e. that a hypothesis is false.		
	Replicability	Being able to repeat an original procedure in exactly the same way.		
	Objectivity	Taking an unbiased external perspective that is not affected by an individual or personal viewpoint, so should be consistent between different researchers.		
	Induction	A scientific method that uses observations to generate testable hypotheses, which are developed into theories.		
	Deduction	A scientific method that develops hypotheses from theories, then tests these hypotheses by 'observation', i.e. empirically.		
	Hypothesis testing	Scientific evidence is gathered by demonstrating objectively that a testable statement (a hypothesis) is either supported or refuted by evidence.		
	Manipulation of variables	To test hypotheses in a valid and reliable way, the IV and DV must be operationally defined.		
	Control of variables	Essential so that extraneous variables could not account for changes in the DV, which would make any apparent effect of the IV invalid.		
	Standardisation	The use of a set procedures for conducting the study and collecting data across different conditions and participants to limit the effects of uncontrolled variables.		
	Quantifiable measurements	Quantifiable measurements (i.e. numerical ones) help to ensure that the DV is being assessed in an objective way.		

Applications of different positions	Comparison with other debates
Both Gould's article on mental testing and Hancock *et al.*'s study on the language of psychopaths have the potential to stigmatise certain groups and lead them to be treated in a negative way. The case study conducted by Freud could be considered socially sensitive as it deals with private information and analysis of psychosexual behaviour, which may be considered 'taboo'.	Closely linked with **ethical considerations** in psychology, but with greater emphasis on the wider implications of the research beyond the immediate involvement of participants. **Ethnocentric** research may relate to issues of cultural diversity and values.
Whether psychology should be considered a science is hotly debated. Some areas and perspectives embrace the principles of hard science, including the use of quantifiable measurements. For example, biological psychologists such as Maguire *et al.* use brain-scanning techniques for analysis to objectively assess neurological function. However, other perspectives in psychology may deliberately avoid such methods, because it is not possible or desirable to study human behaviour using numeric measurement. One example of this is Freud's case study of Little Hans, which relied on qualitative methods such as dream analysis.	Links to the **reductionism/holism** debate as, through the scientific approach of hypothesis testing and variable control, researchers may seek to reduce explanations for behaviour to simple, single factors. Link to **ethical considerations**. Researchers attempt to take an objective approach to the study of human participants, while also considering their well-being and the nature of the researcher–participant relationship and these objectives are often in conflict, for example in the use of deception.

PRACTICE QUESTIONS

Here are some of the sorts of questions that you could be asked in AS-level Psychology H167/02 Psychological themes through core studies.

SECTION B:
AREAS, PERSPECTIVES AND DEBATES

9 (a) Outline how developmental psychology explains behaviour. [2]

(b) Suggest **one** advantage of using an experimental method to investigate behaviour. Support your answer with evidence from **one** appropriate core study. [3]

(c) Suggest **one** advantage of using a non-experimental method to investigate behaviour. Support your answer with evidence from **one** appropriate core study. [3]

(d) Explain the relevance of any **one** core study to the nature-nurture debate. [5]

(e)* Discuss the problems of conducting research with children. Support your answer with evidence from core studies. [12]

SECTION C: PRACTICAL APPLICATIONS

Answer **all** the question parts in Section C.

A robbery took place in a jewellery shop in the Trafford Centre, Manchester, last Friday, witnessed by a large number of shoppers. A number of officers interviewed people at the scene, while others interviewed witnesses later in their own homes. According to our sources, none of the officers had had any training on good questioning techniques. Chief Inspector Becky Durrant of the Manchester Constabulary told us: 'We're doing everything in our powers to catch these criminals, who left with almost half a million pounds' worth of cash and jewels, as well as causing distress to staff and customers. We'd like to appeal for more witnesses to come forward if you were shopping at the Trafford Centre on Friday 21st November between 3.30 and 4.30 in the afternoon. We have been frustrated by the different witness reports we have received so far and are at a loss to understand why people's memories of the incident are so different.'

10 (a) Explain why this article can be viewed as being relevant to cognitive psychology. [4]

(b) Briefly outline **one** core study and explain how it could explain the different witness reports. [5]

(c) Identify **one** psychological issue raised by the above article. Support your answer with evidence from the article. [4]

(d) Use your psychological knowledge to suggest a training programme for the police relevant to the issue you have identified in question 10(c). [6]

(e) Evaluate your suggested training programme. [6]

SECTION B   9 (b) Suggest one advantage of using an experimental method to investigate behaviour. Support your answer with evidence from one appropriate core study. [3]

Rachel's answer:

One advantage is control. There is lots of control in Loftus and Palmer's study and in Bandura *et al.*'s study.

We say: Control is an important advantage of any experimental method and Rachel is correct to select this. However, she needs to explain this in a little more detail. The question asks for only one core study and so there is no need to mention more than one. Rachel needs to expand her answer, as simply saying that there is lots of control without saying what was controlled does not really demonstrate understanding.

Charlotte's answer:

One advantage of experimental methods is that you are able to control extraneous variables. This means that it is easier to draw conclusions about the influence of the IV on the DV. For example, Loftus and Palmer were able to control lots of variables such as the room, the temperature, the background noise and the fact that all their participants were students. This meant that it was much easier to conclude that the wording of the questions really did have an influence on the information that people remembered.

We say: Charlotte's answer is much better. She has given more information about the advantage she has selected and has then given detailed evidence from an appropriate core study. You could use any core study from any of the approaches here so you would have lots to choose from.

9 (c) Suggest one advantage of using a non-experimental method to investigate behaviour. Support your answer with evidence from one appropriate core study. [3]

Rachel's answer:

One advantage of a non-experimental method is that it is much easier to set up as you don't need any complicated equipment. Sperry needed loads of complicated equipment to do his study.

We say: Rachel has made a common mistake here by trying to explain something in terms of what it isn't rather than in terms of what it is. It is not accurate to say that an advantage of a non-experimental method is that it is easy – some are extremely complicated and, while it may be that many do not require complicated equipment, this needs to be evidenced with a core study that does not require complicated equipment rather than one that does.

Charlotte's answer:

One advantage of a non-experimental method could be the fact that they tend to be conducted in more realistic environments and may also collect more qualitative data rather than quantitative data. For example, although there were problems with the way that Freud studied Little Hans, he was in his natural environment and not in a laboratory.

We say: Once again, Charlotte has provided us with the stronger response. The strength is clearer here and the evidence is appropriate. There are fewer non-experimental studies than experimental ones and it is a good idea to make sure that you know which are which.

9 (e)* Discuss the problems of conducting research with children. Support your answer with evidence from core studies. [12]

Rachel's answer:

Children are more difficult to do research with as they may not really understand what is going on and so won't be able to work out what you want them to do. You also can't really explain things to them very easily and so they can't give informed consent as they don't really understand what is going on.

Charlotte's answer:

One problem is that children's language is less sophisticated than adults', and so it might be more difficult to explain to children what you want them to do. This might make some studies quite difficult to conduct. This might also mean that experimenters misunderstand what children are telling them. For example Little Hans' father might well have changed the words that Little Hans used when he reported the conversations to Freud and this may have changed the meaning.

Another problem is ethics. Children can't give consent to take part in studies so their parents have to give consent for them. Children still need to be protected from harm and distress and should be debriefed. Bandura et al. may have caused quite a lot of distress to the children who took part in their study, and there is no mention of debriefing.

Another problem is that children and adults might behave very differently and so it might be problematic to study children and then apply the results to adults. For example, would adults behave the same way in the Bandura et al. study?

We say: Rachel needs to look much more carefully at the question and also at the mark allocation. There are 12 marks for this question, so it is important to cover a number of points in the answer. The question also asks you to support your answer with evidence from core studies and there is no evidence provided in Rachel's answer. Looking at what Rachel has written, it could be argued that the fact that children don't 'work out what you want them to do' is a strength rather than a problem, as it would suggest that they are less likely to respond to demand characteristics. Rachel's second point is also problematic as children don't give consent to participate in research. Their parents or guardians would be asked to give consent on their behalf. Finally, Rachel's answer is quite repetitive and she has written that children 'may not/don't really understand what is going on' twice in this short answer.

We say: This is a better answer from Charlotte who has clearly read the question carefully and has provided evidence from core studies. However, there are still improvements that could be made to this answer. The first point is very good and the example from the Freud study is very clear and detailed. The second paragraph has identified a clear problem and has made some link to the Bandura et al. study although an explanation of how this study might have caused distress would have improved this section. The third point is also a valid one but could have been explained in more detail, and the link to the study is made very weakly. If Charlotte could think of a fourth point it would be worth including another one, especially if she could provide an example from a different core study. Chaney et al. also used children in their studies, so examples could have been drawn from these as well.

SECTION C   10 (a) Explain why this article can be viewed as being relevant to cognitive psychology.

Rachel's answer:

Because it is about memory and how people's memory is not very good.

Charlotte's answer:

This article is relevant to cognitive psychology because it is focusing on the cognitive process of memory and recall and more particularly on factors that affect the accuracy of someone's memory.

We say: This is a very short answer from Rachel and it doesn't really say any more than that the study is about memory. Don't forget that the questions in Section C are worth more than two or three marks, so the examiners will be looking for answers of more than just a sentence. Links to the article would be useful here as well to make sure that you have answered the question properly.

We say: This is a better answer from Charlotte although even this could have been extended and linked more directly to the article. It does make a much more specific point than Rachel's answer, and the link is implied even if it not made explicit.

10 (b) Briefly outline one core study and explain how it could explain the different witness reports. [5]

Rachel's answer:

The core study by Loftus and Palmer is relevant here because it looks at reasons why people remember. The other cognitive study looks at state-dependent learning and this might suggest that people will remember differently in different places.

We say: Rachel hasn't read the question properly. The question asks you to outline **one** core study and explain how it could explain the different witness reports. Rachel has mentioned two studies and it is likely that only one will be credited. There is evidence of some understanding here although this answer needs developing quite a lot more.

Charlotte's answer:

The study by Grant et al. looked at context dependency in memory. In other words whether people remember better when they take in information and try to recall it in the same situation or in different situations. In this study the context was noise or silence so the conditions were:

Learn Silence / Recall Silence (matching)

Learn Noisy / Recall Noisy (matching)

Learn Silence / Recall Noisy (non-matching)

Learn Noisy / Recall Silence (non-matching)

Participants in the matching conditions recalled more information than participants in the non-matching conditions. This could be applied here as some of the witnesses were interviewed at the scene and some at home, so some were interviewed in the same context as when they witnessed the crime (matching) and others were interviewed in different contexts (non-matching).

We say: Charlotte has read the question! This is a nice outline of the study by Grant *et al.* which gives quite a lot of information about the method and the results. The final sentence is a very clear explanation of how this study can be used to explain one issue raised by the article.

10 (c) Identify one psychological issue raised by the above article.

Support your answer with evidence from the article. [4]

Rachel's answer:

One issue is whether people's memories can be relied on in court. You shouldn't be able to convict someone of a crime just because a witness says that they did it because they might be lying.

Charlotte's answer:

One issue is the accuracy of eyewitness testimony and in particular the extent to which information received after the event can influence someone's memory. Loftus and Palmer showed that leading questions could have a powerful influence on people's memory of a car accident, even to the extent that they would say that they had seen something that was not there. The article states that the police conducting the interviews did not have any training in questioning techniques, which supports this issue.

We say: This is not really an issue that is raised by the article although there are links between this article and the issue that Rachel is discussing. The question also asks for the answer to be supported with evidence from the article which Rachel has not done. If she had tried to respond to this part of the question, she would probably have realised that the issue she has selected is not specifically raised in the article.

We say: This answer responds very clearly to the question. The issue is raised by the article and Charlotte has also made reference to Loftus and Palmer in explaining it. She has ended her answer with a piece of evidence from the article that directly links to the issue that she has selected.

10 (d) Use your psychological knowledge to suggest a training programme for the police relevant to the issue you have identified in question 10 (c). [6]

Rachel's answer:

The police need to be trained to recognise when people are lying so that they know who to believe. This could be through training them to recognise body language cues.

Charlotte's answer:

Police need to be trained in interview techniques and especially in avoiding leading questions. They need to realise that even changing a word from 'a' to 'the' could have a big effect on the answers given. They also need to realise that context is important and part of the training should be

We say: Rachel needs to read questions more carefully and also to take note of the numbers of marks available for each question. This is not only too short for an answer to a six-mark question, but also not relevant to the article.

recognising that interviewing people in the same or similar context is likely to produce the best results. One way would be to demonstrate this through studies like the ones by Grant et al. and Loftus and Palmer, but letting the police try out different questioning techniques and collecting their own data. This would have to be in simulations rather than real crimes, for ethical reasons, and would be really difficult to set up.

We say: Charlotte has given a much more thoughtful answer here. The training programme is focusing on a fairly specific issue (questioning techniques) and there is a little bit of detail about how this could be done. However, Charlotte has started to evaluate her suggestions at the end when she mentions ethical reasons and the difficulties of setting this type of situation up, and this is not being asked for in this question.

10 (e) Evaluate your suggested training programme. [6]

Rachel's answer:

This would be really interesting because you could find out whether people did things like blink more when they were lying or fidget a lot. It could be quite complicated though as you would need to know if people were lying or telling the truth.

We say: Rachel needs to think about what she wants to say. To use 'interesting' as an evaluative point is probably not a good idea although 'usefulness' could well be developed into a strong argument. The fact that Rachel is evaluating an inappropriate training programme weakens this further. Her second sentence, where she starts talking about problems in knowing whether people are lying or telling the truth, is the beginning of an interesting point – how can you study body language in people telling the truth or lying unless you know which is which? – but this needs to be developed further.

Charlotte's answer:

This type of training would take quite a long time and it may be difficult for police to attend this type of training because of the job they are supposed to be doing. However, setting up some mock crimes in the real world and allowing the trainees to question witnesses would have good ecological validity although if the witnesses agreed to take part (before witnessing the crime) this would lower the realism because they would be waiting for something to happen and if they didn't know it was a study then this would break ethical guidelines because they could be distressed and they haven't been debriefed. They could also use the trainees as the witnesses so that they could see for themselves how easily their memories can be distorted.

We say: There are some interesting points here and Charlotte has obviously thought carefully about her suggested training programme. However, it looks as though she might have been running out of time as her second sentence is over 70 words long and gets a little difficult to follow. This can easily happen when answering in a rush, but you need to remember that extended answers will also be judged on their clarity. Finally, Charlotte makes a really interesting suggestion but unfortunately this is in the wrong place. This should have been included in the answer to question 10(d), as it is not an evaluative point.

A-LEVEL PRACTICE QUESTIONS

Here are some of the sorts of questions that you could be asked in A-level Psychology H567/02 Psychological themes through core studies. Remember, for Section B you can draw on your learning from Applied psychology studies (looked at in a different book) as well as on the core studies from this book.

SECTION B: AREAS, PERSPECTIVES AND DEBATES

12 (a) Describe the difference between the social approach and the biological approach. [4]

(b) Explain how **one** psychological study can be considered as providing a biological explanation for behaviour. [5]

(c) Evaluate the usefulness of providing a biological explanation for behaviour. Support your answer with evidence from **one** appropriate psychological study. [6]

(d)* Identify and discuss the strengths and weaknesses of providing social explanations for behaviour. Support your answer with evidence from appropriate psychological studies. [20]

SECTION C: PRACTICAL APPLICATIONS

Answer **all** the question parts in Section C.

Is Peppa Pig making toddlers naughty?

Parents despair as children copy cartoon by answering back.

With her cheeky smile, and even cheekier attitude, she has become a hit with children. But it seems a growing number of parents are turning against TV character Peppa Pig, claiming she is a 'bad influence'. Many complain their sons and daughters have started to copy the 'naughty' behaviour of the cartoon pig and her younger brother, George, by answering back to their parents. Some have even banned the programme because they claim it has

made their children misbehave. One father spoke of his despair at how his four-year-old son had taken to splashing in what he gleefully called 'muddy puddles' on his way to school, copying Peppa's favourite pastime. A mother reported, 'My daughter kept saying "no" and "yuk" in a really high-and-mighty way, just like Peppa does, and generally answering back when I ask her to do something.'

Psychologist Dr Aric Sigman said that in recent years there had been a 'significant increase' in children using 'adversarial, snide, questioning, confrontational and disrespectful behaviour' they had copied from cartoons. He added, 'Some 80 per cent of brain development is between birth and three years old, so if they spend a lot of time watching TV, they will copy forms of behaviours that they see on the TV.'

Based on an article by Katherine Faulkner cited in *MailOnline* (News), 9 January 2012

13 (a) Identify **one** psychological issue raised by the above article. Support your answer with evidence from the article. [5]

(b) Briefly outline **one** piece of psychological research and explain how it could relate to the issue you have identified in the above article. [8]

(c) Use your psychological knowledge to suggest how the issue you have identified could be managed. [10]

(d) Evaluate how you would manage the issue you have identified. [12]

SECTION B **12 (a) Describe the difference between the social approach and the biological approach. [4]**

Liam's answer:

The social approach looks at social factors such as other people and the biological approach looks at biological factors such as the way our brains are made.

We say: Liam needs to re-read what he has written. It is important to avoid defining something by using the same words that are in the question. Defining the 'social approach' as looking at social factors and the 'biological approach' as looking at biological factors does not really demonstrate an understanding of what these terms mean. His mention of 'other people' and 'brains' hints at an understanding, but this needs to be extended further.

Rina's answer:

The social approach explains behaviour through external factors such as the presence of other people. This is also sometimes referred to as situational explanations because the assumption is that people's behaviour can be explained by examining the situations they are in rather than their individual characteristics. The biological approach looks at the biological factors such as brain structure and role of nature rather than nurture.

We say: This is a better answer. It is much clearer here that Rina understands what these approaches are although even she is using the phrase biological factors to explain the biological approach. Even changing this to physiology would demonstrate more understanding.

12 (b) Explain how one psychological study can be considered as providing a biological explanation for behaviour. [5]

Liam's answer:

The taxi driver study is a biological study because it shows that our brains change depending on what we do.

Rina's answer:

Sperry's study of the eleven split-brain patients provides a biological explanation for behaviour as it suggests that all of the behaviours seen in the study were a direct result of the disconnection of the two hemispheres. It is not necessary to look at any situational or social factors to explain these behaviours as they can be explained fully in biological terms.

We say: Clearly this is not going to be enough for five marks. The point that Liam is making is a valid one (our brains do change as a result of experience and this is one of the key conclusions of this study) although this could be explained more clearly. It would also be worth explaining how the study chosen is a biological study by relating biological explanations in general to the biological explanations offered in this study. Here, Liam could say that this study explains the taxi drivers' superior navigational skills as a result of physical changes in the hippocampal volume, which is correlated with their driving experience.

We say: Rina has provided a clear link between the notion of a 'biological explanation' and the explanation that is given in the Sperry core study for the behaviours shown by the split-brain patients. It might have been a good idea to include an example of these behaviours together with a more precise explanation (because the information was only seen by one hemisphere and could not travel across the corpus callosum, for example) but the final point about not needing situational or social examples is a good one.

12 (d)* Identify and discuss the strengths and weaknesses of providing social explanations for behaviour. Support your answer with evidence from appropriate psychological studies. [20]

Liam's answer:

Social psychology is useful because it helps us understand social behaviours such as obedience and disobedience and whistle-blowing and helping. All of these behaviours can be seen in the core studies. Social psychology is often unethical because people are deceived about what is going on. Social psychology is expensive because the studies are so complicated.

We say: It is fairly obvious that Liam has not written enough for a question worth 20 marks. It should also be clear that Liam needs to explain the points he is making much more clearly and to give very specific examples from the core studies. For example the studies by Milgram and Bocchiaro et al. could be used as

Rina's answer:

Social psychological explanations are useful. Firstly understanding social behaviours such as obedience and disobedience has very real applications to the world. Milgram's study of obedience not only helped us to understand that the behaviour of the Nazis in the Second World War was not solely a characteristic of a nation but the result of the social environment in which the soldiers were operating. This study is still useful in explaining all kinds of horrific acts where the individuals claim to have been obeying orders. Bocchiaro et al.'s study extends this from Milgram's focus on obedience to a wider focus on why disobedience is so difficult and why whistle-blowing is such a complex act to explain. This is also a useful explanation in that it shows the contrast between what we think we will do and what we will actually do in a situation. Social psychological explanations also help us understand the power of culture and social situation. Piliavin et al.'s study and Levine et al.'s study also show us that the social and cultural situations are crucial in understanding why people behave in the way that they do. However, it could also be argued that social explanations are not all that useful because understanding these behaviours does not always change them. We might think that because we understand how such horrific things happen we could stop them happening but that doesn't seem to be true. Social explanations tend to ignore other explanations such as biological or cognitive factors and maybe this is not always a good idea. Perhaps studying the underlying thought processes or the physiological effects of situations such as those created by Milgram and Piliavin et al. would also be enlightening. A further weakness of social explanations is that the research that is required to investigate these is often unethical and difficult to replicate. Milgram's study deceived participants and caused significant distress and Piliavin et al.'s study also had the potential to distress and in this study it was not possible to debrief participants. Setting up complex situations like these is time-consuming and would be almost impossible to replicate due to the huge number of variables involved.

examples for the first point, and either Milgram or Piliavin *et al.* as examples for the point about ethics. The third point about cost needs to be thought about a bit more carefully. Is this really a fair point about social explanations? An appropriate response to a question like this would be to identify strengths and weaknesses of social explanations (rather than social psychology) and to express each one clearly, backed up with evidence from a core study. Aiming for a balance between strengths and weaknesses would also be a good idea.

We say: There are 20 marks available for this question and this is also one of the questions where the examiners will be assessing the quality of written response (these questions will be marked with an asterisk (*) on the examination paper) so it is important to write clearly and fluently and use psychological terminology wherever appropriate. Rina has made a number of good points and has tried to provide evidence to back these up. One of the strengths of her answer is that she has tried to address both strengths and weaknesses in balance.

SECTION C   13 (a) Identify **one** psychological issue raised by the above article. Support your answer with evidence from the article. [5]

Liam's answer:

The issue is children copying bad behaviour from the television.

We say: This answer is much too short. There are five marks available for this question so it is important to write more than one sentence! This sentence is correct and has identified a broad issue from the article, but Liam has taken no notice of the second part of the question which says 'support your answer with evidence from the article'.

Rina's answer:

The issue is imitation of role models. The article is suggesting that the cartoon character Peppa Pig is a 'bad influence' on children because they are copying her naughty behaviour, such as splashing in puddles and answering back. Social learning theory would say that children are imitating Peppa and George's behaviour because these characters are acting as role models for appropriate behaviour. The behaviour would be even more likely to be imitated if either it is not punished or disapproved of in any way or if it were to be rewarded. This brings in the psychological issue of reinforcement (operant conditioning). The evidence from Dr Sigman suggests that this programme is a specific concern because it is aimed at children of an age where a significant amount of brain development is taking place.

We say: This answer demonstrates that Rina has a very good grasp of psychological terminology ('imitation', 'role models', 'reinforcement') and has included several pieces of evidence from the original article. This is a much more detailed answer than the first one.

13 (b) Briefly outline **one** piece of psychological research and explain how it could relate to the issue you have identified in the above article. [8]

Liam's answer:

The study with the Bobo dolls is relevant here because it shows that children imitate the aggressive behaviour of an adult. The researcher showed children some adults playing aggressively or non-aggressively with a Bobo doll and then let children play with the same toys. The ones who saw the adult being aggressive were more likely to be aggressive themselves.

We say: Overall this is a very short answer for eight marks. The exam paper is two hours long and there are a total of 105 marks, so you have slightly over a minute for each mark. You could spend a couple of minutes thinking and five minutes writing your answer to this question.

Rina's answer:

Bandura conducted a study to see if children would imitate adult role models. He matched children on their pre-existing levels of aggression and then divided them into groups. The children either saw a same-sex role model or an opposite-sex role model behaving aggressively towards a Bobo doll or playing non-aggressively with other toys. Children were tested individually. When they were later allowed to play with a Bobo doll their behaviour was influenced by the role model. Children were more aggressive when they had seen an adult behaving aggressively and imitation was more likely with a same-sex role model. Boys were more likely to be aggressive than girls.

This study does relate to the issue outlined above as it shows that role models can have a significant influence on behaviour. It would suggest that children seeing aggressive behaviour will copy this behaviour. It might also suggest that girls might be more likely to copy Peppa and boys might be more likely to copy George. However, Bandura et al.'s study was with real-life adult role models and this article is discussing the influence of cartoon characters so the application may be limited. Also, the study by Bandura et al. does not look at the consequences of the behaviour so it may be limited in this respect.

We say: This is a much more detailed answer which demonstrates good understanding. The use of Bandura's name right at the beginning of the answer is effective as it means that the examiner knows straight away which study you have chosen. The beginning of the second paragraph also gives a clear signpost to the examiner that Rina has moved on to the second part of the question. The explanation of how this relates to the issue raised in part (a) is also good and the fact that Rina has explicitly related this to Peppa and George is excellent. The next two sentences are an excellent discussion of the limitations of the application of the study by Bandura *et al.* to the issue, but this has not been directly asked for in the question It is possible that this might be seen as relevant (it is a very good set of points) but, as a general rule, stick to what has been specifically asked for in the question.

13 (c) Use your psychological knowledge to suggest how the issue you have identified could be managed. [10]

Liam's answer:

I would suggest that the company that makes Peppa Pig changes the programme so that the negative behaviours are not included and instead Peppa and George do lots of good things. Children will then copy the good behaviours rather than the bad behaviours.

We say: It is fairly obvious that this is not enough for 10 marks. Before going on to read Rina's answer, jot down a few suggestions for improving this answer.

Rina's answer:

I would suggest some applications of behaviourism by the parents. One way of doing this would be to use a token economy system such as a star chart to reward good behaviour. The parents would have to observe their children's behaviour very closely so that they could reward them every time they did something good so that the children learn which behaviours are producing the rewards and then they will produce these behaviours again. Parents should also ignore bad behaviour as much as they can so that children stop producing this behaviour as it is no longer being reinforced. Some children respond to negative attention as well as positive so no response is better. Parents could also ban the programme as it says in the article, but this might make it more attractive to the children. Perhaps they could watch it with their children and respond to the naughty behaviour so that children learn that their parents disapprove of this behaviour.

We say: This starts really nicely by stating clearly that these are applications of behaviourism. Rina has made several appropriate suggestions. They have all been well explained although this could still be more closely related to the article (perhaps mentioning Peppa and George somewhere in the answer would be a good idea!).

13 (d) Evaluate how you would manage the issue you have identified. [12]

Liam's answer:

It would work if the TV companies stopped making anything aggressive or made it impossible for children to watch them but this would be very unlikely to happen. Also children would still see negative behaviours from real people or in the cinema or in computer games and so banning aggression from television wouldn't really work.

This is a very specific command – you are being asked to evaluate here so make sure that you don't include any description. Also 12 marks means at least 12 minutes, so have some thinking and planning time before you start writing.

We say: This is not 12 minutes' work. There are a couple of interesting points here – the first one is that 'this would be very unlikely to happen'. If this candidate took the time to explain why this would be very unlikely to happen (what would the TV companies get out of this, how would you make it impossible for children to see certain things, practical implications such as cost, etc.) this would become an interesting discussion. The second point, that children will still see negative behaviours in other contexts, is also a really important point and could have been discussed in much more detail. It is a shame that Liam has not spent a little more time explaining some very good ideas.

Rina's answer:

Token economy is quite cheap and easy to implement. Parents don't really need any specific training for this and the tokens could be just stars on a chart that add up to a little reward such as biscuits or sweets. There is evidence that token economies are effective in changing behaviour in several contexts such as prisons and psychiatric institutions. However, token economies work best if they are done consistently so that people quickly associate the behaviour with the reward and know which behaviours to produce. However children will have to go to nursery or to school and maybe they wouldn't be rewarded for the same behaviours there and then the way it was done at home would be less effective. It might also be a little bit unrealistic to expect parents to sit and watch everything with their children and even if they ban the programme they will see other children copying these behaviours when they go to school. There are probably more important things to worry about than the behaviour of cartoon pigs.

We say: There is a really nice evaluation of token economy at the start of this answer, and several good evaluation points have been included, such as the comment that rewards are unlikely to be consistent between home and nursery or school. Some evaluation of the other suggestions has been included but this could be expanded. This would be an excellent place for Rina to bring in some psychological terminology such as 'modelling' or 'reinforcement'.

C7
RESEARCH
METHODS

PART 1: UNDERSTANDING RESEARCH METHODS IN PSYCHOLOGY

In this section we are going to explore the research methods that are used in psychological investigations to collect or analyse data – that is, the major techniques that psychologists use to explore behaviour, emotions and cognition.

The major methods are:
- experiment
- observation
- the self-report
- correlation

We will look at each of these in detail.

KEY IDEAS

The **dependent variable (DV)** is the factor in an experiment that is measured by the researcher. Changes in this factor are predicted to be caused by (i.e. *dependent* upon) changes in the independent variable.

The **independent variable (IV)** is the factor in an experiment that is manipulated, changed or compared by the researcher. It is expected to have an influence on the dependent variable.

The different conditions under which participants are tested in an experiment that are manipulated, changed or compared by the researcher are the **levels of the IV**.

An **experiment** is a research method in which the effect of two of more conditions of the IV on a DV is measured, and other variables controlled, in order to investigate a cause-and-effect relationship.

An experiment characterised by the absence of the IV is known as the **control condition**. It is used as a baseline for comparison with an experimental condition.

QUESTION SPOTLIGHT!

Maguire *et al.* (2000) (see page 148) investigated several differences using experimental designs.

Identify the IV and the DV in each of these experiments:

1 A comparison was made between anterior hippocampal volume in taxi drivers and in non-taxi drivers.
2 Total brain volume was measured in taxi drivers and non-taxi drivers.
3 The size of the left and right hippocampus in taxi drivers was compared.

INTRODUCTION

In this section we will be looking at the way in which the experimental method is used in psychology. Specifically, we will explore three types of experimental design and evaluate them. Will also evaluate the experimental method in general.

Experiments

An **experiment** is a way to carry out an investigation in which one variable is manipulated by the experimenter and the effect of this change on another variable is observed or measured. In this way, the experimenter can see whether the variable they are manipulating causes the other variable to change too. If it does, there is said to be a cause-and-effect relationship between the two variables.

In an experiment, the situation allows the effects of one variable on another to be observed and measured. In a true experiment (see page 224) the variations in the first factor, the one causing the difference, are deliberately created by the researcher; in a quasi-experiment these variations arise naturally. In either case, the variable causing the change is called the **independent variable** (or **IV**). The variable being measured, that varies as a consequence of the changes in the IV, is called the **dependent variable** (or **DV**). The measure of the DV provides quantitative data. An experimenter can be sure that it is only the IV that is causing a change in the DV, as all other variables are closely controlled.

An experimental investigation usually has two (or more) conditions or **levels of the IV**, and the DV is measured in each of these situations. To be certain that any changes in the DV arise only because of changes in the IV, the experimenter uses controls to keep constant any other factors that could affect the DV. It is this that ensures they can conclude whether or not there is a cause-and-effect relationship. For example, in a study investigating the effects of hunger on concentration, students could be tested before and after lunch. The time of day would be the IV, with two conditions 'before lunch' and 'after lunch'. The DV (of concentration) would be measured in each condition. It is possible for there to be several levels of the IV. In the first experiment in Loftus and Palmer's study (see page 46), there were five levels – five different verbs were used in a leading question (hit, smashed, collided, contacted, bumped). Each of these was an experimental condition, i.e. one in which the IV was being actively changed. The DV (being measured) was the participant's estimate of speed. In contrast, the second of Loftus and Palmer's experiments used a **control condition**, that is, a condition from which the IV is absent. In this case, they compared two experimental conditions asking about vehicular speed using the verbs 'smashed' (into) and 'hit'; and a control group in which there was no question about vehicular speed. One DV was again the participant's estimate of speed, the other being the response 'yes' or 'no' to the question about broken glass.

QUESTION SPOTLIGHT!

For each of the following experiments, decide whether the conditions are all experimental or whether one or more experimental conditions is being compared to a control condition:

1 A study looks at the difference between eyewitness recall when there are delays of 1, 2, 3 or 4 days between the event and giving the testimony.

2 A test of whether people are more likely to help a stranger who is struggling to get up some steps when the stranger either does or doesn't have a pushchair.

3 An investigation looking at visual development in cats, compares kittens raised in environments with vertical stripes, horizontal stripes, no pattern, and complex patterns with a range of shapes and colours.

Figure 7.1

QUESTION SPOTLIGHT!

Identify whether these experiments used a control condition or only experimental conditions:

1 Blakemore and Cooper (1970) (see page 140).

2 Piliavin *et al.* (1969) (see page 24). There are four IVs and two measures of the DV.

3 Grant *et al.* (1998) (see page 51).

OPERATIONALISING VARIABLES

In order to be certain about the findings of an experiment, we must be sure that we know exactly what has changed. For the IV this means knowing precisely how the variable was manipulated. For the DV this means being confident that any variation is measured accurately. To achieve this, the researcher operationalises both variables. For example, in an experiment testing the effect of leading questions on recall we can identify the two variables: the IV is leading questions and the DV is recall. However, these are not sufficient as definitions – another researcher wouldn't be able to tell what had been changed or how the effect had been observed, hence the need for **operationalisation**. To operationalise the IV we could state that there were two levels of the IV, one that used leading questions, saying 'Did you see the...', and one that used non-leading questions, saying 'Did you see a...'. This could be expanded by giving examples of the items in the questions. Operationalisation of the DV would be errors in recall, i.e. the number of questions incorrectly answered.

EXPERIMENTAL DESIGN

In an experiment, participants may be tested in all, or only one, of the levels of the IV. The different ways that participants are allocated to the levels of the IV are called **experimental designs**. Three common experimental designs are:
* independent measures design
* repeated measures design
* matched participants design.

KEY IDEAS

The definition of variables so that they can be accurately manipulated, measured or quantified and replicated is called **operationalisation**.

STRETCH & CHALLENGE

It is important that you can define variables, as well as identify them. Consider again the IVs and DVs you identified in the question spotlight above.

How was each variable operationalised?

1 Blakemore and Cooper (1970) (IV and DV) (see page 140).

2 Piliavin *et al.* (1969) (4 IVs, 2 DVs) (see page 24).

3 Grant *et al.* (1998) (1 IV, 2 DVs) (see page 51).

KEY IDEAS

The term **'experimental design'** refers to the way in which participants are allocated to levels of the IV.

Independent measures design is an experimental design in which different participants are used for each level of the IV.

Repeated measures design is an experimental design in which each participant performs in every level of the IV.

Matched participants design is an experimental design in which participants are arranged into pairs. Each pair is similar in ways that are important to the study and one member of each pair performs one of the levels of the IV.

Demand characteristics are features of an experimental setting (the 'characteristics') that indicate to participants the aims of the study (hence the 'demands') and so can influence their behaviour.

QUESTION SPOTLIGHT!

As well as being able to understand variables in the core studies, you also need to be able to operationally define new variables.

Write your own operational definitions for the IVs and DVs in the following studies:

1 In a test of memory, recall of long and short words was compared.
2 An investigation aimed to measure whether attachment of 5-year-old boys was stronger to their mother or their father.
3 Some students conducted an experiment to find out if participants are more likely to notice their name or a number in a spoken message that they are not attending to.

Figure 7.2

Independent measures design

In this experimental design, a separate group of participants is used for each level of the IV. This means that the set of data gained for each condition is 'independent' because it is not related to any other pieces of data – they have come from different people. Note that this is not the same use of the word 'independent' as in the 'independent variable'. If we wanted to know whether age affected memory, we could test recall in a group of young people and then wait for them to grow old. However, it is much quicker to compare them to a group of older adults to look at the effect of age. This would be an independent measures design.

This design has the advantage that the participants experience the experimental setting only once. This means that they are less likely to notice clues that might tell them the aims of the experiment (**demand characteristics**) and to respond to them. One disadvantage is that there might be individual differences between participants that could influence the findings. For example, in a study on the effect of repetition, all the people with good memories might end up in the 'no repetition' group. If so, it might look as though repetition was less important than it is in reality. This effect can be reduced by randomly allocating participants to different conditions. This should even out the differences between individuals across the levels of the IV. In order to randomly allocate participants, each is given a number, and the numbers are then randomly divided into two groups. This can be done by putting cards with numbers on into a hat and drawing out two sets, or using a random number generator (e.g. on a computer) to do the same thing.

In order to hide the purpose of the experiment, the researcher may deceive the participants about the aims of the study. For example, in a test on the effect of leading versus non-leading questions on eyewitness memory, the researcher might not want the participants to know it is a test of memory at all, because that would cause them to focus on the task. Instead, the participants might be told that it is a test of hearing or concentration and that they are to watch a film.

This would reduce the risk of demand characteristics affecting performance, but it also raises ethical issues (see page 309). There is clearly a dilemma for researchers between, on the one hand, the need to conduct rigorous studies in which variables are effectively controlled, and, on the other, the need to keep participants informed about the aims and methods of a study.

If possible, only the researcher, and not the participants, should know which condition each individual has been allocated to. This is called a **single blind** procedure and it helps reduce the risk that participants will try to produce the results that they believe the experimenter wants, i.e. it is one way to control researcher effects. These are the negative influences researchers can have on a study by their presence or beliefs. Ideally, someone other than the experimenter should allocate the participants to groups. This arrangement, called **double blind**, means that even the experimenter dealing directly with the participants is unaware of the level of the IV to which each participant belongs. This ensures that the experimenter will not affect the participants' performance by treating them (even unconsciously) in biased ways, i.e. it is another way to limit researcher effects.

KEY IDEAS

A **single blind** experimental procedure ensures that participants are unaware of the level of the IV in which they are performing. This helps to reduce the effect of demand characteristics.

A **double blind** experimental procedure protects against both demand characteristics and researcher bias. It ensures that neither the researcher working with the participants nor the participants themselves are aware of which condition an individual is in.

Researcher effects are the negative influences researchers can have on a study by their presence or beliefs.

QUESTION SPOTLIGHT!

1   Bandura *et al.* (1961) (see page 82) used different children to test the effects of male and female models. *What was this design and why was it chosen?*

2   In study 2, Moray (1959) (see page 62) tested the same people in several conditions including ones where they heard the different versions of the same instruction. '[Own name] you may stop now' appeared in the verbal message they were not attending to in two different conditions, once without their own name and once with. He could have used different people for the 'no name' and 'own name' conditions. *Why was it better to choose the design he did?*

QUESTION SPOTLIGHT!

1   Loftus and Palmer (1974) (see page 45) used an independent measures design to compare the effects of different verbs in leading questions. *Why?*

2   Blakemore and Cooper (1970) (see page 140) used different kittens in their horizontally and vertically striped visual environments. *Why?*

3   Maguire *et al.* (2000) (see page 148) compared the left and right side of taxi drivers' brains using a repeated measures design. *Why did they use this design?*

ACTIVITY

Find the website for the Ignobel awards and have a look at their publications ('The Annals of Improbable Research' and 'MiniAir'). As the title suggests, they publish all kinds of improbable research (not all of which is psychological).

Find an interesting psychology experiment and design a poster or presentation about it, indicating the type of experiment used, the IV and DV, the experimental design and what controls were implemented.

Repeated measures

When the same group of people participate in each level of the IV, this is called a repeated measures design. You can think of this as the participants 'repeating' their performance under different conditions. For example, we could conduct a study to investigate the effects of an orienteering course on hippocampal size. We would measure hippocampal volume in the same group of people before and after the course.

A repeated measures design has the advantage that each person effectively acts as their own baseline. Any differences between participants that might influence their performance will affect both levels of the IV by the same amount, so this is unlikely to bias the findings. Let's suppose that in our experiment on hippocampal volume one person is already very good at orienteering and navigation and another quite poor. This could be a problem if they happened to be in different groups in an independent measures design. In a repeated measures design, however, initial differences between the participants are less important, as both could show an improvement. Individual differences between

KEY IDEAS

Participant variables are individual differences between participants (such as age, skills, personality) that could affect their responses in a study.

In a repeated measures design, **order effects** (either practice or fatigue effects) can produce changes in performance between conditions that are not the result of the IV, so can obscure the effect on the DV.

The **practice effect** refers to the situation where participants' performance improves because they experience the experimental task more than once. They might become more familiar with the task or recall their previous answers.

The **fatigue effect** refers to the situation where the participants' performance declines because they have experienced an experimental task more than once. They might be bored or tired.

Counterbalancing is used to overcome order effects in a repeated measures design. Each possible order of levels of the IV is performed by a different sub-group of participants. This can be described as an ABBA design, as half the participants do condition A then B, and half do B then A.

participants are called **participant variables**. These variables, such as age, gender or intelligence, can affect the participants' score on the DV. It is therefore important to make sure that such differences do not hide, or exaggerate, differences between levels of the IV.

The main problem with this design arises because if each individual participates in every level of the IV they will perform the same or similar tasks two or more times. This repetition can lead to **order effects**. Specifically, repeated performance could cause the participants to improve because they have encountered the task before – a **practice effect**. This would matter because those participants for whom a particular condition was their second test, may well perform better than those for whom it was their first. Alternatively, repetition might make performance worse, perhaps because the participants get bored or tired – a **fatigue effect**. Furthermore, the participants have more opportunity to work out what is being tested, and to see both levels of the IV, and are therefore more likely to respond to demand characteristics.

Order effects can be overcome in two ways: by randomisation or **counterbalancing**. Let's assume that there are two conditions in a memory experiment: 'delay' (D) and 'no delay' (N). In randomisation, participants are randomly allocated to do either condition D followed by N, or vice versa. As some will do each order, any advantage of doing one of the conditions first will probably be evened out in the results. To be more certain that possible effects do even out, counterbalancing can be used. Here, the group of participants is divided into two, and one half will do D followed by N, the other half N followed by D. If on the second test there was a risk of participants muddling up items remembered from the first test, this would be a problem for exactly half the participants in the 'delay' condition, and exactly half in the 'no-delay' condition. Of course, another alternative would be to use a different design.

Matched participants

One way to overcome the problems associated with both independent measures and repeated measures designs is to use a matched participants design. In this situation a different group of participants is used for each level of the IV. However, each participant in one group is matched to a corresponding participant in the other group. This matching is done on relevant variables. For example, in a study looking at the effect of amnesia by measuring recall of words, it would be ideal to compare each amnesic to an unaffected person who was similar in other respects (such as the same age, intelligence or vocabulary). While some factors, such as age or gender, might be important characteristics for matching in many studies, others, such as vocabulary or attitudes, might be very important in specific investigations but unimportant in others. When possible, identical twins make ideal matched participants.

TRUE EXPERIMENTS AND QUASI-EXPERIMENTS

In some experiments it is possible for the researcher to allocate participants to levels of the IV, for example in a laboratory experiment on the effects of group size on bystander apathy, in which the participant is surrounded by a larger or smaller group (of confederates). These are called **true experiments**. In other situations the level of the IV for a participant might be determined before the study, such as having a mental disorder or not doing a certain job, or the species of animal. This is called a **quasi-experiment** because it is not truly experimental, in that the experimenter cannot be absolutely sure that the only difference between the groups is the IV, as they are not actually manipulating the variable themselves.

The laboratory experiment

A **laboratory experiment** is a study in a contrived environment such as a laboratory (but can include other artificial settings). The participants come into this setting in order to be part of the study – they would not be there normally. By creating the situation artificially, the experimenter can control many variables that might influence the participants' behaviour. For example, they can readily ensure that every participant is treated in the same way by using **standardised instructions**. This control of **extraneous variables** is central to a laboratory experiment. It is one of the main reasons that researchers choose to conduct laboratory experiments – they can be confident that if the IV does appear to affect the DV, then the relationship is a causal one. One important variable to control in memory experiments is distractions – rehearsal is important and can be prevented by interference, so in laboratory experiments factors such as noise and the presence of other people is regulated. Factors in the surroundings that can disrupt an experiment, such as noise or light, are called **situational variables**. All the features that make the procedure of laboratory experiments so rigorously controlled also make them easy to replicate. Doing this allows researchers to be more confident about their findings.

The field experiment

An alternative approach to using a laboratory is to conduct a **field experiment**. In a field experiment there is still an IV that is manipulated by the experimenter, and a DV that is measured, but the setting is the participants' normal environment in relation to the behaviour being investigated. For example, the effect of different revision methods on memory might be tested in a classroom. The investigator could set up a situation in which a teacher uses revision diagrams for one topic and revision songs for another. The IV would be the revision strategy, either visual (diagrams) or auditory (songs). The DV would be measured using tests of each topic. As the situation would be familiar to the students, they should be relatively unaffected by being in an experiment,

QUESTION SPOTLIGHT!

Moray (1959) (see page 62) used laboratory experiments to investigate attention using dichotic listening. He controlled many variables, such as the volume of the spoken message, the volume of the key words, such as numbers or the person's own name, and the speed at which the words were said.

All of these controls were implemented by standardised procedures for the experimenter and instructions for the participant. *Why are these important?*

QUESTION SPOTLIGHT!

You need to be able to decide which experimental design to use in different situations.

Would you use an independent measures or repeated measures design in each of these studies, and why?

1 A study into eyewitness testimony looking at the difference between answers to untagged questions ('Did you see the burglar's gun?') and tagged ones ('You saw the burglar's gun, didn't you?').

2 A test of moral development comparing children aged 4 and 6 years.

3 An investigation looking at split-brain patients' comprehension of TV programmes compared to people without split brains.

4 A comparison of the amount of hippocampal tissue in young people before and after learning to drive and passing their driving test.

Figure 7.3
Identical twins make ideal matched participants

TABLE 7.1 STRENGTHS AND WEAKNESSES OF EXPERIMENTAL DESIGNS

	Strengths	Weaknesses
Independent measures	• Different participants are used in each level of the IV so there are no order effects. • Participants see the experimental task only once, reducing the risk of demand characteristics. • The effects of individual differences can be reduced by random allocation to levels of the IV.	• Individual differences could distort results if participants in one level of the IV differ from those in another. • More participants are needed than with repeated measures (may be less ethical or harder to find).
Repeated measures	• Individual differences are unlikely to distort the effect of the IV, as participants do both levels. • Counterbalancing reduces order effects. • Uses fewer participants than repeated measures so is good when participants are hard to find. • Blind procedures can reduce demand characteristics.	• Order effects such as practice and fatigue, and extraneous variables, could distort the results. • Participants see the experimental task more than once, increasing the risk of demand characteristics.
Matched participants	• Participants see the experimental task only once, reducing the risk of demand characteristics. • Controls for individual differences – e.g. identical twins – are excellent matched participants. • No order effects.	• The similarity between pairs is limited by the matching process, which might be flawed if important variables for matching are unknown. • Matching participants is time-consuming and difficult.

compared to a similar test in a laboratory. They may not even know that they are in an experiment at all, so would be unlikely to respond to demand characteristics. When participants are unaware of the experiment, their behaviour is more likely to be representative of real life, and therefore the findings are more likely to generalise to other situations, i.e. to have high **ecological validity**. Of course, the lack of awareness does raise ethical issues.

One clear disadvantage of the field experiment is that it is difficult to maintain control over situational variables. This means that changes in the DV might be caused by factors other than the IV. In the case of the classroom example, the different topics could have been more difficult or interesting, or could have been taught at times in the term when the students were more or less tired. Any of these variables could have caused differences between conditions that would look as though there was an effect on the DV caused by the IV.

The quasi-experiment

A **quasi-experiment** (or natural experiment) differs from a true experiment because the experimenter does not set up the levels of the IV. Quasi-experiments make use of 'natural' (i.e. not artificially produced) changes or differences in circumstances to provide the experimental conditions. They can be conducted in laboratory or field settings. Researchers use quasi-experiments when it would be impractical or unethical to generate the conditions necessary for the different levels of the IV. For example, when comparing witnesses to real crimes who have been frightened or not, we cannot randomly allocate people to the 'frightened' and 'not frightened' conditions. Instead, we would have to search for people who either were, or were not, frightened by their experience as an eyewitness and use them as separate groups of participants.

QUESTION SPOTLIGHT!

Which of the following studies were laboratory experiments and which were field experiments?

1 Baron-Cohen *et al.* (1997) (see page 168): the eyes test study.
2 Chaney *et al.* (see page 88): Funhaler study.
3 Loftus and Palmer (1974) (see page 45): eyewitness testimony study.
4 Piliavin *et al.* (1969) (see page 24): good Samaritan study.
5 Moray (1959) (see page 62): attention study.

Where quasi-experiments are conducted in the field, they have the benefit that the participants are in their usual environment so their behaviour is more likely to be representative of real life. As the participants are not actively allocated to conditions, it is more possible that the existence of the experiment can be hidden from them. This reduces the risk of demand characteristics affecting behaviour. Of course, because participants are not randomly allocated to different levels of the IV, it is difficult to distinguish the effects of any existing differences between groups of participants and those differences that are the result of the experiment. For example, if we were to investigate the effects of organisation on revision using a quasi-experiment we might compare people who revise using cue-cards and mindmaps (high organisation), and those who revise using a highlighter pen to go through their class notes (low organisation). Although the people who used the high-organisation techniques might get better results (i.e. there may be a difference in the DV), we wouldn't know if this was really caused by the revision method (the IV) or whether the participants in the high organisation group were simply more intelligent, or spent more time working, than those in the low organisation group.

ASSESSING RELIABILITY AND VALIDITY IN EXPERIMENTS

Reliability

Laboratory experiments are conducted in an artificial setting, so the researcher can impose controls, for example through standardised procedures. These increase reliability as they ensure that all participants are treated in the same way. As field experiments (and some quasi-experiments) are conducted in the participants' normal environment for the situation or activity being explored, variables within the setting are harder to control, so there is likely to be greater variation between the precise circumstances under which the DV is measured between participants, which lowers their reliability relative to laboratory experiments. Remember, however, that it is still possible to impose some controls. Controls in any experiment make replication easier as researchers can be confident that they are following exactly the same procedure, for example giving identical instructions, using the same stimulus materials and the same timings, and measuring the DV in the same way. If replications produce the same results – i.e. if they demonstrate the same differences between the levels of the IV – a researcher can be confident that their findings are reliable. However, this is likely to be more difficult in a quasi-experiment.

KEY IDEAS

In a **true experiment** a researcher can randomly allocate participants to different levels of the IV.

In a **quasi-experiment** an experimenter makes use of an existing change or difference in situations to create levels of an IV, and then measures the DV in each condition.

A **field experiment** is a study in which the researcher manipulates an IV and measures a DV in the natural setting of the participants for the activity being tested.

A **laboratory experiment** is a study conducted in an artificial environment in which the experimenter manipulates an IV and measures the consequent changes in a DV, while carefully controlling extraneous variables.

Standardised instructions are a set of spoken, written or recorded instructions presented to participants to tell them what to do. This ensures that all participants receive identical treatment and information, so differences between their performance on the DV are more likely to be the result of the IV.

Extraneous variables are factors other than the IV which could affect performance on the DV (and so distort the results).

Situational variables are factors in the environment surrounding participants that can affect their performance on the DV, and so could obscure the effect of the IV.

STRETCH & CHALLENGE ◎

In readiness for your next test in class, prepare for yourself revision materials for two different topics using two different forms, such as mindmaps, cue-cards or summary notes. Consider what controls you should impose to ensure that your comparison will be valid.

Explain what you expect to happen in the test, and why.

If you can, test your methods.

QUESTION SPOTLIGHT!

The eyes test study of Baron-Cohen *et al.* (1997) (see page 168) would be classed as a quasi-experiment, but the study by Loftus and Palmer (1974) (see page 45) on eyewitness testimony would not.

Explain why.

Validity

In laboratory experiments, extraneous variables are controlled, so the researcher can be sure that any changes in the DV can only have been caused by the IV. This certainty is important because it means that the validity of the study is high. The measurement of the DV is typically very accurate, also increasing validity. Although these factors raise confidence that the influence of the independent variable is being measured, rather than the effects of extraneous ones, this does not necessarily mean that the findings really reflect the intended aim of the study. A problem with laboratory experiments is that, in general, the measure of the DV tends to be quite artificial – in other words, the participants' responses are being measured in a way that doesn't reflect day-to-day life. This is described as a lack of **mundane realism**. For example, Loftus and Palmer asked participants to estimate the speed of a filmed car, but we aren't usually asked to respond to film clips in this way. Furthermore, the artificial setting of the laboratory means

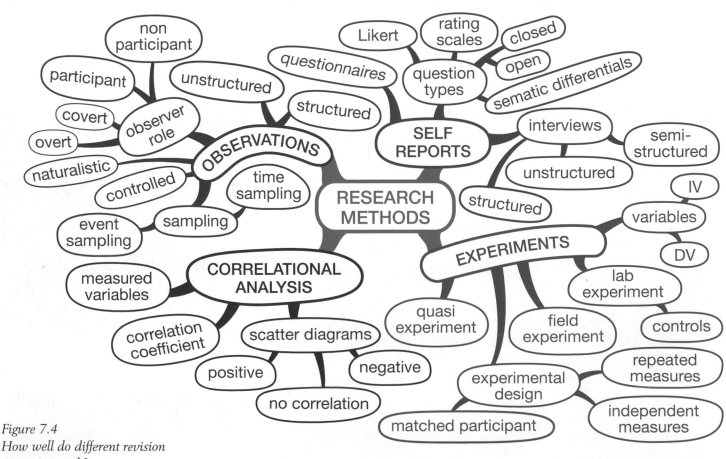

Figure 7.4
How well do different revision strategies work?

that the participants will almost certainly be aware that they are participating in a study (although they might be unaware of its aims), which means that their responses might not be representative of the way they would behave in other situations. This means that the results might not **generalise** beyond the laboratory setting; if so, the findings would be said to lack ecological validity.

The ecological validity of field experiments is likely (but is not guaranteed) to be higher than for laboratory studies as they use less artificial settings, so the participants are more likely to behave in true-to-life ways. Instead, field experiments face a different problem. Precisely because they are set in more authentic environments, situational variables are harder to control, so there is likely to be greater variation between the exact circumstances under which the DV is measured. Importantly, there might be uncontrolled variables arising between levels of the IV, which confound the results. For example, a study about helping behaviour might be conducted in a shopping centre. If the researchers were investigating the effect of crowding on helping, they might compare Saturday mornings (crowded) to Thursday mornings (not crowded). However, a potential confounding variable would be the type of people who were in the shopping centre on those days. Perhaps the shoppers at the weekend would be predominantly families, who might be more helpful, whereas those in the week would be businessmen and businesswomen, who might be too busy to stop and help, or older people, who might have a greater sense of community and be more likely to help. Such effects could skew the results so that it looked as though crowding made people either more or less helpful – in which case neither would be true.

However, in field experiments the effect of demand characteristics would also be lower, as the aims of the study would be less apparent, and because participants might be unaware that the experiment is taking place, their behaviour is also more likely to be realistic. Both of these points increase validity. Nevertheless, not telling the participants about the experiment in advance has disadvantages in terms of ethics. On one hand, it means that they have not been given the opportunity to give their informed consent to participate (see page 309), although conversely there is no need to deceive them about the aims.

In quasi-experiments it is more difficult, if not impossible, to impose controls on the sample. There is therefore less certainty that any observed changes in the DV have necessarily arisen as a consequence of the IV, which potentially lowers validity. However, if the contrasting situations are chosen carefully, there could be very few extraneous variables. As with field experiments, there are advantages in comparison to contrived situations. Because the difference is naturally occurring, it is less likely that demand characteristics will be apparent (although this will also depend on how obviously the measure of the DV is taken). In addition, the ecological validity of the situation is necessarily high, because the change or difference is a real one. It is likely, therefore, that the test will be a valid one and that the findings will be highly representative.

KEY IDEAS

Mundane realism is the extent to which an experimental task represents a real-world situation.

Generalisability is the extent to which findings from one situation or sample will apply to other situations or people.

Figure 7.5
How sure can you be that the IV is the only factor that differs in a field experiment?

TABLE 7.2 STRENGTHS AND WEAKNESSES OF THE EXPERIMENTAL METHOD

	Strengths	Weaknesses
Laboratory experiments	• Good control of extraneous variables. • Causal relationships can be determined. • Strict procedures allow them to be replicated, so researchers can be more confident about their findings. • In a repeated measures design, counterbalancing can be used to reduce order effects.	• The artificial situation could make participants' behaviour unrepresentative. • Participants could respond to demand characteristics and alter their behaviour.
Field experiments	• As participants are in their normal situation, their behaviour is likely to be representative. • Participants could be unaware that they are in a study, so demand characteristics are less problematic than in laboratory experiments.	• Control over extraneous variables is more difficult than in a laboratory, so they are less reliable and replication is more difficult. • The researcher cannot be sure that changes in the DV have been caused by changes in the IV. • Participants are likely to be unaware that they are in a study, which raises ethical issues.
Quasi-experiments	• They can be used to study real-world issues. • If participants are in their normal situation, their behaviour is likely to be representative. • If participants are unaware that they are in a study, demand characteristics will be less problematic. • They enable researchers to investigate variables that could not practically or ethically be manipulated.	• They are only possible when naturally occurring differences arise. • Control over extraneous variables is often very difficult. • As the researcher is not manipulating the IV, they can be less sure of the cause of changes in the DV, i.e. a causal relationship cannot be established. • They are generally hard to replicate.
All experiments	• Using a repeated measures or matched participants design helps to reduce participant variables. • Using an independent measures design helps to avoid the influence of demand characteristics and of order effects.	• If participants are unaware that they are in a study, this raises ethical issues. • The researcher's expectations could lead to biased results.

B – THE OBSERVATIONAL METHOD

INTRODUCTION

In this section we will be looking at the way in which the research method of observations is used in psychology. Specifically, we will look at different ways to organise observations and ways to collect data in observational studies. We will also evaluate each of the techniques and the observational method overall.

THE OBSERVATIONAL METHOD

Observation can be a research method in itself, when the study consists solely of watching participants and recording their behaviour directly to provide data. Alternatively, observation can be used as a technique to collect data about variables within other research methods. For example, observations might be used to measure the dependent variable in an experiment. In this situation, the data collected would be quantitative, although qualitative data can also be collected if appropriate.

Observations were the main way in which data were collected in several of the core studies. For example, observations were used to measure the DV in Bandura et al.'s experiment on aggression, to monitor changes in activity and responses in the kittens in Blakemore and Cooper's study, and to measure the DV in Piliavin *et al.'s* study of helping behaviour. In Sperry's study of split-brain patients, the observations were made in tests requiring a hand-movement response, and in Milgram's study, observational records were kept of participants' behaviour in addition to the measure of obedience. In all of these instances, whether they were in the participants' normal environment (such as in Piliavin *et al.'s* study) or in a laboratory, the situation being observed was artificial. In this respect they were all **controlled observations**. In contrast, it is possible to study behaviour as it occurs normally in real environments. For example, kittens' responses to edges and drops could be observed in pets in the home, childhood aggression could be observed in the playground, and helping behaviour could be observed between shoppers in supermarkets. If the researchers did not interfere with the situation or the behaviours being observed, these would be examples of **naturalistic observations**.

Initially, recordings in an observational study tend to be non-focused, that is, the observer looks at the range of possible behaviours to investigate. In some studies this continues, with any behaviours deemed relevant being recorded. This is called an **unstructured observation**. In contrast, in a **structured observation**, the range of study is narrowed to a smaller set of clearly defined behaviours. The **behavioural categories** must be observable actions rather than inferred, internal states. For example, behaviours such as smiling or

KEY IDEAS

The **observational method** is used when watching participants (human or animal) directly in order to obtain data and gather information about their behaviour.

Participant observation is a way of collecting data such that the participants' behaviour is recorded by a researcher who is engaged with them as part of the social setting.

Non-participant observation is a way of collecting data such that the participants' behaviour is recorded by a researcher who is not engaging with them as part of the social setting. The observer may be overt or covert.

Overt observation (or disclosed observation) is research in which the role of the observer is known to participants.

Covert observation (or non-disclosed observation) is research in which participants are unaware that they are being watched. The observer may be participant or non-participant.

Controlled observation is a research method in which behaviours seen are recorded by the researchers in situations in which there has been some manipulation (e.g. of the social or physical environment) by the researchers. Such observations may be conducted in either the participants' normal environment or in an artificial situation such as a laboratory.

Naturalistic observation is a research method in which behaviours seen in the participants' normal environment are recorded without interference from the researchers in either the social or the physical environment.

laughing can be observed, but 'being happy' cannot. This might seem to be a disadvantage of observations, but it can also be seen as a strength – helping to make data recording objective.

TABLE 7.3 STRENGTHS AND WEAKNESSES OF NATURALISTIC AND CONTROLLED OBSERVATIONS

	Strengths	Weaknesses
Naturalistic observations	• Participants are in their normal environment so are more likely to react in realistic ways. • Participants are less likely to be aware that they are being observed so are more likely to react in a genuine way. • Reactions can be observed within a complete and complex social setting. • Useful for obtaining observations in situations where intervention would be unethical or when co-operation would be unlikely.	• Extraneous variables can rarely be controlled so represent a considerable threat to validity. • It may be difficult to ensure reliability of data collection as recording equipment would be obvious, as would overt note-taking by observers (although this can be overcome with concealed videos). • If observers are identified or even suspected by the participants, validity is compromised.
Controlled observations	• Data recording is likely to be reliable as equipment can be used and researchers can be obvious. • As extraneous variables can be controlled, validity can be high compared to naturalistic observations. • Compared to experiments, a greater range of behaviours may be explored.	• Participants are in an unfamiliar environment so may react differently from how they would normally. • Participants will be aware that they are in an artificial situation (even if they are unaware of the real reason for being there) so their responses may not reflect what they would normally do. • The social situation is limited so cannot completely represent the reality of a complex social setting.

DO IT YOURSELF 🔍

Find an animal to watch, such as a pet cat or dog, or a squirrel out of the window. Try to record everything it does, in sequence.
What problems did you have?

Possibly, you found that:
- Behaviours happen too fast for you to keep track of them.
- It is hard to break the stream of behaviour into discrete events.
- Even when discrete behaviours can be identified, they may overlap.
- You were tempted to record states (which can only be inferred, not actually observed) in addition to behaviours (which can be seen).
- Your presence altered the behaviour of the animal.

Observational techniques attempt to overcome problems such as these.

Figure 7.6
Observations can be used with animals as well as humans

A **coding frame** makes recording the behavioural categories easier. It represents the different behaviours as abbreviations or 'codes', such as the first two letters of the word. In addition, it allows for other variables about the behaviours to be recorded, such as their severity or duration. Third, the coding frame may also include the operational definitions of the behavioural categories. For example, in recording observations of children's aggression, a researcher might have behavioural categories of 'hitting', 'biting' and 'shouting'. The coding frame could summarise these to H, B and S. When each one is recorded, further details might be scored on a scale indicating where the victim was hit (face, arms, legs) and how loudly the perpetrator shouted (on a scale of 1 to 3).

Box 7.1

Behavioural categories and coding frames

In a study of helping behaviour, a student defines three behavioural categories, each of which has two possible codes:

- *verbal comments* (VC): any speech that is supportive
  - questions to see if help is needed (Qu)
  - offering to help (Of)
- *immediate assistance* (IA): any action that is intended to be helpful
  - helping the individual by doing the *same* as they are doing (Sa)
  - doing something *different* to help them at that time and place (Di)
- seeking *further aid* (FA): any action that is intended to obtain additional help
  - *going* to get someone or something else to help (Go)
  - *phoning* for assistance (Ph)

The data record sheet could look like this:

Behavioural category	Codes	Participant number		
		1	2	3
VC	Qu, Of	Qu	Ot	x
IA	Sa, Di	Di	Di	Di
FA	Ga, Ph	Go	Ph	x

THE ROLE OF THE OBSERVER IN THE SOCIAL CONTEXT

The role of the observer in the social setting might be either participant or non-participant. A **participant observer** is part of the social setting, for example, when a researcher investigating helping in a supermarket is both an observer and a shopper. Alternatively, a non-participant observer is not involved in the situation being observed, for example, a researcher observing kittens or one watching children through a one-way glass.

In addition, an observer may be either **overt** (their role as an observer is apparent) or **covert** (they are hidden or disguised). Often a participant observer is overt, for example, when the researcher is holding a clipboard. Alternatively, they might be covert, for example, if they are disguised as a member of the social group (such as the observers in Piliavin *et al.'s* study, who appeared to be

---

STRETCH & CHALLENGE

Draw a coding frame for the example from the text on observing children's aggression, and add one more behavioural category along with possible codes.

KEY IDEAS

Unstructured observation is a research method in which an observer records a non-specified, wide range of behaviours including any that seem relevant.

Structured observation is a research method in which an observer records a specified range of behaviours in pre-decided and pre-defined categories.

Behavioural categories are the operationally defined units of events used in a structured observation to break a continuous stream of activity into discrete recordable events. They must be observable actions rather than inferred states.

A **coding frame** is a system for differentiating behaviours to be recorded in an observation, which uses abbreviations to represent different behavioural categories and their dimensions (such as severity). It may also include the operational definitions of the behavioural categories.

TABLE 7.4 STRENGTHS AND WEAKNESSES OF PARTICIPANT AND NON-PARTICIPANT OBSERVATION

	Strengths	Weaknesses
Participant observation	• Being involved in the social group can give the observer insight into the real participants' emotions and motives. • If the participants are unaware of the observer's dual role they might behave more normally than they would otherwise, thus increasing validity. • If the participants are unaware of the observer's dual role, they might reveal more than they would otherwise.	• Participants will be aware that they are being observed (even if they are unaware of the real reason for this) so their responses may not reflect what they would normally do. • Being involved in the social group can make the observer subjective. • If a participant observer has to be hidden, this raises practical and ethical issues, as the participants cannot give informed consent, and they may reveal more than they otherwise would.
Non-participant observation	• If non-participant observers are covert, e.g. hidden behind a one-way screen, data recording can use equipment to make accurate and detailed records. • Observers can remain objective about the situation as they are not involved.	• If participants are unaware that they are being observed this raises ethical questions about informed consent and the right to withdraw. • However, if participants are aware of a non-participant observer, this is likely to have an impact on behaviour, making it less typical of the normal situation.

TABLE 7.5 STRENGTHS AND WEAKNESSES OF OVERT AND COVERT OBSERVATION

	Strengths	Weaknesses
Overt observation	• As participants are aware of the observer's presence, the technique is more ethical than covert observation.	• Participants will be aware that they are being observed (even if they are unaware of the real reason for this) so their responses may not reflect what they would normally do.
Covert observation	• Participants are less likely to be aware that they are being observed so are more likely to react in a genuine way. • If covert observers are non-participant, e.g. hidden behind a one-way screen, data recording can use equipment to make accurate and detailed records.	• If observers are identified or even suspected by the participants validity is compromised. • As participants are unaware that they are being observed this raises ethical questions about informed consent and the right to withdraw. • If covert observers are also participant observers it may be difficult for them to record data accurately but unobtrusively.

 **KEY IDEAS**

Observer effects are the influences that the presence of an observer can have on participants in a situation where the observer is overt, or their role becomes apparent. The participants' awareness that they are being watched prompts changes in their behaviour.

normal passengers), or if they are physically hidden (e.g. when using CCTV). As a consequence, the participants would not know that they were being watched. This increases validity as it is unlikely that participants would be affected by **observer effects** such as demand characteristics or social desirability. However, it raises practical issues, as the observer must be either hidden, far away or disguised in their role. Covert participant observation also presents ethical problems as the participants cannot give informed consent, and if they work out the observer's role this can cause distress.

Participant observations are harder to conduct than non-participant ones as the observer cannot concentrate exclusively on recording behaviours –

they must engage in social behaviour as well. They might also find it difficult to focus on one individual or behaviour and actually record behaviours, as in doing so they might draw attention to their role as an observer. It is also harder for the observer to remain objective if they are participating – that is, they risk becoming biased as they develop a personal viewpoint. However, their involvement can also be a benefit: by engaging in the social situation, they might be able to gain greater insight into the participants' feelings and motives than a non-participant observer could.

QUESTION SPOTLIGHT!

In Bandura *et al.*'s study (see page 82), behaviours were observed through a one-way screen.

Is this participant or non-participant observation?

TABLE 7.6 STRENGTHS AND WEAKNESSES OF STRUCTURED AND UNSTRUCTURED OBSERVATIONS

	Strengths	Weaknesses
Structured observations	• Operational definitions can be developed in a pilot study before data collection begins, to be certain that they include all the key actions. This improves validity. • Operationally defined behavioural categories agreed between observers are likely to be reliable. • Practising the use of data-collection techniques further improves inter-rater reliability. • Photographic and video data collection allows re-analysis of data, which improves validity as rapidly occurring behaviours are less likely to be missed.	• Simple definitions of behaviour may not convey sufficient meaning, e.g. 'lifting a hand' could be a friendly wave or an intimidating threat. This lowers validity. • Total numbers of behaviours within a category may be relatively meaningless without the context in which they occurred. This lowers validity. • Having predetermined behavioural categories may be limiting if new behaviours become apparent during the study.
Unstructured observations	• Without the limitation of specific categories, any relevant behaviours can be recorded, so the data are richer and more complete. • Detailed descriptions of behaviours, rather than simple category totals, mean that observations give a more complete picture of the situation.	• By attempting to record everything, observers may miss or ignore important aspects. • Some of the data collected may be irrelevant or detract from the important features. • Without operational definitions, recoding may be inconsistent and subjective.

ACTIVITY

Imagine the following studies. Would each be a participant or a non-participant observation? Is the observer overt or covert?

1 A study of eyewitness testimony in which the researcher interviews witnesses to real crimes.

2 An investigation into navigation in an unknown environment in which a researcher who is part of a rambling group goes out for a walk with them and records the group's route-finding decisions, without telling them what he is doing.

Figure 7.7
Observations in the field can be naturalistic or controlled

KEY IDEAS

Observer bias is the tendency of an observer to record behaviours that they believe should or will occur, or to identify behaviours within the context of their subjective perspective, rather than recording those behaviours that are actually occurring.

QUESTION SPOTLIGHT!

Photographs and videos of behaviour can be analysed after the event. This is useful as analyses can be revisited and shared between observers.

Suggest one other advantage and one disadvantage of using a camera compared to simply watching.

STRUCTURED OBSERVATIONS

The environment in which observations take place can be naturalistic, such as in a familiar work environment, or controlled, such as in a university laboratory. In either situation, observations may be unstructured or structured, i.e. restricted to pre-decided and pre-defined behavioural categories. This helps to reduce the impact of the observer's personal opinion — that is, to limit the effect of **observer bias**. These behavioural categories must be operationalised, i.e. clearly defined (see page 221). For example, Bandura *et al.* (see page 82) studied aggression in children by exposing them to a fixed sequence of behaviours performed by an adult model. They then gave the children toys, such as a large inflatable 'Bobo doll', a mallet and a dart gun, and recorded specific aggressive behaviours. Their behavioural categories included:

* striking the Bobo doll with the mallet
* sitting on the doll and punching it in the nose
* kicking the doll
* tossing the doll in the air
* repeating the phrases: 'Sock him', 'Hit him down', 'Kick him', 'Throw him in the air', or 'Pow'
* striking, slapping or pushing the doll aggressively
* shooting darts with the gun
* aiming the gun and firing imaginary shots.

The method of data recording within these behavioural categories is also important. Techniques can include photographs, video, audio recordings (of spoken descriptions), handwritten notes or direct records inputted into a computer. Handwritten and computerised data collection can take the form of descriptions, ratings or codings (checklists).

If there is more than one observer they should record the same information when observing the same events. To achieve this, they are trained in the use of the behavioural categories. They practise the data-gathering techniques by simultaneous observation or repeated use of recorded video sequences, as well as by discussion of the definitions, so that they achieve a high level of agreement before the collection of data for the study begins. This serves to improve the data collected by raising inter-rater reliability.

DATA COLLECTION IN OBSERVATIONS: EVENT AND TIME SAMPLING

Data collection may be driven by the occurrence of, or changes in, the events, when each occurrence of a behaviour being tailed, this is called **event sampling**. Alternatively, data collection may be driven by time, i.e. recording when events happen. This is called **time sampling**.

In its simplest form, event sampling involves using a checklist, and whenever an event happens it is ticked on an observation sheet (or keyed in directly on a computer). This generates a total number of occurrences for each behavioural category. However, this technique does not indicate how long each event lasted or when in time it occurred. For example, an event sample of students' behaviour in the classroom might indicate how often each member of the class looked out the window or yawned, but it wouldn't tell us how long they spent gazing or whether the yawns were all towards the end of the lesson.

ACTIVITY ✳

Imagine the following studies. Consider whether each one is set in a naturalistic or controlled environment, is a structured or unstructured observation, would involve overt or covert observation, and would use a participant or a non-participant observer. For each example, identify three of these features.

1 A teacher organises a group of students to sit in their common room and occasionally say the name of a student sitting elsewhere in the room. They have to watch what the named student does.

2 A study of taxi drivers' navigation in which a researcher sits beside the driver on specified, complex routes and notes the number of times they frown or scratch their head.

3 A researcher investigating helpful behaviour arranges to watch from a closed shop till, dressed as an assistant. On a day when lots of elderly people shop, they observe how shoppers react towards the elderly, including impatience, understanding, and assistance.

4 An observer studies obedience by pretending to be a new army recruit. They watch what the other recruits do when ordered to do impossibly difficult physical tasks.

For example 3, identify the behavioural categories and suggest how a coding frame might be developed.

Figure 7.8
Could you test Moray's ideas about attention in a natural setting?

Box 7.2

Observation checklist for event sampling

Imagine a rabbit which, over the course of one minute, eats, hops, eats, hops, stands still for a long time, hops, hops again, eats, stands still for a long time, runs down into its burrow, runs out again, hops, hops again, eats, sniffs, eats, then stands still until the end of the minute. The checklist would look like this:

Behaviour	hop	eat	stand	down into burrow	out of burrow	sniff
tally	⊬⊬ I	⊬⊬	III	I	I	I

KEY IDEAS

Inter-observer reliability is the extent to which two observers will produce the same records when they watch the same event.

Event sampling is a data-collection technique that uses a checklist of possible activities, which are tallied as they occur.

Time sampling is a data-collection technique that uses a limited list of possible activities. The occurrence of these activities is recorded in relation to short, specified time intervals.

A **checklist** is a list or table of behavioural categories used to tally each event as it occurs.

There are several different ways to conduct time sampling, although all involve dividing the observation period into recording intervals such as every ten seconds. A mechanism for timing the interval must be used in addition to an observation sheet. In general, fewer behaviours can be time-sampled in any one session than can be event sampled. In **instantaneous scan sampling** only the action being performed at the start of each preset interval is recorded. For example, if an observer were watching one child's aggressive behaviour in the playground, they might record at 10, 20, 30, 40 seconds, etc., whether he or she was behaving aggressively, non-aggressively, or was not interacting with others, and they would ignore the child's activity at any other time. In **predominant activity sampling**, the same time periods and behavioural categories can be used, but instead of recording only the single behaviour occurring at the moment the time interval ends, the observer watches throughout the interval and records the behaviour that the individual performed the most during that time. In **one-zero sampling**, again the same time periods and behavioural categories can be used, but here the researcher would record whether behaviour occurred within the time period.

TABLE 7.7 STRENGTHS AND WEAKNESSES OF EVENT AND TIME SAMPLING

	Strengths	Weaknesses
Event sampling	• It can record every occurrence of each behaviour to give a complete record. • Records are easy to obtain and to analyse as they are just totals.	• It gives no indication of the relative time spent on each behavioural category. • It gives no indication of the order in which events from each behavioural category occur.
Time sampling	• It can give an indication of the order in which events happen. • It can give an indication of the relative time spent on each behaviour. • Instantaneous scan sampling can be highly reliable. • Predominant activity scans provide a estimate of time spent on each behaviour. • One-zero scans can record the occurrence of infrequent behaviours.	• Even with computerised systems, it is difficult to record as many different behaviours in time sampling as can be recorded in event sampling. • Records are more difficult to obtain as timings have to be precise and if they are indicated by a timer that makes a noise, this can lead to demand characteristics. • Predominant activity scans provide only a relative estimate of time spent on each behaviour, not an actual measure.

ASSESSING RELIABILITY AND VALIDITY IN OBSERVATIONS

Reliability

Remember that reliability is about consistency (see page 250). A single observer must record their observations consistently from one participant to another. They can improve this by working with operational definitions of behavioural categories and using sampling methods such as instantaneous scan time sampling, which offers high reliability. Where there is more than one observer, high inter-rater reliability is important. This is achieved by observers working together on their operational definitions and practising the use of the data-collection technique prior to the study. This is usually done by each observer scoring the same section of recorded behaviour on video.

Box 7.3

Time-sampling techniques compared

Imagine the rabbit again. Here are three possible time-sampling records:

INSTANTANEOUS SCAN

Behaviour	Time interval					
	10	20	30	40	50	60
Hop						
Eat	✓		✓	✓		
Stand		✓			✓	✓
Sniff						

PREDOMINANT ACTIVITY SCAN

Behaviour	Time interval					
	10	20	30	40	50	60
Hop						
Eat				✓		
Stand	✓	✓	✓		✓	✓
Sniff						

ONE-ZERO SCAN

Behaviour	Time interval					
	10	20	30	40	50	60
Hop	✓	✓		✓		
Eat	✓		✓	✓	✓	
Stand	✓	✓	✓	✓	✓	✓
Sniff					✓	

Note that:
- in the instantaneous scan, no record is made of hopping or sniffing because they happened not to occur at the precise moment of the end of any intervals
- only the predominant activity scan shows that the rabbit spent most of its time standing still (although this is only an estimate)
- only the one-zero scan records the occurrence of sniffing, as it was infrequent and brief.

KEY IDEAS

Social desirability is a potential source of bias, as participants tend to respond in ways that they think reflect what is acceptable in society rather than how they necessarily believe they should or want to.

QUESTION SPOTLIGHT!

Observations are commonly used in developmental psychology.

Can you suggest why this is the case?

Validity

Remember that validity is about being sure that you are measuring what you intended to measure (see page 251). To produce valid data in an observational study, a researcher must be confident that the behaviours they are recording are a true representation of the participants' normal behaviour. It is therefore important that appropriate behavioural categories are chosen, and that the definitions reflect the intended activities. To achieve this, behavioural categories should be mutually exclusive, i.e. a particular activity of interest would appear in one, and only one, category. For example, returning to the observation of a rabbit on page 237, if the rabbit hopped down into its burrow, would that be recorded as a 'hop' or as going 'down into the burrow'? Valid operational definitions of the categories would overcome this problem, for example by saying that 'down into the burrow' is any activity resulting in movement that takes the rabbit's ears past the burrow entrance. The 'hop' would therefore be scored as 'down into the burrow'.

Several other factors can reduce validity, including demand characteristics and **social desirability**. To reduce the effects of these, observers can keep their role hidden — as in a covert participant observation — so the participants are unaware that they are being observed. Finally, using a realistic setting is important so that the behaviours reflect normal activities.

TABLE 7.8 STRENGTHS AND WEAKNESSES OF OBSERVATIONAL TECHNIQUES

Strengths	Weaknesses
• Participant observers may benefit from being involved in the social experience by gaining insights into the emotions or motivation felt by participants making the data more detailed and more valid.	• Participant observers may be biased if they become involved in the social situation they are observing.
• In naturalistic settings and with covert observers behaviour is likely to be highly representative of real life, unlike questionnaires or interviews in which people might report different behaviours than they would actually do in real life.	• If multiple observers are used, inter-observer reliability may be low. • Ethical issues arise when participants are unaware that they are being observed.
• The technique allows for data collection from participants who are unable to contribute to interviews, questionnaires or experimental testing, such as animals and children.	• It is harder to control extraneous variables, even in a structured observation, than in a laboratory experiment. • In an observation, the researcher cannot be certain about the reasons for the behaviours seen.
• Observations can be preferable when direct methods are impractical, e.g. because they would induce demand characteristics or because they would be unethical, e.g. if they deliberately produced a stressful situation.	• Observations are limited to the recording of overt actions rather than states, emotions, attitudes or beliefs.

C – THE SELF REPORT

INTRODUCTION

In this section we will be looking at the way in which self-reports as a research method, such as questionnaires and interviews, are used in psychology. Specifically, we will explore the use of rating scales and Likert scales, and two types of question – open and closed – in the collection of data in self-reports. We will also evaluate each of these techniques individually, and the method of self-reports overall.

THE SELF-REPORT

Self-report techniques are so called because the participant is reporting their own beliefs, thoughts or feelings to the researcher, rather than the researcher measuring aspects of the participant's behaviour (which reflect their thoughts or feelings). The methods include **questionnaires** and **interviews**. In both of these, the researcher presents the participant with questions. In a questionnaire, these are on paper (or on a computer) and the participant fills them in. In an interview, the questions are asked by an interviewer, usually face to face or by telephone. The methods share some basic question types, although there are some differences too.

Self-report can be a research method in itself, when the study consists solely of a questionnaire, for example. In other situations, self-report is used as a way to collect data. The latter approach is illustrated in several of the core studies, for example by the descriptions given by Little Hans to his father (Freud, 1909), by the answers to questions asked by Simons and Chabris (1999), by much of the data with the questionnaires used by Chaney *et al.*, in the interviews with murderers conducted by Hancock *et al.*, and the responses to interview questions given by participants in Piliavin *et al.*'s study.

RATING SCALES

A **rating scale** is a simple numerical scale on which a participant can indicate the extent or strength of some measure. They therefore generate **quantitative** data. Examples could include:

- indicating to what extent you agree with a statement by picking a number between 1 and 5
- identifying how likely you are to do something on a scale of 0 to 10
- stating your preference for something from a choice of 1, 2, 3 or 4.

To be valid, a rating scale should be able to discriminate between different responses. Participants' responses might tend to cluster in the middle, so, to

 KEY IDEAS

Qualitative and quantitative data
Investigations using self-report can produce two types of data. Numerical data, or **quantitative data**, indicate the *quantity* of a psychological measure. Examples include time, or a numerical score on a personality test. These kinds of measures are associated with research methods such as experiments and correlations. It is, however, possible to produce quantitative data from observations, questionnaires or interviews, for example by recording the number of times a behaviour is observed or by counting responses to closed questions. On page 282 we look in more detail at quantitative data and how they are analysed.

Qualitative data indicate the *quality* of a psychological characteristic, and come from research that generates in-depth, descriptive findings. This is typical of observations, in which particular behaviours are the focus of an observer's detailed account, or of questionnaires, interviews and case studies, in which responses to open questions elicit elaborate reporting of feelings, beliefs or opinions. For example, rather than counting the number of times a behaviour occurs, behaviours may be described in detail.

Self-report methods are ways to obtain data by asking participants to provide information about themselves.

A **questionnaire** is a self-report method that uses written questions.

An **interview** is a self-report method in which participants reply verbally to questions asked by an interviewer.

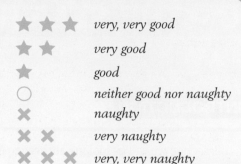

Box 7.4
Rating scales in the core study
In the contemporary study by Lee *et al.* (1997) (see page 103), the children indicated goodness/naughtiness using a 7-point **rating scale** of words and pictures. Their scores were converted to numbers from 3 to −3.

★★★   *very, very good*
★★   *very good*
★   *good*
○   *neither good nor naughty*
✕   *naughty*
✕✕   *very naughty*
✕✕✕   *very, very naughty*

KEY IDEAS

A **pilot study** is a small-scale trial run of a method to identify and resolve any problems with the procedure.

QUESTION SPOTLIGHT!

In the Chaney *et al.* (2004) study of children with asthma (see page 88), the children's parents were given a questionnaire about their child. The study was investigating how a spacer device, with incentive toys (spinner and whistle), might encourage better adherence to treatment and improved breathing patterns through the device.

Using these ideas as guidance, write five possible rating scale questions that Chaney et al. could have used. Ensure some are reverse scored.

Explain why some items should be reverse scored.

avoid this, the scale must offer a range of values (e.g. 11, as an odd number gives a middle score). If several rating scales are used, then there is a risk that participants might exhibit a response bias, tending towards one extreme or the other. Ideally, on some scales, the meaning of a high score should be reversed to reduce this (these are called positive and negative scales). However, in practice this can confuse participants and reduce the validity of the scale. When scales are used in this way, the numerical score must be reversed for the negative statements before analysis. The totals can then be added up to give a single score.

Scales should also be reliable. To check this, a **pilot study** can be done to test and retest the same participants to ensure that they do give the same answers. If there are scales that are unreliable (i.e. on which participants give different answers the second time), they should be amended or removed (see also page 281).

ACTIVITY ✳

Devise rating scales to measure each of the following:
- How confident an eyewitness is that they saw a tattoo on a suspect's face
- The extent to which a bystander to an event feels obliged to help
- The likelihood that a participant believes that they would follow orders from someone
- The certainty with which an individual thinks they will win a particular game of poker.

TABLE 7.9 STRENGTHS AND WEAKNESSES OF RATING SCALES

Strengths	Weaknesses
• They are easy for participants to respond to, so large amounts of data can be collected quickly, making the data more reliable and, if a wide sample is found, more generalisible. • They produce quantitative data, which are easy to analyse, e.g. to find modes, medians and to use to plot graphs. • They can be tested for reliability (by test-retest) and improved by changing or removing unreliable items. • When several are used, their validity can be improved by reversing some items to reduce response bias.	• They produce only quantitative data, which lack detail, so participants cannot express opinions fully, thus lowering validity. • There is a risk of response biases, such as consistently giving answers in the middle of the scale or at one extreme end. • The points on the scale are only relative (ordinal data), i.e. the gaps between the points are not equal. This means that the data should not be used to calculate a mean, a standard deviation or in parametric tests. • They cannot be used to measure complex variables that require more than a simple numerical response, such as attitudes.

LIKERT SCALES

We can elicit people's attitudes by asking them open questions, but their responses could be very varied, making them hard to compare. By using **Likert scales**, we can produce quantitative data that are much easier to analyse. A Likert scale begins with a statement and asks the participant to respond to that statement by saying how much they agree with it. For example, in a questionnaire-based test similar to Hare's PCL used by Hancock *et al.* (2011), called the Self-Report Psychopathy Scale, the following items appear:

- I think I could 'beat' a lie detector.
- My friends would say that I am a warm person.
- I always plan out my weekly activities.
- I have tricked someone into giving me money.

As with rating scales, it is important to prevent participants from developing a 'response set', such as always agreeing with the statement. To achieve this, about half of the statements should be 'reversed'. For example, when Likert scales are being used to measure attitudes to violent TV and aggressive behaviour, some should express a 'positive' opinion, such as 'I think an unnecessary fuss is made over the effect of violent TV', and others a 'negative' view, such as 'Violence on TV is to blame for the rise in crime'. In the Web Watch example, 'strongly agree' for the first and last questions would correspond with higher psychopathy and would score 5. However, to score the middle two questions, 'reverse scoring' would be applied – that is, 'strongly disagree' would score 5, and 'strongly agree' would score only 1.

Reverse scoring ensures that similar, 'positive' or socially acceptable statements are neither always associated with agreement, nor always at the same side of the page. The principle of reversing scales is applied to many other kinds of questions and helps to avoid bias in the way the participants respond. Likert scales generate quantitative data because, although each participant's response is to a named category, the number of agreements and disagreements can be added up. Ultimately, this produces a single number for each participant for the attitude (or attitudes) tested. When the scales are scored, the responses

KEY IDEAS

A numerical scale on which a participant indicates a choice by selecting one number, so providing quantitative data, is called a **rating scale**. Rating scales can be used to give a numerical answer to a question or to indicate the extent to which the participant agrees with a statement.

A **Likert scale** is a type of question that measures attitudes using a statement to which participants respond by choosing an option, typically from choices of 'strongly agree', 'agree', 'don't know', 'disagree' or 'strongly disagree'.

WEB WATCH @

You can download the Self-Report Psychopathy Scale (SRS-III), complete with a scoring key, here:

http://dionysus.psych.wisc.edu/MediaWiki/index.php?title=Self-Report_Psychopathy_(SRP-III)

These items measure four subscales: 'Interpersonal Manipulation', 'Callous Affect', 'Erratic Life Style' and 'Anti-Social Behavior' and the participant chooses from 'strongly disagree', 'disagree', 'don't know', 'agree' or 'strongly agree' for each statement.

WEB WATCH @

You can download the 60-item personality test that was used by Bocchiaro *et al.* (2012) Go to:

http://hexaco.org and select 'Take the HEXACO-PI-R' on the left-hand side.

STRETCH & CHALLENGE

Look at the examples of Likert scales in Box 7.5.

1   Decide which one measures each of the factors named in the text.

2   Decide which one would need to be 'reverse scored' and explain why.

3   Think of one more statement for each factor that could be used in this test.

ACTIVITY ✳

Devise Likert scales to measure each of the following:

•   The likelihood of an individual helping someone in distress

•   Attitudes towards obeying regulations, such as specifically allocated mother-and-baby parking spaces

•   A person's feelings towards their father.

are allocated numbers (from 1 to 5). For the negative scales, the scoring is reversed. So, in the examples above, responding 'strongly agree' to 'I think an unnecessary fuss is made over the effect of violent TV', would score 5. In contrast, for 'Violence on TV is to blame for the rise in crime', the response 'strongly agree' would score 1, whereas 'strongly disagree' would score 5.

> Box 7.5
> **Likert scales in the core studies**
> Bocchiaro *et al.* (2012) (see page 14), used 5-point Likert scales to measure several aspects of personality, such as Emotionality, Extraversion and Agreeableness. Examples of questions (from the English version), which were rated from 1 (strongly disagree) to 5 (strongly agree), include:
> •   I would be quite bored by a visit to an art gallery.
> •   I feel like crying when I see other people crying.
> •   Most people tend to get angry more quickly than I do.

TABLE 7.10 STRENGTHS AND WEAKNESSES OF LIKERT SCALES

Strengths	Weaknesses
• They are easy for participants to respond to, so large amounts of data can be collected quickly, making the data more reliable and, if a wide sample is found, more generalisible. • They produce quantitative data, which are easy to analyse, e.g. to find modes, medians and to use to plot graphs. • They can be tested for reliability (by test-retest) and improved by changing or removing unreliable items. • They allow the measurement of more complex attitudes than rating scales can. • When several are used, their validity can be improved by reversing some items to reduce response bias.	• They produce only quantitative data, which lack detail, so participants cannot express opinions fully, thus lowering validity. • There is a risk of response biases, such as consistently giving answers in the middle of the scale or at one extreme end. • The points on the scale are only relative (ordinal data), i.e. the gaps between the points are not equal. This means that the data should not be used to calculate a mean, a standard deviation or in parametric tests. • The meaning of the middle value is ambiguous. It could indicate no opinion or undecided.

SEMANTIC DIFFERENTIALS

A different type of rating scale allows participants to choose on a scale between two extremes. In a **semantic differential**, the participant rates their response between an opposing pair of descriptive words (bipolar adjectives), such as 'weak' and 'strong' or 'honest' and 'dishonest'. Data are gathered from the participant's cross on one of several positions between the adjectives, usually 5 or 7 and, like other scales, some of these should be reversed. Semantic differentials are often used to measure attitudes, the original intention of the scale being to test the meanings that the participant associated with a concept. For example, in a study of the effect on adolescents of viewing cigarette smoking in a film trailer, a semantic differential was used to measure perceptions of the character on measures such as 'sexy/unsexy' and 'social/antisocial' (Hanewinkel, 2009) (see Box 7.6).

Box 7.6

The semantic differential

boring	_ _ _ _ _ _ _	exciting
friendly	_ _ _ _ _ _ _	unfriendly
young	_ _ _ _ _ _ _	old
cool	_ _ _ _ _ _ _	uncool
beautiful	_ _ _ _ _ _ _	ugly

QUESTION SPOTLIGHT!

Decide which of the following are rating scales, Likert scales, semantic differentials or none of these question types.

1. 'I think all little boys are "mummy's boys".' strongly agree / agree / don't know / disagree / strongly disagree
2. On a scale of 1 to 7, how good are you at judging the speed of a vehicle? (1 = very good)
3. Describe your how you feel when you choose to do something that you know is wrong.
4. Use this scale to indicate how likely you would be to find a destination you had visited only once before.

5. Put a mark on this line to indicate how you are currently feeling:
   calm _____ tense
6. Rate your asthmatic child's attitude to using their inhaler:
   willing 1 2 3 4 5 unwilling
   suspicious 1 2 3 4 5 accepting
7. If you were a juror, would you trust evidence from an eyewitness? yes / no

KEY IDEAS

Closed questions are questions that offer a small number of explicitly stated alternative responses and no opportunity to expand on answers. They generate quantitative data.

Open questions are questions that allow participants to give full and detailed answers in their own words, i.e. no categories or choices are given. They generate qualitative data.

OPEN AND CLOSED QUESTIONS

Both open and closed questions can be used in either questionnaires or interviews. A closed question gives the participant little choice and requires one of a small number of alternative answers. In a questionnaire these might be presented as words or numbers to circle, or as boxes to cross or tick (see Box 7.8).

One advantage of using **closed questions** is that the results they generate are easy to analyse because they are simple numbers, i.e. they are quantitative. For example, we could ask a group of mothers and fathers whether their children imitated specific behaviours, by using a yes/no format. This would allow us to say that X% of mothers and X% of fathers reported that children copied particular acts, such as cuddling a toy, playing with bricks or banging the computer mouse to make it work.

An **open question** does not require a fixed response and gives the participant the chance to offer an extended answer (see Box 7.7). For example, an open question such as 'How does your asthmatic child respond when you tell them to use their inhaler?' will supply much more information than would be gained from ticking boxes about sitting down or running away. Unlike the numbers produced by closed questions, the results generated by open questions are qualitative, that is, they are detailed and descriptive. These data are more difficult to analyse, the aim being to look for common themes across different participants' responses. For example, if the parents of asthmatic children were interviewed about how their children responded to other situations, important themes might emerge. For example, two alternative themes could suggest that the children were afraid or were bored. Another pair could suggest the children deliberately avoided using their inhaler, or did so accidentally (e.g. they forgot). Patterns emerging in the themes might show that there were differences in emotional or cognitive processing in the two groups.

Box 7.7

Examples of open questions

1　Thinking back to when you saw the accident, can you describe what other vehicles and people were around at the time?
2　Write an account of what you could hear at the time of the accident.
3　If you try to recall what happened immediately before the accident, what can you remember?

Box 7.8

Examples of closed questions

1　If you were trying to remember the details of a crime you had witnessed, would you: Tick all that apply
   a)　write a list of the things that happened ☐
   b)　draw a map of where people and objects were ☐
   c)　repeat things over and over again ☐
   d)　tie a knot in your handkerchief? ☐

2　Do you work in a legal or police-related occupation?
Yes ☐　No ☐

3　Was the car involved in the accident:
   a)　an estate ☐
   b)　a hatchback ☐
   c)　a sports car ☐
   d)　a people carrier ☐
   e)　none of the above? ☐

Both qualitative and quantitative data can be collected using either questionnaires or interviews. In practice, researchers mainly use questionnaires to gather specific, quantitative information, and interviews to gather more in-depth, qualitative data.

TABLE 7.11 STRENGTHS AND WEAKNESSES OF OPEN AND CLOSED QUESTIONS

	Strengths	Weaknesses
Open questions	• Open questions produce qualitative data, which provides detail, so participants can express opinions fully, raising validity. • Analysis retains detail of participants' answers, so information, such as variation in responses, is not 'lost' through averaging.	• They produce qualitative data, which are time-consuming to analyse as themes need to be identified and extracted. • Interpretation of qualitative data can be subjective, leading to bias from individual researchers and potentially reducing inter-rater reliability. • Findings are individual so may be less generalisible.
Closed questions	• Closed questions are easy for participants to respond to, so large amounts of data can be collected quickly, making the data more reliable and, if a wide sample is found, more generalisible. • They produce quantitative data, which are easy to analyse, e.g. to find modes, medians and to plot graphs using data from many questions.	• They produce only quantitative data, which lack detail and meaning, so participants cannot express opinions fully, thus lowering validity. • There is a risk of response biases, such as consistently saying 'yes'. • The score for all participants on each question is only a total (nominal data), so the data can be used only to calculate a mode.

QUESTIONNAIRES

In a questionnaire the questions are generally strictly ordered, so it is 'structured', i.e. every participant answers the same questions in the same order. It is possible, especially using computers, to tailor questions to individual participants (e.g. when a questionnaire says 'Leave out this section if...'), making the questionnaire 'semi-structured'. In general, therefore, questionnaires are necessarily more structured than interviews. However, a greater variety of closed questions can be used in a questionnaire than in an interview because it is possible to offer a variety of choices for responses in written form, including closed questions and rating scales as well as open questions.

Questionnaires often end with an invitation that reads: 'Please tell us anything else you would like to about this topic'. This is an open question, allowing the

QUESTION SPOTLIGHT!

In Freud (1909) (see page 164), Hans' father asked both open and closed questions. The conversations reported by Freud included the following examples of open questions:

- 'Why did you come into our room?'
- 'What can it mean: a crumpled giraffe?'
- 'What did you do with the crumpled one?'
- 'Why did the big one call out?'

Ensure that you can identify examples of open and closed questions from each relevant study.

Figure 7.9

QUESTION SPOTLIGHT!

A

Simons and Chabris (1999) (see page 69) interviewed each participant after they had watched the video. The participant was asked four questions, always in the same order. They were: (i) While you were doing the counting, did you notice anything unusual on the video? (ii) Did you notice anything other than the six players? (iii) Did you see anyone else (besides the six players) appear on the video? (iv) Did you see a gorilla [woman carrying an umbrella] walk across the screen? If the participant gave a 'yes' response to any question, they were asked to provide details of what they noticed.

- *Which of these are open questions and which are closed questions?*
- *Is this a structured, semi-structured or unstructured interview protocol?*

Figure 7.10
Simons and Chabris interviewed participants about the unexpected event in their video

researchers to collect some qualitative data. However, this is likely to be much less effective than qualitative research conducted through interviewing, as, in the absence of prompts from the interviewer, the participant might give very little information.

Finally, some questionnaires contain 'filler' and 'lie detector' questions. Fillers are questions that will not be used in the analysis. They are there simply to disguise the true purpose of the questionnaire, reducing demand characteristics (see page 222). Lie detector questions are included to try to identify participants whose responses reflect a social desirability bias. For example, a questionnaire about drug use in teenagers included a closed question asking which drugs the individual had taken from a list of 11, one of which was made up. Results from participants who said 'yes' to the fictitious drug were ignored, as it was likely that they were lying about their drug use in general.

QUESTION SPOTLIGHT!

The Army Alpha test, described by Gould (1982) (see page 178) claimed to test native intelligence. Some questions were:

- Five hundred is a game played with *rackets / pins / cards / dice*
- Carrie Nation is known as a *singer / temperance agitator / suffragist / nurse*
- 'There is a reason' is an 'ad' for a *drink / revolver / flour / cleanser*

Are these open or closed questions?

TEST 8

Notice the sample sentence:

People **hear** with the   eyes   <u>ears</u>   nose   mouth

The correct word is **ears**, because it makes the truest sentence.

In each of the sentences below you have four choices for the last word. Only one of them is correct. In each sentence draw a line under the one of these four words which makes the truest sentence. If you can not be sure, guess. The two samples are already marked as they should be.

SAMPLES {
People **hear** with the   eyes   <u>ears</u>   nose   mouth
France is in   <u>Europe</u>   Asia   Africa   Australia
}

1. The apple grows on a   <u>shrub</u>   vine   bush   tree 1
2. Five hundred is played with   rackets   <u>pins</u>   cards   dice 2
3. The Percheron is a kind of   <u>goat</u>   horse   cow   sheep 3
4. The most prominent industry of Gloucester is   fishing   packing   <u>brewing</u>   automobiles.. 4
5. Sapphires are usually   blue   <u>red</u>   green   yellow 5
6. The Rhode Island Red is a kind of   horse   granite   cattle   <u>fowl</u> .... 6 C
7. Christie Mathewson is famous as a   writer   artist   baseball player   <u>comedian</u> 7
8. Revolvers are made by   Swift & Co.   Smith & Wesson   <u>W. L. Douglas</u>   B. T. Babbitt. 8
9. Carrie Nation is known as a   singer   temperance agitator   <u>suffragist</u>   nurse 9
10. "There's a reason" is an "ad" for a   <u>drink</u>   revolver   flour   cleanser .... 10 C
11. Artichoke is a kind of   hay   corn   <u>vegetable</u>   fodder .... 11 C
12. Chard is a   fish   lizard   vegetable   <u>snake</u> 12
13. Cornell University is at   Ithaca   Cambridge   Annapolis   New Haven 13
14. Buenos Aires is a city of   Spain   Brazil   Portugal   <u>Argentina</u> .... 14 C
15. Ivory is obtained from   <u>elephants</u>   mines   oysters   reefs .... 15 C
16. Alfred Noyes is famous as a   painter   poet   musician   sculptor 16
17. The armadillo is a kind of   ornamental shrub   <u>animal</u>   musical instrument   dagger...... 17
18. The tendon of Achilles is in the   <u>heel</u>   head   shoulder   abdomen ..... 18 C
19. Crisco is a   patent medicine   <u>disinfectant</u>   tooth-paste   food product.......... 19
20. An aspen is a   <u>machine</u>   fabric   tree   drink 20
21. The sabre is a kind of   musket   <u>sword</u>   cannon   pistol .... 21 C
22. The mimeograph is a kind of   typewriter   copying machine   <u>phonograph</u>   pencil......... 22
23. Maroon is a   food   fabric   drink   <u>color</u> .... 23 C
24. The clarionet is used in   <u>music</u>   stenography   book-binding   lithography .... 24 C
25. Denim is a   <u>dance</u>   food   fabric   drink 25
26. The author of "Huckleberry Finn" is   Poe   Mark Twain   Stevenson   <u>Hawthorne</u> 26
27. Faraday was most famous in   literature   war   religion   science 27
28. Air and gasolene are mixed in the   accelerator   carburetor   gear case   differential....... 28

Figure 7.11
An original Army Alpha test paper

INTERVIEWS

The interview as a research method uses questions spoken by an interviewer to a participant. These questions might be structured, but can be much less so than in a questionnaire. In an **unstructured interview** (or a semi-structured one) new questions can be incorporated in response to the participant's answers, which cannot be done in a questionnaire. This makes interviews particularly useful for gaining in-depth information about individuals and for new topics of investigation.

One advantage of an unstructured interview is that if new themes arise they can be thoroughly explored, whereas a questionnaire would be unable to delve further. For example, in a questionnaire or structured interview with a parent about the behaviour of their asthmatic child, they could be asked 'Does the child display any resistance to taking their medication?', and then 'If yes, indicate which of the following', with a list including items such as 'running away', 'crying', and 'hiding'. Here, the possible answers are limited, whereas an unstructured interview could pursue lines such as whether the child is afraid, bored, or being silly. This would give a much fuller picture of the social interaction and possible routes for intervention.

Structured interviews are the kinds of interviews you might have encountered outside supermarkets or in town centres. Everyone is treated in the same way, and numerical data are generated. In unstructured and **semi-structured interviews**, more open questions are used, generating detailed, descriptive responses, i.e. qualitative data. These are the type of interview that a patient has with a doctor, which might begin with 'How are you feeling?' The questions that follow depend on the symptoms the patient describes. The quantitative data produced by questionnaires and structured interviews are relatively easy to analyse because they are numerical. In contrast, the findings of unstructured interviews contain a great deal of information in the form of continuous speech. This has to be analysed by identifying themes, i.e. ideas within the respondent's comments that can be classified or interpreted, so are more difficult to analyse and are open to investigator bias as the responses might need interpreting.

There are some potential problems with interviews as a research method. People might be less likely to be honest in an interview than in answering a questionnaire. Imagine how a respondent in a questionnaire study, compared to one in an interview study, might feel towards questions about punishing their child. There is likely to be a greater effect of social desirability when the respondent is face-to-face with the investigator. Conversely, participants in questionnaire studies might develop a different sort of response bias – one in which they tend always to give the same kind of answer (see page 241). Have you ever done a quiz in a magazine that asks you questions with answers 'a', 'b' or 'c'? After a few responses you might have decided which 'type' you are, which will affect the way you answer the remaining items.

Participating in a questionnaire or interview study requires time and effort from participants, and a willingness to divulge things about themselves. People can be reluctant to participate, especially if questions might invade privacy or

QUESTION SPOTLIGHT!

The revised Hare Psychopathology Checklist (PCL-R) is a 20-item inventory intended to be used as a semi-structured interview. Although it can be administered only by trained individuals, and copies of the exact questions are not generally available, you can see the style of the questions and the items being investigated (see Web watch on page 243).

Suggest two reasons why it would be more useful in research with psychopaths – such as that carried out by Hancock et al. (see page 184) – to use a semi-structured interview rather than a structured one.

KEY IDEAS

A **structured interview** asks predominantly closed questions in a fixed order. The questions are likely to be scripted so they are standardised, and consistency might even be required for the interviewer's posture, etc.

A **semi-structured interview** uses a fixed list of open and closed questions, although the interviewer can introduce additional questions if required.

An **unstructured interview** generally begins with a standard question for all participants but from there on, questions depend on the respondent's answers. There might be a list of topics for the interviewer to cover.

Figure 7.12
Interviews tend to be more flexible than questionnaires as they can be unstructured

STRETCH & CHALLENGE

Look though a magazine or search the Internet for some psychological tests in the form of questionnaires. Try to find examples of each question type (open, closed, rating scales, semantic differentials, Likert scales).

- Are the rating scales and Likert scales sometimes presented reversed? Why?
- Can you identify any filler or lie detector questions? If so, why is this a potential problem? If not, suggest questions that could be used as fillers or lie detectors.

KEY IDEAS

Test-retest is a measure of reliability that uses the same test twice. If the participants' two sets of scores correlate well, the measure has good reliability.

Split-half is a measure of reliability that compares two halves of a test, e.g. odd- and even-numbered questions. If the participants' scores on the two halves correlate well, the measure has good reliability.

Correlation coefficient is a measure of the strength of a correlation, usually expressed as an 'r' value between 0 and 1. A high value, e.g. $r=0.8$, means that there is a strong correlation, and $r=0$ means there is no correlation. This is often used to indicate reliability, so a higher value suggests better reliability.

Reliability is the consistency of a measure, e.g. whether results from the same participants would be similar each time.

Validity is the extent to which a test or tool measures what it claims to measure.

be stressful: think about participants being asked about losing a parent, a severe addiction, or about crime. This means that the people who do volunteer are probably not representative of the whole population. In a questionnaire study, participants also have to return the completed questionnaire. Even when given a postage-paid envelope, many potential participants do not return them. The percentage of non-returners is called the drop-out or 'attrition rate', and it adds a further bias to the sample.

ASSESSING RELIABILITY AND VALIDITY IN SELF-REPORTS

Reliability

Psychologists need to measure variables consistently. This is called **reliability**. If you are a reliable student, you regularly turn up to lessons or hand in your homework. Like a reliable student, a reliable psychological test or measure is also consistent: it will always produce the same results in the same situation with the same people. This aspect of consistency is called **external reliability**. Reliability is used to assess both experimental procedures and 'tools', such as tests, interviews and behavioural categories in observations, so the consistent behaviour of the researcher plays a part in making sure that the results are consistent. In a reliable self-report the same person would give the same responses to the same questions each time. This is assessed by a **test-retest** assessment. If the same participants respond to the same test twice in a similar way, the test has external reliability. The two sets of scores can be correlated, and a high correlation (close to 1) shows good reliability (see pages 253–7 for an explanation of correlations).

In self-reports we are also concerned about the consistency of items within the measure itself (i.e. the questions). This is its **internal reliability** and shows that items within the self-report tool are measuring the same phenomenon. A **split-half** assessment is a measure of internal reliability in which scores from two halves of a test (e.g. all the even and all the odd numbered questions) are compared. For example, a questionnaire testing extraversion might contain 20 questions. If scores from the first half of these are correlated with the scores from the second half, the measure has good reliability (see pages 253–7 for an explanation of correlations). Such correlations can be used to identify specific items that do not produce consistent responses. These unreliable items can then be changed or removed, improving the overall reliability of the measure.

To maintain high reliability, researchers must interview in standardised ways and interpret the responses to open questions consistently – this is **inter-rater reliability**. It is checked by each researcher assessing the same self-reports (e.g. producing a numerical score from each interview transcript) and then correlating their ratings. If there is a strong positive correlation, the researchers are reliable.

Validity

Validity is another concept which applies to all psychological research. To be valid, a questionnaire or interview must be reliable, but other factors affect the validity of self-reports too. Validity is the extent to which a technique is capable of achieving the intended purpose: if a questionnaire measures the aspect of beliefs or behaviours it is supposed to, it is valid. If a score in an experiment task is a valid indicator of the DV, it measures the variable under scrutiny rather than varying because of demand characteristics, fatigue or the effect of the experimenter. (See Key Ideas, page 222.)

Internal validity refers to the test or measure being used; for example, in an experiment, whether changes in the DV are caused by the IV rather than sources of error. For self-reports, we can consider this problem in several ways:

- **Face validity** is whether a measure appears, at face value, to test what it claims to.
- **Criterion validity** indicates whether a phenomenon measured in one way will relate to, or predict, some other related variable. This relationship can be co-existing either at the same time (i.e. concurrent – see below) or in the future, which is described as predictive validity – the extent to which the measure can indicate what will happen in the future, and is correct in this forecast.
- **Concurrent validity** (a type of criterion validity) is whether a measure will produce a similar score for a particular individual as another test that claims to assess the same phenomenon. This can be assessed by comparing the results to a measure known to be effective.
- **Construct validity** is a wider idea, looking at whether a measure is based on some certain-to-exist phenomenon, which it tests. It arises as a consequence of combined theoretical and empirical research, rather than being the product of a single measure or procedure.

External validity relates to issues beyond the investigation, particularly, whether the findings will generalise to other populations, location, contexts and times than the ones investigated. This includes the concept of ecological validity (see page 226). One specific aspect of importance to self-reports is the idea of **population validity** – the extent to which findings from one sample can be generalised to the whole of the population from which the sample was taken, and to other populations. Many factors affect whether such generalisations can be made, such as the sampling method used, the size of the sample, the narrowness (or otherwise) of the sample and the nature of the phenomenon being tested. So, if the sample is deemed to be representative, i.e. to have the range of relevant characteristics that are found in the wider population, then the findings should generalise from the sample to that population. However, historically, this was rarely the case in psychology, as so much research was based on students who, being mainly young, white and Western, were not typical of the range of people in the wider population. So, to achieve **representativeness**, the sample tested should include a good cross section of the population, so that all the different categories of people within in it are included.

QUESTION SPOTLIGHT!

Which is face validity and which is concurrent validity?

- An interview about helping genuinely measures behaviours such as carrying bags for elderly people and holding doors open for wheelchair users, rather than eliciting socially desirable responses.
- Clinicians working with patients who have mental-health disorders use a range of standardised diagnostic self-report tools that make the same diagnoses.

TABLE 7.12 STRENGTHS AND WEAKNESSES OF SELF-REPORT TECHNIQUES

	Strengths	Weaknesses
Questionnaires	<ul><li>They are relatively easy to administer and can be sent or emailed to participants, making them time- and cost-efficient.</li><li>Respondents might be more truthful than in an interview, especially if their answers are personal or socially sensitive.</li><li>Data are relatively easy to analyse as they are usually quantitative.</li></ul>	<ul><li>Response biases – such as tending always to answer 'no', or always ticking the box on the left – can lead to invalid results.</li><li>They are limited because, unlike unstructured interviews, there is no flexibility to allow for the collection of useful but unexpected data, as new questions cannot be added.</li></ul>
Interviews	<ul><li>Structured interview data are relatively easy to analyse as they are quantitative.</li><li>Semi-structured or unstructured interviews enable the researcher to gain specific and detailed information from the respondent that could be missed in structured techniques.</li><li>Face-to-face, an interviewer can respond more flexibly to gain useful, detailed information when this is difficult to obtain.</li></ul>	<ul><li>Structured interviews are limited by fixed questions.</li><li>Investigator bias can be a problem, as the expectations of the interviewer can either alter the way in which they ask questions, thus unconsciously affecting the respondents' answers, or affect they way in which responses are interpreted.</li></ul>
Both questionaires and interviews	<ul><li>Generate quantitative and/or qualitative data.</li><li>Structured questionnaires and interviews can be easily repeated to generate more data or check findings.</li><li>Structured questionnaires and interviews can be readily assessed for reliability and improved by removing inconsistent items.</li></ul>	<ul><li>Participants can be affected by biases such as social desirability, and might be influenced by leading questions.</li><li>As only some people are willing to fill in questionnaires or be interviewed, the participants might not be representative of the majority of the population.</li></ul>

D – THE CORRELATIONAL ANALYSIS

INTRODUCTION

In this section we will be looking at the way in which the research method of **correlational analysis** is used in psychology. Specifically, we will explore positive and negative correlations and the production and interpretation of scatter diagrams. We will also evaluate the method of correlational analysis.

CORRELATIONAL ANALYSIS

A correlational analysis aims to investigate whether two variables are related. A correlational design is useful in situations in which it is only possible for the variables to be measured, rather than manipulated or compared, i.e. when it is not possible to conduct an experiment. This might be the case where changing the variables would not be practical, such as attempting to vary the amount of pre-school exposure to TV, or where it would be unethical, such as increasing real-life exposure to violence.

Obtaining data for correlational analysis

In order to look for a correlation between two variables, each must exist over a range and it must be possible to measure them numerically, i.e. the data must be quantitative. This means that the participants' scores cannot just be in named categories (see page 282 for a description of different kinds of data). Although the scales for each variable may be different, they both need to be numerical (or it must be possible to convert them to numbers).

For example, variables such as 'brain weight' or IQ are numerical and could be used in a correlation, as could scores from rating scales (see page 241). However, responses to the question 'What's your favourite colour?' would produce data only in named categories, which could not be used in a correlation. Similarly, the question 'What is your employment status?' could generate answers of 'employed', 'self-employed', 'student', 'retired' or 'at-home mum', and although this gives a range of responses, we cannot put them in order, so they could not be used in a correlation.

A range of techniques can be used in correlational analyses to collect appropriate data. For example, self-reports, such as interviews and questionnaires, may collect ordinal data through rating scales, by adding together the scores from several simple closed questions. Observations can also produce ordinal data, as can many kinds of tests. Some tests, such as intelligence tests, are treated as equal interval data, and many scientific measurements used in psychological investigations, such as reaction time, pulse rate and galvanic skin resistance (a measure of stress), also produce equal interval data.

 **KEY IDEAS**

Correlational analysis is a technique used to investigate a link between two measured variables.

Figure 7.13
My goldfish lives in a tank on my desk. The more fizzy drinks I consume, the more active my fish is. It's tempting to assume there is a causal relationship (see page 254) – seeing the bubbles in my glass makes her excited. In reality, there is no causal relationship; both variables are affected by a third factor – temperature. The hotter the weather, the more I drink, and fish are more active in warmer water.

KEY IDEAS

A relationship between two variables such that a change in one is responsible for a change in the other is known as a **causal relationship**.

A **correlation** is a relationship between two measured variables.

STRETCH & CHALLENGE

Dan and Alysha have a car wash company in their local town. When they study the variation in their takings over time they discover a pattern. Dan thinks it matches one he's seen in the local police station about car theft. When they look at the incidence of thefts and of their car washing, there is a clear positive correlation. The more cars they wash, the higher the number of thefts. Alysha wonders whether the thieves are more likely to steal clean cars!

In reality, it is unlikely that this apparent relationship is causal.

Suggest a third factor that could increase both the incidence of car theft and the likelihood of people having their car washed.

Figure 7.14
Correlations cannot tell us about causal relationships

Drawing conclusions in correlational analysis

It is important to note that a correlational analysis looks for a relationship between two measured variables. These are sometimes called co-variables because a correlation cannot investigate which of them is causing the other to change. Although we might have a strong suspicion which variable is responsible, a simple correlation cannot help us to be sure: it can tell us only whether the two variables are related. As a consequence, you must not refer to them as the independent variable and dependent variable!

We cannot say from one correlation that an increase in one variable has caused an increase (or decrease) in the other, because it is possible that the changes in both variables could be the result of another factor. Suppose we measure two variables – memory and number of GCSE passes – and find that they are positively correlated. It might be tempting to say that a good memory is responsible for getting better grades, but we cannot be sure of this. It is possible that both of these factors depend on a third variable, such as the amount of practice at learning and recall the individual has had in their lifetime. All we can conclude is that the two factors we have measured vary together, not that there is a cause-and-effect relationship between them. If we want to make judgments about causality, we need to conduct an experiment in which we can be sure that it is the manipulation of one variable that is responsible for the change in the other. Of course, if we conduct a correlational analysis and find that there is no relationship between two variables, then we can conclude that there is no **causal relationship**.

QUESTION SPOTLIGHT!

Remember that correlations find relationships between variables, not causal relationships, so we don't use the terms IV and DV.
Judging only by the way these sentences are worded, decide which are proposing correlational relationships, and which are proposing causal relationships:

1 When taking medication is fun, children are more likely to adhere to treatment than with standard procedures.
2 The hippocampal size of animal species is related to their need to hide and find winter food stores.
3 There is a link between the size of the hippocampus in the brain and a person's navigational ability.
4 Children are more likely to copy the behaviour of same-sex adults than that of opposite-sex adults.
5 Males and females differ in their navigational ability.
6 Children who watch more violent television are more likely to engage in aggressive play.

POSITIVE AND NEGATIVE CORRELATIONS

The findings of a correlational analysis are used to assess the nature of the relationship between the two variables. This can be described in two ways, by the direction and the strength of the link. In a **positive correlation**, both variables increase in the same direction – that is, higher scores on one variable correspond with higher scores on the other. For example, we would expect to find a positive correlation between exposure to aggressive models and violent behaviour, such that greater exposure to models is linked to a higher incidence of violence. When two variables are **negatively correlated**, higher scores on one variable correspond with low scores on the other. For example, we might predict a negative correlation between number of years of education and level of obedience, such that as the amount of education increases, the likelihood of blind obedience decreases. Alternatively, there might be no correlation at all between two variables; this lack of relation is sometimes called a zero correlation.

 KEY IDEAS

A **positive correlation** is a relationship between two variables such that an increase in one accompanies an increase in the other.

A **negative correlation** is a relationship between two variables such that an increase in one accompanies a decrease in the other.

A **scatter diagram** is a graph used to display the data from a correlational study. Each point on the graph represents the participant's score on scales for each of the two measured variables.

ACTIVITY

Look at the two sets of correlational data below.
Which one do you think is a positive correlation, and which one do you think is a negative correlation?

TABLE 7.13A									
Reaction time (secs)	78	71	69	86	98	65	70	69	71
Hours of sleep	6	9	7	5	4	7	8	9	8

TABLE 7.13B									
Attendance (%)	41	19	85	90	54	82	79	89	61
Exam score	3	3	9	10	5	9	8	8	6

QUESTION SPOTLIGHT!

Maguire *et al.* (2000) (see page 148), investigated several correlational relationships between the volume of different brain areas and time spent working as a taxi driver.
Identify whether the following were positive or negative correlations:

1 As posterior hippocampal size increased, so did years spent driving a taxi.
2 As years spent driving a taxi increased, the size of the anterior hippocampus decreased.

Scatter diagrams

The different relationships can be illustrated visually on a scatter diagram (or scattergram). This is a graph with one variable along each of the axes on which each point represents one pair of scores. These two scores usually relate to one participant. However, in some situations they might not, e.g. when comparing data from pairs of twins or when testing reliability between two researchers' scoring or rating of the same observation or interview (see pages 231 and 247).

A scatter diagram readily indicates whether a correlation is positive or negative. For example, if we were to collect data on the variables of brain volume and braininess, we might expect both to increase together. This would be a positive correlation and the general line of the pattern of the points would slope

MATHS MOMENT

Using the two sets of correlational data from the activity above, sketch a scatter diagram for each correlation, labelling the variables on each axis.

QUESTION SPOTLIGHT!

On page 255, two correlational relationships from Maguire *et al.* (2000) are described.

Sketch a scatter diagram for each correlation, labelling the variables on each axis.

upwards from left to right (see Figure 7.15a). Alternatively we could measure brain volume and reaction time. Now we would expect faster speeds (i.e. smaller reaction times) with bigger brains. This would be a negative correlation and the line made by the points would slope downwards from left to right (see Figure 7.15b).

Another aspect of the findings of a correlation is the strength of the relationship. If a correlation is very strong, the two variables are closely related. This can also be readily seen on a scatter diagram. The closer the points are to the 'imaginary line', the stronger the correlation (see Figures 7.15c and d). This measure of 'strength' can also be described numerically, as a correlation coefficient (see page 250). When there is no correlation between two variables, the points on a scatter diagram are randomly spread, with no obvious line (see Figure 7.15e).

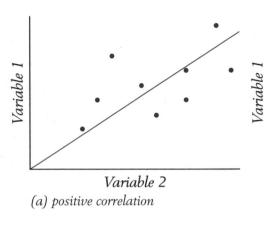

(a) *positive correlation*

(b) *negative correlation*

(c) *a weak positive correlation*

Figure 7.15
A scatter diagram is used to represent the results of a correlational analysis

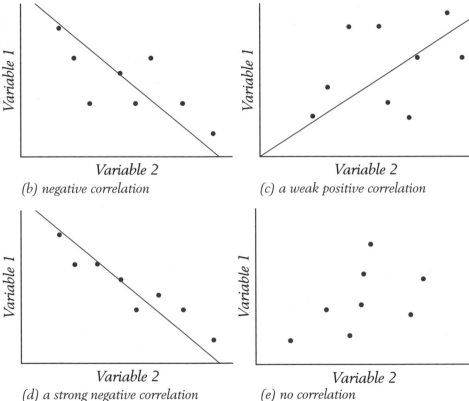

(d) *a strong negative correlation*

(e) *no correlation*

ASSESSING RELIABILITY AND VALIDITY IN CORRELATIONS

Reliability

Remember that reliability is about consistency (see page 250). In correlational analyses we are concerned about the consistency of the measures used. The findings of a correlational analysis will be reliable only if the measures of both variables are consistent. Thus, for some correlations, such as those using scientific scales (such as volume or time), the measures will be highly reliable. In other cases, such as studies correlating variables measured using self-reports, observations or estimates, reliability will potentially be lower.

Validity

Remember that validity is about being sure that you are measuring what you intended to measure. To be valid, a correlational analysis must be reliable, but other factors affect validity too. As with reliability, the findings of a correlational analysis will be valid only if the measures of both variables measure real phenomena in effective ways. To achieve this, the variables must be defined and measured effectively.

ACTIVITY ✳

How would you operationalise (see page 221) the two variables in each of the possible correlations described below?

1 People are more likely to offer to help when in smaller groups.
2 An increase in aggressiveness and the amount of Internet use.
3 A relationship between eyewitness accuracy and post-event exposure to media reports about the crime.

WEB WATCH @

Look at the scatter diagrams on the following websites:

- www.intropsych.com/ch01_psychology_and_science/01drinkingandgpanegcorrelation.jpg
- http://origin-ars.sciencedirect.com/content/image/1-s2.0-S0738399199000476-gr2.gif
- www.holah.co.uk/images/correlationquestion2.png
- www.ecs.org/html/educationIssues/Research/images/primer/example_understanding7.gif

Which are positive correlations and which are negative?

Which of the correlations look the strongest and which look the weakest?

TABLE 7.14 STRENGTHS AND WEAKNESSES OF CORRELATION ANALYSIS

Strengths	Weaknesses
• A correlational study can be conducted on variables that can be measured but not manipulated, i.e. when experimentation would be impractical or unethical.	• A single correlational analysis cannot indicate whether a relationship is causal, so when a relationship is found this might be due to one of the measured variables or alternatively another, unknown, variable might be responsible.
• A correlation can demonstrate the presence or absence of a relationship so is useful for indicating areas for subsequent experimental research.	• Correlational analysis can be used only with variables that can be measured on a scale.

C7
RESEARCH
METHODS

PART 2: RESEARCH METHODS IN ACTION

In this section we will explore how research in psychology happens: the role of scientific enquiry, how research reports are written, ethics and the analysis of data. We will explore in detail the planning and evaluation processes that are common to all psychological investigations, the particular design decisions required in planning studies using each of the four research methods and how these can be evaluated. We will look at general issues pertinent to all of the methods, including research aims and questions, hypotheses, sampling and variables as well as ways to improve research.

E – PSYCHOLOGY AS A SCIENCE

INTRODUCTION

This section explores the details you need to design and evaluate your own studies and those presented in a source in an examination.

Science in psychology

Throughout this book you have been reading about the process of scientific enquiry. What does that actually mean? If you were asked to name the most scientific research method you know, you would probably have little difficulty identifying the laboratory experiment, and you would be right. But why is this the case? In this section you will find out.

CAUSAL RELATIONSHIPS: THE STUDY OF CAUSE AND EFFECT

In a laboratory experiment, the intention is to investigate the effect the IV has on the DV. When the IV is carefully manipulated and other potential **extraneous variables** are controlled, the researcher can be fairly sure that any changes in the DV are the consequence of the deliberate variation in the IV. This is a causal, or **cause-and-effect**, relationship. This contrasts with the situation in a quasi-experiment, where deliberate manipulation of the IV is not possible so changes in the DV may be due to **confounding variables**. Similarly, in a field experiment, where the possibility of controlling extraneous variables is limited, confounding variables may disguise the effect of the IV. Imagine a field experiment into the effects of studying in silence versus with music, that was conducted when some building work was being done. In the 'music' condition, the students were able to concentrate because the music covered up the banging noise of the building work. In the 'silent' condition the students could not concentrate. This might result in the conclusion that working in silence is ineffective. The confounding variable of being disturbed by the building work acted against the (potential) effect of the IV of silence. Conversely, if the music played was too loud, or of a type that the students disliked (perhaps it was chosen by the experimenter and wasn't to their taste), working in silence would appear to be highly effective. In fact, the IV of silence might not be important at all, the difference could simply be due to the students being unable to work with the terrible choice of music.

In correlational studies, there is a temptation to conclude that if two variables change together, one is responsible for the change in the other. Unlike in an experimental situation, such cause-and-effect conclusions cannot be drawn from a correlational analysis. This is because other factors are not controlled, so the researcher cannot be sure that any correspondence between variables is not due to some other factor (see pages 267–9).

(see pages 267–9).

KEY IDEAS

The study of **cause and effect** is the investigation of a causal relationship, i.e. the search for a link between two variables such that a change in one variable can be demonstrated to be responsible for changes in another variable, as is seen in experiments in which the IV causes changes in the DV.

Extraneous variables are any factors that can affect the outcome of an investigation other than those being tested. Their influence may be systematic, i.e. have a consistent effect on one level of the IV, or may not be (non-systematic). In either case, they threaten the validity of the findings.

A **confounding variable** is a factor in an experiment that confounds (i.e. confuses) the results because it masks the effect of the IV on the DV as its effects are systematic. This can arise either because the additional variable acts in the same way as the IV, making the IV appear to be important when it is not, or because it works in the opposite way from the IV, making the IV appear to be unimportant when it is. One way to overcome such problems is through random allocation.

KEY IDEAS

Induction – a scientific method that uses observations to generate testable hypotheses, which are developed into theories.

Deduction – a scientific method that develops hypotheses from theories, then tests these hypotheses by 'observation', i.e. empirically.

Falsification – being able to demonstrate that something is not the case, i.e. that a hypothesis is false.

It is the manipulation of the independent variable, therefore, that gives us the capacity to study cause and effect in experiments. As a consequence, the precision with which variables are manipulated and measured in investigations is important – see opposite page.

THE PRINCIPLES OF SCIENTIFIC ENQUIRY

The scientific method is about 'knowing' rather than just 'believing'. This leads to two ideas: that scientific knowledge is somehow different from non-scientific information, and that it is obtained through a different (i.e. 'scientific') process. This process, called the **scientific method** is important and, confusingly, can again mean several things. 'Scientific methods' are ways of collecting data, such as experiments, for example. A 'scientific method' is a process of developing knowledge in one of two scientific ways (see Figure 7.16). In **induction**, observations of real-world phenomena lead to an analysis of the patterns that can be seen. Generalisations from these patterns lead to the development of testable hypotheses which can be used to build a theory. In **deduction**, observations lead directly to the generation of theories, from which testable hypotheses are developed. These are used to make predictions which are tested by observation.

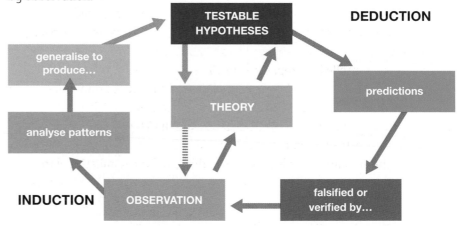

Figure 7.16
Two views of the scientific method

HYPOTHESIS TESTING

It is important to the scientific nature of this process that the hypotheses are testable, i.e. that evidence can be found that would demonstrate them to be true or false. This is called **falsification**. If it is not possible for the statement in a hypothesis to be shown to be false, then we cannot have confidence in evidence that supports it. One of Freud's suggestions was about defence mechanisms, unconscious ways to hide our real feelings. Two defence mechanisms were repression (pushing feelings deep into the unconscious) and reaction formation (behaving in the opposite way to our feelings). Imagine a man who appears to be heterosexual. He may be so, or he may be a gay man who is demonstrating reaction formation. It would be impossible to tell, i.e. the ideas cannot be falsified.

As we will see on pages 262–6, we use pairs of hypotheses – the alternative and null – so that whether we support (confirm) or refute (reject) our hypothesis, we can still draw a conclusion. In order to give mathematical precision to this process, we can also use inferential statistics (see page 294).

As we have already seen, when conducting experiments, we need to ensure that our tests are valid and reliable. So, in order that the hypotheses we are proposing can be tested effectively, the **manipulation of variables** must be carefully controlled, that is, we must be certain that the IV is being changed as intended, and that nothing else is varying with it. For example, in an experiment investigating the effect of group size in a study on helping on trains, we might choose to test different group sizes in different carriages. However, if the smaller group sizes are always found in first-class or 'quiet-zone' carriages, these factors, rather than the IV, might be affecting the outcome, i.e. they would be a confounding variable.

Control of extraneous variables

The controlling of variables helps to improve the validity and reliability of hypothesis testing. A **control** is a factor that is kept constant, so is essential to being able to establish cause-and-effect relationships. If uncontrolled variables could account for changes in the DV, it would not be possible to draw valid conclusions about the action of the IV. For example, in a test of the effect on obedience to teachers who mark their authority by wearing academic gowns compared to wearing ordinary clothes, it would be essential that other aspects, such as how experienced the teacher was and how well known they were to their students, were controlled, i.e. kept the same. The obvious way to do this would be to use the same teacher and dress them differently. However, sometimes this is not possible. In a study comparing the extent to which TV disrupts studying compared to music, the music played and the TV programme could not be identical. Instead, various controls would need to be imposed, such as the volume, the amount of words that were audible, and the familiarity of the material being presented. As well as improving validity by ensuring differences are more likely to be due to the IV, such controls also raise reliability, as they make it easier to set up the same situation for each participant.

Standardisation helps to improve reliability by establishing identical procedures for different conditions and for each participant or group. Spoken or written instructions, the process of presenting stimuli and the recording of data can all be standardised. This is much easier to achieve when **quantifiable measurements** are being used to assess the DV. Remember, quantitative data are numerical (see page 282). For example, in a study involving the assessment of IQ, the use of a tool that provides a numerical score, such as an IQ test, will lead to better reliability than a judgment based on an essay or a task involving a creative solution to a problem. In these cases the score would be decided by a more **subjective** process than adding up the number of correct answers – that is, it would depend to an extent on the personal opinion of the researcher scoring the test. In contrast, science requires objectivity in data collection – that is, it should be free from personal opinion. One way to improve **objectivity** in data collection, especially where qualitative data are being collected, is to use operational definitions (see page 267).

KEY IDEAS

Control – a way to keep a potential extraneous variable constant so that it does not affect the DV in addition to or instead of the IV to ensure that a cause-and-effect relationship can be established.

Standardisation – the use of set procedures for conducting the study and collecting data across different conditions and participants to limit the effects of uncontrolled variables.

Subjectivity – taking a biased personal viewpoint that may be influenced by one's own beliefs or experiences, so may differ between individual researchers, i.e. is not independent of the situation.

Objectivity – taking an unbiased external perspective that is not affected by an individual or personal viewpoint, so should be consistent between different researchers.

Replicability – being able to repeat an original procedure in exactly the same way.

WEB WATCH @

In your examination, you will be required to respond to a source. It is important that you practise reading about psychological investigations and applying your knowledge of research methods to them.

Go to the website of the British Psychological Society 'Research Digest' and read about some recent investigations.

http://digest.bps.org.uk

If you find this interesting, you can follow the Research Digest on Twitter.

Replicability

Highly controlled and standardised procedures, and the collection of data using quantifiable measurements all lead to the capacity to repeat a study in exactly the same way. This is the essence of replicability. Being able to conduct studies again enables psychologists to demonstrate the reliability and validity of an effect by repeating it. This is particularly so when other people replicate studies – ensuring that the finding is not due to an unspecified influence of a particular researcher.

THE RESEARCH PROCESS

How does psychological knowledge end up in a book like this? This question is really asking how the 'scientific enquiry' described on page 260 leads to access to psychological knowledge. Researchers not just in universities, but also in hospitals, schools, industry and many other locations, conduct studies and make their findings available to others. This is done through the publication of studies in journals. A journal is essentially a professional 'magazine' that invites researchers to submit 'papers'. A paper is a written article describing a study (or theoretical contribution), like each of the core studies. Some journals are very general, such as the *British Journal of Psychology* or *Nature*, while others, such as the *Journal of Neuropsychology*, are very specific. Submitted papers are scrutinised by a panel of experts in the academic area. The process of **peer review** allows the panel of experts to judge whether the article makes a significant contribution to the body of psychological knowledge. In order to do so, the research must be highly regarded in terms of its methodology, its data analysis, and the conclusions that are drawn. It should also demonstrate that it has followed appropriate ethical guidelines. Once it has been published, an article is subject to further peer review. Ongoing scrutiny by other researchers allows them to comment on the work and follow it up, either to produce replications and extensions, or to contradict its findings. The latter would be an example of falsification in practice.

When journal articles (or 'papers') report a piece of empirical research, they tend to follow a fairly standard pattern – one that you can use if you write up practical reports. The layout typically includes the following sections. A paper starts with an *abstract*, a summary that includes the aim, method, results and conclusion. This is followed by the *introduction*, which places the study in the context of relevant theories and research, leading to a justification of what is being done and why. The next section, the *method*, includes details such as the design, the sample and sampling method, the procedure (which may include reference to ethics) and apparatus and materials (e.g. stimuli, questionnaires, etc). This is followed by a *results* section, which is likely to contain both descriptive and inferential statistics, then by a *discussion*, which considers the results in the light of the context presented in the introduction to draw conclusions about the meaning of the results. This section may include important failings of the study and ideas for future study. Finally, a section entitled *references* lists all the other journal articles that have been referred to in the introduction and the discussion.

When articles are referred to, or 'cited', in academic writing, they are always written in a precise way – although there are several standard formats. One commonly used format is the Harvard system. When the article is quoted, the author's surname is given, followed by the year of publication. If there are two or three authors, all the names are cited, but for four or more only the first is given, followed by '*et al.*' (see Box 7.9). In the references section, full references are given, which state all the authors' names and initials, the year of publication, the title of the article and the journal the article appears in, with the volume and page numbers. You will notice that references to other books appear slightly differently, following the pattern: author(s) name(s) and initial(s), the year of publication, the title of the book, the name of the publisher and the town in which the publisher is located.

Following the references section, there may be an additional *appendices* section. An appendix can include original materials, such as stimuli or questionnaires, or raw data tables or examples of the results.

Box 7.9

Writing references: The Harvard System

When you refer to a study or theory, you tell the reader whose work you are talking about. This is done using a formal citation, giving their name(s) and the date of publication. In the Harvard system, if there are one, two or three authors, all the names are cited, but for four or more only the first is given, followed by '*et al.*'.

You can see detailed instructions here: http://www.staffs.ac.uk/assets/harvard_quick_guide_tcm44-47797.pdf

In the Harvard system, this book would be referenced as:
Jarvis, M., Russell, J., Gauntlett, E. and Lintern, F (2015) *OCR A Level Psychology: AS and Year 1*. 2nd Ed. Oxford, Oxford University Press.

HYPOTHESES

A **hypothesis** is a testable statement of the investigator's predictions about the results of their study. In most published research the hypotheses are not stated so you are unlikely to have encountered them even if you have read original journal articles. Instead, an *aim* is typically stated, i.e. the purpose of the study is given, or a *research question* (a question that illustrates what the study intends to investigate) is posed. Hypotheses are, however, useful in the process of drawing conclusions from research, which you need to understand.

The alternative hypothesis

Most studies have a hypothesis as well as an aim, but some, for example some observations, are not testing a particular idea so they do not. The aim in an experiment is very specific. If you conduct an experiment to find out whether increasing arousal with loud music makes recall of words better or worse, your

 KEY IDEAS

Hypothesis (plural: hypotheses) – a testable statement predicting a relationship between variables, such as in an experiment, where a change in the IV will produce an increase or a decrease in the DV, or in a correlation, where an increase in one variable will be linked to an increase or a decrease in another variable.

Alternative hypothesis – a testable statement predicting that there will be a relationship between variables in an investigation.

This is a two-tailed hypothofish – which way will it go?

This is a one-tailed hypothofish – which way will it go?

Figure 7.17
One-tailed and two-tailed hypotheses: in how many directions could each fish swim?

KEY IDEAS

Two-tailed (or non-directional) hypothesis – a statement predicting how one variable will be related to another, e.g. whether there will be a difference in the DV between levels of the IV (in an experiment), or that there will be a relationship between the measured variables (in a correlation).

One-tailed (or directional) hypothesis – a statement predicting the direction of a relationship between variables, e.g. in an experiment whether a change in the IV will produce an increase or a decrease in the DV, or in a correlation whether an increase in one variable will be linked to an increase or a decrease in another variable.

aim would be to test this effect. You would need a corresponding hypothesis, for example: *There is a difference between the number of words recalled when listening to loud or quiet music.* This is called the **alternative hypothesis**, and states the difference you expect to find between levels of the IV.

> **Box 7.10**
> **Why are there two names for the types of alternative hypothesis?**
> When hypotheses are tested for significance by putting the data into an inferential statistical test (see sections for different tests on pages 297–308), they are given different names. A non-directional hypothesis is referred to as a two-tailed hypothesis, and a directional hypothesis is referred to as a one-tailed hypothesis. This is simply because the different types of hypotheses consider the spread of possible scores over either both 'tails' or ends of the distribution or range of scores, or only the top or the bottom. A hypothesis considering the results in only one 'direction' (e.g. whether the IV improves scores) uses only one of the two possible 'tails' of the distribution, so is called a directional or one-tailed hypothesis. A hypothesis considering the results in both 'directions' (e.g. whether the IV changes scores, causing them to go up or down) uses both of the possible 'tails' of the distribution, so is called a non-directional or two-tailed hypothesis.

Direction in hypotheses: directional and non-directional hypotheses

The alternative hypothesis (sometimes written as H_1) above is **a non-directional (two-tailed) hypothesis** (see Figure 7.17). In an experiment, we expect that the IV will change the DV, but we may not be sure whether the effect will be an increase or a decrease, in which case we use a non-directional hypothesis. We would probably choose this type of hypothesis if we were testing the effect of a variable that had not been investigated before. For example, if we were investigating the effect of eating jelly babies on recall, they might help us to remember, or they might distract us.

If most previous research suggests that we can be confident about the nature of an effect, we can use a **directional (one-tailed) hypothesis**. For example, in a test of how post-event information from talking to other witnesses affects testimonies we could be confident that talking would make them less accurate. This is a directional prediction so a hypothesis might be: '*Testimonies from eyewitnesses who have discussed events with others are less accurate than those of witnesses who have not discussed events.*' The corresponding non-directional hypothesis would have been: '*There is a difference in accuracy of testimonies from witnesses who have and have not discussed events.*'

A non-directional hypothesis in a correlational study simply predicts that there will be a relationship between the two measured variables. A directional hypothesis states whether this relationship will be a positive or a negative correlation (see page 255). For example, in a study looking for a relationship between brain volume and braininess, we might say: '*There will be a relationship between brain volume and braininess.*' This would be a non-directional hypothesis. Alternatively we could suggest a directional hypothesis, such as: '*There will be a positive correlation between brain volume and braininess.*' We could also say: 'As brain volume increases brainmness increases.' This would be a directional hypothesis too. Remember that m in a correlational study, we cannot say that one factor causes the change in the other. Directional hypotheses for negative correlations follow the same pattern, for example: 'As brain size increases reaction time decreases.' This could alternatively be written as: 'There will be a negative correlation between brain size and reaction time.'

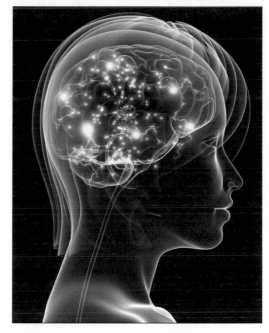

Figure 7.18
Is brain size related to braininess?

QUESTION SPOTLIGHT!

1   Imagine an experiment testing the effect of eating either healthy or unhealthy food on concentration.
    Write a non-directional hypothesis for this study.

2   Charlotte predicts that listening to music will make students quicker at completing dot-to-dots.
    Write a directional hypothesis for this experiment.

3   A teacher thinks that there might be a correlation between the amount her students have eaten and their concentration. She isn't sure whether eating more will make them less hungry, so they will concentrate better, or that eating more will make them sleepy, so they will concentrate less.
    Write a non-directional hypothesis for her study.

4   A watchdog organisation is concerned about a possible relationship between eyewitness accuracy and the amount of post-event exposure to media reports about the crime.
    Write a directional hypothesis for this correlation.

The null hypothesis

As well as the alternative hypothesis, you also need to be clear about the **null hypothesis**. This states that any difference in the DV between levels of the IV is so small that there is a high probability that it has arisen by chance. This is an important idea because it is used in statistical testing. These tests help you to decide whether it is likely that the null hypothesis is correct. A typical null hypothesis (H_0) would be: 'There will be no difference in accuracy of testimonies from witnesses who have or have not discussed events.' Sometimes you will see null hypotheses written in this form: 'Any difference in the accuracy of testimonies from witnesses who have and have not discussed events is due to chance.'

The null hypothesis in an experiment says, basically: 'There will be no difference between condition X and condition Y' (or that: 'Any difference in the DV between condition X and condition Y is due to chance'). If we were investigating the effect of age on eyewitness memory, for example, a suitable null hypothesis would be: 'Any difference in recall between older and younger witnesses is due to chance.' So that the sentence makes sense, it is sometimes better to swap the order of the IV and DV around. So a slightly different way to write this null hypothesis would be: 'There will be no difference between older and younger witnesses' recall' (or 'Any difference between older and younger witnesses' recall is due to chance'). However, always make sure that you state both of the levels of the IV and the DV otherwise it won't make sense. For example a null hypothesis that states 'There is no difference between eyewitness recall and age' is meaningless.

KEY IDEAS

Null hypothesis – a testable statement saying that any difference or correlation is due to chance, i.e. that no pattern in the results has arisen because of the variables being studied.

QUESTION SPOTLIGHT!

The experiments by Loftus and Palmer (1974) (page 45) expected eyewitness testimony to be less accurate with leading questions.

Explain whether the hypothesis would have been directional or non-directional.

As with experimental studies, correlational studies need to have a null hypothesis. These also predict no link or that any relationship could have occurred by chance. A typical null hypothesis for a correlational study reads: '*There will be no relationship between variable X and variable Y*' (or '*Any relationship between variable X and variable Y is due to chance*'). For example: '*There will be no relationship between brain volume and braininess*' (or '*Any relationship between brain volume and braininess is due to chance*').

QUESTION SPOTLIGHT!

Read each of the following hypotheses.
Which are alternative and which are null hypotheses?

1 Any difference between test scores of students who have learned using mindmaps or mnemonics is the to chance.
2 There will be a difference between the helpfulness of people who own pets and people who do not.
3 There will be no correlation between time spent doing homework and achievement.
4 Students who do their homework on the bus or train will get lower scores than those who sit at a desk.
5 There will be a negative correlation between number of hours spent doing a part-time job and module grades.
6 Students who play a musical instrument will concentrate better in class than those who do not.

STRETCH & CHALLENGE

Which of the alternative hypotheses in the Question Spotlight are directional and which are non-directional?

Operationally define the variables in each of the null hypotheses.

F – ISSUES IN DESIGNING STUDIES

INTRODUCTION

For most investigations, researchers must consider how variables will be measured and how a sample will be obtained. The different research methods also have specific design requirements and potential flaws, although all share the need for strong reliability and validity. This section explores these issues.

VARIABLES

The key things you need to remember about variables are that experiments have independent and dependent variables, and that correlations have two measured variables. The variables in correlations are sometimes called 'co-variables'.

Operationalising and measuring variables: the independent and dependent variable

Experiments investigate changes or differences in the dependent variable (DV) between two or more levels of the independent variable (IV), which are set up by the experimenter. In an experiment it is important that the IV is clearly defined, or 'operationalised', so that the manipulation of the conditions provides a valid representation of the intended differences. For example, in a study with an IV of age, where there are 'young' and 'old' groups, it is important to know how old the groups are. It is also essential that the DV is operationalised, so that it can be effectively measured. In a study comparing recall of old and young witnesses, we might operationalise 'young' as under 20, and 'old' as over 70 years of age. We could operationalise our measure of the DV by counting the number of things they remember correctly or the number of errors they make.

Measuring variables: the levels of measurement

Experiments and correlational analyses produce quantitative data, i.e. they generate one or more 'scores' or numerical values for each participant. Observations and self-reports may also produce quantitative data. There are different types of quantitative data, which differ in their relative strengths and weaknesses and in the way in which they are analysed (see pages 282–3).

Quantitative data can be recorded in many different ways. Although it is usually numerical, sometimes this is not obvious. For example, when a researcher uses Likert scales (see page 243) the results are points on a scale, usually from 'strongly agree' to 'strongly disagree'. However, these can be allocated numbers so that the scores can be counted up, making the data quantitative. There are three different types of numerical data, referred to as different **levels of measurement**. These are:

- nominal
- ordinal
- interval

QUESTION SPOTLIGHT!

Look back at the situations described in the Question Spotlight on page 265.

Identify the IV and DV in each study.

Operationalise each of these variables.

 KEY IDEAS

Levels of measurement – the types of quantitative data obtained (see nominal, ordinal or interval data).

Nominal data – data as totals of named categories such as the number of kittens who respond to visual stimuli of lines, spots or squares, or the number of participants saying 'yes' or 'no'.

Ordinal data – data as points along a scale, such as a rating or Likert scale, such that the points fall in order but there are not necessarily equal gaps between those points.

Interval data – data as points on a scale that has equal gaps between the points, e.g. standardised measures such as IQ tests or scientific scales such as centimetres and beats-per-minute.

Nominal data

Results that are just totals in two or more named categories that are unrelated are called **nominal data**. These include answers to simple questions – for example, saying 'yes' or 'no' – although there can be more than two categories. For example, in a study of childhood aggression, researchers might score physical aggression as hit/kick/bite or verbal aggression as shout/swear/make nasty comments. The important idea is that these scores are not related in a way that would allow them to lie along the same scale. Closed questions in interviews or on questionnaires often generate nominal data. (To help you to remember that *nom*inal data are scores in *nam*ed categories, think of 'nom' meaning 'name'.)

QUESTION SPOTLIGHT!

What level of measurement was used to score the DV in each of the following studies?

1   Baron-Cohen *et al.* (1997) (page 168) measured identification of emotions in 25 photographs of eyes, from a choice of two for each photograph.
2   Maguire *et al.* (2000) (page 148) measured hippocampal volume in taxi drivers.
3   Piliavin *et al.* (1969) (page 24) measured train passengers' response time.
4   Grant *et al.* (1998) (page 51) measured recognition using a 16-question multiple-choice test.

Ordinal data

In **ordinal data**, the results are points from a scale. The results themselves may be numbers, or words that can be allocated numbers because the points relate to one another, allowing them to be put in order, e.g. from smallest to biggest, or from worst to best. There needs to be a clear increase in the value of points along the scale, but the size of each increase does not have to be equal, i.e. the gaps between the points on the scale do not have to be the same. For example, we could ask participants to rate how good they think their memory is, on a scale that reads: 'very poor', 'poor', 'average', 'good', 'very good'. We would know that people who rated themselves as 'very good' were much better than average, but we would not know for sure if they were twice as good as people who said they were 'quite good'. Numerical scales can also produce ordinal data, for example if an eyewitness indicates how certain they are that their recall is accurate on a scale of 1 to 10. Because the participants are only estimating, we cannot be sure that one person's interpretation of the scale is the same as another's, so the absolute value of each point may not be the same. (To help you to remember that *ord*inal data are points in *ord*er along a scale, look at the first three letters.)

Interval data

Like ordinal data, **interval data** are scores on a linear scale – the points increase in value. However, on an interval scale, the divisions between the points are equal. For example, if participants in a memory test have to recall nonsense items, such as FZC, DMP, WBR, HTG, LXV, SQJ, each one is equally memorable as they are all unfamiliar. The same may be true for some word lists, such as ant, cat, dog, hen, fox, pig, as they are all familiar three-letter, one-syllable animal names. These would be interval scales. However, on a word list that included rhinoceros or porcupine it is unlikely that each item would be equally memorable so the gaps between the points on the scale of 'the number of words

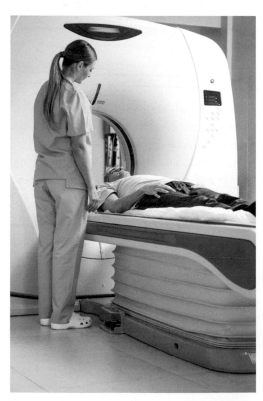

Figure 7.19
The measures of hippocampal volume taken with the MRI scanner in Maguire et al.*'s study produced equal interval data*

recalled' would not all be equal. This would mean that the scale could not be described as an interval level of measurement. In psychology, commonly used equal interval scales include measures of intelligence and personality as well as all scientific scales, such as time, volume or speed. (To help you to remember *interval* scales remember that there are equal *intervals* between the points.)

TABLE 7.15 STRENGTHS AND WEAKNESSES OF DIFFERENT WAYS TO MEASURE VARIABLES

Level of measurement	Strengths	Weaknesses
Nominal	<ul><li>Easy to generate from closed questions, so large amounts of data can be collected quickly, increasing reliability.</li><li>Quick to find the mode to assess central tendency.</li></ul>	<ul><li>Without a linear scale, participants may be unable to express degrees of response.</li><li>Points are not on a linear scale so medians and means cannot be used to assess central tendency.</li><li>Can only use the mode as a measure of spread.</li></ul>
Ordinal	<ul><li>More informative than nominal data, as it indicates relative values on a linear scale rather than just totals.</li><li>Easy to generate from Likert and rating scales.</li><li>Points are on a linear scale so a median can be used as well as a mode to assess central tendency.</li></ul>	<ul><li>As the gaps between the points are only relative, comparisons between participants may be invalid as they may interpret the scale differently.</li><li>Gaps between the points are not equal so a mean cannot be used to assess central tendency.</li></ul>
Interval	<ul><li>More informative than nominal and ordinal data as the points are directly comparable because all the points are of equal value.</li><li>Easy to generate from closed questions.</li><li>Points are on a linear scale, with equal gaps between the points so a mean can be used as well as the mode and median to assess central tendency and variance or standard deviation can be used as measures of spread.</li><li>Scientific measurements are highly reliable and have an absolute zero baseline.</li></ul>	<ul><li>In interval scales that are not scientific measures there is no absolute baseline to the scale so scoring zero may not mean that the participant does not demonstrate that variable at all, merely that the scale does not measure it.</li></ul>

SAMPLES AND SAMPLING

The group of participants in a study are called the **sample**. They are selected from the **target population** and should represent that population. Details about the sample that indicate its diversity, such as age, ethnicity and gender, are important in most investigations. Depending on the study, many other characteristics of the sample may be relevant, such as socio-economic status, education, employment, geographical location, occupation, etc. Sample size also matters. Small samples are less reliable and also less likely to be representative. In addition, different sampling methods produce samples that vary in their representativeness.

Opportunity sampling

Researchers often choose a sample simply by using those people who are around at the time. This is called **opportunity sampling** and is unlikely to fairly represent the population. Think about any studies you have done. You probably conducted them on your class, friends, family, or students in the canteen.

QUESTION SPOTLIGHT!

Look back to your operationalisation of the DV for the situations described in the Question Spotlight on page 267.

Would your proposed measures of the DV in each study have collected nominal, ordinal or interval data?

KEY IDEAS

Sample – the group of people selected from a population to represent that population in a study.

Target population – the group from which a sample is drawn.

STRETCH & CHALLENGE ◎

Rachel decides to use social media to ask for participants for her study. What sampling method is she using?

What disadvantages might there be to this sampling technique?

These people will tend to be very alike – they won't include the variety that exists in the population from which they come. For example, your classmates are probably all in the same year, doing similar subjects, and may be predominantly of one gender. This means that your results may not reflect the scores that people of different ages and interests at your school or college might produce. Despite this potential problem, opportunity sampling is the most common method, even for professional psychologists, many of whom rely on university students for participants. This is acceptable where the results are unlikely to be affected by age or education.

Self-selected sampling

Rather than asking people directly, you might request volunteers. This might be done by putting up a notice, making an announcement or posting a request on the Internet. The people who respond and become participants choose to do so, and are described as a **self-selected sample**. This sampling technique is also unrepresentative of the population. Volunteers are likely to have more free time than average and, apart from being willing, tend to have other characteristics in common, such as being better educated. However, it is a very useful technique when looking for participants who are unusual in some way, for example, in Sperry's study of split-brain patients (page 116).

Snowball sampling

When participants are hard to find, or when researchers need a particular kind of person, one way to obtain more participants is to ask those participants you already have to find further participants for you. Additional members of the sample are therefore in some way connected to the original participants. This has certain advantages, such as allowing access to hard-to-reach groups, but also the disadvantage that the participants may be all very similar – in ways that they do not need to be – reducing the representativeness of the sample and hence the generalisability of the results. Imagine a researcher investigating navigation, who needs a sample of bus drivers and starts with one or two they know. Using snowball sampling, the sample is likely to end up being made up of drivers from one bus station, who perhaps mainly drive on the same route, or in the same town.

Random sampling

Opportunity, self-selected and snowball samples all run the risk of being biased – they will probably contain very similar people and are unlikely to include the spread characteristics in the population. A better way to obtain participants is by **random sampling**, which ensures that each person in the population has an equal chance of being chosen. This means that the sample is much more likely to be representative. This is quite different from the previous types of sample. Imagine you are looking for a sample of students at your college. If you place an advert for volunteers on the library notice board, students who never go to the library cannot be included. If you find people by opportunity at the start of the day, the students who are always late cannot be included. If you start with two sporty students and ask them to find more participants, you are likely to end up with a more-sporty-than-average sample. However, if you take a numbered list of all students and use a random number generator to chose the sample, any individual is equally likely to be chosen. For a small population this can be done by allocating each person a number, putting pieces of paper with each number on in a hat, and drawing out numbers until there are enough for the sample.

Stratified sampling

Another way to obtain a representative sample is by **stratified sampling**. In this method, individuals are taken to represent each major strata, or layer, within the population. The subdivisions can include socio-economic groups, ages, geographical locations and ethnic groups. For example, a study conducted in a school to investigate levels of obedience should ensure that children from each academic year are selected.

In proportionate strata sampling, individuals from the different strata are selected according to the incidence of that subgroup within the population. For example, in a town with a lot of retired residents, the sample should be skewed in favour of elderly participants in the same way as the parent population. In disproportionate strata sampling, the relative incidence of subgroups is not reflected in the sample. This may be deliberate in order to ensure that there is some representation for particularly 'rare' groups, or unequal weighting may be given to subgroups that are known to be more variable.

Figure 7.20
How varied would a snowball sample of bus drivers be?

TABLE 7.16 STRENGTHS AND WEAKNESSES OF SAMPLING TECHNIQUES

Technique	Strengths	Weaknesses
Opportunity sample – participants are chosen because they are available, e.g. university students selected because they are around at the time.	Quicker and easier than other methods as the participants are readily available.	Non-representative as the kinds of people available are likely to be limited, and therefore similar, making the sample biased.
Self-selected sample – participants are invited to participate e.g. through advertisements via email or notices. Those who reply become the sample.	Relatively easy because the participants come to you and are committed, e.g. likely to turn up for repeat testing.	Non-representative as the kinds of people who respond to requests are likely to be similar, e.g. have free time.
Snowball sample – from a very small number of participants, more are contacted through the initial group.	Relatively easy because you have to find only the first few. A convenient way to find a sample of a particular kind of participant.	Non-representative as they are likely to be similar in ways other than any common characteristics needed for the study.
Random sample – all members of the population (i.e. possible participants) are allocated numbers, and a fixed amount of these are selected in a unbiased way, e.g. by taking numbers from a hat.	Should be representative as all types of people in the population are equally likely to be chosen.	Hard to ensure everyone is equally likely to be chosen, e.g. due to lack of information or access, and the sample may be biased, e.g. if only girls happen to be selected, especially if the sample is small.
Stratified sample – all types of members of the population (i.e. possible subgroups) are represented by deliberately selecting participants from all strata, often in proportion to their existence in the population.	Should be representative as all types of people in the population are represented.	Difficult, as all the subgroups in the population must be known and accessible.

STRETCH & CHALLENGE

Which sampling method would have been used in Grant *et al.* if the original eight people who each found five friends had been participants themselves rather than experimenters?

QUESTION SPOTLIGHT!

Which sampling method was used in each of the following studies?

1 Chaney *et al.* (2004) (page 88) selected children from those with prescriptions for asthma, which suggests that each child with such a prescription had an equal chance of being chosen.

2 Grant *et al.* (1998) (page 51) – the eight experimenters (not the participants) each found five friends.

A

3 Maguire *et al.* (2000) (page 148) used a group of taxi drivers who volunteered for the study.

4 Piliavin *et al.* (1969) (page 24) observed subway train passengers who happened to be in the carriage.

THE PROCEDURE: DESIGNING PSYCHOLOGICAL INVESTIGATIONS

When designing the procedure of a study, researchers have to consider the relative importance of ethics (see Section 7G) and scientific rigour. In the previous sections we discussed four different research methods:

- experiments (pages 220–30)
- observational studies (pages 231–40)
- self reports (pages 241–52)
- correlational analyses (pages 253–7)

In this section we will remind you about these and explore how an appropriate technique is selected and applied to a research problem. The most commonly used method is the experiment. This is a study in which an independent variable (IV) is manipulated and consequent changes in a dependent variable (DV) are measured in order to establish a cause-and-effect relationship. Different experimental designs may be used in which participants are allocated to levels of the IV in different ways. These include:

- independent measures design – different groups of participants are used for each level of the IV.
- repeated measures design – each participant performs in every level of the IV.
- matched participants design – participants are arranged into pairs, each pair is similar in ways that are important to the study and the members of each pair perform in the two different levels of the IV.

When any of the research methods listed above and in Table 7.17 (see page 274) are employed, a number of different design decisions need to be considered.

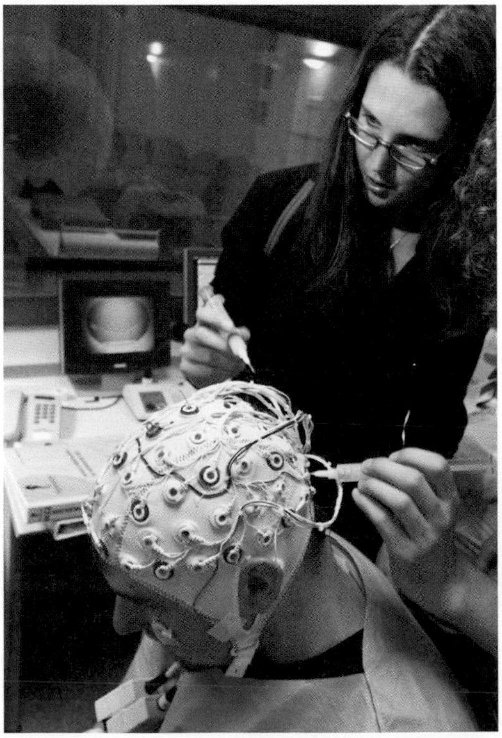

Design decisions in experiments
Lab, field or quasi-experiment?
The first decision is whether the IV can be manipulated at all. If the IV will change during the experiment, but this is not under the control of the researcher, then it will be a quasi-experiment. This method tends to be used when it is unethical or impractical to manipulate the IV. The following is an example of a quasi-experiment. A researcher believes that high stress levels will lead to a greater incidence of depression. It would clearly be unethical to deliberately

Figure 7.21
Sometimes only a laboratory experiment is possible

increase stress with the intention of inducing depression. However, the incidence of depression in students could be measured immediately before their exams and some time afterwards.

In true experiments the researcher actively allocates participants to conditions or manipulates the situation to create different conditions. These conditions may be set up either in a contrived environment (a laboratory experiment), or in the participants' normal surroundings for the activity being tested (a field experiment). A laboratory environment is used when a high level of control over the situation, accurate measurement of the DV, and the potential to use specific apparatus is required. For example:

- presenting stimuli at a fixed distance or for a specific length of time can only practically be achieved in laboratory conditions
- timing participants' reactions requires precision that can only be achieved in the laboratory
- using a brain scanner requires participants to come to a laboratory.

A laboratory experiment is therefore chosen when practicality or the need for experimental rigour exceeds the importance of reducing demand characteristics. When, however, it is more important that the participant is responding without the influence of an artificial setting, or may even be unaware that they are participating in an experiment at all, a field experiment would be chosen if this were possible.

If a researcher conducts a laboratory experiment they have the advantage of rigorous control over the situation and their participants. They can control precisely the nature and presentation of stimuli, sources of distraction, and the order of conditions (see counterbalancing below). However, they also have some hurdles. Demand characteristics can be a risk as they indicate to the participants the aims of the study which, in turn, affect the participants' behaviour. Clearly this should be avoided. A researcher can minimise the effects of demand characteristics by disguising the purpose of the experiment, for example by using 'filler' questions between the critical ones in a questionnaire. Such distractions make it harder for the participants to correctly guess the experimental aims. Alternatively, participants can be deliberately deceived about the aims. This is likely to be effective but also raises ethical issues (see page 309).

A **pilot study** is often conducted prior to an experiment. The purpose of this is to investigate whether there are any problems with the procedure. It enables the experimenter to establish that their operational definition of the IV does produce two different conditions, and that they can measure the DV over a range of scores. Importantly, it also allows them to identify and introduce controls for any extraneous variables that could confound the results.

Another risk in laboratory studies is that of **researcher bias**, for example the distortions that arise because the experimenter responds differently to participants in the different levels of the IV because of their expectations. This response may be unconscious but can subtly alter participant responses, creating or hiding patterns in the results. Imagine a researcher looking for differences between participants with and without an eating disorder, who acts in a kinder way to the participants with mental health problems. This might

KEY IDEAS

Pilot study – a small-scale trial run of a method to identify problems and resolve them.

Researcher bias – an unconscious tendency of the researcher to act in ways that alter the results, often in the expected direction.

QUESTION SPOTLIGHT!

Which type of experiment would you choose to use in each of the following studies and why?

1 Does watching a physically violent TV programme lead to immediate increases in verbally aggressive behaviour?
2 Are five-year-old children more likely to talk about their fantasies to their mum or their dad?
3 Are students more obedient than factory workers?
4 Do marathon runners who exercise listening to music perform better in competitions if they are listening to music?

TABLE 7.17 WHEN ARE DIFFERENT RESEARCH METHODS USED?

Research method	Description of the method	When is the method used?
Laboratory experiment	A true experiment, conducted in an artificial environment, in which the experimenter manipulates an IV and measures the consequent changes in a DV while carefully controlling extraneous variables. Participants are allocated to conditions by the experimenter.	When looking for differences, comparisons or cause-and-effect relationships. It must be possible to actively change the levels of the IV, i.e. to allocate participants to conditions, and to record the DV accurately. It is important that the behaviour is likely to be relatively unaffected by a contrived environment.
Field experiment	A true experiment in which the researcher manipulates an IV and measures a DV in the natural setting of the participants. Participants are allocated to conditions by the experimenter.	When looking for differences, comparisons or cause-and-effect relationships. It must be possible to actively change the levels of the IV and record the DV accurately. It is preferable when it is likely that behaviour could be affected by a contrived environment, or would be impossible to replicate in the laboratory.
Quasi-experiment	A study in which an experimenter makes use of an existing change or difference in situations to provide levels of an IV and then measures the DV in each condition. Participants cannot be allocated to conditions so it is not a true experiment.	When looking for differences or comparisons between variables that cannot be artificially controlled or manipulated.
Correlational analysis	A technique used to investigate a link between two measured variables.	When looking for relationships between variables. Can be used when it is unethical or impractical to artificially control or manipulate variables. There must be two variables that can be measured on ordinal or interval scales.
Observation	A technique in which the researcher watches and records behaviours in a structured or unstructured way. The observation may be overt or covert, the observer may be participant or non-participant, and the situation may be controlled or naturalistic.	When seeking to record specific, observable behaviours (rather than inferred states). This may also include variables that cannot be measured by asking questions, or when recording from infants or animals.
Questionnaire	A self-report method used to obtain data by asking participants to provide information about themselves using written questions.	When aiming to collect data about opinions or attitudes from a large sample and when the questions to be asked are largely straightforward and the same for every participant. Also if face-to-face contact might reduce the response rate or honesty, or if participants are geographically spread out.
Interview	A self-report method used to obtain data by asking participants to provide information about themselves by replying verbally to questions asked by an interviewer.	When aiming to collect data from individuals using questions that may require explanation, or when the questions may need to vary between participants.

make them feel more confident or positive about completing the experimental task so they try harder or persist for longer. Any differences in the results could be caused by researcher bias so would be erroneous.

Which experimental design?

In any true experiment, a decision has to be made about the experimental design. There are good reasons for choosing each design. By having different participants in each level of the IV, an independent measures design, the researcher avoids order effects. In addition, the participants have less opportunity to become aware of the aims so will be less likely to respond to demand characteristics than in a repeated measures design. It is also possible for all conditions to be tested simultaneously. This is sometimes an advantage. Imagine a field experiment comparing attention to hearing the word 'help', in younger and older people, which uses the social context of a staged distraction. As there may be many variables that could affect attention, it might be better to have all the participants, from both levels of the IV, together.

Sometimes a repeated measures design is preferable as it overcomes problems with individual differences. If there are different participants in each level of the IV, any differences found between these conditions could be due to the people rather than the variable being manipulated. Returning to the example of older and younger people, any differences found in identifying the target word in a field experiment might be the result of poorer hearing in the older people rather than differences in attention.

In a repeated measures design any differences between performance in each level of the IV should be due to the experimenter's manipulation. However, it is also possible that differences may arise because an individual experiences the same (or similar) tasks more than once, i.e. order effects. These cannot be avoided but can be cancelled out using counterbalancing (or lessened by randomisation of the order of conditions for different participants).

Ideally, researchers would like to avoid the problems of both individual differences and order effects. This is, to an extent, possible with a matched participants design. To set up a study using matched participants the researcher decides on the important ways in which participants could differ. Consider a study about eating disorders that is investigating the influence of a big meal on body image. What design would be best? In repeated measures the aim would be obvious, so demand characteristics would be a problem. Using an independent measures design would be possible, but variables other than the meal size – such as age, gender, educational level, or socio-economic group – could affect vulnerability to eating disorders. In a matched participants design, participants are identified who share important characteristics so that one of each similar pair can be placed into each level of the IV. So, in this case, if two 25-year-old male students from the same socio-economic group were found, one would be allocated to each group. As you can imagine, this procedure is time-consuming and is not without risk – it relies on the assumption that the criteria being used for matching are those that are most important – and this may not be the case. Nevertheless, once established, the two matched groups have the advantages of both independent measures and repeated measures designs.

Design decisions in observations

Observations are chosen when records are needed of actual behaviours rather than, say, what people think they would do, which they would report in a questionnaire. Having access to physical responses – rather than verbal ones, scores on tests, or performance on experimental tasks – means that researchers can investigate participants who cannot follow instructions or give spoken responses, for example, animals, very young children, or non-verbal adults.

QUESTION SPOTLIGHT!

1 What factors might affect the attention to the surprising but non-frightening event in Figure 7.22?

Figure 7.22

2 Rachel wants to compare attention to the word 'help' in younger and older participants. Why might it be better to conduct a laboratory experiment than a field experiment?

DO IT YOURSELF 🔍

Look back at the experimental ideas in the Question Spotlights on page 265.

Design and conduct an experiment to test one of these. Your answer should state a hypothesis, operationally define the IV and the DV, identify at least two controls, describe the procedure and materials, and explain how you would obtain your sample. Justify your decisions, such as the choice of experimental method (lab, field or quasi), the choice of design, and why the controls you have suggested are important.

ACTIVITY ✸

Staff in a primary school want to investigate whether the children copy the bad habits they see in each other.

Design an observation to test this. Your answer should state a hypothesis, the procedure, and how you obtain your sample. Justify your decisions, such as the choice of behavioural categories and whether the observation will be participant.

Figure 7.23
In a participant observation, the observer can become part of the situation being observed

One ethical concern in designing an observation is the need to protect people's privacy. Participants should either give their consent to be observed, or observations should take place only in situations where the individuals would reasonably expect to be watched by others.

A researcher has to decide whether to observe in a naturalistic or contrived situation. If the behaviour is very infrequent and its appearance is dependent on a certain set of circumstances, a contrived situation will employ deliberate manipulation of the setting to ensure that the behaviours are seen. This would be preferred in circumstances such as recording the responses of children to real-life moral dilemmas, or scoring changes in aggressive behaviour following prosocial or antisocial television programmes.

Another question is whether to conduct an unstructured or a structured observation. When the range of possible behaviours of interest is already known, or is likely to be limited and easily determined in a pilot study, a structured observation would be conducted. However, if the situation is relatively unexplored, or if the range of potential behaviours that might be of interest is huge, an unstructured observation would allow the researchers to consider and record any interesting behaviour that arises. This might be preferred in a situation such as when trying to find out how patients respond to an entirely new drug delivery method, for example if a drug were being tested that was sniffed rather than swallowed or inhaled orally.

Participant or non-participant, covert or overt?

If the researcher knows that their participants will be affected by being observed, they may conduct a covert observation. This is where the participants are unaware that they are being observed and is useful if their expectations or beliefs would affect their behaviour. For example, if we want to investigate the behaviour of a child faced with the dilemma of leaving alone something they really want, we would be more likely to obtain representative information by observing them covertly than if they were aware of our role.

Covert observations clearly raise both ethical and practical issues. In general, a covert observer is physically hidden, or far away. However, awareness of the observer can also be avoided if the observer is 'disguised' within the observed group, i.e. by carrying out a participant observation. In the situation of a child in a classroom facing a dilemma about stroking a rabbit it has been told not to touch, the observer could perhaps appear to be a cleaner. This is advantageous for the researcher as they can more easily conduct a controlled observation, for example by modelling the behaviour of stroking the rabbit to observe the effect on the participant. Participants can alternatively be made aware that they are going to be observed. This is an overt observation and raises fewer ethical issues. Participants can be asked for their informed consent, so can be observed in a greater range of environments.

A non-participant design helps the observer to concentrate on the behaviours of interest, as they do not have to pay attention to maintaining their role in the social situation. It is also easier for the non-participant observer to remain objective, so, when subjectivity is a potential risk, this is preferable. In contrast, participant observation may be more useful for exactly the opposite reason – by becoming involved in the social situation the observer may gain greater insight into the participants' feelings or motives than a non-participant observer could.

Preparing to collect data

In an observation, design decisions also have to be made about how data will be collected. These include:

- the sampling strategy
- behavioural categories
- coding frames.

In event sampling, the observer uses a checklist and tallies each occurrence of a behaviour. Alternatively, records may be taken at fixed time intervals, such as every 10 seconds – this is called time sampling. In either case, each behaviour or 'behavioural category' should be operationally defined. This ensures that the observer is consistent in their recording of each type of event and that, if there is more than one observer, their records are also consistent (see inter-observer reliability, page 238). It is important at the design stage that each behavioural category is independent and observable – that is, that they can be readily separated from the continuous stream of events and are reliably identifiable (they must be directly observable and not inferred). For example, recording a child left with a marshmallow 'being tempted' would not be a valid category as 'temptation' itself cannot be seen, whereas an observable product of that temptation, such as sniffing it, would be a valid category.

If appropriate, a coding frame should also be developed once the behavioural categories have been decided (see page 233). Memorable codes should be assigned to each behavioural category, so that these can be used to simplify data recording in time or event sampling.

When time sampling is going to be used, the researcher has to make decisions about:

- the time sampling technique
- the length of the time intervals.

The choice of time-sampling technique (instantaneous scan, one-zero or predominant activity) will be determined in part by the type of information required (e.g. about duration versus frequency of behaviours) and in part by the nature of the behaviours themselves. When some very frequent and some infrequent behaviours are of interest, instantaneous scan sampling would not be used. Conversely, it would be ideal when there are many behaviours of similar duration. This can be assessed in a pilot study. The ideal length of the time intervals themselves can also be determined in a pilot study. They should be long enough to gather data over a range of behaviours, but short enough to detect changes in patterns of behaviour.

Design decisions in self-report studies

Self-report studies are those in which the participant reports their beliefs, thoughts or feelings to the researcher. They include questionnaires and interviews. In both techniques the researcher presents the participant with questions.

Interview or questionnaire?

The first decision to be made here is whether to collect data face-to-face (by interview) or in writing (using a questionnaire). If the nature of the investigation is socially sensitive a questionnaire may be preferable. Respondents are less

DO IT YOURSELF 🔍

Felicity is planning the timetable in a college and thinks each subject should have some morning and some afternoon lessons. This is because she believes that students don't concentrate as well in the afternoon as they do in the morning.

Design and conduct an observation to test this. Your answer should define the behavioural categories, describe the procedure, including whether the observers will be overt or covert and participant or non-participant and why, and justify your choice of behavioural categories and sampling strategy (time or event sampling).

Figure 7.24
If people are likely to clam up under the scrutiny of an interviewer, a questionnaire is a better choice

ACTIVITY ✳

Derek is a careers officer and is deciding what career guidance to offer students on different courses. He suspects that science students have a greater number of clear career goals than arts students.

Design a self-report to test this. Your answer should state the hypothesis, whether you are planning a questionnaire or interview, the procedure, and how you will obtain your sample. Justify your decisions, such as the choice of questions and question types.

likely to be affected by social desirability, and lie or omit answers, if they do not feel judged because they are not face-to-face with a researcher. For example, interviewees may under-report childhood abuse because they are embarrassed. Conversely, spending time building up a trusting relationship may help an interviewer to elicit more information.

Structured, semi-structured or unstructured?

Although different questions can be given to different individuals in a questionnaire, in general everyone's questions are identical. This is an example of a structured design because the structure remains the same for every participant. In a semi-structured design, the same questions are used for each respondent, but additional questions can be used, so there is some tailoring of the questions to the individual on the basis of the answers given. Interviews can alternatively be unstructured – these are entirely variable, so in response to answers a participant gives, the interviewer can present different questions. This adaptable technique is more likely to gain useful, detailed information when this is difficult to obtain. For example, with a reticent participant with mental-health problems, more is likely to be learned using a flexible approach than by sticking rigidly to a set of predetermined questions.

Open or closed questions?

A researcher may choose to use closed questions as the results are easy to analyse because they generate simple numbers. For example, we could ask 'do you believe that you would help a stranger in distress in the street?' using a yes/no format. Alternatively, we could ask: 'How many of the following strangers have you ever helped: an elderly person, a child, a person with a pushchair, an ill person?' This would allow us to say that x% of participants reported particular altruistic behaviours. Another kind of closed question is the Likert-style question. This is used to elicit attitudes. When using Likert scales some of the statements must be 'reversed' so that the 'positive' or socially acceptable response is not always at the same side of the page.

Closed questions, including Likert and rating scales, and semantic differentials all produce results that are numerical or 'quantitative' (see page 282). If, however, the nature of the research requires detailed, in-depth answers, then open questions are more appropriate as they can elicit an extended answer. An open question posed to an 11-year-old – such as 'how do you feel when you tell a lie?' – will supply more detailed information than ticking boxes about guilt or fear. Unlike the numbers produced by closed questions, the results generated by open questions are qualitative, that is, they are detailed and descriptive. These data are more difficult to analyse, and this would be a consideration for researchers who wanted to collect a wide range of information from a large sample of participants.

Both qualitative and quantitative data can be collected using either questionnaires or interviews. In practice, researchers would generally choose questionnaires to gather specific, quantitative information, and interviews to gather more in-depth, qualitative data.

Design decisions in correlational analyses

Remember that a correlational study looks for relationships between two variables. Both variables must exist over a range and it must be possible to measure them numerically. This means that the participants' scores cannot just be in named categories, they must be on an ordinal or interval scale, i.e. one that is numerical, or can be converted to numbers. The two scales can, however, be different. The choice of scales will depend on the variables being tested. Ideally, interval scales would be used as the data from these allows more detailed analyses to be conducted on the results (such as parametric statistics, see page 298). However, many psychological variables cannot be measured in this way. For example, in a study of childhood aggression, the amount of time a child was being aggressive for could be measured in hours and minutes (an equal interval scale), but any detail of how aggressive they were being (how hard they were hitting or the nastiness of the words they were saying) would only provide ordinal scores, as each 'hit' isn't necessarily the same. Nevertheless, this is an ordinal scale, so the two could be used together in a correlation.

DO IT YOURSELF

Charlotte believes that tidiness of her friends' notes and files relates to their test results.

Design and conduct a correlation to test this. Your answer should state a hypothesis, operationally define the two variables, describe the procedure, and explain how you would obtain your sample. Justify your decisions, such as the choice of variables and whether you are predicting a positive or negative correlation.

A researcher is likely to choose to conduct a correlational study when the variables they are investigating cannot be manipulated for practical or ethical reasons. This would apply to variables such as the length of time a person has had a mental illness, or its severity. A correlational design is also used to measure inter-rater reliability, i.e. to see whether two researchers are consistent in their rating of responses from participants in a self-report or observational study. In addition, correlations are used to assess the reliability of tools such as questionnaires. If participants are assessed on the same variable twice, the two sets of scores should correlate.

DEVELOPING A PLAN

When designing a study, a researcher needs to work through several important steps to plan effectively. They should:
- decide on their aim and, if appropriate, develop hypotheses to test
- select the most appropriate research method
- identify and operationalise the variables
- make design decisions (including considering which controls are necessary)
- ensure the design is ethically sound
- devise appropriate materials or apparatus
- use a pilot study to resolve any practical issues
- identify the target population
- decide which sampling method to use and the sample size they will need.

QUESTION SPOTLIGHT!

Suggest how the variables in the following correlations might be measured.
1 TV-viewing and rule-breaking at school.
2 Intelligence and healthiness of diet.

Figure 7.25
Is there a link between healthy eating and intelligence?

3 Dexterity and texting.
4 Popularity and gossiping.

QUESTION SPOTLIGHT!

Look back to your answers to the Question Spotlights on page 265 and 266.
1 Using your operational definitions, describe what apparatus or materials would be needed to create the levels of the IV and measure the changes in the DV in each case.
2 Suggest at least two controls for each study and explain why they are necessary.

Finally, the researcher should decide how the results will be analysed, choosing which descriptive and inferential statistics they will use once the data have been collected (see pages 282–312).

Research method	Check:
Experiment	<ul><li>the participants can follow the standardised instructions.</li><li>that the apparatus and materials are appropriate.</li><li>that the DV covers the full range of scores.</li><li>for any possible extraneous variables that need to be controlled.</li><li>whether any aspects of the procedure will lead to demand characteristics.</li><li>whether there are any order effects in a repeated measures design.</li></ul>
Observation	<ul><li>that observers agree on operational definitions of behavioural categories.</li><li>inter-observer reliability – do they need practice?</li><li>that the behavioural categories include all the important behaviours and do not overlap.</li><li>that the coding frame is effective.</li><li>whether the participants are affected by the observers – should they be covert?</li></ul>
Self-report	<ul><li>that the participants understand the questions and are prepared to answer them.</li><li>that closed questions offer suitable options.</li><li>whether open questions are also needed to elicit unpredictable responses.</li><li>that response biases are limited, e.g. through the use of filler questions and reversal of positive and negative 'ends' of Likert scales, rating scales and semantic differentials.</li><li>whether the reporting method is appropriate, e.g. if a face-to-face interview is too intimidating should it be changed to a questionnaire?</li></ul>
Correlation	<ul><li>that the participants can follow the standardised instructions.</li><li>that the apparatus and materials are appropriate.</li><li>that the measures of the two variables cover the full range of scores.</li></ul>

TABLE 7.18 USING A PILOT STUDY TO CHECK THE METHOD: WHAT TO LOOK FOR

IMPROVING INVESTIGATIONS

Once a study has been designed, and especially when a pilot study has been conducted, the procedure can often be refined to improve reliability and/or validity.

In order to be reliable, a measure must be consistent. Imagine trying to work out the dimensions of a box with a ruler that could only measure 'short' and 'long', or one that was made of elastic. These would be nominal and ordinal measures respectively. Because the elastic ruler might stretch by different amounts each time you used it, your judgments would lack consistency (a reliability problem). The short/long ruler wouldn't tell you what you wanted to know – i.e. how big the box was (a problem of validity).

One way to raise reliability and validity is to change the way in which variables are measured. If possible, 'better' levels of measurement can be used. For example, in a study investigating visual development in kittens, this might be assessed by observing whether the kitten's head would follow a hopping rabbit or not (a nominal measure). Alternatively, the researchers could use a controlled laboratory situation to record whether the movement of the kitten's head when tracking a rolling ball head looked smooth or jumpy (an ordinal scale, 0–5), or measure the fastest speed of rolling ball they could successfully track visually (an equal interval scale). These data would be more informative than simply whether the kitten could track a moving object or not. However, such changes are only improvements if they are genuinely more useful. It may be, for example, that factors other than visual competence affect how well kittens respond, such as how motivated they are – is the object important enough? A kitten might be motivated to track a rabbit much more effectively than a ball. So, although as a measure it would be more reliable, it might not necessarily be more valid. Reliability and validity can also be improved by refining the way in which variables are defined. For example, in an experiment recording aggressive behaviour (e.g. Bandura *et al.*, page 82), fighting might include 'pushing, pulling or hitting another individual'. However, such behaviours might also be seen in play. A good operational definition would distinguish between these, perhaps by adding 'in the absence of smiling or laughter'. This would increase the consistency of observations as some researchers might have been including play and others not, thus raising reliability. It would also mean that the records reflected purely aggressive behaviours rather than a mixture of aggression and play, so would also improve validity.

In experiments, several other procedures can improve validity. These include imposing more controls, using standardised instructions, blind and double-blind procedures, random allocation in independent measures designs, and counterbalancing in repeated measures designs (or, alternatively, using a matched participants design). In any study, if the sample is unrepresentative, an improvement in sampling method to obtain a larger and/or wider sample will make the findings more representative. In general, improvements to mundane realism and ecological validity work against these changes to improve other aspects of the study, so a balance must be achieved between scientific rigour and validity in terms of real life.

QUESTION SPOTLIGHT!

For each of the proposed improvements below, decide whether they would improve reliability, validity, or both, and explain why.

1   Najia is recording social and emotional behaviour in people with autism. She asks them if they ever cry when they hurt themselves. Rachel suggests that sometimes crying in this situation is more biological than emotional and suggests she adds a question about whether they cry when they see a sad film.

2   Sonny is testing children's understanding of morals by asking them whether they feel remorseful when they are unkind to their friends. He decides they don't understand the question, so instead shows them a picture story about a boy who hits his friend on the head with the ball, either accidentally or deliberately. He asks them which boy is naughtier.

3   Charlotte is investigating auditory attention to significant information so is testing how well people identify their own name versus numbers in the rejected message. She decides to have extra conditions that include the person's own home town or irrelevant place names.

STRETCH & CHALLENGE

There is at least one problem with each of the proposed changes in the Question Spotlight above.

Identify two of these problems and explain whether they are issues of reliability, or of validity

G – DEALING WITH DATA: DESCRIPTIVE AND INFERENTIAL STATISTICS

INTRODUCTION

The purpose of research is to test hypotheses. In order to do this, investigations generate data and this must be analysed to decide whether the findings support the alternative hypothesis. This section looks at some ways to present and analyse data.

QUANTITATIVE AND QUALITATIVE DATA

Quantitative data, mainly associated with experiments, correlations, category totals in observations and closed questions in self reports, are numerical. The strengths of quantitative data tend to come from having high **objectivity** and reliability. Qualitative data, being in-depth and descriptive, are typically more **subjective**, but may often be more representative and therefore higher in validity. (See page 261 for the distinction between subjectivity and objectivity, and page 241 for more about the distinction between qualitative and quantitative data.)

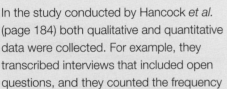

QUESTION SPOTLIGHT!

In the study conducted by Hancock *et al.* (page 184) both qualitative and quantitative data were collected. For example, they transcribed interviews that included open questions, and they counted the frequency of references to various needs, such as food, drink, money and religion.

Identify which of these data are qualitative and which are quantitative.

TABLE 7.19 STRENGTHS AND WEAKNESSES OF QUALITATIVE AND QUANTITATIVE DATA

Data type	Strengths	Weaknesses
Quantitative	• Tends to be collected using objective measures. • Data collection tends to be highly reliable. • Data can be analysed using inferential statistics.	• Method of measurement may limit participants' responses, making the data less valid, e.g. if appropriate response options are not available.
Qualitative	• Data collection may be highly valid as it is likely to be possible for participants to express themselves exactly as they want to. • It is less likely that key or rare observations will be 'lost' through the process of averaging or simplifying data.	• Tends to be collected using relatively subjective measures. • Data collection may be invalid as recording or interpretation of responses may be biased by the researcher's opinions or feelings. • Data are individual so it may be difficult to make generalisations from the findings.

QUESTION SPOTLIGHT!

In a study about obedience in school, a researcher found that only half of the first 20 participants tested obeyed an order. Of the next 20, almost all obeyed. *Estimate the modal response, to obey or not, for the whole sample of 60.*

Converting qualitative data to quantitative data

When qualitative data are collected, it is sometimes useful to convert them into quantitative data. This means that patterns in the data can be illustrated using graphs, comparisons can be made more easily, and statistical analyses can be conducted. Qualitative data can come from interviews (transcripts of what a participant has said – such as on page 249), from open questions in questionnaires, from case studies, and from descriptions from observations. One way to convert these into quantitative data is to identify simple categories into which the descriptive responses fall, and the wider key themes that these represent. The number of examples of items from each category are then counted, as well as the total numbers of items identified in each theme. For example, in an article commenting on altruism in modern and earlier times, two obvious themes might be increased altruism and decreased altruism. Within these categories different kinds of helping behaviour might be included, such as giving others food or money, looking after elderly relatives or neighbours, or donating kidneys. The number of instances of each kind of helpful behaviour – and possibly examples of selfish behaviour – might be counted up. This process is the essence of a research method called content analysis, which aims to extract the meaning behind written (or sometimes visual) material. It can, for example, be used to identify bias in the way newspaper articles, websites or television programmes are presented.

PRIMARY AND SECONDARY DATA

There are many ways to conduct research and there are many different ways to classify different types of research. One way is to distinguish between the collection of primary and secondary data. Researchers who are working with participants – for example, through experiments, correlations, observations, case studies or self-report methods – are collecting **primary data**, that is, their results are coming straight from the source (the people in their studies). In other cases, researchers may be using data originally obtained by other people, perhaps for different reasons, to re-analyse, combine or compare results. As they have not collected the results themselves – or it was not collected for the explicit reasons of their research – this is referred to as **secondary data**. Most commonly, this is where researchers take data obtained by other psychologists that is relevant to their research, and they re-analyse it, either in a different way, for a different purpose, or in combination with results from other, similar, studies. When the data from several studies (sometimes hundreds) are combined to produce a larger sample and re-analysed, this is called a *meta-analysis*.

ESTIMATION

It is often useful to make estimations from the results of studies. It can help to decide, for example, what graphs to draw or statistics to do. Estimations are more than a 'guess', they are based on some data or information, but they are short cuts that do not involve calculations. For example, in a study about visual adaptation, using adults looking in a mirror while drawing, the first 10 participants all performed well, scoring between 35 and 45 out of 50. The next two participants scored 11 and 9. An estimate of the mean score for the whole sample of 50 participants would suggest a figure of about 30, i.e. closer to 50 than to 0, because most of the scores were large.

WEB WATCH @

To practise extracting quantitative data from qualitative material, use these two articles as secondary sources. Decide on two general themes and count up the number of statements in each article that illustrate each theme. Plot these data on two pie charts or a single bar chart (you may want to use or paired or stacked bar chart).

http://www.dailymail.co.uk/sciencetech/article-2588864/Violent-video-games-makes-children-grow-aggressive-adults-study-claims.html

http://www.dailymail.co.uk/sciencetech/article-2598914/Violent-video-games-DONT-make-players-aggressive-lack-practice-difficult-levels-do.html

 **KEY IDEAS**

Primary data – the results of a first-hand investigation; collecting qualitative or quantitative information directly from a sample.

Secondary data – information that is obtained about the results of an investigation that has already been conducted by another researcher, possibly for a different purpose. This can then be re-used in a new analysis.

Figure 7.26
How well can adult humans adapt to visual changes?

KEY IDEAS

Frequency table (tally chart) – a grid showing the possible categories of results in which a tick or tally is made each time the item is scored. These can be added together to give a total in each category.

DO IT YOURSELF

Try doing a quick survey with your class or friends by devising questions about keeping to homework deadlines or doing extra reading. Write a hypothesis to consider differences between boys and girls, or between students taking sciences or humanities subjects. Draw a tally chart and ask at least 10 people your questions, then see if you can answer the questions above from your raw data table.

TABULATING DATA

Psychological investigations that collect quantitative data tend to generate quite a lot of results – one or more scores from each participant. In order to summarise these - to make any patterns easy to see – researchers use various tables and graphs. In this section we will consider two uses of tables: in data collection and to illustrate the findings of studies.

Raw data tables

Tables used to collect data are often **frequency tables** or **tally charts**. These have a number of rows with headings for scoring, which are filled in with a tally mark each time the item being scored occurs. This type of table is useful for checklists in observations and for counting responses to closed questions in questionnaires. An example of a tally chart can be seen in Box 7.2 on page 237. It is conventional to score each tally as a vertical line, making every fifth one into a 'five-bar gate'. This makes counting the totals easier and more reliable.

Raw data from other sources, such as scores for each participant from a test or task in an experiment, is also tabulated. Columns for each level of the IV are completed with the scores for each participant. In such cases, the participants' names should not be recorded, to preserve their confidentiality (see page 310). In this way, the scores are conveniently arranged for future calculations.

For any table, it is important to give the table itself an informative title and to label each row and column with a heading. If the figures in the table are measured in specific units (such as seconds) or as a percentage, this should be written just once, in the heading, rather than alongside each score.

Once the results of a study have been collected, it is often useful to be able to make estimations from the data. For example: Which responses were the most and the least common? Were the scores in the two levels of the IV different? Which level of the IV had the highest scores? Is the difference in the direction predicted by the hypothesis or not? Roughly how much higher were they than the other condition(s)?

Summary tables

So that other people can clearly see the outcome of a study, a summary of the findings is usually presented in a table. Tables should always have an informative title and clear headings for each row and column, which include units of measurement if appropriate. Results such as totals or frequencies, percentages, means, medians and modes can all be tabulated. For example, a researcher might measure self-reported navigational ability in bus drivers and non-bus drivers. The median and range of self-report scores could be presented as in Table 7.20.

TABLE 7.20 NAVIGATIONAL ABILITY IN BUS DRIVERS AND NON-BUS DRIVERS		
Navigational ability	**Bus drivers**	**Non-bus drivers**
Median	21	22
Range	20	39

KEY IDEAS

Using different numerical forms

The results of experiments are often whole numbers, decimals or minutes and seconds. However, the data you encounter in published research may be presented in many different ways, such as:

Fractions: A way of representing portions of whole numbers such that the number on the top (the numerator) is divided by the number on the bottom (the denominator). For example, $\frac{1}{2}$ means '1 divided by 2', which makes 0.5. Similarly, $\frac{2}{4}$ means '2 divided by 4', which also makes 0.5.

Decimal form: This is a different way of representing portions of whole numbers, using only $\frac{1}{10^{th}}$, $\frac{1}{100^{th}}$ etc. Each digit past the decimal point (full stop in a number) is a tenth of the size of the one before. So, 0.5 equals five tenths, 0.6 equals 6 tenths, 0.05 equals 5 hundredths, 0.06 equals 6 hundredths, etc.

Standard form: This is a way of representing very small or very large numbers by showing how many 'times tens' the number is multiplied by. For example, 3×10^4 means '3 multiplied by four tens', i.e. $3 \times (10 \times 10 \times 10 \times 10)$, or $3 \times 10,000 = 30,000$. When the number to be represented is very small, the 'power' that 10 is raised to (4 in the example above) is negative.

Percentage: This is a special fraction in which the denominator is always 100. The resulting number is followed by the sign '%'. So, a half would be written as 50% (because $\frac{1}{2} = \frac{50}{100}$). To convert a fraction to a percentage, you multiply 100 by the fraction (e.g. $\frac{1}{2}$ times 100 = 50, so $\frac{1}{2}$ is the same as 50%). To convert a percentage to a fraction, you divide by 100 (e.g. 25% is $\frac{25}{100} = \frac{1}{4}$). To change a decimal to a percentage, multiply by 100 (e.g. $0.75 = 0.75 \times 100 - 75\%$). To change a percentage to a decimal, divide by 100, e.g. 90% = $\frac{90}{100} = 0.9$.

Ratio: A comparison between values of different categories, e.g. a sports club has 3 trainers and 27 players. The trainer:player ratio is 3:27, which is the same as 1:9 (as both numbers can be divided by 3).

Significant figures: This is a way to simplify a long number. The first digit is the most important, as it tells us the most about the ball-park amount. This makes it 'significant', but watch out for the next number too. If it is 5 or more, you round up. If it is 4 or less you don't. So, 7640 becomes 8000 to one significant figure, or 0.0336 becomes 0.03 to one significant figure. These numbers would be 7600 and 0.034 to two significant figures.

Percentages are often used to represent the proportion of scores in different categories. An alternative way to express information in categories, such as the number of male and female participants in a study is as a **ratio**. A ratio is simply a comparison between values of different categories. It is important to ensure that the order is the same for both the order of the words and the order of the numbers. Imagine a study with 60 male and 40 female participants. This is the ratio of the absolute numbers, but these should be simplified or 'reduced' by dividing both values by the same number. In general, ratios are quoted as the smallest possible whole numbers. The example of the gender ratio can be easily be simplified to a ratio of 6:4, by dividing both numbers by 10. However, it can be simplified again by dividing by two, leaving a ratio of 3:2 males to females.

DESCRIPTIVE STATISTICS

Averages: measures of central tendency

One way to analyse quantitative data is to work out the **measure of central tendency**, or 'average'. This is a single number that indicates the 'middle' or typical point in a set of data. There are different measures of central tendency to use with different levels of measurement: the mode, median and mean.

ACTIVITY

If you collected data about student study habits as suggested in the Do-it-yourself box on the opposite page, construct a summary table of the data showing totals or percentages for each question and for each level of the IV.

QUESTION SPOTLIGHT!

A study is comparing four- and seven-year-olds' lying about eating sweets. There were 45 seven-year-olds and 10 four-year-olds. What is the ratio of four- to seven-year-olds?

QUESTION SPOTLIGHT!

From Table 5.4 on page 185, identify the modal type of crime.

STRETCH & CHALLENGE

Calculate the means for the two sets of scores in the section on the median.

Why might it be mathematically incorrect to calculate the mean on the self-report data, but okay to calculate the mode?

 KEY IDEAS

Measure of central tendency – a mathematical way to describe a typical or average score from a data set (such as using the mode, median or mean).

Mode – a measure of central tendency worked out as the most frequent score(s) in a set of results.

Median – a measure of central tendency worked out as the middle score in the list when the data are in rank order (from smallest to largest). If there are two numbers in the middle they are added together and divided by two.

Mean – a measure of central tendency worked out by adding up all the scores and dividing by the number of scores.

The mode

The **mode** is the most frequent score in a set of results. If two (or more) scores are equally common there will be two (or more) modes. For example, a school decides to ask the pupils which type of teacher they are most likely to obey, ones who are *stern, interesting, in senior positions*, or *old*. They find that out of 50 people, 17 say *stern*, 20 say *interesting*, 11 say *in senior positions*, and 2 say *old*. So, in this case, the mode is 'interesting', because this is the most frequent response. The mode can be used with any kind of data but it is the only measure of central tendency that can be used with nominal data.

The median

The median is found by putting all the scores in a set into order, from smallest to largest, and finding the one in the middle of the list. When the scores in a group with an even number of participants are put in order (i.e. 'ranked'), there will be two numbers in the middle. These should be added together and divided by two to find the median. The median cannot be used with nominal data but can be used with data of any other level of measurement, such as with data generated from rating scales, Likert scales and semantic differentials. Returning to the example of self-reported navigational ability in bus drivers and non-bus drivers, the medians for the two groups of participants would be calculated in the following way:

> Bus drivers: 11, 12, 13, 15, 20, 22, 25, 26, 28, 30
>
> $20 + 22 = 42$, $\frac{42}{2} = 21$, so the median = 21
>
> Non-bus drivers: 1, 4, 9, 15, 20, 24, 25, 30, 37, 39
>
> $20 + 24 = 44$, $\frac{44}{2} = 22$, so the median = 22

The medians for the two sets of data above are very similar. This suggests that there is no difference in navigational ability between bus drivers and non-bus drivers.

The mean

The **mean** is the measure of central tendency we usually call the 'average'. It is worked out by adding up all the scores in the data set and dividing by the total number of scores (including any that were zeros). The mean is the most informative measure of central tendency because it takes every score into account, but it should only be used with equal interval data. Since many memory studies use interval scales from carefully controlled lists of stimuli – such as numbers, nonsense syllables or equal frequency and length words – the mean is often used as the measure of central tendency.

A researcher might measure navigational ability in bus drivers and non-bus drivers by timing how long they take to find their way through a virtual maze in the laboratory. The mean from their time in minutes would be calculated in the following way:

Bus drivers: 2, 15, 6, 8, 14, 19, 9, 4, 8, 13

total = 98, $\frac{98}{10}$ = 9.8, so the mean is 9.8 minutes

Non-bus drivers: 14, 3, 6, 18, 2, 18, 13, 5, 1, 15

total = 95, $\frac{95}{10}$ = 9.5, so the mean is 9.5 minutes

The means for the two sets of data above are very similar. This again suggests that there is no difference in navigational ability of bus drivers and non-bus drivers.

QUESTION SPOTLIGHT!

1   Work out the total for the scores in each set of data below about obedience to police officers and community police officers (CPOs). Now estimate the mean for each of the two data sets below.

Authority figure	Seconds to obey order
Police officer	6, 5, 3, 8, 3, 7, 9, 2, 3, 4
CPO	12, 14, 2, 6, 9, 5, 8, 2, 10, 15

2   Calculate the mode, median and mean for the set of data above.
3   In another study, many more participants were used. The total score for 78 participants in the 'police officer' condition was 800 seconds. Estimate the mean for this group. In the 'CPO' condition, 91 participants were tested, and the total of these scores was 1320 seconds. Estimate the mean score for this group. Is the difference in the same direction as in the first study?

MEASURES OF DISPERSION

A measure of dispersion gives an indication of how spread out the results within a data set are – that is, how much they vary around the measure of central tendency, are they clustered together or widely dispersed? Two data sets of the same size, with the same average, could vary considerably in terms of how close the majority of data points were to that average. Such differences can be described by the measures of spread: the range, the variance and the standard deviation.

Range
This is the simplest measure of spread and can be used with ordinal or interval data. The range is calculated in the following way:

1   Find the largest and smallest value.
2   Subtract the smallest value from the largest then add 1.

You may have learned to calculate the range without adding 1. We add 1 because scales measure the gaps between points, not the points themselves. Imagine

STRETCH & CHALLENGE

How does the mode distort the apparent difference between the data sets in the table on the left?

STRETCH & CHALLENGE

Although it is not appropriate to use the range with nominal data as the categories are not related in any linear way, an indication of the spread across categories (rather than within) can be obtained using the variation ratio. If you have collected nominal data in your own investigation, you may wish to try out this simple calculation. To work out the variation ratio, the total number of non-modal scores in the data set is divided by the total number of scores.

What kind of pattern do you find in the size of the variation ratio with more or less varied results?

 **KEY IDEAS**

Measure of dispersion – a mathematical way to describe the variation or spread in the scores from a data set.

Range – a measure of dispersion based on the biggest and smallest values in the data set.

Variance – a measure of dispersion that calculates the average difference between each score in the data set and the mean. Bigger values indicate greater dispersion.

Standard deviation – a measure of dispersion that calculates the average difference between each score in the data set and the mean, and represents this in the same units as the mean itself. Bigger values indicate greater dispersion.

a scale of attentiveness in class from 1 (not paying attention) to 5 (paying full attention). This can be represented on a line:

If we say someone is concentrating at a level of 2, they could be anywhere between 1.5 and 2.5, and someone scoring 4 has a concentration level somewhere between 3.5 and 4.5. So, if they were the highest and lowest scores, the real spread extends to those limits, i.e. 1.5 and 4.5. Therefore, we have a possible maximum spread of 1.5 to 4.5, giving us 4.5 – 1.5 = 3. This figure is one more than the biggest (4) minus the smallest (2) = 2.

Looking back to page 286, the range for the two sets of data would be calculated in the following way:

> Bus drivers: 11, 12, 13, 15, 20, 22, 25, 26, 28, 30
>
> 30 – 11 = 19, 19 + 1 = 20, so the range = 20
>
> Non-bus drivers: 1, 4, 9, 15, 20, 24, 25, 30, 37, 39
>
> 39 – 1 = 38, 38 + 1 = 39, so the range = 39

So, although the medians and means for these two data sets were very similar, the ranges were quite different. This tells us that the diversity in navigational ability in non-bus drivers is greater than that of bus drivers, in other words, bus drivers are all quite similar and 'averagely good' in their navigational skills, whereas non-bus drivers vary from quite poor navigators to very good ones.

One problem with the range is that it may not be very representative of the data set when there is a single very large or very small score, i.e. an outlier. Look at the data table on page 287 and imagine that there was one participant in the 'police officer' condition with a time of 15 seconds. This would make the range much larger than before, and the same as for the 'CPO' condition, so it would no longer show that obedience to a police officer was much more similar, whereas obedience to a CPO was generally more variable. The next measures of dispersion we will discuss overcome this problem by taking every score into account, not just the two extreme ones.

If you have ordinal data in named categories, you can calculate a range by allocating numerical values to the named categories in rank order. This is how Likert scales are analysed, for example (see page 243).

Variance

Just as the mean can tell us more than the mode, a measure called the **variance** can tell us more than the range. Rather than looking only at the extremes of the data set, the variance (given the name s^2) considers the difference between each data point and the mean – this is called the deviation. These deviations are then

QUESTION SPOTLIGHT!

Calculate and comment on the range for the data on page 287 about obedience to Police Officers and Community Police Officers (CPOs).

squared, added together and the total is divided by the number of scores in the data set, minus 1. This is represented by the formula:

$$s^2 = \frac{\Sigma(x - \bar{x})^2}{n - 1}$$

The main advantage of the variance (and the standard deviation below), is that they take every score into account so, unlike the range, are not distorted by outliers.

Before using the formula to calculate the variance, be sure that you understand the meaning of the brackets. In maths, you always do the parts of a sum in brackets first. So, in this case, each $x - \bar{x}$ subtraction is performed before the total is squared (i.e. you do not square $\bar{x}$ first).

Taking the 'bus driver' set of scores from the study described on page 287, we calculate the variance like this:

x	$x - \bar{x}$	$(x - \bar{x})^2$
2	7.8	60.84
15	5.2	27.04
6	3.8	14.44
8	1.8	3.24
14	4.2	17.64
19	9.2	84.64
9	0.8	0.64
4	5.8	33.64
8	1.8	3.24
13	3.2	10.24
		255.6

Bus drivers: 2, 15, 6, 8, 14, 19, 9, 4, 8, 13

1 Calculate the mean ($\bar{x}$).
   in this case: total = 98, $\frac{98}{10}$ = 9.8, so $\bar{x}$ = 9.8

2 Write down the number of scores (n):
   in this case: $n = 10$

3 Draw a table with 3 columns, and write the scores (the values of x) down the first column.

4 Work out the difference between each score and the mean and ignore the sign, i.e. whether it is a positive or a negative number ($x - \bar{x}$)

5 Square each of these differences $(x - \bar{x})^2$

6 Add together the column of differences $\Sigma (x - \bar{x})^2$
   in this case: $\Sigma (x - \bar{x})^2$ = 255.6

7 Take this total and divide it by $n-1$ in this case $\frac{255.6}{10 - 1} = \frac{255.6}{9}$ = 28.4.
   This is the value of s^2, so here s^2 = 28.4.

ACTIVITY ✳

Calculate the variance for the non-bus driver data on page 287. Explain the value you find in relation to the value for bus drivers from the text.

The variance tells us the dispersion of a group. Looking at the two data sets on page 286, the bus drivers' scores are much closer together, i.e. have less dispersion. This means that the variance would be smaller than for the non-bus drivers.

Standard deviation

One problem with the variance is that the final answer is a squared number, so is not in the same units as the mean. The standard deviation, because it uses the square root, returns the figure to the same units as the mean. As a consequence it is easier to make direct judgements about the data set. This becomes important when we are looking at the percentage of scores that fall either side of the mean (see the section on normal distribution on page 294).

Like the variance, the standard deviation works out the average amount of spread around the mean. Similarly, a larger value for standard deviation indicates that the scores are spread out a long way from the mean, a smaller value shows that the scores are generally clustered close to the mean.

KEY IDEAS

s^2	=	the variance
X	=	each score in the data set, i.e. a figure for the variable being measured
$\bar{X}$	=	the mean of the data set (called the 'sample mean')
Σ	=	the Greek letter Sigma, meaning 'the sum of', i.e. 'add them all up'
n	=	the number of scores in the data set
d	=	the deviation, is sometimes used in place of the difference between each score in the data set and the mean ($X-\bar{X}$) in the formula above.

So, like the variance the **standard deviation** (given the name **s**, **SD** or σ) finds the deviations, squares them and adds them together, and the total is divided by the number of scores in the data set, minus 1. The final step is then to find the square root, so you need to recognise just one extra symbol (√). The standard deviation is represented by the formula:

$$s = \sqrt{\frac{\Sigma(x-\bar{x})^2}{n-1}}$$

Starting with the variance from the formula above, the last step to find the standard deviation is to take the square root: √28.4 = 5.33, so **σ = 5.33**. We will return to the concept of standard deviation when we look at the normal distribution on page 294.

ACTIVITY ✳

The table on the right gives some of the means and standard deviations from the study by Bocchiaro *et al.* (2012), which looked for (but didn't find) personality differences between obedient and disobedient participants.

1 In which personality dimension were the whistle-blowers most similar?

2 Which group of participants had the greatest variation in terms of agreeableness?

3 Describe the differences in dispersion of the emotionality scores for the three types of participants.

TABLE 7.21 MEANS AND STANDARD DEVIATIONS FOR THREE OF THE SIX PERSONALITY DIMENSIONS MEASURED BY BOCCHIARO *et al.* (2012)

Personality dimension	Obedient participants		Disobedient participants		Whistle-blowers	
	mean	SD	mean	SD	mean	SD
Emotionality	3.08	0.64	2.94	0.70	2.76	0.53
Extraversion	3.65	0.50	3.49	0.52	3.74	0.37
Agreeableness	3.01	0.57	2.99	0.83	3.09	0.55

ACTIVITY ✳

Calculate the standard deviations for the two sets of data about obedience to police officers on page 287. Explain the difference between the two values you find.

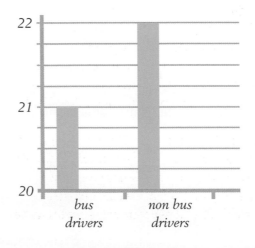

Figure 7.27
Navigational ability in bus drivers and non-bus drivers

GRAPHS AND TABLES

Graphs are used to illustrate findings. They may illustrate totals or frequencies, percentages or any of the measures of central tendency. Different graphs are used for different types of data. You need to know which to choose and how to sketch them.

Bar chart

A bar chart is used when the data are in discrete categories, that is, when the scores are not on a continuous scale. For example, bar charts would be used for the totals of nominal data and for all measures of central tendency (modes, medians or means). The bars on a bar chart must be separate (see figure 7.27). This is because the x axis represents distinct groups not a linear scale. If you are plotting the results of an experiment, the levels of the IV go along the bottom (on the x axis) and the DV goes on the y axis. (To help you to remember which is the x axis and which is the y axis, think 'X is a-cross'.)

Stacked bar charts are a special kind of bar chart in which different bars relating to the same category of data are put on top of each other. This can be seen in Figure 2.7 on page 55. This is useful when the levels of the IV are compiled from two or more conditions (as in Grant *et al.*), or when more than one measure of the DV has been taken in different levels of the IV. Another special kind of bar chart is the paired bar chart, which is used in similar way to the stacked bar chart but is more useful if two (or more) levels of the IV are to be compared in several ways as the height of the bars can be compared directly. An example can be see in Figure 4.29 on page 152.

Pie chart

A pie chart is a circular graph divided into sectors. Each portion of the circle represents a numerical proportion of a whole. To use a pie chart, therefore, you have to be confident that your data fairly reflect the 'whole', and for this reason they are often rejected by psychologists. In addition, it may be more difficult to make direct comparisons between data in different pie charts (unlike bar charts), although some more complex comparisons of sector area may be easier in pie charts.

To draw a pie chart, the data must consist of frequencies or proportions that can be expressed as a fraction. These figures must then be converted to angles (proportions of $360°$) to ensure the pie chart is full. For example, if the number of boys and girls in a class is equal, this would appear on a pie chart as half the circle for boys and half for girls, i.e. $180°$ each. To calculate the proportion of the circle in degrees we multiply the fraction by 360 (the number of degrees in a whole circle). A protractor is then used to mark each segment of a circle. You should be aware of how a pie chart is constructed even though you will probably use a computer to draw them.

In the study on obedience conducted by Bocchiaro *et al.* (2012), three options were given to 149 participants in the actual study and in an independent sample of 138 people were asked to predict what they themselves would do and what they thought most students at the university would do in the experimental situation (see Table 7.22). Their results for each of these parts of the study can be

STRETCH & CHALLENGE

Draw either a paired or a stacked bar chart for the data in Table 2.3 on page 48. Justify your choice of chart.

ACTIVITY ✳

Look at the bar chart on page 37. What are the units on the y axis? What are the categories on the x axis? Are they the conditions of the IV or something else? If so, what?

Draw a bar chart for the data in Table 180.

STRETCH & CHALLENGE

If you have not yet drawn the pie chart in the Maths Moment on page 186, draw it now. Draw a bar chart of the same data. Which do you think makes it easier to compare the proportion of each crime type? Then draw bar charts and pie charts for the data in Table 3.1 on page 85. These data offer more complex comparisons. Which do you think is easier to understand here? Is a pie chart acceptable for these data?

represented on a pie chart. The data given are percentages from the results of the study. To write these as fractions, they have been divided by 100. To calculate the degrees for each sector, 360 is multiplied by the fraction. This is rounded to the nearest whole number so that it is possible to draw it on a pie chart. Note that in a normal results table, you would not write '/100' in each cell of the table.

TABLE 7.22 CALCULATING THE SECTORS FOR A PIE CHART TO REPRESENT THE RESULTS OF BOCCHIARO *et al.* (2012)

		Obedience	Disobedience (refusal)	Disobedience ('whistle-blowing')
Experimental study results	Fraction of participants	76.5/100	14.1/100	9.4/100
	Proportion of the participants in degrees	275	51	34
Predicted results for themselves	Fraction of participants	3.6/100	31.9/100	64.5/100
	Proportion of the participants in degrees	13	115	232
Predicted results for a typical student	Percentage of participants	18.8/100	43.9/100	37.3/100
	Proportion of the participants in degrees			

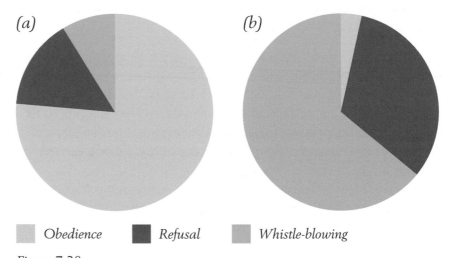

ACTIVITY ✳

Calculate the proportion of the participants in each of the outcomes of obedience and disobedience for the predicted typical student results in Table 7.22 above. Draw a pie chart to illustrate these results, and compare it to the two pie charts shown in Figure 7.28.

(a)   *(b)*

☐ *Obedience*   ■ *Refusal*   ▨ *Whistle-blowing*

Figure 7.28
Pie charts to illustrate the results of Bocchiaro et al. *(2012)*
(a) Experimental results
(b) Student samples' predicted results for themselves

Histogram

Histograms are used to show the pattern in a whole data set, where this is continuous data, i.e. data measured on an ordinal or interval scale. Histograms may be used to illustrate the distribution of a set of scores.

In an experiment, the DV is plotted along the *x* axis and the frequency of each score is plotted up the y axis. The scores along the *x* axis may be grouped into categories (e.g. if the DV is age, the data may be grouped into 0–10 years, 11–20 years, 21–30 years, etc.). Because the scale being represented on the x axis is continuous, the bars are drawn next to each other, unlike in a bar chart. This means that if there are no scores in a category, a gap must be left to show that the category is empty. For example, a histogram of the distribution of Eyes Test scores for non-autistic participants looks like Figure 7.29.

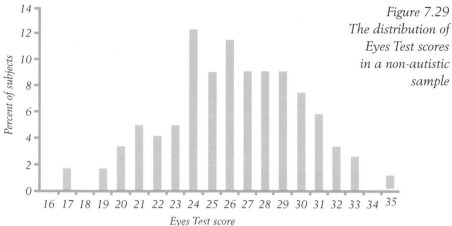

Figure 7.29 The distribution of Eyes Test scores in a non-autistic sample

Line graph

An alternative way to present the same frequency data as can be drawn on a histogram is to use a line graph. This is constructed on similar axes but instead of drawing columns, a point is marked at the height of the frequency of each score. These points are then joined to form a line. This type of graph is a frequency polygon. If a smooth line is drawn as a line of best fit between the points, it is called a frequency distribution curve. A normal distribution curve is an example of a frequency distribution curve (see page 294).

Scatter diagrams

Scatter diagrams were discussed on page 255. They are used to display the findings of correlational studies. To construct a scatter diagram, a dot is plotted at the point where each individual's scores on each variable cross. When you see a 'line of best fit' on a scatter diagram, its position has been calculated, you it cannot be drawn just by looking. However, this line is drawn at an angle such that it comes close to as many points as possible (see Figure 7.30). In a strong correlation all the data points lie close to the line, in a weak correlation they are more spread out. Where there is no correlation, the points do not form a clear line at all.

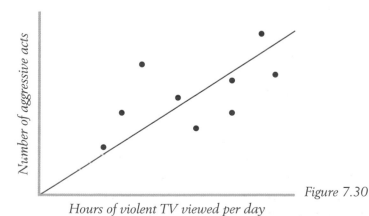

Figure 7.30

STRETCH & CHALLENGE

If you have not yet drawn the bar chart in the Maths Moment on page 47, draw it now. Why is a bar chart more appropriate than a histogram here? Why would a histogram be appropriate if only the data for the first three films were included?

ACTIVITY

Look at the histogram in Figure 7.29, and read off the height of each column. Put these data into a table for the frequency of each Eyes Test score. Use this table to draw a line graph. It should have exactly the same shape as Figure 7.29.

KEY IDEAS

A graph of the **normal distribution** is sometimes called 'the bell curve' because of its shape, which rises gradually and symmetrically to a maximum at the point of the mean, median and mode.

QUESTION SPOTLIGHT!

1 How strong is the positive correlation shown in the scatter diagram in Figure 7.30 compared to the one in Figure 7.15a?
2 What conclusion would you draw from these data?

Remember that you cannot draw a causal conclusion from a correlational study, so the scatter diagram in Figure 7.30, which shows a positive correlation, tells us that there is a relationship between aggression and viewing of violent TV, but not which (if either) of these variables is the cause of this link. We would have to conduct an experiment to find this out.

QUESTION SPOTLIGHT!

Draw a scatter diagram using the data below.
Does the scatter diagram show a positive or a negative correlation?
What conclusion would you draw from these data?

IQ	103	119	98	121	101	125	109	132
Memory test score	14	17	11	17	9	16	16	19

INFERENTIAL STATISTICS

The normal distribution curve

Look at the graph in Figure 7.31, you will see that it is 'bell-shaped'. This is typical of a **normal distribution**, a frequency distribution that:
* has the mode, median and mean together in the centre
* has 50% of the scores to the left and 50% to the right of the mean
* is symmetrical.

An important property of the normal distribution is that the proportion of scores falling either side of the mean is always the same. On pages 289–90 we discussed calculating the standard deviation, which measures how spread out the scores are from the mean. Remember also that, unlike the variance, the standard deviation returns the figure to the same range of values as the scores themselves. This is important here. The figure for any data set is 'standard' in

STRETCH & CHALLENGE

Look again at the core study by Baron-Cohen *et al*. Imagine a histogram for the Eyes Test results of an autistic group. How would it be different? Sketch what you think it would look like and explain how it would differ from Figures 7.29 and 7.31.

STRETCH & CHALLENGE

Why would the general pattern be easier to see if you drew a curve rather than joining all the points with straight lines?

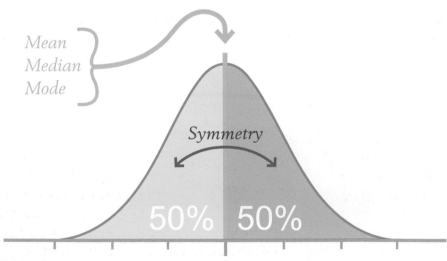

Figure 7.31
The shape of the normal distribution

that, once calculated, it always demonstrates the same pattern. In a normal distribution, 68% of the scores lie within one standard deviation from the mean, 95% within two standard deviations from the mean, and 99.7% within three standard deviations from the mean. For example, Charlotte and Rachel have been timing people on a test and have worked out the mean and standard deviation of their participants' scores. The mean is 15 minutes, and the standard deviation is 2 minutes. This means that 68% of the participants have scores between 13 minutes and 17 minutes, i.e. 2 minutes above and below the mean.

We can also make generalisations using the normal distribution. One of Charlotte and Rachel's participants took only 11 minutes, which is 2 standard deviations below the mean. We can work out what percentage of people would take longer than this participant. For normally distributed scores, we know that 95% lie within two standard deviations from the mean. However, there are also the people who took even longer in the 'tail' to the right of two standard deviations, which is half of the remaining 5%, i.e. another 2.5%. So, in total, 97.5% of the population would be slower than the person who took only 11 minutes.

STRETCH & CHALLENGE

If you sketched the histogram in the Maths Moment on page 144 look back at it. If not, read the question and imagine it. What shape is it and why do you think it has that shape?

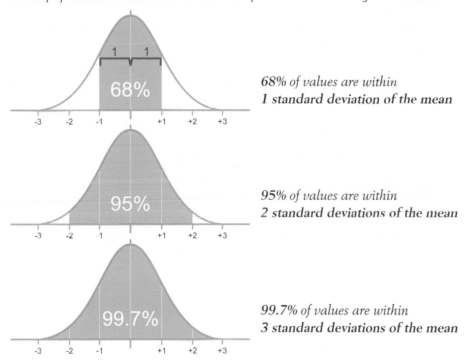

68% of values are within **1 standard deviation of the mean**

95% of values are within **2 standard deviations of the mean**

99.7% of values are within **3 standard deviations of the mean**

Figure 7.32
Standard deviations from the mean in a normally distributed population

Skewed distributions

In a normal distribution, all the measures of central tendency lie together in the middle of the graph. This is not so in skewed distributions because there is a greater spread of scores on one side. In distributions with a positive skew, the long tail is to the right (a 'positive' direction), in a distribution with a negative skew, the long tail is to the left (a 'negative' direction). As a consequence, the mean, median and mode all lie in different places, so the rules about standard deviations from the mean we discussed above no longer apply.

A useful way of looking at skewed distributions is to remember what each measure of central tendency tells us. The mode is the most frequent score, so is always the highest point of a distribution, whether it is normal or skewed (remember there may be two modes, so there would be two bars, or points, of equal height). The median is the middle point of the data, with 50% of the scores either side. In a skewed distribution the median will be towards the tail, as there will be more scores on the 'long' side than the short side. However, the measure of central tendency that is affected the most is the mean. Because the mean takes the value of every score into account, it lies the furthest along the tail.

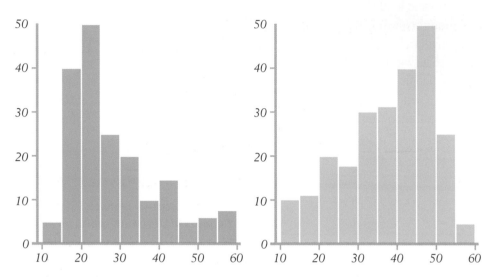

Figure 7.33
(a) A positively skewed frequency distribution
(b) A negatively skewed frequency distribution

Why do we use inferential tests?

Inferential statistics helps us to make *inferences* about our data – that is, to draw meaningful conclusions from numbers. Only quantitative data can be used in statistical tests so they tend to be used on the results of experimental and correlational studies. Where questionnaires, interviews or observations are used to generate numerical data in experimental or correlational designs, these data can be analysed statistically. Different inferential tests are used in different situations, for example with different levels of measurement and experimental designs.

Hypotheses in inferential analysis

On pages 264–5 we discussed writing hypotheses. When we test our findings using inferential statistics, we use two hypotheses. The alternative hypothesis, which states the anticipated results of an investigation, and the null hypothesis, which suggests the non-existence of such a pattern.

Consider an investigation into the effects on levels of aggression of watching TV. An experimenter might use the null hypothesis: 'There is no difference in aggression between people who watch TV for an hour or less per day and those who watch for more than five hours per day.' In a correlational study, a researcher might ask participants to say how long they watch TV per day, and to estimate

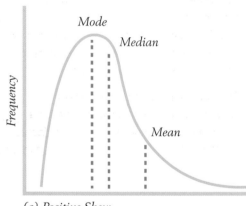

(a) Positive Skew

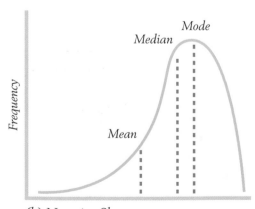

(b) Negative Skew

Figure 7.34
Measures of central tendency in skewed distributions

how many fights they have ever been in. The null hypothesis might be: 'There is no relationship between the amount of time people spend watching TV and the number of fights they have been in.'

In statistical testing we are aiming to reject the null hypothesis. This is what we will do if our results fit the expected pattern. If we can show that it is *unlikely* that the pattern we have found could have arisen by chance, then we can confidently reject the null hypothesis. In this case we would then be able to accept the alternative hypothesis. This is important because it means that we can satisfy the falsifiability requirement of the scientific method (see page 260).

PROBABILITY AND SIGNIFICANCE

Statistical tests aim to find out whether it is likely that any pattern in the data could have arisen by chance or is more likely to be due to the variable(s) under investigation. If the test shows that the pattern is likely to be due to the variable(s) being investigated it is described as *significant*. A statistical test therefore compares the mathematical probability of any pattern in our results arising by *chance*.

Each test calculates a single number, called the **observed value** from the scores found, or *observed,* in the study. A comparison between this value and a **critical value** from a table tells us whether the pattern is significant or not significant. However, the key to this comparison is the **significance level**. This is the probability, set by the researcher (and reflected in the critical value tables), at which they are prepared to accept the risk that a pattern could have occurred by chance. In most psychological research this is set at $p \le 0.05$, which means there is a 5% probability that a pattern could simply have arisen by chance. Conversely, if the test says the pattern in our results is significant, we can be 95% sure that this could not have arisen by chance.

If a psychologist wanted to be more sure than this, they could set the significance level at a probability of 1% ($p \le 0.01$) or even 0.1% ($p \le 0.001$). In fact, $p \le 0.05$ is generally chosen when there is evidence, such as previous research, to suggest that the predicted difference or correlation will arise. More stringent significance levels are used in studies requiring greater certainty (e.g. where errors could have dangerous implications), or in replications to verify the findings of previous research. The significance level therefore represents how confident we are about the pattern in our results and indicates the level of risk that we will tolerate. At any significance level there is a possibility that our conclusion could be wrong (we will discuss this on pages 307–8).

CHOOSING AND USING A STATISTICAL TEST

You need to know when to use five different non-parametric inferential tests and how to interpret their results. You also need to know when you could choose to do a parametric test. Several factors affect your choice:
- *Research method:* correlation or experiment (i.e. test of difference)
- *Design of an experimental study:* if it was repeated measures (or matched participants) or independent measures

KEY IDEAS

Significance level – the probability that a pattern in the results (a difference in an experiment or relationship in a correlation) could have arisen by chance. It is usually set at $p \le 0.05$.

Observed value – the single number calculated by a statistical test from the scores found (observed) in the study. It is compared to a critical value to determine whether the pattern in the results is significant.

Critical value – a value from a table for the appropriate statistical test to which an observed value is compared. This indicates whether the pattern in the results is significant.

KEY IDEAS

Some useful mathematical symbols

+   This is a 'plus' sign, which means 'add together'. Remember to add together numbers inside brackets first.

<   This means 'less than'. Remember that the 'small' end of the arrowhead is first, so it's less.

>   This means 'greater than'. Remember that the 'big' end of the arrowhead is first, so it's greater.

<<   This double arrowhead means 'much less than'.

>>   This double arrowhead means 'much greater than'.

~   This sign is called a 'tilda' and can mean many different things in the context of statistics. However, you are most likely to see it being used to mean either 'roughly equivalent to' or 'the same order of magnitude as'. Note that this is different from the 'bar' sign that is used over the letter x when referring to the mean (see page 290).

≈   This sign means 'approximately equal to'.

≥   This combination of a 'greater than' arrowhead and an equals sign means 'greater than or equal to'.

p The letter p is used to represent a probability.

≤   This combination of a 'less than' arrowhead and an equals sign means 'less than or equal to'.

KEY IDEAS

Degrees of freedom – in the Chi-square test this is used instead of N. It is the number of categories of data minus one and is calculated using the formula: (number of rows in the table – 1)×(number of columns in the table – 1).

- *Level of measurement:* nominal or ordinal/interval data
- *Distribution and spread:* if the sample scores appear to come from a normally distributed population with even spread.

Each test produces a single number, the observed value. This is given a 'name' (e.g. χ^2 for Chi-square). To be significant, the observed value must be greater than or equal to the critical value for tests in purple, and smaller than or equal to the critical value for tests in black.

A key decision is whether it is possible to use a parametric test. These tests are more powerful than non-parametric tests but have more stringent requirements for their use. As with non-parametric tests, there are a range of choices for different designs, however, all require that the data are from an equal-interval scale and that the sample scores appear to come from a normally distributed population with even spread. The tests are also much more complex to calculate and you are not required to learn any of these. You do, however, need to be able to decide which non-parametric test to use, and you can either use Table 7.23 or follow the flowchart in Figure 7.35. All of these tests generate an observed value with a special name (see Table 7.23).

As we said on page 297, significance is judged by comparing the observed value (from the test) to a critical value (from a table). To look up a critical value you need to know three pieces of information:

TABLE 7.23 CHOOSING A NON-PARAMETRIC INFERENTIAL TEST

Method/design	Nominal data	Ordinal or interval data
Correlation		Spearman's Rho test (r or r^s)
Experiment: independent measures	Chi-square test (χ^2)	Mann Whitney U test (U)
Experiment: repeated measures or matched pairs	Bionomial Sign test (s)	Wilcoxon Signed Ranks test (T)

- whether the *hypothesis* is directional (in which case we do a one-tailed test) or non-directional (so we do a two-tailed test)
- *significance* level: e.g. $p \leq 0.05$
- the *number of participants* in the sample, which is generally written as '**N =**' followed by a number. However:
  - for the Mann Whitney test, the two samples may have different numbers of participants, so N_1 and N_2 may be used to distinguish them, and
  - for the Chi-square test, '**degrees of freedom**' is used instead of N. This is the number of categories of data minus one.

Using this information and the correct table for the test, you can find the relevant critical value. For some tests (indicated in purple on Table 7.23) the observed value must be greater than, or equal to, the critical value in order to be significant; for the remainder, it is the other way round. If the difference or correlation is significant then we can reject the null hypothesis and accept the alternative hypothesis. However, even if the test indicates significance, a directional alternative hypothesis can be accepted only if the difference or correlation is in the predicted direction.

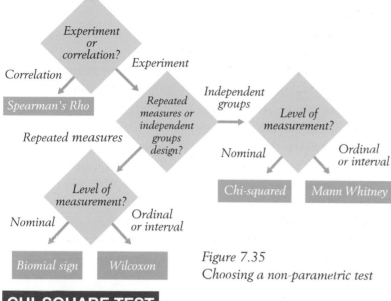

Figure 7.35
Choosing a non-parametric test

CHI-SQUARE TEST

When is the Chi-Square test used?

The Chi-square test is a test of association which looks for patterns in nominal data. It produces an observed value given the name 'x^2'. It tests whether the distribution of results in an experiment differs from what would be expected on the basis of chance alone. It does this by comparing the data actually collected with a data set based on the null hypothesis.

The criteria for using the Chi-square test are:
*   dependent variable has *nominal* level of measurement
*   design of the research is *independent measures*
*   looking for an association between the independent variable and the dependent variable.

How is the Chi-square test used?

To enter data into a Chi-square test, a table of totals is needed.

TABLE 7.24 A TABLE OF EXPERIMENTAL RESULTS FOR THE CHI-SQUARE TEST

	Ability to chase a ball rolled along the ground	Ability to jump up to catch a ball in their mouth in the air	Ability to follow a scent trail
Dogs raised in a vertically striped environment	61	15	24
Dogs raised in a horizontally striped environment	27	25	38

The data in the table are used in the formula:

$$\chi^2 = \sum \frac{(O - E)^2}{E}$$

You would not be asked to calculate χ^2 in an exam, although you may be asked to put numbers into the equation. However, you might want to use the test on real data. When psychologists conduct statistical tests, they use computers to work out the observed value.

The formula produces the observed value for this test, called χ^2. To compare this to a critical value, you need the following information:

* *degrees of freedom* (df) – this is calculated using the formula: (number of rows in the table – 1) $\times$ (number of columns in the table – 1)
* *alternative hypothesis* – directional or non-directional
* level of significance – the '*p*-value' e.g. $p \leq 0.05$

If the observed value is greater than the critical value, then the association is significant, so the null hypothesis is rejected and the alternative hypothesis is accepted. If the observed value is less than the critical value, then the association is not significant, so the null hypothesis is accepted and the alternative hypothesis is rejected.

If the degrees of freedom for the test equal 1, then the test calculation requires a correction factor (Yate's Correction) and a slightly different formula is used:

$$\chi^2 = \sum \frac{(O - E - \frac{1}{2})^2}{E}$$

(The '|' symbol indicates the modulus – that is, it is calculated ignoring the sign.)

If the data collected consist of only one row of data, for example comparing the number of aggressive acts in four different TV programmes, a χ^2 'Goodness of Fit' test is performed. In this case, the degrees of freedom are calculated by subtracting 1 from the number of categories present. So, in the TV example, the degrees of freedom would be 4–1 = 3. The critical values are read from the table as for the χ^2 test of association.

THE MANN WHITNEY U TEST

When is the Mann Whitney test used?

The Mann Whitney test is used to find out whether there is a significant difference between two sets of data and produces an observed value given the name 'U'. The test uses several pieces of information, including the number of participants in each of the two levels of the IV, which may be the same or different.

The criteria for using the Mann Whitney test are:

* dependent variable has an *ordinal* or *equal interval* level of measurement
* design of the research is *independent measures*
* looking for a *difference* between the effect each level of the independent variable has on the dependent variable.

QUESTION SPOTLIGHT!

Bandura *et al.* (1963) investigated imitation of aggression and used a Mann Whitney test in their comparison of imitation by boys and girls. Justify this choice of test.

DO IT YOURSELF

To run a Chi-square test online, go to http://faculty.vassar.edu/lowry/VassarStats.html. Follow the link to 'frequency data' on the navigation bar, scroll down to 'Chi-Square, Cramer's V, and Lambda' and click on it. The first thing you will have to do is select the number of rows and columns. If you wanted to enter the data in Table 7.24, you would click on 2 rows and 3 columns then enter the data into the rows provided. You then click on 'Calculate' and look for the Chi-square box. The figure here is your observed value for Chi-square, which should be 13.05 if you have used the data in Table 7.24. So, in this case, we would say that the observed value of $\chi^2 = 13.05$. You also need to find the figure labelled 'df', which you will need to look up the critical value. In this case, it is $(2 – 1) \times (3 – 1) = 2$ The table below contains an extract from a table of critical values for Chi-square. Let's assume that $p \leq 0.05$, as we have evidence to suggest what will happen in studies such as this, i.e. that there will be differences between dogs raised in different visual environments. The researchers would also have a null hypothesis and an alternative hypothesis which could be directional or non-directional. Let's assume in this case it was directional (so we must do a one-tailed test). We now have all the information we need to look up the critical value:

- df=2
- $p \leq 0.05$
- one-tailed test.

To look up the correct critical value for our test, we need to find the row corresponding to df=2, then the column for a one-tailed test at $p \leq 0.05$.

The critical value is 5.991. In order to decide what the results mean, this must be compared to the observed value. If the observed value is greater than or equal to the critical value, then the pattern in the results is significant. As the observed Chi-square value ($\chi^2 = 13.05$) is greater than the critical value (5.991), we can conclude that there is a significant pattern. This means that the null hypothesis can be rejected and the alternative hypothesis can be accepted.

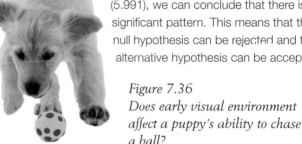

Figure 7.36
Does early visual environment affect a puppy's ability to chase a ball?

TABLE 7.25 A TABLE OF EXPERIMENTAL RESULTS FOR THE CHI-SQUARE TEST

df	Level of significance for a two-tailed test				
	0.2	0.1	0.05	0.02	0.001
	Level of significance for a one-tailed test				
	0.1	**0.05**	0.025	0.01	0.0005
1	2.706	3.841	5.024	6.635	7.879
2	4.605	**5.991**	7.378	9.210	10.597
3	6.251	7.815	9.348	11.345	12.838
4	7.779	9.488	11.143	13.277	14.860

How is the Mann Whitney test used?

Two sets of data are assembled, one for each level of the independent variable. The Mann Whitney test then involves ranking the data set and examining how the ranks are spread across the two levels of the independent variable. To retain the null hypothesis, which states that there is no difference, we would expect the ranks to be randomly distributed between the two levels of independent variable. If the distribution of ranks is predominantly in one direction (e.g. participants in condition A generally score higher than those in condition B), the Mann Whitney test will detect a significant difference between the two conditions.

This calculation produces two values, the smaller of which is the observed value of U. To compare this to a critical value, you need the following information:

- N_a and N_b: the number of participants (i.e. scores) in each of the two levels of the IV
- *alternative hypothesis*: directional or non-directional
- *level of significance*: the '*p*-value' e.g. $p \leq 0.05$.

If the observed value is less than or equal to the critical value, then the difference between the sets of scores is significant so the null hypothesis is rejected and the alternative hypothesis is accepted. If the observed value is greater than the critical value then the difference is not significant so the null hypothesis is accepted and the alternative hypothesis is rejected. You can try an example of the Mann Whitney test in the 'Do it yourself' box.

DO IT YOURSELF

To calculate a Mann Whitney test you will first need to work out the mean for each group. To calculate the observed value online, go to: http://faculty.vassar.edu/lowry/VassarStats.html. Follow the link to Ordinal Data on the navigation bar, scroll down to Mann Whitney test and click on it. You should then see an extra box asking for the number of participants in group A (n_a), type in 10. A second box should then appear asking for the number of participants in group B (n_b), type in 10 again. (If this doesn't happen, you need to go back and do a browser check on the home page and allow your computer to accept browser windows.) Once you have entered the number of participants in each group you will arrive at the main Mann Whitney test page. Don't be put off by the formulae – just scroll down the page until you come to 'Data Entry'. In the right-hand columns labelled 'Raw Data for' enter the data for 'Sample A' and 'Sample B'. Then click on 'Calculate from Raw Data'. The observed value (U) will appear in the box labelled 'U_a ='.

Here is an example. A study investigated the difference in ability to exercise restraint from using an appealing computer game, between people who were good, and not so good, at resisting tempting food. A Mann Whitney test was used to see whether there was a significant difference in computer-game restraint between the two groups:

- Group a: the control group (who were able to resist tempting food)
- Group b: the experimental group (who were not able to resist tempting food).

The ability to restrain their use of the computer game was better in the 'good food resisters' than in the 'weak food resisters' – but was the difference small enough to have arisen just by chance? The Mann Whitney test produced a U value of 2. This is compared to a critical value found from the table.

To look up the critical value we need to know:

- the level of significance ($p \leq 0.05$)
- whether the test is comparing a directional or non-directional prediction (directional – so we use a one-tailed test)
- the number of participants (n) in each group (n_a=5, n_b=4)

TABLE 7.26 CRITICAL VALUES FOR THE MANN WHITNEY TEST: ONE-TAILED TESTS AT $p \leq 0.05$, AND TWO-TAILED TESTS AT $p \leq 0.1$

n1a → nb ↓	3	4	**5**	6
3	0	0	1	2
4	0	1	**2**	3
5	1	2	4	5
6	2	3	5	7

The critical value is 2.

For the Mann Whitney test to be significant, the observed value must be smaller than or equal to the critical value.

Since the observed value of 2 is the same as the critical value of 2, we can conclude that there is a significant difference in computer-game restraint between two groups of participants. Before we can decide whether to accept the alternative hypothesis, we must be sure that this difference is in the predicted direction. The mean restraint by the 'good food-resisters' was better than by the 'weak food-resisters', so the researchers could reject their null hypothesis and accept the alternative hypothesis. They could therefore conclude that there is a difference in ability to restrain computer game use between people who are good at, and not so good at, resisting tempting food.

THE BINOMIAL SIGN TEST

When is the Binomial Sign test used?

The Binomial Sign test is used to find out whether there is a significant difference between two sets of data. These must come from the same participants. It produces an observed value given the name 's'.

The criteria for using the Binomial Sign test are:
*   dependent variable has a *nominal* (or *ordinal* or interval) level of measurement. If the data are nominal, the possible scores must be assigned to 'higher'/'better' or 'lower'/'worse'. If scores are ordinal or interval, the value of the numerical scores are used to judge 'better' or 'worse'.
*   design of the research is repeated measures
*   looking for a difference between the effect each level of the independent variable has on the dependent variable.

For example, the Binomial Sign test could be used to compare people's ability to detect the name of their home town compared to another place name in an unattended message in a shadowing task. The Binomial Sign test would only consider whether a participant heard the name of their home town or not, rather than how many times they heard it or how quickly they responded to it.

How is the Binomial Sign test used?

This is a very simple test. It just compares the number of differences in one direction to the number in the other direction in the whole data set. It does not consider how big each difference is. As a consequence, it is not very powerful, so it may fail to find a significant difference that another test would be able to detect.

Two sets of data are assembled in a table, one column for each level of the independent variable, with each row representing a pair of scores from the same participant. Each pair is compared, to decide whether the score in first column is bigger than the one in the second column (given a '+'), or whether the score in first column is smaller than the one in the second column (given a '–'). If a participant's scores are equal in both conditions, the data from this participant are not used. The number of pluses and minuses is then counted, and whichever is the smaller number is called 's', the observed value for the Binomial Sign test. To retain the null hypothesis, which states that there is no difference between the groups, we would expect the number of pluses and minuses to be about the same between the two levels of independent variable. If the distribution of scores is predominantly in one direction (e.g. participants generally score higher (more pluses) in the first condition than in the second), the Binomial Sign test will detect a significant difference between the two conditions.

The value of s is the observed value for the Binomial Sign test. It is compared to a critical value, which is found using the following information:
*   N: the number of participants (counting only those who did not have the same score in both conditions)
*   alternative hypothesis: directional (one-tailed) or non-directional (two-tailed)
*   level of significance: the '*p*-value', e.g. $p \leq 0.05$.

If the observed value is less than or equal to the critical value then the difference between the sets of scores is significant, so the null hypothesis is rejected and the alternative hypothesis accepted. If the observed value is greater than the critical value then the difference is not significant, so the null hypothesis is accepted and the alternative hypothesis is rejected. You can see an example of the Binomial Sign test in the 'Do it yourself' box.

DO IT YOURSELF 🔍

To calculate a Binomial Sign test, follow these steps:

1 Draw up a table with two columns, one for the scores for each condition.
2 Fill in each participant's scores in a new row.
3 Cross out the scores for any participant who gave the same response in both conditions.
4 Count up the number of participants who remain. This is your value for 'N'.
5 Decide which values will be assigned to '+' and which to '−'.
6 Add a third column, marking '+' or '−' to indicate the direction of the difference between each participant's scores.
7 Count up the number of participants given a '+' and the number given a '−'.
8 Record the smaller of these two totals, this is the observed value of 's'.

Helped when with familiar people	Helped when with strangers	Direction
no	yes	-
yes	no	+
~~no~~	~~no~~	~~xxx~~
no	yes	-
no	yes	-
no	yes	-
~~no~~	~~no~~	~~xxx~~
yes	no	+
no	yes	-
~~yes~~	~~yes~~	~~xxx~~
no	yes	-
no	yes	-

- The table above gives data for the two conditions (of being in a group with familiar people and being with strangers) for the 12 participants.
- The participants with 'tied' scores (who responded in the same way in both conditions) are crossed out (there were three of them).
- There is a the third column for pluses and minuses, which is filled in with 'helped only with people they knew' as '+' and 'helped only with people they did not know' as '−'.
- Adding up the pluses and minuses gives us: pluses = 2, minuses = 7.
- The observed value of 's' is the smaller value, i.e. s=2.

So there seems to be difference, but is it small enough to have arisen just by chance?

Figure 7.37
Who gets helped? Friends or strangers?

Here is an example. A study tested whether people were more likely to help others when surrounded by people they knew, compared to when with people they did not know. Everyone was tested in both conditions. They used a Binomial Sign test to see whether there was a significant difference in helping between the two conditions.

The binomial test produced an s value of 2. This is compared to a critical value found from the table. To look up the critical value we need to know:

- the level of significance ($p \leq 0.05$)
- it was a non-directional prediction (two-tailed test)
- the number of participants whose scores were used = 9 (N=9)

TABLE OF CRITICAL VALUES FOR BINOMIAL SIGN S:

	Levels of significance for a one-tailed test		
	0.05	0.025	0.01
	Levels of significance for a two-tailed test		
N	0.1	**0.05**	0.02
8	1	0	0
9	1	**1**	0
10	1	1	0
11	2	1	1
12	2	2	1

The critical value is 1.

For the Binomial Sign test to be significant, the observed value must be smaller than or equal to the critical value.

Since the observed value of 2 is the larger than the critical value of 1, we must conclude that there is no significant difference in helping when in a familiar group of people or when with strangers. We must therefore accept the null hypothesis and reject the alternative hypothesis. This might seem surprising but remember that the sign test is a very simple test and the sample was quite small. A bigger sample, or a more powerful test, might have found a significant difference.

THE WILCOXON SIGNED RANKS TEST

When is the Wilcoxon test used?

The Wilcoxon test is used to find out whether there is a significant difference between two sets of data. These must come from the same participants (or from matched participants). It produces an observed value given the name 'T' or 'W'.

The criteria for using the Wilcoxon test are:
- dependent variable has an ordinal or interval level of measurement
- design of the research is either repeated measures or matched participants
- looking for a *difference* between the effect each level of the independent variable has on the dependent variable.

How is the Wilcoxon test used?

Two sets of data are assembled in a table, one column for each level of the independent variable, with each row representing a pair of scores from the same participant (or matched pair). As with the Mann Whitney test, the formula involves ranking the data. To retain the null hypothesis, which states that any difference is due to chance, we would expect the ranks to be randomly distributed between the two levels of independent variable. If the distribution of ranks is predominantly in one direction (e.g. participants generally score higher in one condition than the other), the Wilcoxon test will detect a significant difference between the two conditions.

The number of ranks relating to the least direction of difference generates an observed value for the test, called 'W' (or 'T'). It is compared to a critical value, which is found using the following information:

- N: the number of participants (or the number of matched pairs if it is being used for an experiment with a matched participants design)
- *alternative hypothesis*: directional (one-tailed) or non-directional (two-tailed)
- *level of significance:* the 'p-value' e.g. $p \leq 0.05$.

If the observed value is less than or equal to the critical value then the difference between the sets of scores is significant, so the null hypothesis is rejected and the alternative hypothesis accepted. If the observed value is greater than the critical value then the difference is not significant, so the null hypothesis is accepted and the alternative hypothesis is rejected. You can see an example of the Wilcoxon test in the 'Do it yourself' box.

DO IT YOURSELF

To run a Wilcoxon test online, go to: http://www.fon.hum.uva.nl/Service/Statistics/Signed_Rank_Test.html . You will see a box labelled 'The observation pairs'. Enter the pairs of scores, each pair along one line with a single space between the two numbers. Then click on 'Submit'. Above the box, four numbers will appear. 'W–' is your observed value. (Ignore 'W+', this is an alternative way of expressing the observed value.) There will also be a value for N, the number of participants or paired scores. This will be the same as the number of rows in the table unless there are any pairs in which both numbers are identical – these will have been excluded.

Figure 7.38
Are ear witnesses influenced by leading questions?

If you enter the numbers in the table below, you should obtain the following three figures: W+=68, W–=10, N=12.
Below is a table of data about an experiment conducted on 'ear witnesses', ones who have heard a crime being committed (rather than having seen it).

The table to the right contains an extract from a table of critical values for Wilcoxon. Let's assume that $p \leq 0.05$ and that there will be differences between the ability of participants to correctly answer questions that are leading or non-leading. However, as testing ear-witnesses in this way is new, we are not sure which will be better, so the alternative hypothesis would be non-directional. We now have all the information we need to look up the critical value:

- N=12
- $p \leq 0.05$
- two-tailed test.

To look up the correct critical value for our test, we need to find the row corresponding to N=12, then the column for a two-tailed test at $p \leq 0.05$.

	Level of significance for a two-tailed test			
	0.1	**0.05**	0.02	0.01
	Level of significance for a one-tailed test			
N	0.05	0.025	0.01	0.005
9	8	6	3	2
10	11	8	5	3
11	14	11	7	5
12	17	**14**	10	7
13	21	17	13	10

The critical value is 14. In order to decide what the results mean, this must be compared to the observed value. If the observed value is less than or equal to the critical value, then the difference is significant. Since the observed Wilcoxon value, W– =10, is less than the critical value (14), we can conclude that there is a significant difference. This means that the null hypothesis can be rejected and the alternative hypothesis can be accepted.

Participant number	1	2	3	4	5	6	7	8	9	10	11	12
Number of correct answers to non-leading questions	28	18	17	14	7	18	17	22	34	14	14	23
Number of correct answers to leading questions	26	14	19	3	6	14	16	21	32	11	15	22

THE SPEARMAN'S RHO TEST

When is Spearman's Rho used?

Spearman's Rho is used to find out whether there is a relationship between two variables. It produces an observed value given the name 'r', 'r_s' or 'rho'.

The criteria for using the Spearman's Rho test are:
- two variables with an *ordinal* or *interval* level of measurement
- design of the research is a correlation
- looking for a *relationship* between the two variables

Two sets of paired scores are used. These are usually two scores from every participant gathered from two different scales. Alternatively, they can be pairs of scores on the same scale, one from each twin, for example to compare intelligence or severity of a mental illness. When Spearman's Rho is used to test for reliability, the pairs of scores come from different researchers, e.g. interviewers or observers, or from different versions of a test.

How is Spearman's Rho used?

The Spearman's Rho test initially rank orders each variable separately. If the rank orders for each variable are very similar then a positive correlation is expected. If the rank orders appear to be a mirror image of one another, then a negative correlation is expected. If the rank orders appear to be randomly distributed and there are large differences in rank for each participant's scores, then no correlation is expected.

The formula for the Spearman's Rho produces an observed value for the test (the correlation coefficient), which is given the term rho (r or r_s). It is compared to a critical value, which is found using the following information:
- N: the number of participants (or pairs of scores)
- *alternative hypothesis:* directional (one-tailed) or non-directional (two-tailed)
- *level of significance:* the 'p-value' e.g. $p \leq 0.05$.

If the observed value is greater than the critical value then the relationship is significant, so the null hypothesis is rejected and the alternative hypothesis accepted. If the observed value is less than the critical value then the relationship is not significant, so the null hypothesis is accepted and the alternative hypothesis is rejected. You can see an example of the Spearman's Rho test in action in the 'Do it yourself' box.

You may remember from page 250 that a correlation coefficient is always a number between $+1$ and -1. When there is no correlation (a zero correlation) $r = 0$. A perfect positive correlation is $r = +1$ and a perfect negative correlation is $r = -1$. The closer the correlation coefficient is to plus or minus 1, the stronger the correlation. For example, a strong positive correlation would be $r = 0.85$. A weak negative correlation $r = -0.4$.

QUESTION SPOTLIGHT!

Bandura *et al.* (1963) investigated imitation of aggression by matching children between groups seeing different models. To compare the effect of different models they used a Wilcoxon test.
Justify their use of this test.

Figure 7.39
If we raise the significance level we increase the risk of a type one error (rejecting the null hypothesis when it is true), but if we lower the significance level, we risk making a type two error (accepting the null hypothesis when it is false). We have to find a balance.

DO IT YOURSELF

To run a Spearman's Rho test online, go to: http://faculty.vassar. edu/lowry/VassarStats.html. Follow the link to 'Correlation and Regression' on the navigation bar, scroll down to 'Rank Order Correlation' and click on it. The first thing you will have to do is say how many participants you wish to enter data for. Enter 10 and scroll down the page until you come to 'Data Entry'. In the 'Raw Data' columns enter the following data.

Click on 'Calculate from Raw Data' and look for the r_s box. The figure here is your correlation coefficient, in this case 0.97. Being almost +1, this is a very strong positive correlation. The critical value for N=10, for a one-tailed test at $p \leq 0.05$ is 0.56. Since the observed value of r_s =0.97, and this is greater than the critical value of 0.56, this is a significant relationship.

Participant number	1	2	3	4	5	6	7	8	9	10
Frequency of childhood TV-viewing (X)	6	9	2	8	5	7	6	4	2	6
Criminality in adulthood (Y)	23	30	12	30	20	26	26	15	10	25

KEY IDEAS

Some useful mathematical symbols

α   This is the Greek letter Alpha and is used to refer to an unknown angle. You could encounter it in relation to a pie chart. It is also used to refer to the probability of making a type one error.

TYPE 1 AND TYPE 2 ERRORS

As we saw on page 297, even if we conclude from an inferential test that the pattern in the results is significant, we cannot be certain that this conclusion is correct. This is because the tests are only calculating the probability that the distribution of scores could have arisen by chance. This is not a certainty: there are two possible problems here.

If the alternative hypothesis is accepted when, in fact, the distribution of results is due to chance, we have made an 'optimistic' error. We have concluded that there is a difference or correlation between variables when there is not. This is called a **type one error**. The probability of making a type one error is sometimes referred to as 'α'. (It might help you to remember that both 'optimistic' and 'one' begin with the letter 'O'.) Type one errors are more likely at higher (less stringent) significance levels. For example, we are more likely to make a type one error at $p \leq 0.05$ than at $p \leq 0.01$. This is because there is a greater margin for generous errors; it is easier to accept the alternative hypothesis at $p \leq 0.05$ than at $p \leq 0.01$.

Conversely, we may accept the null hypothesis when, in fact, the distribution of results is not due to chance. In this case we would be making a 'pessimistic' error, that is, erring on the safe side by not accepting results that might be right. We will conclude that there is not a difference or correlation between variables when there is one. This is called a **type two error**. (To help you to remember this, think of 'It is better 2 be safe than 2 be sorry'.) Type two errors are more likely at lower (more stringent) significance levels. For example, we are more likely to make a type two error at $p \leq 0.01$ than at $p \leq 0.05$. This is because there is a smaller margin of error – it is harder to accept the alternative hypothesis at $p \leq 0.01$ than at $p \leq 0.05$.

It is important to note that if we try to cut the risk of making a type one error, by reducing the significance level from $p \leq 0.05$ to $p \leq 0.01$, then we *increase* the risk of making a type two error.

ETHICAL ISSUES RELATING TO PSYCHOLOGICAL RESEARCH WITH HUMAN PARTICIPANTS

You will have already encountered ethical issues raised in earlier chapters. Here we will look at the ethical dilemmas that psychologists face and how they can deal with them effectively.

BPS guidelines

To help psychologists to cope with ethical issues arising in research and professional practice, the British Psychological Society (BPS) regularly updates its ethical guidelines. As psychologists are concerned with people's welfare, it is important that these guidelines are followed. When research is conducted at institutions such as universities, the planned study must be approved by an ethics committee. This ensures that these guidelines are being followed. While the primary concern is for the welfare of individuals, another issue is the perception of psychology in society. Participants who are deceived or distressed may not want to participate again, may portray psychology in a poor light to others, and are unlikely to trust the findings of psychological research. These are all outcomes we would want to avoid.

The current BPS Code of Ethics and Conduct identifies four key ethical principles. These are:

- **Respect**: valuing the dignity and worth of all individuals. This includes an awareness of how psychologists may influence people and appear to have authority, and of people's rights to privacy and self-determination. Of particular importance are the standards of informed consent, right to withdraw and confidentiality.
- **Competence**: valuing continuing development as a psychologist and the maintenance of high standards of work. This includes functioning optimally and within the limits of one's own knowledge, skill, training, education and experience.
- **Responsibility**: valuing the responsibilities of being a psychologist – to clients, the public, and the profession and the science of psychology. This includes the avoidance of harm and the prevention of misuse or abuse of one's contributions to society. Of particular importance are the standards of protection of participants and the role of the debrief.
- **Integrity**: valuing honesty, accuracy, clarity, and fairness in interactions and seeking to promote these in scientific and professional work as a psychologist. Of particular importance is adherence to the standard relating to deception.

Informed consent and deception

As we saw on page 222, it is important in experiments to hide the aims from participants, or even to deceive them, in order to reduce demand characteristics. However, potential participants also have the right to know what is going to happen so that they can give their informed consent. These two opposing needs mean that it may be hard to get genuine consent. Ideally, researchers should obtain valid and informed consent from participants by giving them sufficient information about the procedure to decide whether they want to participate.

WEB WATCH

Look on the BPS website for its most up-to-date ethical guidelines, currently the Code of Ethics and Conduct (2009) and the Code of Human Research Ethics (2014).

Why is it necessary to update the guidelines?

KEY IDEAS

Ethical guidelines

Informed consent – having sufficient knowledge about a study to know whether you want to agree to participate.

Presumptive consent – gaining agreement to participate, in principle, from a group of people similar to the intended participants, by asking them if they would object to the procedure. It can be used when to gain informed consent from the participants themselves would lead to their working out the aim of the study.

Debrief – full explanation of aims and potential consequences of a study given to participants after participation to ensure that they leave in at least as positive a condition as they arrived.

Protection of participants – participants should not be put at any greater physical or psychological risk than they would expect in their day-to-day lives.

Deception – participants should not be deliberately misinformed (lied to) about the aim or procedure of the study. If this is unavoidable, steps should be taken beforehand to ensure they are unlikely to be distressed, and afterwards to ensure they are not.

Confidentiality – individuals' results and personal information should be kept safely and not released to anyone outside the study.

Right to withdraw – a participant should be aware that they can remove themselves, and their data, from the study at any time.

QUESTION SPOTLIGHT!

Milgram (1963) (page 6) investigated obedience.

Why was it necessary to use deception in this study?

QUESTION SPOTLIGHT!

A researcher is working with a person who is in prison.

What steps should they take to ensure:
- the individual has given their consent
- their confidentiality
- the individual is given the right to withdraw?

Figure 7.40
Privacy and confidentiality should still be maintained even when consent cannot be obtained

QUESTION SPOTLIGHT!

A researcher is designing a field experiment about emotions and death in which participants will see a staged violent crime in which someone appears to be shot dead.

How should they deal with the following ethical issues:
- informed consent
- privacy
- protection from harm?

However, in some situations the researcher cannot ask for consent. This is often (but not always) the case in naturalistic observations and field experiments and in laboratory experiments where deception is essential to the aims. In these situations, a researcher can attempt to decide whether participants in the sample would be likely to object by asking other people. Using a group of people similar to those who will become participants, the researcher can ask whether they would find the study acceptable if they were involved. This is called **presumptive consent** because it allows the researcher to presume that the actual participants would also be happy to participate.

Deception should be avoided. If used, participants should be told the real aim as soon as possible and be allowed to take their results away. When participants know that they have been in a study they should be fully debriefed quickly to ensure that they leave in at least as positive a mood as they started.

Right to withdraw

Participants can leave a study at any time if they wish. This is their **right to withdraw** and it must be observed even if this means data are lost. While participants can be offered incentives to join a study, these cannot be taken back if they leave – so they do not feel compelled to continue. Nor should researchers use their position of authority to encourage participants to continue beyond the point where they want to stop. In practice, this means that researchers must make the right to withdraw explicit to participants and be prepared to relinquish data if a participant chooses to withdraw.

Privacy and confidentiality

Studies that ask for personal information or observe people risk invading privacy. A researcher should make clear to participants their right to ignore questions that they do not want to answer, thus protecting their **privacy**. When completing a questionnaire in a laboratory situation, participants should be given an individual space and assured of the confidentiality and security of their data.

All data should remain **confidential** (e.g. by not storing names with data) unless participants have agreed otherwise. Participants' identities can be protected by allocating each person a number and using this to identify them. In experiments with an independent measures design, this helps to identify and keep a record of which condition each participant was in. In repeated measures designs, participant numbers are essential for pairing up an individual's scores in each condition.

In observations, people should only be watched in situations where they would expect to be on public display. This ensures their privacy. When conducting a case study, including those of larger groups such as institutions, confidentiality is still important and identities must be hidden. For example, the identities of schools or hospitals should be concealed.

The only exceptions to this general principle are that personally identifiable information can be communicated when the individual gives their informed consent to do so or in exceptional circumstances when the safety or interests of the individual or others may be at risk.

Protection of the participant

Studies have the potential to cause participants **psychological harm** (e.g. distress) or **physical harm** (e.g. engaging in risky behaviours such as taking drugs). In these situations, participants have the right to be protected and should not be exposed to any greater risk than they would be in their normal lives. Experienced researchers should be used in risky procedures and studies should be stopped if unexpected risks arise.

Debrief

If participants have been negatively affected by a study the researcher has a responsibility to return them to their previous condition. This is one of the functions of the **debrief** but this is not an alternative to designing an ethical study. The debrief is an explanation given to the participants at the end of the study to explain fully the aims of the study and to ensure that they do not want to withdraw their data and that their condition is at least as good as when they began the study. As debriefing is not an alternative to designing an ethical study, it is important to consider all the ways in which a study could cause distress and to minimise them.

HOW DOES PSYCHOLOGY CONTRIBUTE TO THE SUCCESS OF THE ECONOMY AND SOCIETY?

As we have seen in the last section, one of the reasons that psychologists must behave in ethically sound ways is so that members of society see their findings as trustworthy. Similarly, one reason for the focus on rigorous scientific methods is so that the findings of psychological research are considered to provide a credible basis on which to make important decisions. How, then, does psychology contribute to the success of the economy and society? If you look back through the 'practical applications' sections at the end of each core study, and the comparison between pairs of core studies, you will see many examples, although there are, of course, many others. If you continue your studies to complete the A level, you will learn in detail about more contributions of psychology, to mental health and to two other applied areas from child, criminal, environmental, and sports and exercise psychology.

How does psychology contribute to the economy?

If we first focus on possible problems with the economy, we can readily see some examples. The work of Milgram and of Moray have important implications for the prevention of air and road accidents, which are costly in practical terms as well as in terms of lives. Research on attention, such as that of Simons and Chabris, has applications in health-care settings, for example, in identifying possible causes of errors in doctors' judgements. This raises similar issues relating to both the economy, in terms of cost-effectiveness, and society, in relation to well-being.

More positively, psychology can also offer ways to improve practice before problems arise. Again in the health-care setting, the research of Bocchiaro *et al.* helps to highlight the importance of whistle-blowing. Efficiency in the workplace is an area of relevance to the economy, and the research of Grant *et al.* relates to

WEB WATCH

To find out about how the government engages society in decision-making about scientific issues, have a look at this website:

https://www.gov.uk/government/policies/engaging-the-public-in-science-and-engineering--3

All of the national academies conduct some research linked to psychology (the Royal Academy of Engineering in the field of ergonomics, for example). You might be interested in the surveys conducted to monitor public opinion (an example of self-report data), as well as the programme of events to inspire students.

STRETCH & CHALLENGE ◎

On the website indicated above, there is a link to the Charter for Science and Society in the UK, or you can find it directly, at:

https://scienceandsociety.blog.gov.uk

Look at some of the survey links and their conclusions. What types of questions can you see in the questionnaires? To what extent do you think the surveys are valid and reliable? What do the comments about the findings suggest about the way science is portrayed to the public?

WEB WATCH @

Employment is often difficult for people on the autistic spectrum, but some IT firms are recognising that they have particular strengths, and are actively recruiting people with autism and helping them to cope. Find an article about this using the link below. Identify the strengths that people on the autistic spectrum may have in the IT field and the ways in which they can be helped to integrate into the workplace.

http://www.news.com.au/finance/business/german-software-company-sap-recruits-autistic-staff/story-fnda1bsz-1226661672010

Figure 7.41
What help with social communication might people on the autistic spectrum need in the workplace?

A this, showing that, at least in some situations, working in silence is best.

Many days' work are lost through physical and mental ill-health: psychological research and practice can help to reduce these. For example, Chaney *et al.* demonstrated a way to improve childhood adherence to medical regimes. While Funhalers are inappropriate for adults in the workplace, controlling childhood asthma leads to better adult health, and many other psychological studies have demonstrated ways to improve adult compliance. In the domain of mental health, Freud has made an enormous contribution to the understanding and treatment of mental disorders, with the study of Little Hans still playing a role in the training of psychotherapists today. Similarly, Baron-Cohen *et al.*'s study points towards ways to enable high-functioning people with autism to cope in the workplace, for example, by using different visual cues to judge emotions of co-workers, or to help co-workers of those on the spectrum to give clear signals about their feelings.

How does psychology contribute to society?

Thinking about possible problems in society, one obvious one is crime. In courts of law, mistakes can be made when eyewitness testimony is trusted too much, as the work of Loftus and Palmer has shown. Such findings have led to changes in both police and court procedures. The findings of Piliavin *et al.* can also help us to understand why, in the face of apparent need, and even when someone might be the victim of a crime, people may not offer help. From Hancock *et al.*'s research on psychopaths we can learn how they differ in terms of emotions and motivations. This, in turn, helps the criminal justice system to develop more effective rehabilitation strategies for psychopathic criminals.

The role of parents, and of the media, in influencing children is highlighted by research such as that of Bandura *et al.* This leads to useful advice for parents themselves and for society as a whole, for example in the importance of the TV watershed and of certification on films and computer games. The study alerts us particularly to the risk for boys, but also suggests that perhaps children could be influenced by role models in positive as well as negative ways. This could offer opportunities to use real-life and media models to encourage pro-social behaviour.

Children have also been the recipients of the product of years of development of psychometric tests. The work of Yerkes, and the caution advised by Gould, has led to more effective and fair IQ testing, which is today used widely in schools and in the workplace.

For individuals with developmental or acquired perceptual or brain disorders, psychological research about brain structure and function is beginning to provide a foundation for understanding what is going wrong, and how those disorders might be avoided or improved. While we are far from being able to cure many such problems, the findings of studies such as Sperry, Blakemore and Cooper, and Maguire *et al.* have all contributed to underpinning knowledge that has implications for the detection and rehabilitation of people who have suffered brain damage from injury or disease.

PRACTICE QUESTIONS

Here are some of the sorts of questions you could be asked for AS Level Psychology H167/01. Answers to section A can be found on p.319. Further practice questions for A Level can be found in OCR Psychology Year Two.

SECTION A: MULTIPLE CHOICE

1 Which is a type of experiment in psychological research?
- **A** Classroom
- **B** Field
- **C** Library
- **D** Park [1]

2 Which of the following is not an experimental design?
- **A** Repeated measures
- **B** Independent measures
- **C** Quasi-experiment
- **D** Matched participants [1]

3 What is always included in an academic reference?
- **A** Participants used in the research
- **B** Method used in the research
- **C** The location of the research
- **D** The date of publication [1]

4 Which of the following would be a strength of questionnaire research?
- **A** The amount of control
- **B** The ability to infer cause-and-effect relationships
- **C** The ability to compare responses
- **D** The high response rates [1]

5 Which of these is not a section in a practical report?
- **A** Author biography
- **B** Introduction
- **C** Abstract
- **D** Results [1]

6 Where would details of a sampling technique be found in a practical report?
- **A** Introduction
- **B** Abstract
- **C** Method
- **D** Discussion [1]

7 Which is a null hypothesis?
- **A** 'Footballers will not perform significantly better when in front of an audience compared to no audience
- **B** 'There will be a significant difference between the performance of footballers with or without an audience.'
- **C** 'There will be a significant negative correlation between how footballers perform with and without an audience.'
- **D** 'There will be no significant difference between the performance of footballers with and without an audience.' [1]

8 Which of these is a weakness of observational research?
- **A** A risk of observer bias
- **B** High ecological validity
- **C** High levels of control
- **D** Demand characteristics [1]

SECTION B: RESEARCH DESIGN AND RESPONSE

A psychologist conducted an experiment to see if the promise of chocolate made A level psychology students work faster at a task. She conducted her experiment in a sixth-form college and used two different psychology classes. In the first class she told them that there would be a reward of a bar of chocolate for every student who successfully completed a series of multiple-choice questions about a topic they had recently studied. The students in the other group were not told about any reward and were simply asked to complete the multiple-choice questions. The time that it took each student to complete the multiple-choice task was recorded.

1 State an appropriate alternative hypothesis for this experiment. [3]

2 Identify the independent variable and the dependent variable in this experiment. [2]

3 (a) Identify the sampling method used in this study. [1]
   (b) Suggest **one** weakness of the sampling method used in this study. [2]

4 (a) Name the experimental design used in this study. [1]
   (b) Outline **one** strength and **one** weakness of the experimental design used in this study. [4]

5 Outline how each of the following ethical considerations could have been dealt with in this study:
   (a) Informed consent [2]
   (b) Right to withdraw [2]

6 (a) Suggest **one** extraneous variable that may affect the results of this study. [2]
   (b) Suggest how this variable could be controlled if the study were to be repeated. [3]
   (c) In which section of a report would a researcher discuss possible improvements? [1]

7 You have been asked to carry out a follow-up study to investigate the effect of positive reinforcement (reward) in A level students' learning experiences. Explain how you would carry out an observation to investigate if there is a difference or not. Justify your decisions as part of your explanation. [12]

You must refer to:

- participant or non-participant observations
- time or event sampling
- collection of data.

You should use your own experience of carrying out an observation to inform your response.

SECTION C: DATA ANALYSIS AND INTERPRETATION

A psychologist carried out a quasi-experimental study to investigate if there is a difference in job satisfaction levels depending on working environment. He looked specifically at whether there was a difference between office workers who could work flexibly (vary their start and finish time and sometimes work from home) and those who needed to work to a very rigid time structure (for example, 9am to 5.30pm every day).

He approached two separate graphic design companies – one that allowed workers to work flexible hours and one that did not. Both companies agreed to give a random sample of 10 staff a questionnaire designed by the psychologist, which would be completed by the workers and collected by the psychologist a week later. One of the questions asked the worker to rate how satisfied they were with their job using a scale from 1 to 10, with 10 indicating high job satisfaction and 1 indicating low satisfaction. The results from the study are shown in the table below.

1 Outline how a mean is calculated. [2]

2 Outline **one** conclusion that can be drawn from the above table. Refer to the mean ratings as part of your answer. [2]

3 State which office had a greater dispersion of scores. Justify your answer. [2]

4 Draw an appropriate graph to show the difference in mean ratings for the two offices. [4]

5 (a) Outline what is meant by a quasi-experiment. [2]

(b) Explain why this investigation is an example of a quasi-experiment. [2]

6 The psychologist used a questionnaire to collect the data. Describe **one** weakness of using a questionnaire in this investigation. [3]

7 (a) Outline the purpose of peer review in psychological research. [3]

(b) Following a peer review, the following statement was made about the study above:

'There is a potential issue with the representativeness of the sample when considering these findings.'

Explain what this statement means in relation to this study. [5]

A table to show the job satisfaction ratings given by 10 staff in each organisation			
Participant number	Flexible working satisfaction rating	Participant number	Non-flexible working satisfaction rating
1	6	1	6
2	6	2	6
3	7	3	5
4	8	4	5
5	6	5	7
6	8	6	3
7	8	7	9
8	8	8	4
9	7	9	6
10	9	10	5
Mean	7.3	Mean	5.6

SECTION B 1 State an appropriate alternative hypothesis for this experiment. [3]

Rachel's answer:

Rewards make people work better.

We say: This is not clear enough. The alternative hypothesis must include a clear statement of both the independent variable and the dependent variable. The independent variable is the promise of a reward (rather than the reward itself) and the dependent variable is the time that it took each person to complete the task.

Charlotte's answer:

Students who are promised a reward for completing a multiple-choice task will complete this task faster than students who are not promised a reward.

We say: That's better. This is a very clear and specific statement of what the experimenter is predicting.

2 Identify the independent variable and the dependent variable in this experiment. [2]

Rachel's answer:

The independent variable is the reward and the dependent variable is the chocolate.

We say: Oh dear, Rachel has got a little bit confused here. The independent variable is the promise of the reward (which is the chocolate) and the dependent variable is the variable that the researcher measures. In this study, this is the time taken to complete the multiple-choice task.

Charlotte's answer:

The independent variable is the promise of the reward (or no promise of a reward) and the dependent variable is the time that each person took to complete the multiple-choice task.

We say: Good, Charlotte has got these the right way around and has given a precise description of each.

4 (a) Name the experimental design used in this study. [1]

(b) Outline one strength and one weakness of the experimental design used in this study. [4]

Rachel's answer:

(a)   This was a field experiment

(b)   It is a strength because the participants are in their natural environment and it was a weakness because the experimenter didn't have very much control.

Charlotte's answer:

(a)   The experimental design is independent measures as different people are being used in each group.

(b)   A strength of independent measures is that participants only take part in one of the conditions. This means that they are less likely to figure out the aim of the study or to suffer from order effects by doing both conditions. A weakness is that there are different people in each condition and there may be individual differences between them.

We say: The experimental design refers to how the participants are allocated to conditions. Are the same people tested in both conditions or are different people tested in each condition? Field experiment refers to the type of method being used rather than the type of experimental design. Because Rachel was mistaken in giving the answer 'field experiment' in part (a), she has gone on to discuss in part (b) the strengths and weaknesses of field experiments rather than the strengths and weaknesses of the experimental design that was used.

We say: A good answer from Charlotte for part (a). Her answer to part (b) shows very good knowledge of the strengths and weaknesses of independent measures, although unfortunately Charlotte has not related her answer specifically to this study. The examiner won't assume that you can do this and if the question says something like 'in this study' it is important to make these links explicitly. Charlotte could have said that participants in the control group didn't know that the other group had been offered a reward so couldn't have worked out that this was an experiment looking at the effect of promising a reward.

---

6 (a) Suggest one extraneous variable that may affect the results of this study. [2]

(b) Suggest how this variable could be controlled if the study were to be repeated. [3]

(c) In which section of a report would a researcher discuss possible improvements? [1]

Rachel's answer:

(a)   Some people might not like chocolate.

(b)   You could have a choice of rewards for people to choose from so there would be something for everyone.

(c)   The method.

We say: Rachel's answer to part (a) is an interesting suggestion, and it is certainly true that if someone in the experimental group didn't like chocolate (or was on a diet!) then this would be a confounding variable, as the promise of the reward would not be equal across all participants. Rachel needs to give just a little bit more information to explain her suggestion more clearly.

For part (b), Rachel gives a reasonable suggestion, although choices could, in themselves, create further problems. If she gave a little bit more information about what she is thinking of here it might improve this answer. Unfortunately Rachel has given an incorrect answer for part (c). You would describe the procedure in the method section of a report but you would discuss improvements to the procedure in the discussion.

Charlotte's answer:

(a) It is not clear whether the experimenter tested both groups at the same time or not. If one group had been tested just before lunch and one after lunch this might have been why one group completed the task faster than another group. The promise of the reward might have had nothing to do with this.

(b) You could make sure that both groups were tested at the same time of day to make sure that this did not influence the time it took them to complete the multiple-choice task.

(c) The discussion.

We say: Charlotte's suggestion for part (a) is an appropriate one, and she has clearly explained why testing at different times of the day might have created an extraneous variable in the study. For part (b) she gives a clear suggestion for overcoming the problem that was identified in the previous question. Her part (c) answer is correct; there is no need to give any elaboration here.

SECTION C   1 Outline how a mean is calculated. [2]

Rachel's answer:

By adding them all up and then dividing them.

We say: Rachel needs to re-read her answer. Has she really explained how to calculate a mean? The first part of her answer is fine but she needs to explain the second part. You need to divide by the number of scores and this has not been made clear.

Charlotte's answer:

You add up all the results and then divide by the number of pieces of data, so if there were ten scores you would add them up and divide by ten.

We say: This is much clearer. The reader would be able to calculate a mean based on these instructions.

2 Outline one conclusion that can be drawn from the above table. Refer to the mean ratings as part of your answer. [2]

Rachel's answer:

Flexible working is better than non-flexible working.

Charlotte's answer:

People who are able to work flexibly have a higher mean rating of job satisfaction than people who are not able to work flexibly.

> **We say:** You need to take care when answering questions like this. It is not strictly true to say that flexible working is better than non-flexible working as this is not what has been measured. Rachel has also failed to refer to the mean ratings as part of her answer.

> **We say:** This is much clearer conclusion which is focusing specifically on the measurements taken, which were of job satisfaction. Charlotte has mentioned 'mean rating' but it would probably have been wise for her to include the actual mean scores to ensure that she had done what the examiner has asked for.

4 Draw an appropriate graph to show the difference in mean ratings for the two offices. [4]

Rachel's answer:

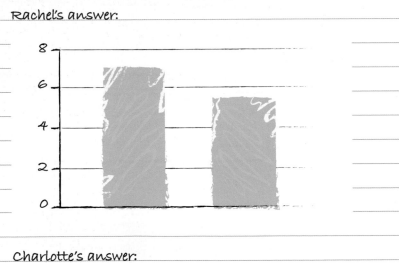

> **We say:** Rachel has drawn the graph accurately but as she has not included a title or any labels, it is impossible to know what the graph is representing.

Charlotte's answer:

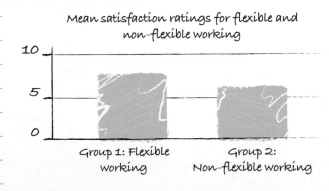

Mean satisfaction ratings for flexible and non-flexible working

Group 1: Flexible working

Group 2: Non-flexible working

> **We say:** Charlotte's graph is a lot more informative than Rachel's because she has labelled the horizontal axis and has given her graph a very clear title. However, she hasn't labelled the vertical axis and even though we might think it is perfectly clear that this is the rating of satisfaction, it is still necessary to label this.

5 (a) Outline what is meant by a quasi-experiment. [2]

(b) Explain why this investigation is an example of a quasi-experiment.[2]

Rachel's answer:

(a) A quasi-experiment is where the experimenter doesn't make the groups.

(b) Because the experimenter didn't make the groups.

Charlotte's answer:

(a) A quasi-experiment is one where the experimenter does not manipulate the independent variable but takes advantage of an already manipulated variable in the real world.

(b) In this study the independent variable of being able to work flexibly or not was not manipulated for the purposes of the experiment but already existed. The experimenter simply took advantage of the fact that these groups already existed.

We say: As with many of her other answer, Rachel has hinted at the right answer but has not explained herself clearly enough. For part (a), she is right to say that the experimenter doesn't 'make the groups' but this needs to be expanded upon. If Rachel explained that the groups already exist naturally then this would have been clearer. For part (b), Rachel is just repeating herself. She needs to explain that the experimenter simply took advantage of the fact that there are groups of people who work flexibly and groups of people who do not and this meant that the groups already existed.

We say: This is an excellent answer! Well done, Charlotte.

Answers to the Section A multiple-choice questions on page 313: 1b, 2c, 3d, 4c, 5a, 6c, 7d, 8a

As you get to the end of your Year 1, or alternatively you have taken psychology AS level and realise you have fallen in love with the subject, this is a good time to start thinking about careers. If you're applying to University in the Autumn, time will soon creep up on you, and it is advisable to prepare an early application. If you're going to manage that, you need to get planning now.

Making the most of Year 2

Psychology is one of the most popular and competitive subjects at degree level, and obtaining a place to study psychology is now as tough as obtaining a place to study medicine or law. Any offers you are given next year will be conditional on your overall A level grades, so it is critical to get the highest grades that you can next year. The best thing you can do about that at this point is to get your careers research done now and your application in as early as possible in the Autumn. This will leave you free to focus on your A levels.

If you are coming to the end of Year 1 of A level, how you experience the second year will depend very much on how your teacher has planned the split of work. If you have completed your core studies and you are taking on applied psychology, you can expect more breadth and less depth. There will also be rather more emphasis on theory and less on detailed coverage of studies.

If you took on psychology as an AS level and now find you can't live without it, remember that your AS exams won't count towards your A level. This is a major change to the system – you may have older siblings and friends who had that luxury, but be clear that the situation is different now. You can make use of the psychology that you have studied, but you'll need to take all the A level exams at the end of your course. For you there are additional core studies as well as applied psychology topics to learn. However, you may find that the biggest difference in A level is actually in the exam questions you'll be faced with. These require longer answers with more emphasis on evaluation and analysis.

Undergraduate psychology

Although we recommend studying psychology, you should be aware that most psychologists who teach undergraduates don't think that A level psychology is particularly good preparation. Many psychology undergraduates are surprised at how scientific university psychology is. There will be little or no Freud! You will spend a lot of time carrying out experiments and other types of study, and a considerable amount of time learning about research methodology and statistics. There is also less opportunity at first- and second-year undergraduate level to choose interesting-sounding options, and you may come to realise that your A level teacher has chosen the most interesting and 'sexy' options that protect you from some of the more dry and technical aspects of psychology.

The other key difference between any study at A level and undergraduate level – and this is true in any subject area – is the requirement for independent study. The emphasis at A level is on learning and knowing well a particular body of information and being able to demonstrate that you can think analytically about this material. This necessarily means that your teacher will provide you with everything you need to know, or will at least prescribe reading that will give you all the answers. At undergraduate level, there is far greater emphasis on your locating and processing information for yourself and developing your own skills.

Psychology careers

Do you want to be a professional psychologist? If the answer to this is 'yes', then you really need to start with a psychology degree. If, however, you don't yet have a firm career plan, but you are looking for an interesting degree that is well regarded by a range of employers, then you would also do well to consider a degree in psychology. It is important to know that the vast majority of people with psychology degrees never go on to become professional psychologists. This means that you don't have to worry that you are limiting yourself to a career as a psychologist if you take a psychology degree. People who study psychology at degree level can end up working in a huge variety of fields, including health, sport, education, criminal justice or business. Detailed information about different psychology careers can be found here:

http://www.bps.org.uk/careers-in-psychology

Choosing a psychology degree
Accredited degrees

At the time of writing there are 452 degrees in the United Kingdom accredited by the British Psychological Society.

Some of these are straight psychology, but you can also opt for a range of joint or combined honours courses, if that suits you better. If you are likely to want to be a professional psychologist it is important to choose a degree that is accredited by the British Psychological Society. You can see a list of these here:

http://www.bps.org.uk/bpslegacy/ac

Entry requirements

Psychology is now extremely popular, and you will find that entry grades are correspondingly high. For the most popular courses, this can mean up to three A grades at A level. You can see an up-to-date list of entry requirements here:

http://search.ucas.com

You will see that there is wide variation in entry grades from one course to another. Remember that the most sought-after courses are not necessarily those that will suit you best as an individual. The courses that are hardest to get into are likely to be those where the most famous researchers work. This may or may not be important to you; you might place more emphasis on quality of teaching.

It is also worth remembering that the popularity of a course might be determined as much by the location of the university, as by the quality of the course itself. Pretty campus universities in the home counties are most popular – but beware that rural campuses can be miles from the nearest pub! If you're willing to live in the rougher part of a city, at a university that has no landscaped grounds, you might be able to get into a decent course with lower grades (and perhaps have more fun).

Measures of course quality

There are two major published figures that are used to define the quality of a university department.

1   The Research Excellence Framework (REF). This is a measure of how successful the department is in publishing influential research. At the time of writing the first REF results are awaiting publication. You should be able to find out about these here:

http://www.ref.ac.uk/

2   The National Student Surveys. You can read summaries of survey results in various places, but we recommend the Unistats site:

http://unistats.direct.gov.uk/

We hope you have enjoyed your first year of psychology and that you will decide to take it further.

Matt, Julia, Lizzie and Fiona

INDEX

REFERENCES

Alexander, J.F. (2009) The international criminal court and the prevention of atrocities: predicting the court's impact. *Villanova Law Review*, **54**, 1–56.

Bateson, P. (1986) When to experiment on animals. *New Scientist*, **1496**, 30–2.

Baynes, K., Eliassen, J.C. and Gazzaniga, M.S. (1997) Agraphia without alexia: isolation of graphemic output in a split brain patient. 26th Annual Meeting of the Society for Neuroscience, November 1996.

Becklen, R. and Cervone, D. (1983) Selective looking and the noticing of unexpected events. *Memory and Cognition*, **11**, 601–8.

Benefiel, A.C. and Greenough, W.T. (1998) Effects of experience and environment on the developing and mature brain: Implications for laboratory animal housing. *ILAR Journal*, **39** (1), 5–11.

Binet, A. and Simon, T. (1913) *A method of measuring the development of the intelligence of young children*. Lincoln, IL: Courier.

Casey, B.J., Tottenham, N. and Fossella, J. (2002) Clinical, imaging, lesion, and genetic approaches toward a model of cognitive control. *Developmental Psychobiology*, **40**, 237–54.

Casey, B.J., Somerville, L.H., Gotlib, I.H., Ayduk, O., Franklin, N.T., Askren, M.K., Jonides, J., Berman, M., Wilson, N., Teslovich, T., Glover, G., Zayas, V., Mischel, W. and Shoda, Y. (2011) Behavioural and neural correlates of delay of gratification 40 years later. *Proceedings of the National Academy of Sciences*, **108** (36), 14998–15003.

Celano, M., Phillips, K.M. and Ziman, R. (1998) Treatment adherence among low-income children with asthma. *Journal of Pediatric Psychology*, **23** (6), 345–9.

Chabris, C.F., Weinberger, A., Fontaine, M. and Simons, D.J. (2011) You do not talk about Fight Club if you do not notice FightClub: Inattentional blindness for a simulated real-world assault. *i-Perception*, **2**, 150–3.

Chapman, K. R., Walker, L., Cluley, S. and Fabbri, L. (2000) Improving patient compliance with asthma therapy. *Respiratory medicine*, **94** (1), 2–9.

Cheng, L., Gosseries, O., Ying, L., Hu, X., Yu, D., Gao, H., He, M., Schnakers, C., Laureys, S. and Di, H. (2013) Assessment of localisation to auditory stimulation in post-comatose states: use the patient's own name. *BMC Neurology*, **13**, 27.

Cherry, E.C. (1953) Some experiments on the recognition of speech, with one and with two ears. *The Journal of the Acoustical Society of America*, **25** (5), 975–9.

Chiu, M.M. and Chow, B.W.Y. (2011) Classroom discipline across forty-one countries: School, economic and cultural differences. *Journal of Cross-Cultural Psychology*, **42** (3), 516–33.

Dharmani, I., Leung, J., Carlile, S. and Sharma, M. (2013) Switch attention to listen. *Scientific Reports*, **3**, 1297.

Dragnaski, B., Gaser, C., Busch, V, Schuierer, G., Bogdahn, U. and May, A. (2004) Neuroplasticity: Changes in grey matter induced by training. *Nature*, **427**, 311–2.

Eigsti, I.M., Zayas, V., Mischel, W., Shoda, Y., Ayduk, O., Dadlani, M.B., Davidson, M.C., Lawrence Aber, J., Casey, B.J. (2006) Predicting cognitive control from preschool to late adolescence and young adulthood. *Psychological Science*, **17**, 478–84.

Elms, A.C. and Milgram, S. (1966) Personality characteristics associated with obedience and defiance toward authoritative command. *Journal of Experimental Research in Personality*, **1**, 282–9.

Fillmore, C.J. (1971) Types of lexical information. In *Semantics: An interdisciplinary reader in philosophy, linguistics, and psychology*, Eds. D.D. Steinberg and L.A. Jakobovits. Cambridge: Cambridge University Press.

Gaser, C. and Schlaug, G. (2003) Gray matter differences between musicians and nonmusicians. *Annals of the New York Academy of Sciences*, **999**, 514–7.

Godden D.R. and Baddeley, A.D. (1975) Context-dependent memory in two natural environments: on land and underwater. *British Journal of Psychology*, **66**, 325–31.

Hare, R.D. (2006) Psychopathy: A clinical and forensic overview. *Psychiatric Clinics of North America*, **29**, 709–24.

Hare, T.A., Tottenham, N., Davidson, M.C., Glover, G.H. and Casey, B.J. (2005) Contributions of amygdala and striatal activity in emotion regulation. *Biological Psychiatry*, **57**, 624–32.

Hayden, M., Levy, J. and Thompson, J. (Eds.) (2007) *The SAGE Handbook of Research in International Education*, pp. 267–80. London: Sage Publications Ltd.

Held, R. and Hein A. (1963) Movement-produced stimulation in the development of visually guided behavior. *Journal of Comparative and Physiological Psychology*, **56** (5), 872–6.

Hirsch, H.V.B. and Spinelli, D.N. (1970) Visual experience modifies distribution of horizontally and vertically oriented receptive fields in cats. *Science*, **168** (3933), 869–71.

Hubel, D.H. and Wiesel, T.N. (1962) Receptive fields, binocular interaction and functional architecture in the cat's visual cortex. *Journal of Physiology*, **160** (1), 106–54.

Hubel, D.H. and Wiesel, T.N. (1970) The period of susceptibility to the physiological effects of unilateral eye closure in kittens. *Journal of Physiology*, **206** (2), 419–36.

Isarida, T.I., Isarida, T.K. and Sakai, T. (2012) Effects of study time and meaningfulness on environmental context-dependent recognition. *Memory and Cognition*, **40**, 1225–34.

Johnson, M.K., Hashtroudi, S. and Lindsay, D.S. (1993) Source monitoring. *Psychological Bulletin*, **114**, 3–28.

Ke, C. (1992) Dichotic listening with Chinese and English tasks. *Journal of Psycholinguistic Research*, **21**, 463–71.

Kohlberg, L. (speaker) (1975) *Education for a Society in Moral Transition*. The 30th Annual Conference for the Association for Supervision of Curriculum Development, cassette recording no. AC 120 24, 15–19 March. New Orleans: Louisiana

Latane, B. and Darley, J.M. (1968) Group inhibition of bystander intervention. *Journal of Personality and Social Psychology*, **10**, 215–21.

Lee, D.W., Miyasato, L.E. and Clayton, N.S. (1998)

Neurobiological bases of spatial learning in the natural environment: Neurogenesis and growth in the avian and mammalian hippocampus. *NeuroReport Review*, **9**, 15–27.

Lüttke, H.B. (2004) Experiments within the Milgram Paradigm. *Gruppendynamik und Organisationsberatung*, **35**, 431–64.

Mack, A. and Rock, I. (1998) *Inattentional Blindness*. Cambridge, MA: MIT Press.

Maguire, E.A., Burgess, N. and O'Keefe, J. (1999) Human spatial navigation: Cognitive maps, sexual dimorphism, and neural sub-strates. *Current Opinion in Neurobiology*, **9**, 171–7.

Maguire, E.A., Spiers, H.J., Good, C.D., Hartley, T., Frackowiak, R.S.J. and Burgess, N. (2003) Navigation expertise and the human hippocampus: A structural brain imaging analysis. *Hippocampus*, **13**, 208–17.

Marshall, J. (1969) *Law and psychology in conflict*. New York: Anchor Books.

Maslow, A.H. (1943) A theory of human motivation. *Psychological Review*, **50**, 370–96.

Masuda, T. and Nisbett, R.E. (2006) Culture and change blindness. *Cognitive Sciences*, **30**, 381–99.

Metcalfe, J. and Mischel, W. (1999) A hot/cool-system analysis of delay of gratification: Dynamics of willpower. *Psychological Review*, **106**, 3–19.

Milgram, S. (1970) The experience of living in cities. *Science*, **167**, 1461–8.

Mischel, W., Shoda, Y., Rodriguez, M.I. (1989) Delay of gratification in children. *Science*, **244**, 933–8.

Mohan, D., Angus, D.C., Ricketts, D., Farris, C., Fischhoff, B., Rosengart, M.R., Yealy, D.M., Barnato, A.E. (2014) Assessing the validity of using serious game technology to analyze physician decision making. *PLOS ONE*, **9** (8), e105445.

Moray, N. (1990) Designing for transportation safety in the light of perception, attention and mental models. *Ergonomics*, **33** (10/11), 1201–13.

Moreno, V. and di Vesta, F.J. (1991) Cross-cultural comparisons of study habits. *Journal of Educational Psychology*, **83** (2), 231–9.

Munte, T.F., Altenmuller, E. and Jannke, L. (2002) The musician's brain as a model of neuroplasticity. *Nature Reviews, Neuroscience*, **3**, 473–8

Neisser, U. (1979) The control of information pickup in selective looking. In *Perception and its Development. A Tribute to Eleanor J Gibson*, Ed. A.D. Pick, pp. 201–21. Hillsdale, NJ: Lawrence Erlbaum Associates.

Oxman, T.E., Rosenberg, S.D., Schnurr, P.P. and Tucker, G.J. (1988) Diagnostic classification through content analysis of patients' speech. *American Journal of Psychiatry*, **145**, 464–8.

Piaget, J. (1932/1965) *The moral judgment of the child*. London: Free Press.

Porter, S., ten Brinke, L. and Wilson, K. (2009) Crime profiles and conditional release performance of psychopathic and non-psychopathic sexual offenders. *Legal and Criminological Psychology*, **14**, 109–18.

Raine, A., Ishikawa, S.S., Arce, E., Lencz, T., Knuth, K.H., Bihrle, S. and Colletti, P. (2004) Hippocampal structural asymmetry in unsuccessful psychopaths. *Biological Psychiatry*, **55**, 185–91.

Sharpless, S.K. and Jasper, H.H. (1956) Habituation of the arousal reaction. *Brain*, **79**, 655–69.

Simons, D.J. and Chabris, C.F. (1999) Gorillas in our midst: Sustained inattentional blindness for dynamic events. *Perception*, **28**, 1059–74.

Smith, N.A., Seale, J. and Shaw, J. (1984) Medication compliance in children with asthma. *Journal of Paediatrics and Child Health*, **20** (1), 47–51.

Smith, S.M. (1986) Environmental context-dependent recognition memory using a short-term memory task for input. *Memory and Cognition*, **14**, 347–54.

Smith, S.M. (1988) Environmental context-dependent memory. In *Memory in context: Context in memory*, Ed. G.M. Davies and D.M. Thomson, pp. 13–34. New York: Wiley.

Smith, S.M., Vela, E. and Williamson, J.E. (1988) Shallow input processing does not induce environmental context-dependent recognition. *Bulletin of the Psychonomic Society*, **26**, 537–40.

Smulders, T.V., Sasson, A.D. and DeVoogd, T.J. (1995) Seasonal variation in hippocampal volume in a food-storing bird, the black-capped chickadee. *Journal of Neurobiology*, **27**, 15–25.

Somerville, L.H., Hare, T. and Casey, B.J. (2011) Frontostriatal maturation predicts cognitive control failure to appetitive cues in adolescents. *Journal of Cognitive Neuroscience*, **23**, 2123–34.

Soveri, A., Laine, M., Hämäläinen, H. and Hugdahl, K. (2011) Bilingual advantage in attentional control: Evidence from the forced-attention dichotic listening paradigm. *Bilingualism: Language and Cognition*, **14** (3), 371–8.

Tabri, D., Abou Chacra, K.M. and Pring, T. (2011) Speech perception in noise by monolingual, bilingual and trilingual listeners. *International Journal of Language and Communicational Disorders*, **46** (4), 411–22.

Tarnow, E. (2000) Self destructive obedience in the airplane cockpit and the concept of obedience optimisation. In *Obedience to authority*, Ed. T. Blass. Mahwah, NJ: Lawrence Erlbaum.

Thompson, C.K. (2000) Neuroplasticity: Evidence from aphasia. *Journal of Communication Disorders*. **33** (4), 357–66.

Triandis, H.C. (1995) *Individualism and collectivism*. Boulder, CO: Westview Press.

Tulving, E. (1972) Episodic and semantic memory. In *Organization of memory*, Ed. E. Tulving and W. Donaldson, pp. 381–403. New York: Academic Press.

Watson, J.B. (1930) *Behaviourism*. Chicago: University of Chicago Press

Welsh, T.N. and Elliot, D. (2001) Gender differences in a dichotic listening and movement task: Lateralization or strategy? *Neuropsychologia*, **39**, 25–35.

Whipple, G.M. (1909) The observer as reporter: A survey of the 'psychology of testimony'. *Psychological Bulletin*, **6** (5), 153–70.

Williamson, S. E. (1993) Cohesion and coherence in the speech of psychopathic criminals [Abstract]. *Dissertation Abstracts International*, **53**, 6579.

Wimmer, H., Gruber, S. and Perner, J. (1984) Young children's conception of lying: Lexical realism—moral subjectivism. *Journal of Experimental Child Psychology*, **37** (1), 1–30.

Wolfe, J.M. (1999) Inattentional amnesia. In *Fleeting memories: Cognition of brief visual stimuli*, Ed. V. Coltheart, pp. 71–94. Cambridge, MA: MIT Press.

Yerkes, R.M. (Ed.) (1921) *Psychological Examining in the United States Army*, Vol. 15. US Government Printing Office.

Zaidel, E. (1978) Lexical structure in the right hemisphere. In *Cerebral Correlates of Conscious Experience*, Eds. P. Buser and A. Rougeul Buser, pp. 177–97. Amsterdam: Elsevier North-Holland Biomedical Press.

Meet the authors

Matt Jarvis

Matt Jarvis is an experienced psychology teacher, trainer and researcher. He is a Chartered Psychologist, currently teaches part time and holds a Research Fellowship in Psychology.

Fiona Lintern

Fiona Lintern is an experienced teacher of psychology at A level, undergraduate and postgraduate levels. She is a Lecturer at Walford and North Shropshire College and Programme Leader for the MSc Teaching of Psychology at Glyndwr University and has extensive examining and authoring experience.

Julia Russell

Julia Russell is Head of Psychology at The Queen's School, Chester, and a lecturer on the MSc in Teaching of Psychology at Glyndwr University. She has extensive examining experience and has authored many successful learning resources.

Lizzie Gauntlett

Lizzie Gauntlett is an experienced teacher of psychology. She is an experienced examiner and is currently undertaking a PhD in Education at Bournemouth University.

Also available from Oxford...

OCR A Level Psychology Year 2
978 019 833276 3

Matt Jarvis • Julia Russell
Lizzie Gauntlett • Fiona Lintern
OXFORD

- Offers comprehensive coverage of the **applied psychology** content for A level study, including key research, links to debates and issues and **practice exam questions**

- Includes an **A to Z of research methods**, a helpful summary of the terms and techniques needed to master **research skills for psychological investigations**

- Has a section dedicated to **revision skills** to fully prepare students for the challenge of linear assessment

The *OCR A Level Psychology AS and Year 1 Student Book* and *OCR A Level Psychology Year 2 Student Book* are both available in eBook format.

eBook Available

The Research Methods Companion (Second Edition) 978 019 835613 4 is also available.

OXFORD UNIVERSITY PRESS

tel +44 1536 452620
fax +44 1865 313472

email schools.enquiries.uk@oup.com
web www.oxfordsecondary.co.uk/ocr-psychology